LECTURES ON LITERATURE

Vladimir Nabokov

LECTURES ON LITERATURE

EDITED BY Fredson Bowers

INTRODUCTION BY John Updike

A HARVEST/HBJ BOOK
HARCOURT BRACE JOVANOVICH, PUBLISHERS
BRUCCOLI CLARK   NEW YORK AND LONDON

Excerpts from "The Metamorphosis" by Franz Kafka are reprinted by permission of Schocken Books, Inc., from his book *The Penal Colony*, and Martin Secker & Warburg Limited, from *In the Penal Settlement*, both editions translated by Willa and Edwin Muir, copyright © 1948 by Schocken Books, Inc., copyright renewed © 1975 by Schocken Books, Inc. Excerpts from *Swann's Way* by Marcel Proust, translated by C. K. Scott Moncrieff, copyright © 1928, 1934, 1956, 1962 by the Modern Library, Inc., are reprinted by permission of Random House, Inc., Mrs. Eileen Scott Moncrieff, and Chatto and Windus Ltd; those from *Ulysses* by James Joyce, copyright © 1914, 1918 by Margaret Caroline Anderson, copyright © 1934 by the Modern Library, Inc., copyright © 1942, 1946 by Nora Joseph Joyce, copyright © 1962 by Lucia and Giorgio Joyce, by permission of Random House, Inc., and The Bodley Head.

Library of Congress Cataloging in Publication Data
Nabokov, Vladimir Vladimirovich, 1899-1977.
Lectures on literature.
(A Harvest/HBJ book)
1. Fiction—19th century—History and criticism—Addresses, essays, lectures.   2. Fiction—20th century—History and criticism—Addresses, essays, lectures.
I. Bowers, Fredson Thayer.   II. Title.
PN3499.N3   1980   809.3   79-3690   ISBN 0-15-649589-9

HBJ   Printed in the United States of America

First Harvest/HBJ edition 1982
A B C D E F G H I J

Contents

Editor's Foreword
by Fredson Bowers

In 1940, before launching on my academic career in America, I fortunately took the trouble of writing one hundred lectures—about 2,000 pages—on Russian literature, and later another hundred lectures on great novelists from Jane Austen to James Joyce. This kept me happy at Wellesley and Cornell for twenty academic years.[*]

Vladimir Nabokov arrived in America in May 1940. After lecturing on the road for the Institute of International Education and teaching a summer course in Russian literature at Stanford University, he was at Wellesley College from 1941 to 1948. Initially he was the Wellesley Russian Department and taught courses in language and grammar; but he also developed Russian 201, a survey of Russian literature in translation. In 1948 Nabokov was appointed Associate Professor of Slavic Literature at Cornell University where he taught Literature 311-312, Masters of European Fiction, and Literature 325-326, Russian Literature in Translation. The catalogue description for Literature 311-312 was almost certainly written by Nabokov: "Selected English, Russian, French, and German novels and short stories of the nineteenth and twentieth centuries will be read. Special attention will be paid to individual genius and questions of structure. All foreign works will be read in English translation." This course included *Anna Karenin*, "The Death of Ivan Ilyich," *Dead Souls*, "The Greatcoat," *Fathers and Sons*, *Madame Bovary*, *Mansfield Park*, *Bleak House*, "The Strange Case of Dr. Jekyll and Mr.

---

[*]*Strong Opinions* (New York: McGraw-Hill, 1973), p. 5.

Hyde," *Swann's Way*, "The Metamorphosis," and *Ulysses*.* Nabokov was prohibited from teaching American works at Cornell because he was not a member of the English Department. He was a visiting lecturer at Harvard University in the spring of 1952.

After he left teaching in 1958, Nabokov planned to publish a book based on his lectures, but he never began the project. (The lectures on *Dead Souls* and "The Greatcoat" were incorporated in *Nikolai Gogol* [1944].) These volumes preserve his lectures in their classroom form. Apart from the happy circumstance that here we have a major writer responding to the masterpieces of four literatures, his lectures merit wide availability because they are enduring guides to the art of fiction. Contemptuous of school-and-movement approaches to literature and scornful of critics who treated literature as a medium for socio-political messages, Nabokov tried to reveal how masterpieces work: "In my academic days I endeavored to provide students of literature with exact information about details, about such combinations of details as yield the sensual spark without which a book is dead. In that respect, general ideas are of no importance. Any ass can assimilate the main points of Tolstoy's attitude toward adultery but in order to enjoy Tolstoy's art the good reader must wish to visualize, for instance, the arrangement of a railway carriage on the Moscow-Petersburg night train as it was a hundred years ago. Here diagrams are most helpful. Instead of perpetuating the pretentious nonsense of Homeric, chromatic, and visceral chapter headings, instructors should prepare maps of Dublin with Bloom's and Stephen's intertwining itineraries clearly traced. Without a visual perception of the larch labyrinth in *Mansfield Park* that novel loses some of its stereographic charm, and unless the façade of Dr. Jekyll's house is distinctly reconstructed in the student's mind, the enjoyment of Stevenson's story cannot be perfect."**

The lectures collected in these two volumes represent Vladimir Nabokov's teaching at Wellesley and Cornell—with four lectures prepared for special occasions. For the convenience of readers, the lectures have been separated into two volumes: 1. British, French, and German Writers; 2. Russian Writers.

At the first meeting of Literature 311 in September 1953 Vladimir Nabokov asked the students to explain in writing why they had enrolled in

---

*Mrs. Nabokov is certain that Chekhov was taught in Literature 311-312, but the student class notes we have consulted do not include Chekhov. It may be that he was not taught every year.

**Strong Opinions, pp. 156-157.

the course. At the next class he approvingly reported that one student had answered, "Because I like stories."

EDITORIAL METHOD

The fact cannot and need not be disguised that the texts for these essays represent Vladimir Nabokov's written-out notes for delivery as classroom lectures and that they cannot be regarded as a finished literary work such as he produced when he revised his classroom lectures on Gogol for publication as a book. The lectures exist in very different states of preparation and polish, and even of completed structure. Most are in his own handwriting, with only occasional sections typed by his wife Vèra as an aid to delivery; but some lectures are completely in autograph form, as is true for the Stevenson, Kafka, and substantially for the series on Joyce. The *Bleak House* series is very much of a mixture, but with autograph predominating. Ordinarily the handwritten pages give every indication of rough initial composition, and as a result Nabokov might work them over extensively, not only during the first writing-out but also on review, when on some occasions he further revised both style and content. However, the alterations, whether substitutions or simple additions, were not always fully fitted syntactically into the context, or else further necessary adjustment in unaltered readings was not made. As a result, when the revision was heavy, the holograph portions of the texts require frequent editorial intervention, in order to prepare for reading what was no doubt easily adjustable or would pass unnoticed in oral delivery.

On the other hand, typed pages can represent a considerable part of a lecture, as for *Mansfield Park* but more substantially in the *Madame Bovary* series. The frequent contrast between the comparative roughness of much of the holograph, even when revised, and the relative smoothness of the typed pages suggests that in the process of typing parts of her husband's lectures, Mrs. Nabokov exercised normal editorial discretion in preparing the pages for delivery. Even so, Nabokov might work over some pages of the typing in order to add fresh comments or to revise phrases for felicity.

As a whole, it would be impractical to offer these manuscripts to the reading public in verbatim form, either structurally or stylistically. The Stevenson essay exists in what can described only as rough notes; hence the present ordering of its material is almost entirely the responsibility of the editor. In the other lectures, however, the general order of delivery is not usually in question since it is ordinarily a chronological working through of the book. Problems may arise, however, which make the editorial process one of synthesis and redaction. Various separate groups of pages in the folders represent simple background notes made in the initial stages of preparation and either not utilized or else revised and incorporated subsequently into the lectures themselves. Other of these independent sections are more ambiguous, and it is not always demonstrable whether they reflect stages of amplification during the course of repeated delivery in different years or else jottings for possible use in a future version. Certain problems of organization seem to result from added or alternate parts of some of the lectures, possibly intended for different audiences. Whenever possible the editor has salvaged all such material not manifestly background and preparatory memoranda and has worked it into the texture of the lecture discourse at appropriate places. Omitted, particularly, however, are pages of quotations from critics, which Mrs. Nabokov typed for her husband's use in the Proust, Jane Austen, Dickens, and Joyce lectures, as well as chronologies of the action of novels that Nabokov constructed for his own information.

However, the problem of structure goes deeper than this incorporation of pertinent material from what might be called Nabokov's files. In various of the lectures Nabokov interspersed his chronological narrative with discrete sections of remarks on theme or style or influence. Where these interpolations were intended to be placed is usually far from clear; moreover, they are often incomplete and can even represent little more than jottings, though some may actually form charming little separate essays. It has devolved upon the editor to insert these sections when simple bridge passages are possible or, when the materials are in somewhat fragmentary form, to break up their separate elements for insertion in the discourse elsewhere as appropriate. For instance, the connected account of Stephen's interview with Mr. Deasy in part one, chapter 2 of the *Ulysses* lectures has been assembled from three different parts of the manuscript. The main quotation (here editorially supplied) seems not to have been read in class, but the students, with their books open, were referred to its pertinent points, provided in the next paragraph about the shell of Saint James (see p. 299). The rest of the text, however, comes from two parts of a separate section that begins with notes on structure, passes to miscellaneous comments on beauties and defects in the novel, to parallels in themes, and then to notes such as the reference to the conversation with Deasy as illustrating Flaubertian counterpoint and another note about Joyce's parodic style, citing the Deasy letter as an example. By such means, whenever the material permitted, the editor has been able to flesh out narrative and to preserve in a connected context a maximum of Nabokov's discussion of authors, their works, and the art of literature in general.

Quotation bulked large in Nabokov's teaching methods as an aid in his effort to transmit his ideas of literary artistry. In the construction of the present reading edition from the lectures, Nabokov's method has been followed with very little cutting except of the most extended quoted illustrations, for the quotations are most helpful in recalling a book to the reader's memory or else in introducing it to a fresh reader under Nabokov's expert guidance. Quotations, therefore, ordinarily follow Nabokov's specific instructions to read certain passages (usually marked also in his own teaching copy) with the effect that the reader may participate in the discourse as if he were present as a listener. On occasion Nabokov's copies of his teaching books have passages marked for quotation although not mentioned in his lecture text. When these could be worked into the text as an aid to the reader, the quotations have been provided. Moreover, some few quotations have been selected by the editor although not called for either in the lectures or in the teaching copies when the occasion seemed to require illustration of a point that Nabokov was making. Nabokov's students were expected to follow his lectures with their books open before them. Hence they could be referred to points in the text by allusions in a manner impossible for a reader to follow, who must be supplied with extra quotation as a substitute. Molly's final soliloquy in *Ulysses* is an example. A unique instance, however, occurs at the end of the lectures on Proust. Nabokov had chosen for his text *Swann's Way*, the first volume of *Remembrance of Things Past*. The last lecture on Proust ends with an extended quotation from Marcel's meditations in the Bois de Boulogne on his memory of the past that concludes the novel. It is an effective ending to the novel but it leaves Marcel (and the reader) only a short way along the road to the full understanding of the functions and operations of memory as the key to reality, the meaning of the whole work. The musings in the Bois, indeed, are only one of the different aspects of viewing the past that in the gradual building up of Marcel's understanding prepare him for the final experience that reveals the reality for which he had been searching through the preceding volumes. This event takes place in the great third chapter, "The Princesse de Guermantes Receives," of the final volume, *The Past Recovered*. Since the revelation found in this chapter is the key to the cumulative meaning of the whole series of novels, any consideration of Proust that did not analyze it in explicit terms and make clear the difference between its full flowering and the early seed dropped in *Swann's*

Way would fail in its essential purpose. Although Nabokov's lectures on Proust ended with the quotation of the episode in the Bois, a random sentence or two unconnected directly with his lectures suggests that he may have taken up the matter with his students, the more especially since the extensive typed quotations from Derrick Leon's book on Proust tend to concentrate on this final episode and its explanation. Nabokov's disjunct remark that "a nosegay of the senses in the present *and* the vision of an event or sensation in the past, this is when sense and memory come together and lost time is found again" is essentially true and an excellent encapsulation of Proust's theme; but it would not be very illuminating to anyone who had not read this final volume without the full explanation Proust himself provides in *The Past Recaptured*. The editor in this extraordinary case has felt justified, therefore, in extending the Nabokov ending by fortifying with quotation from the final volume of *Remembrance of Things Past* the incomplete Nabokov notes in an attempt to focus more sharply the essence of the revelation that came to Marcel by providing excerpts from Proust's own account of the transformation of memory into reality and into material for literature. The editorial augmentation fulfills the spirit of Nabokov's jottings and should be of some help in rounding out the understanding, in turn, of *Swann's Way*, which was, after all, designed as the opening of a series.

The reader of these lectures should take special note that quotations from Flaubert reproduce Nabokov's frequent alterations of the translation that he made throughout his teaching copy of the novel, whereas those from Kafka and Proust take account of the less systematic changes marked in his books.

The teaching copies for all the novels in this volume have been preserved. As remarked, the translated books may be interlined or marginally annotated with his own translations of words and phrases. All of the books are marked for quotation and contain notes about the context, most of these notes also being present in the written-out lectures but others clueing Nabokov in on some oral comment to make about the style or the content of certain passages. Whenever possible, comments in the annotated copies have been worked into the texture of the lectures as appropriate occasion arose.

Nabokov was acutely conscious of the need to shape the separate lectures to the allotted classroom hour, and it is not unusual to find noted in the margin the time at which that particular point should have been reached. Within the lecture text a number of passages and even separate sentences or phrases are enclosed in square brackets. Some of these brackets seem to indicate matter that could be omitted if time were pressing. Others may represent matter that he queried for omission more for reasons of content or expression than for time restrictions; and indeed it is not unusual to find some of these bracketed queries subsequently deleted, just as some, alternatively, are removed from the status of queries by the substitution for them of parentheses. All such undeleted bracketed material has been faithfully reproduced but without sign of the bracketing, which would have been intrusive for the reader. Deletions are observed, of course, except for a handful of cases when it has seemed to the editor possible that the matter was excised for considerations of time or, sometimes, of position, in which latter case the deleted matter has been transferred to a more appropriate context. On the other hand, some of Nabokov's comments directed exclusively to his students and often on pedagogical subjects have been omitted as inconsistent with the aims of a reading edition, although one that otherwise retains much of the flavor of Nabokov's lecture delivery. Among such omissions one may mention overobvious explanations for an undergraduate audience such as "Trieste (Italy), Zurich (Switzerland) and Paris (France)" from the Joyce lectures, or admonitions to use a dictionary to look up unfamiliar words, and similar comments suitable only for students' ears and not for the printed page. Various of the addresses to the class as *you* have been retained as not inappropriate on some occasions for a reader, but these have been changed in some instances to a more neutral form of address.

Stylistically the most part of these texts by no means represents what would have been Nabokov's language and syntax if he had himself worked them up in book form, for a marked difference exists between the general style of these classroom lectures and the polished workmanship of several of his published lectures. Since publication without reworking had not been contemplated when Nabokov wrote out these lectures and their notes for delivery, it would be pedantic in the extreme to try to transcribe the texts *literatum* in every detail from the sometimes rough form found in the manuscripts. The editor of a reading edition may be permitted to deal more freely with inconsistencies, inadvertent mistakes, and incomplete inscription, including the need sometimes to add bridge passages in connection with quotation. On the other hand, no reader would want a manipulated text that endeavored to "improve" Nabokov's writing in any intrusive way even in some of its unpolished sections. Thus a synthetic approach has been firmly rejected, and Nabokov's language has been reproduced with fidelity save for words missing by accident and inadvertent repetitions often the result of incomplete revision.

Occasionally some tangles either in language or in syntax have needed straightening out, chiefly when Nabokov had interlined additions or substitutions and neglected to delete parts of the original to make it conform to the revised readings. In a few cases syntactical constructions that would pass unnoticed in oral delivery have been adjusted for a reading audience. Minor slips such as inadvertent singulars for plurals, misspellings, omitted opening or closing quotation marks, missing necessary punctuation, erratic capitalization, unintentional verbal repetition, and the like have all been set right unobtrusively. For the purposes of this edition Nabokov's few British spellings and punctuational usages have been modified for American publication: these were not always consistent, anyway. A very few times English idioms have been rectified, but borderline cases are retained such as Nabokov's idiosyncratic use of the verb *grade*. Mostly, however, usage that a reader might be inclined to query will be found to have dictionary authority, for Nabokov was a careful writer. Titles of books have been italicized and shorter pieces placed within quotation marks. It would be tedious for a reader to be presented with all of Nabokov's underlined words in italics, most of which were directions to himself for verbal emphasis, not necessarily of the kind to be transferred to the printed page. Correspondingly, his dependence upon the dash for punctuating oral delivery has been somewhat reduced by the substitution of more conventional punctuation.

Corrections and modifications have been performed silently. It has seemed to be of no practical value to a reader to know, for instance, that in one place in a Joyce lecture Nabokov slipped and wrote "Irishman" when "Irishmen" was required, that he once forgot that Bloom had lived at the "City Arms" and called it the "King's Arms," that he ordinarily wrote "Blaze" for Blazes Boylan and often "Steven" for Stephen Dedalus. Thus the only footnotes are either Nabokov's own or else occasional editorial comments on points of interest such as the application of some isolated jotting, whether among the manuscripts or in the annotated copy of the teaching book, to the text of the lecture at hand. The mechanics of the lectures, such as Nabokov's notes to himself, often in Russian, have been omitted as have been his markings for correct delivery of the vowel quantities in pronunciation and the accenting of syllables in certain names and unusual words. Nor do footnotes interrupt what one hopes is the flow of the discourse to indicate to the reader that an unassigned section has been editorially inserted at a particular point.

The opening essay on "Good Readers and Good Writers" has been reconstructed from parts of his untitled written-out opening lecture to the class before the exposition began of *Mansfield Park*, the first book of the semester. The final "L'Envoi" is abstracted from his untitled closing remarks at the end of the semester after completing the last lecture on *Ulysses* and before going on to discuss the nature of the final examination.

The editions of the books that he used as teaching copies for his lectures were selected for their cheapness and the convenience of his students. Nabokov did not hold in high regard the translations that he felt obliged to employ and, as he remarked, when he read passages from the foreign-language authors he altered them at will for reading aloud. The texts from which the quotations are taken are as follows: Jane Austen, *Mansfield Park* (London: Dent; New York: Dutton, 1948), Everyman's Library #23; Charles Dickens, *Bleak House* (London: Dent; New York: Dutton, 1948), Everyman's Library #236; Gustave Flaubert, *Madame Bovary*, trans. Eleanor Marx Aveling (New York & Toronto: Rinehart, 1948); Robert Louis Stevenson, *The Strange Case of Dr. Jekyll and Mr. Hyde and Other Stories* (New York: Pocket Books, 1941); Marcel Proust, *Swann's Way*, trans. C. K. Scott Moncrieff (New York: Modern Library, 1956); Franz Kafka, *Selected Short Stories of Franz Kafka*, trans. Willa and Edwin Muir (New York: Modern Library, 1952); James Joyce, *Ulysses* (New York: Random House, 1934).

ACKNOWLEDGMENTS

The assistance provided during the preparation of this book by Vladimir Nabokov's wife, Vèra, and their son Dmitri cannot be adequately acknowledged here. From the inception of this project, the Nabokovs invested untold hours advising the editor and publisher on virtually every facet of the editorial process. They patiently and tirelessly answered numerous questions about such matters as the structure of Nabokov's lectures and his preferences in matters of diction. Their painstaking advice has made this volume better than it could have been without them.

Grateful acknowledgment is due as well to the following persons: Else Albrecht-Carrie, Permissions Editor, New Directions Publishing Corporation; Alfred Appel, Professor of English, Northwestern University; Brian Boyd, Professor of English, University of Auckland; Donald D. Eddy, Professor of English, Cornell University; Richard Ellman, Professor of English, Oxford University; Paul T. Heffron, Acting Chief, Manuscript Division, Library of Congress; Cathleen Jaclyn, Cornell University Libraries; Joanne McMillan, The Children's Hospital Medical Center; Nina W. Matheson; Myra Orth; Stephen Jan Parker, Editor *Vladimir Nabokov Research Newsletter*; and Stephanie Welch, Wellesley University.

Introduction
by John Updike

Vladimir Vladimirovich Nabokov was born on Shakespeare's birthday in 1899, in St. Petersburg (now Leningrad), into a family both aristocratic and wealthy. The family name, indeed, may stem from the same Arabic root as the word *nabob*, having been brought into Russia by the fourteenth-century Tatar prince Nabok Murza. Since the eighteenth century the Nabokovs had enjoyed distinguished military and governmental careers. Our author's grandfather, Dmitri Nikolaevich, was State Minister of Justice for the tsars Alexander II and Alexander III; his son, Vladimir Dmitrievich, forsook a certain future in court circles in order to join, as politician and journalist, the doomed fight for constitutional democracy in Russia. A courageous and combative liberal who was sent to prison for three months in 1908, he without misgiving maintained himself and his immediate family in a life of upper-class luxury divided between the townhouse built by his father in the fashionable Admiralteiskaya region of St. Petersburg, and the country estate, Vyra, brought by his wife—of the immensely rich Rukavishnikov family—to the marriage as part of her dowry. Their first surviving child, Vladimir, received, in the testimony of his siblings, a uniquely generous portion of parental love and attention. He was precocious, spirited, at first sickly and then robust. A friend of the household remembered him as "the slender, well-proportioned boy with the expressive, lively face and intelligent probing eyes which glittered with sparks of mockery."

V. D. Nabokov was something of an Anglophile, and his children were tutored in English as well as French. His son, in his memoir *Speak, Memory*, claims, "I learned to read English before I could read Russian," and remembers an early "sequence of English nurses and governesses," as well as a procession of comfortable Anglo-Saxon artifacts: "All sorts of snug, mellow things came in a steady procession from the English Shop on Nevski Avenue: fruitcakes, smelling salts, playing cards, picture puzzles, striped blazers, talcum-white tennis balls." Of the authors lectured upon in this volume, Dickens was probably the first encountered. "My father was an expert on Dickens, and at one time read to us, children, aloud, chunks of Dickens, in English, of course," Nabokov wrote to Edmund Wilson forty years after the event. "Perhaps his reading to us aloud, on rainy evenings in the country, *Great Expectations* . . . when I was a boy of twelve or thirteen, prevented me mentally from re-reading Dickens later on." It was Wilson who directed his attention to *Bleak House* in 1950. Of his boyhood reading, Nabokov recalled to a *Playboy* interviewer, "Between the ages of ten and fifteen in St. Petersburg, I must have read more fiction and poetry— English, Russian, and French—than in any other five-year period of my life. I relished especially the works of Wells, Poe, Browning, Keats, Flaubert, Verlaine, Rimbaud, Chekhov, Tolstoy, and Alexander Blok. On another level, my heroes were the Scarlet Pimpernel, Phileas Fogg, and Sherlock Holmes." This last level of reading may help account for Nabokov's surprising, though engaging, inclusion of such a piece of late-Victorian fog-swaddled Gothic as Stevenson's tale of Jekyll and Hyde within his course of European classics.

A French governess, the stout, well-memorialized Mademoiselle, took up abode in the Nabokov household when young Vladimir was six, and though *Madame Bovary* is absent from the list of French novels which she so trippingly ("her slender voice sped on and on, never weakening, without the slightest hitch or hesitation") read aloud to her charges—"We got it all: *Les Malheurs de Sophie, Le Tour du Monde en Quatre Vingts Jours, Le Petit Chose, Les Miserables, Le Comte de Monte Cristo,* many others"— the book undoubtedly existed in the family library. After V. D. Nabokov's senseless murder on a Berlin stage in 1922, "a fellow student of his, with whom he had gone for a bicycle trip in the Black Forest, sent my widowed mother the *Madame Bovary* volume which my father had had with him at the time and on the flyleaf of which he had written 'The unsurpassed pearl of French literature'—a judgment that still holds." Elsewhere in *Speak, Memory,* Nabokov writes of his rapturous reading of the work of Mayne Reid, an Irish author of American Westerns, and states of a lorgnette held by one of Reid's beleaguered heroines, "That lorgnette I found afterward in the hands of Madame Bovary, and later Anna Karenin had it, and then it passed into the possession of Chekhov's Lady with the Lapdog and was lost by her on the pier at Yalta." At what age he might have first perused Flaubert's classic study of adultery, we can only guess a precocious one; he read *War and Peace* for the first time when he was eleven, "in Berlin, on a Turkish sofa, in our somberly rococo Privatstrasse flat giving on a dark, damp back garden with larches and gnomes that have remained in that book, like an old postcard, forever."

At this same age of eleven, Vladimir, having been tutored entirely at home, was enrolled in St. Petersburg's relatively progressive Tenishev School, where he was accused by teachers "of not conforming to my surroundings; of 'showing off' (mainly by peppering my Russian papers with English and French terms, which came naturally to me); of refusing to touch the filthy wet towels in the washroom; of fighting with my knuckles instead of using the slaplike swing with the underside of the fist adopted by Russian scrappers." Another alumnus of the Tenishev School, Osip Mandelstam, called the students there "little ascetics, monks in their own puerile monastery." The study of Russian literature emphasized medieval Rus—the Byzantine influence, the ancient chronicles—and proceeded through study of Pushkin in depth to the works of Gogol, Lermontov, Fet, and Turgenev. Tolstoy and Dostoevsky were not in the syllabus. At least one teacher, Vladimir Hippius, "a first-rate though somewhat esoteric poet whom I greatly admired," impressed himself forcibly on the young student; Nabokov at the age of sixteen published a collection of his own poems and Hippius "brought a copy with him to class and provoked the delirious hilarity of the majority of my classmates by applying his fiery sarcasm (he was a fierce man with red hair) to my most romantic lines."

Nabokov's secondary education ended as his world was collapsing. In 1919, his family became émigrés. "It was arranged that my brother and I would go up to Cambridge, on a scholarship awarded more in atonement for political tribulations than in acknowledgment of intellectual merit." He studied Russian and French literature, much as at the Tenishev School, and played soccer, wrote poetry, romanced a number of young ladies, and *never once* visited the University Library. Among his desultory memories of his college years there is one of "P.M. storming into my room with a copy of *Ulysses* freshly smuggled from Paris." In a *Paris Review* interview Nabokov names the classmate, Peter Mrosovsky, and admits that he did not read the book through until fifteen years later, when he "liked it enormously." In Paris in the mid-thirties he and Joyce met a few times. Once Joyce attended a reading Nabokov gave. The Russian was pinch-hitting for a suddenly indisposed Hungarian novelist before a sparse and motley crowd: "A source of unforgettable consolation was the sight of

Joyce sitting, arms folded and glasses glinting, in the midst of the Hungarian football team." On another inauspicious occasion in 1938, they dined together with their mutual friends Paul and Lucie Léon; of their conversation Nabokov remembered nothing and his wife Vèra recalled that "Joyce asked about the exact ingredients of *myod*, the Russian 'mead,' and everybody gave him a different answer." Nabokov distrusted such social conjunctions of writers and in an earlier letter to Vèra had recounted a version of the legendary single, fruitless encounter between Joyce and Proust. When did Nabokov first read Proust? The English novelist Henry Green in his memoir *Pack My Bag* wrote of Oxford in the early twenties that "anyone who pretended to care about good writing and who knew French knew his Proust." Cambridge was likely no different, though as a student there Nabokov was intent upon his own Russian-ness to an obsessive degree—"my fear of losing or corrupting, through alien influence, the only thing I had salvaged from Russia—her language— became positively morbid. . . ." At any rate, by the time he granted his first published interview, in 1932, to a correspondent for a Riga newspaper, he can say, rejecting the suggestion of any German influence on his work during the Berlin years, "One might more properly speak about a French influence: I love Flaubert and Proust."

Though Nabokov lived for over fifteen years in Berlin, he never learned—by his own high linguistic standards—German. "I speak and read German poorly,' he told the Riga interviewer. Thirty years later, speaking in a filmed interview for the Bayerischer Rundfunk, he expanded upon the question: "Upon moving to Berlin I was beset by a panicky fear of somehow flawing my precious layer of Russian by learning to speak German fluently. The task of linguistic occlusion was made easier by the fact that I lived in a closed émigré circle of Russian friends and read exclusively Russian newspapers, magazines, and books. My only forays into the local language were the civilities exchanged with my successive landlords or landladies and the routine necessities of shopping: *Ich möchte etwas Schinken.* I now regret that I did so poorly; I regret it from a cultural point of view." Yet he had been acquainted with German entomological works since boyhood, and his first literary success was a translation, in the Crimea, of some Heine songs for a Russian concert singer. In later life, his wife knew German, and with her help he checked translations of his own works into that language and ventured to improve, in his lectures on "The Metamorphosis," upon the English version by Willa and Edwin Muir. There is no reason to doubt the claim he makes, in his introduction to the translation of his rather Kafkaesque novel *Invitation to a Beheading*, that at the time of its writing in 1935 he had read no Kafka. In 1969 he told a BBC interviewer, "I do not know German and so could not read Kafka before the nineteen thirties when his *La métamorphose* appeared in *La nouvelle revue française*"; two years later he told Bavarian Broadcasting, "I read Goethe and Kafka *en regard* as I also did Homer and Horace."

The first author herein lectured upon was the last Nabokov enrolled among his subjects. The event can be followed with some closeness in *The Nabokov-Wilson Letters* (Harper & Row, 1978). On 17 April 1950, Nabokov wrote to Edmund Wilson from Cornell, where he had recently taken academic employment: "Next year I am teaching a course called 'European Fiction' (XIX and XX c.). What English writers (novels or short stories) would you suggest? I must have at least two." Wilson promptly responded, "About the English novelists: in my opinion the two incomparably greatest (leaving Joyce out of account as an Irishman) are Dickens and Jane Austen. Try rereading, if you haven't done so, the later Dickens of *Bleak House* and *Little Dorrit*. Jane Austen is worth reading all through—even her fragments are remarkable." On 5 May, Nabokov wrote back, "Thanks for the suggestion concerning my fiction course. I dislike Jane, and am prejudiced, in fact, against all women writers. They are in another class. Could never see anything in *Pride and Prejudice*. ... I shall take Stevenson instead of Jane A." Wilson countered, "You are mistaken about Jane Austen. I think you ought to read *Mansfield Park*. ... She is, in my opinion, one of the half dozen greatest English writers (the others being Shakespeare, Milton, Swift, Keats and Dickens). Stevenson is second-rate. I don't know why you admire him so much—though he *has* done some rather fine short stories." And, uncharacteristically, Nabokov capitulated, writing on 15 May, "I am in the middle of *Bleak House*—going slowly because of the many notes I must make for class-discussion. Great stuff. ... I have obtained *Mansfield Park* and I think I shall use it too in my course. Thanks for these most useful suggestions." Six months later, he wrote Wilson with some glee:

I want to make my mid-term report on the two books you suggested I should discuss with my students. In connection with *Mansfield Park* I had them read the works mentioned by the characters in the novel—the two first cantos of the "Lay of the Last Minstrel," Cowper's "The Task," passages from *King Henry the Eighth*, Crabbe's tale "The Parting Hour," bits of Johnson's *The Idler*, Browne's address to "A Pipe of Tobacco" (Imitation of

Pope), Sterne's *Sentimental Journey* (the whole "gate-and-no-key" passage comes from there—and the starling) and of course *Lovers' Vows* in Mrs. Inchbald's inimitable translation (a scream).... I think I had more fun than my class.

Nabokov in his early Berlin years supported himself by giving lessons in an unlikely quintet of subjects: English, French, boxing, tennis, and prosody. In the latter years of exile, public readings in Berlin and in such other centers of émigré population as Prague, Paris, and Brussels earned more money than the sales of his works in Russian. So, but for his lack of an advanced degree, he was not unprepared, arriving in America in 1940, for the lecturer's role that was to provide, until the publication of *Lolita*, his main source of income. At Wellesley for the first time, in 1941, he delivered an assortment of lectures among whose titles—"Hard Facts about Readers," "A Century of Exile," "The Strange Fate of Russian Literature"—was one included in this volume, "The Art of Literature and Commonsense." Until 1948 he lived with his family in Cambridge (at 8 Craigie Circle, his longest-maintained address until the Palace Hotel in Montreux received him for keeps in 1961) and divided his time between two academic appointments: that of Resident Lecturer at Wellesley College, and as Research Fellow in Entomology at Harvard's Museum of Comparative Zoology. He worked tremendously hard in those years, and was twice hospitalized. Besides instilling the elements of Russian grammar into the heads of young women and pondering the minute structures of butterfly genitalia, he was creating himself as an American writer, publishing two novels (one written in English in Paris), an eccentric and witty book on Gogol, and, in *The Atlantic Monthly* and *The New Yorker*, stories, reminiscences, and poems of an arresting ingenuity and elan. Among the growing body of admirers for his English writings was Morris Bishop, light-verse virtuoso and head of the Romance Languages Department at Cornell; he mounted a successful campaign to hire Nabokov away from Wellesley, where his resident lectureship was neither remunerative nor secure. According to Bishop's reminiscence "Nabokov at Cornell" (*TriQuarterly*, No. 17, Winter 1970: a special issue devoted to Nabokov on his seventieth birthday), Nabokov was designated Associate Professor of Slavic and at first gave "an intermediate reading course in Russian Literature and an advanced course on a special subject, usually Pushkin, or the Modernist Movement in Russian Literature.... As his Russian classes were inevitably small, even invisible, he was assigned a course in English on Masters of European Fiction." According to Nabokov, the nickname by which Literature 311-312 was known, "Dirty Lit," "was an inherited joke: it had been applied to the lectures of my immediate predecessor, a sad, gentle, hard-drinking fellow who was more interested in the sex life of the authors than in their books."

A former student from the course, Ross Wetzsteon, contributed to the *TriQuarterly* special issue a fond remembrance of Nabokov as teacher. " 'Caress the details,' Nabokov would utter, rolling the r, his voice the rough caress of a cat's tongue, 'the divine details!' " The lecturer insisted on changes in every translation, and would scribble an antic diagram on the blackboard with a mock plea that the students "copy this exactly as I draw it." His accent caused half the class to write "epidramatic" where Nabokov had said "epigrammatic." Wetzsteon concludes, "Nabokov was a great teacher not because he taught the subject well but because he exemplified, and stimulated in his students, a profound and loving attitude toward it." Another survivor of Literature 311-312 has recalled how Nabokov would begin the term with the words, "The seats are numbered. I would like you to choose your seat and stick to it. This is because I would like to link up your faces with your names. All satisfied with their seats? O.K. No talking, no smoking, no knitting, no newspaper reading, no sleeping, and for God's sake take notes." Before an exam, he would say, "One clear head, one blue book, ink, think, abbreviate obvious names, for example, Madame Bovary. Do not pad ignorance with eloquence. Unless medical evidence is produced nobody will be permitted to retire to the W. C." As a lecturer he was enthusiastic, electric, evangelical. My own wife, who sat in the last classes Nabokov taught—the spring and fall terms of 1958—before, suddenly enriched by *Lolita*, he took a leave of absence that never ended, was so deeply under his spell that she attended one lecture with a fever high enough to send her to the infirmary immediately afterward. "I felt he could teach me how to read. I believed he could give me something that would last all my life—and it did." She cannot to this day take Thomas Mann seriously, and has not surrendered a jot of the central dogma she culled from Literature 311-312: "Style and structure are the essence of a book; great ideas are hogwash."

Yet even his rare ideal student might fall prey to Nabokov's mischief. When our Miss Ruggles, a tender twenty, went up at the end of one class to retrieve her blue book from the mess of graded "prelims" strewn there, she could not find it, and at last had to approach the professor. Nabokov stood tall and apparently abstracted on the platform above her, fussing with his papers. She begged his pardon and said that her exam didn't seem to be here. He bent low, eyebrows raised. "And what is your name?" She told him, and with prestidigitational suddenness he produced her blue book from behind his back. It was marked 97. "I wanted to see," he informed her, "what a genius looked like." And coolly he looked her up and down, while she blushed; that was the extent of their conversation. She, by the way, does not remember the course being referred to as "Dirty Lit." On campus it was called, simply, "Nabokov."

Seven years after his retirement, Nabokov remembered the course with mixed feelings:

> My method of teaching precluded genuine contact with the students. At best, they regurgitated a few bits of my brain during examinations. . . . Vainly I tried to replace my appearances at the lectern by taped records to be played over the college radio. On the other hand, I deeply enjoyed the chuckle of appreciation in this or that warm spot of the lecture hall at this or that point of my lecture. My best reward comes from those former students of mine who ten or fifteen years later write to me to say that they now understand what I wanted of them when I taught them to visualize Emma Bovary's mistranslated hairdo or the arrangement of rooms in the Samsa household. . . .

In more than one interview handed down, on 3 x 5 cards, from the Montreux-Palace, the publication of a book based upon his Cornell lectures was promised, but (with such other works in progress as his illustrated treatise on *Butterflies in Art* and the novel *Original of Laura*) the project still hovered at the air at the time of the great man's death in the summer of 1977.

Now here, wonderfully, the lectures are. And still redolent of the classroom odors that an authorial revision might have scoured away. Nothing one has heard or read about them has quite foretold their striking, enveloping quality of pedagogic warmth. The youth and, somehow, femininity of the audience have been gathered into the urgent, ardent instructor's voice "The work with this group has been a particularly pleasant association between the fountain of my voice and a garden of ears—some open, others closed, many very receptive, a few merely ornamental, but all of them human and divine." For longish stretches we are being read to, as young Vladimir Vladimirovich was read aloud to by his father, his mother, and Mademoiselle. During these stretches of quotation we must imagine the accent, the infectious rumbling pleasure, the theatrical power of this lecturer who, now portly and balding, was once an athlete and who partook of the Russian tradition of flamboyant oral presentation. Elsewhere, the intonation, the twinkle, the sneer, the excited pounce are present in the prose, a liquid speaking prose effortlessly bright and prone to purl into metaphor and pun: a dazzling demonstration, for those lucky Cornell students in the remote, clean-cut fifties, of the irresistibly artistic sensibility. Nabokov's reputation as a literary critic, heretofore circumscribed, in English, by his laborious monument to Pushkin and his haughty dismissals of Freud and Faulkner and Mann, benefits from the evidence of these generous and patient appreciations, as they range from his delineation of Jane Austen's "dimpled" style and his hearty identification with Dickens's gusto to his reverent explication of Flaubert's counterpoint and his charmingly awed—like that of a boy dismantling his first watch—laying bare of Joyce's busily ticking synchronizations. Nabokov took early and lasting delight in the exact sciences, and his blissful hours spent within the luminous hush of microscopic examination carry over into his delicate tracing of the horse theme in *Madame Bovary* or the twinned dreams of Bloom and Dedalus; lepidoptery placed him in a world beyond common sense, where on a butterfly's hindwing "a large eyespot imitates a drop of liquid with such uncanny perfection that a line which crosses the wing is slightly displaced at the exact stretch where it passes through," where "when a butterfly has to look like a leaf, not only are all the details of a leaf beautifully rendered but markings mimicking grub-bored holes are generously thrown in." He asked, then, of his own art and the art of others a something extra—a flourish of mimetic magic or deceptive doubleness—that was supernatural and surreal in the root sense of these degraded words. Where there was not this shimmer of the gratuitous, of the superhuman and nonutilitarian, he turned harshly impatient, in terms that imply a lack of feature, a blankness peculiar to the inanimate: "Many accepted authors simply do not exist for me. Their names are engraved on empty graves, their books are dummies...." Where he *did* find this shimmer, producing its tingle in the spine, his enthusiasm went far beyond the academic, and he became an inspired, and surely inspiring, teacher.

Lectures that so wittily introduce themselves, and that make no secret of their prejudices and premises, need little further introduction. The fifties, with their emphasis upon private space, their disdainful regard of public concerns, their sense of solitary, disengaged artistry, and their New-Criticism faith that all essential information is contained within the work itself, were a more congenial theatre for Nabokov's ideas than the following decades might have been. But in any decade Nabokov's approach would have seemed radical in the degree of severance between reality and art that it supposes. "The truth is that great novels are great fairy tales—

and the novels in this series are supreme fairy tales. . . . literature was born on the day when a boy came crying wolf wolf and there was no wolf behind him." But the boy who cried wolf became an irritation to his tribe and was allowed to perish. Another priest of the imagination, Wallace Stevens, could decree that "if we desire to formulate an accurate theory of poetry, we find it necessary to examine the structure of reality, because reality is a central reference for poetry." Whereas for Nabokov, reality has less a structure than a pattern, a habit, of deception: "Every great writer is a great deceiver, but so is that arch-cheat Nature. Nature always deceives." In his aesthetic, small heed is paid to the lowly delight of recognition, and the blunt virtue of verity. For Nabokov, the world—art's raw material—is itself an artistic creation, so insubstantial and illusionistic that he seems to imply a masterpiece can be spun from thin air, by pure act of the artist's imperial will. Yet works like *Madame Bovary* and *Ulysses* glow with the heat of resistance that the will to manipulate meets in banal, heavily actual subjects. Acquaintance, abhorrence, and the helpless love we give our own bodies and fates join in these transmuted scenes of Dublin and Rouen; away from them, in works like *Salammbô* and *Finnegans Wake*, Joyce and Flaubert yield to their dreaming, dandyish selves and are swallowed by their hobbies. In his passionate reading of "The Metamorphosis," Nabokov deprecates as "mediocrity surrounding genius" Gregor Samsa's philistine and bourgeois family without acknowledging, at the very heart of Kafka's poignance, how much Gregor needs and adores these possibly crass, but also vital and definite, inhabitants of the mundane. The ambivalence omnipresent in Kafka's rich tragi-comedy has no place in Nabokov's credo, though in artistic practice a work like *Lolita* brims with it, and with a formidable density of observed detail—"sense data selected, permeated, and grouped," in his own formula.

The Cornell years were productive ones for Nabokov. After arriving there he completed *Speak, Memory*. It was in an Ithaca backyard that his wife prevented him from burning the difficult beginnings of *Lolita*, which he completed in 1953. The good-humored stories of *Pnin* were written entirely at Cornell, the heroic researches attending his translation of *Eugene Onegin* were largely carried out in her libraries, and Cornell is reflected fondly in the college milieu of *Pale Fire*. One might imagine that his move two hundred miles inland from the East Coast, with its frequent summer excursions to the Far West, gave him a franker purchase on his adopted "lovely, trustful, dreamy, enormous country" (to quote Humbert Humbert). Nabokov was nearly fifty when he came to Ithaca, and had ample reason for artistic exhaustion. He had been exiled twice, driven from

Russia by Bolshevism and from Europe by Hitler, and had created a brilliant body of work in what amounted to a dying language, for an émigré public that was inexorably disappearing. Yet in this his second American decade he managed to bring an entirely new audacity and panache to American literature, to help revive the native vein of fantasy, and to bestow upon himself riches and an international reputation. It is pleasant to suspect that the rereading compelled by the preparation of these lectures at the outset of the decade, and the admonitions and intoxications rehearsed with each year's delivery, contributed to the splendid redefining of Nabokov's creative powers; and to detect, in his fiction of those years, something of Austen's nicety, Dickens's *brio*, and Stevenson's "delightful winey taste," added to and spicing up the Continental stock of Nabokov's own inimitable brew. His favorite American authors were, he once allowed, Melville and Hawthorne, and we may regret that he never lectured upon them. But let us be grateful for the lectures that *were* called into being and that are here given permanent form, with another volume to come. Tinted windows overlooking seven masterpieces, they are as enhancing as "the harlequin pattern of colored panes" through which Nabokov as a child, being read to on the porch of his summer home, would gaze out at his family's garden.

LECTURES ON LITERATURE

*My course, among other things, is
a kind of detective investigation of
the mystery of literary structures.*

Good Readers
and Good Writers

"How to be a Good Reader" or "Kindness to Authors"—
something of that sort might serve to provide a subtitle for these various
discussions of various authors, for my plan is to deal lovingly, in loving and
lingering detail, with several European masterpieces. A hundred years ago,
Flaubert in a letter to his mistress made the following remark: *Comme l'on
serait savant si l'on connaissait bien seulement cinq à six livres*: "What a
scholar one might be if one knew well only some half a dozen books."

In reading, one should notice and fondle details. There is nothing wrong
about the moonshine of generalization when it comes *after* the sunny
trifles of the book have been lovingly collected. If one begins with a ready-
made generalization, one begins at the wrong end and travels away from
the book before one has started to understand it. Nothing is more boring or
more unfair to the author than starting to read, say, *Madame Bovary*, with
the preconceived notion that it is a denunciation of the bourgeoisie. We
should always remember that the work of art is invariably the creation of a
new world, so that the first thing we should do is to study that new world as
closely as possible, approaching it as something brand new, having no
obvious connection with the worlds we already know. When this new
world has been closely studied, then and only then let us examine its links
with other worlds, other branches of knowledge.

Another question: Can we expect to glean information about places and
times from a novel? Can anybody be so naive as to think he or she can learn
anything about the past from those buxom best-sellers that are hawked
around by book clubs under the heading of historical novels? But what

about the masterpieces? Can we rely on Jane Austen's picture of landowning England with baronets and landscaped grounds when all she knew was a clergyman's parlor? And *Bleak House*, that fantastic romance within a fantastic London, can we call it a study of London a hundred years ago? Certainly not. And the same holds for other such novels in this series. The truth is that great novels are great fairy tales—and the novels in this series are supreme fairy tales.

Time and space, the colors of the seasons, the movements of muscles and minds, all these are for writers of genius (as far as we can guess and I trust we guess right) not traditional notions which may be borrowed from the circulating library of public truths but a series of unique surprises which master artists have learned to express in their own unique way. To minor authors is left the ornamentation of the commonplace: these do not bother about any reinventing of the world; they merely try to squeeze the best they can out of a given order of things, out of traditional patterns of fiction. The various combinations these minor authors are able to produce within these set limits may be quite amusing in a mild ephemeral way because minor readers like to recognize their own ideas in a pleasing disguise. But the real writer, the fellow who sends planets spinning and models a man asleep and eagerly tampers with the sleeper's rib, that kind of author has no given values at his disposal: he must create them himself. The art of writing is a very futile business if it does not imply first of all the art of seeing the world as the potentiality of fiction. The material of this world may be real enough (as far as reality goes) but does not exist at all as an accepted entirety: it is chaos, and to this chaos the author says "go!" allowing the world to flicker and to fuse. It is now recombined in its very atoms, not merely in its visible and superficial parts. The writer is the first man to map it and to name the natural objects it contains. Those berries there are edible. That speckled creature that bolted across my path might be tamed. That lake between those trees will be called Lake Opal or, more artistically, Dishwater Lake. That mist is a mountain—and that mountain must be conquered. Up a trackless slope climbs the master artist, and at the top, on a windy ridge, whom do you think he meets? The panting and happy reader, and there they spontaneously embrace and are linked forever if the book lasts forever.

One evening at a remote provincial college through which I happened to be jogging on a protracted lecture tour, I suggested a little quiz—ten definitions of a reader, and from these ten the students had to choose four definitions that would combine to make a good reader. I have mislaid the list, but as far as I remember the definitions went something like this. Select four answers to the question what should a reader be to be a good reader:

1. The reader should belong to a book club.
2. The reader should identify himself or herself with the hero or heroine.
3. The reader should concentrate on the social-economic angle.
4. The reader should prefer a story with action and dialogue to one with none.
5. The reader should have seen the book in a movie.
6. The reader should be a budding author.
7. The reader should have imagination.
8. The reader should have memory.
9. The reader should have a dictionary.
10. The reader should have some artistic sense.

The students leaned heavily on emotional identification, action, and the social-economic or historical angle. Of course, as you have guessed, the good reader is one who has imagination, memory, a dictionary, and some artistic sense—which sense I propose to develop in myself and in others whenever I have the chance.

Incidentally, I use the word *reader* very loosely. Curiously enough, one cannot *read* a book: one can only reread it. A good reader, a major reader, an active and creative reader is a rereader. And I shall tell you why. When we read a book for the first time the very process of laboriously moving our eyes from left to right, line after line, page after page, this complicated physical work upon the book, the very process of learning in terms of space and time what the book is about, this stands between us and artistic appreciation. When we look at a painting we do not have to move our eyes in a special way even if, as in a book, the picture contains elements of depth and development. The element of time does not really enter in a first contact with a painting. In reading a book, we must have time to acquaint ourselves with it. We have no physical organ (as we have the eye in regard to a painting) that takes in the whole picture and then can enjoy its details. But at a second, or third, or fourth reading we do, in a sense, behave towards a book as we do towards a painting. However, let us not confuse the physical eye, that monstrous masterpiece of evolution, with the mind, an even more monstrous achievement. A book, no matter what it is—a work of fiction or a work of science (the boundary line between the two is not as clear as is generally believed)—a book of fiction appeals first of all to the mind. The mind, the brain, the top of the tingling spine, is, or should be, the only instrument used upon a book.

Now, this being so, we should ponder the question how does the mind work when the sullen reader is confronted by the sunny book. First, the sullen mood melts away, and for better or worse the reader enters into the spirit of the game. The effort to begin a book, especially if it is praised by people whom the young reader secretly deems to be too old-fashioned or too serious, this effort is often difficult to make; but once it is made, rewards are various and abundant. Since the master artist used his imagination in creating his book, it is natural and fair that the consumer of a book should use his imagination too.

There are, however, at least two varieties of imagination in the reader's case. So let us see which one of the two is the right one to use in reading a book. First, there is the comparatively lowly kind which turns for support to the simple emotions and is of a definitely personal nature. (There are various subvarieties here, in this first section of emotional reading.) A situation in a book is intensely felt because it reminds us of something that happened to us or to someone we know or knew. Or, again, a reader treasures a book mainly because it evokes a country, a landscape, a mode of living which he nostalgically recalls as part of his own past. Or, and this is the worst thing a reader can do, he identifies himself with a character in the book. This lowly variety is not the kind of imagination I would like readers to use.

So what is the authentic instrument to be used by the reader? It is impersonal imagination and artistic delight. What should be established, I think, is an artistic harmonious balance between the reader's mind and the author's mind. We ought to remain a little aloof and take pleasure in this aloofness while at the same time we keenly enjoy—passionately enjoy, enjoy with tears and shivers—the inner weave of a given masterpiece. To be quite objective in these matters is of course impossible. Everything that is worthwhile is to some extent subjective. For instance, you sitting there may be merely my dream, and I may be your nightmare. But what I mean is that the reader must know when and where to curb his imagination and this he does by trying to get clear the specific world the author places at his disposal. We must see things and hear things, we must visualize the rooms, the clothes, the manners of an author's people. The color of Fanny Price's eyes in *Mansfield Park* and the furnishing of her cold little room are important.

We all have different temperaments, and I can tell you right now that the best temperament for a reader to have, or to develop, is a combination of the artistic and the scientific one. The enthusiastic artist alone is apt to be too subjective in his attitude towards a book, and so a scientific coolness of judgment will temper the intuitive heat. If, however, a would-be reader is utterly devoid of passion and patience—of an artist's passion and a scientist's patience—he will hardly enjoy great literature.

Literature was born not the day when a boy crying wolf, wolf came running out of the Neanderthal valley with a big gray wolf at his heels: literature was born on the day when a boy came crying wolf, wolf and there was no wolf behind him. That the poor little fellow because he lied too often was finally eaten up by a real beast is quite incidental. But here is what is important. Between the wolf in the tall grass and the wolf in the tall story there is a shimmering go-between. That go-between, that prism, is the art of literature.

Literature is invention. Fiction is fiction. To call a story a true story is an insult to both art and truth. Every great writer is a great deceiver, but so is that arch-cheat Nature. Nature always deceives. From the simple deception of propagation to the prodigiously sophisticated illusion of protective colors in butterflies or birds, there is in Nature a marvelous system of spells and wiles. The writer of fiction only follows Nature's lead.

Going back for a moment to our wolf-crying woodland little woolly fellow, we may put it this way: the magic of art was in the shadow of the wolf that he deliberately invented, his dream of the wolf; then the story of his tricks made a good story. When he perished at last, the story told about him acquired a good lesson in the dark around the camp fire. But he was the little magician. He was the inventor.

There are three points of view from which a writer can be considered: he may be considered as a storyteller, as a teacher, and as an enchanter. A major writer combines these three—storyteller, teacher, enchanter—but it is the enchanter in him that predominates and makes him a major writer.

To the storyteller we turn for entertainment, for mental excitement of the simplest kind, for emotional participation, for the pleasure of traveling in some remote region in space or time. A slightly different though not necessarily higher mind looks for the teacher in the writer. Propagandist, moralist, prophet—this is the rising sequence. We may go to the teacher not only for moral education but also for direct knowledge, for simple facts. Alas, I have known people whose purpose in reading the French and Russian novelists was to learn something about life in gay Paree or in sad Russia. Finally, and above all, a great writer is always a great enchanter, and it is here that we come to the really exciting part when we try to grasp the individual magic of his genius and to study the style, the imagery, the pattern of his novels or poems.

The three facets of the great writer—magic, story, lesson—are prone to blend in one impression of unified and unique radiance, since the magic of art may be present in the very bones of the story, in the very marrow of thought. There are masterpieces of dry, limpid, organized thought which provoke in us an artistic quiver quite as strongly as a novel like *Mansfield Park* does or as any rich flow of Dickensian sensual imagery. It seems to me that a good formula to test the quality of a novel is, in the long run, a merging of the precision of poetry and the intuition of science. In order to bask in that magic a wise reader reads the book of genius not with his heart, not so much with his brain, but with his spine. It is there that occurs the telltale tingle even though we must keep a little aloof, a little detached when reading. Then with a pleasure which is both sensual and intellectual we shall watch the artist build his castle of cards and watch the castle of cards become a castle of beautiful steel and glass.

And there is beauty, emotion, magic

In order to experience that base in that magic,
~~and to magnify many times the idea~~

a wise reader reads the book of genius
not with his heart, not ~~so much~~ with his brain
— but with his spine. It is there that occurs
the tell tale tingle — [~~while the brain attends~~
~~with a smile and the heart tiptoes in the wings~~]
~~In a later lecture I shall discuss this~~
~~business of the spine.~~ ~~So to unclose his~~
~~talk is not our knowledge bears, do no~~
~~sound again~~
Let us keep a little aloof, a little detached
when reading, ~~let us hold~~ and then
with a pleasure ^which is both^ sensual ~~as~~ intellectual ~~and~~
~~and not unquizzical~~ we shall watch the
artist build his castle of cards and
watch the castle of cards ^become^ ~~turn into~~ a
castle of ~~marble has~~ beautiful steel and glass

12.3

Portsmouth is in Hampshire

at least from which it could be distant

Fanny is born in 1790 Arrives 1800

mark action in 1808 (the ball
at M.P. being Thursday, 22. XII)
— which could be only 1808
George III (reign 1760 - 1820)

CHAPTER I

1811-13 — 50 = 1781

ABOUT thirty years ago, Miss Maria Ward, of Huntingdon,
with only seven thousand pounds, had the good luck to captivate Sir Thomas Bertram, of Mansfield Park, in the county of
Northampton, and to be thereby raised to the rank of a baronet's
lady, with all the comforts and consequences of an handsome
house and large income. All Huntingdon exclaimed on the
greatness of the match, and her uncle, the lawyer, himself, allowed
her to be at least three thousand pounds short of any equitable
claim to it. She had two sisters to be benefited by her elevation;
and such of their acquaintance as thought Miss Ward and Miss
Frances quite as handsome as Miss Maria, did not scruple to
predict their marrying with almost equal advantage. But there
certainly are not so many men of large fortune in the world, as
there are pretty women to deserve them. Miss Ward, at the end
of half a dozen years, found herself obliged to be attached to the
Rev. Mr. Norris, a friend of her brother-in-law, with scarcely
any private fortune, and Miss Frances fared yet worse. Miss
Ward's match, indeed, when it came to the point, was not
contemptible, Sir Thomas being happily able to give his friend
an income in the living of Mansfield; and Mr. and Mrs. Norris
began their career of conjugal felicity with very little less than a
thousand a-year. But Miss Frances married, in the common
phrase, to disoblige her family, and by fixing on a Lieutenant
of Marines, without education, fortune, or connections, did it
very thoroughly. She could hardly have made a more untoward
choice. Sir Thomas Bertram had interest, which, from principle

I

3 clergymen Grant, Norris and Sir Thomas son Edmund

influence

Mansfield Park
(1814)

Mansfield Park was composed in Chawton, Hampshire. It was begun in February 1811 and finished soon after June 1813; that is to say, it took Jane Austen about twenty-eight months to complete a novel containing some 160 thousand words divided into forty-eight chapters. It was published in 1814 (the same year as Scott's *Waverley* and Byron's *Corsair*) in three volumes. These three parts, though the conventional method of publication at the time, in fact stress the structure, the playlike form of the book, a comedy of manners and mischief, of smiles and sighs, in three acts made up, respectively, of eighteen, thirteen, and seventeen chapters.

I am averse to distinguishing content from form and to mixing conventional plots with thematic currents. All I need say at the present time, before we have plunged deep into the book and bathed in it (not waded through it), is that the superficial action in *Mansfield Park* is the emotional interplay between two families of country gentlefolks. One of these two families consists of Sir Thomas Bertram and his wife, their tall athletic children, Tom, Edmund, Maria, and Julia, and their gentle niece Fanny Price, the author's pet, the character through whom the story is sifted. Fanny is an adopted child, an impecunious niece, a gentle ward (notice that her mother's maiden name was Ward). This was a most popular figure in the novels of the eighteenth and nineteenth centuries. There are several reasons why a novelist would be tempted to use this ward of literature. First, her position in the tepid bosom of an essentially alien family yields the little alien a steady stream of pathos. Second, the little stranger can be easily made to go the romantic way in regard to the son of

Opening page of Nabokov's teaching copy of *Mansfield Park*.

the family and obvious conflicts can result. Third, her dual position of detached observer and participant in the daily life of the family make of her a convenient representative of the author. We find the gentle ward not only in the works of lady authors but also in those of Dickens, Dostoevski, Tolstoy, and many others. The prototype of these quiet maidens, whose bashful beauty finishes by shining in full through the veils of humility and self-effacement—shining in full when the logic of virtue triumphs over the chances of life—the prototype of these quiet maidens is, of course, Cinderella. Dependent, helpless, friendless, neglected, forgotten—and then marrying the hero.

Mansfield Park is a fairy tale, but then all novels are, in a sense, fairy tales. At first sight Jane Austen's manner and matter may seem to be old-fashioned, stilted, unreal. But this is a delusion to which the bad reader succumbs. The good reader is aware that the quest for real life, real people, and so forth is a meaningless process when speaking of books. In a book, the reality of a person, or object, or a circumstance depends exclusively on the world of that particular book. An original author always invents an original world, and if a character or an action fits into the pattern of that world, then we experience the pleasurable shock of artistic truth, no matter how unlikely the person or thing may seem if transferred into what book reviewers, poor hacks, call "real life." There is no such thing as real life for an author of genius: he must create it himself and then create the consequences. The charm of *Mansfield Park* can be fully enjoyed only when we adopt its conventions, its rules, its enchanting make-believe. Mansfield Park never existed, and its people never lived.

Miss Austen's is not a violently vivid masterpiece as some other novels in this series are. Novels like *Madame Bovary* or *Anna Karenin* are delightful explosions admirably controlled. *Mansfield Park*, on the other hand, is the work of a lady and the game of a child. But from that workbasket comes exquisite needlework art, and there is a streak of marvelous genius in that child.

———

"About thirty years ago. . . ." So the novel begins. Miss Austen wrote it between 1811 and 1813 so that "thirty years ago" would mean, when mentioned at the beginning of the novel, 1781. About 1781, then, "Miss

———

Nabokov's map of England locating the action of *Mansfield Park*

———

VLADIMIR NABOKOV

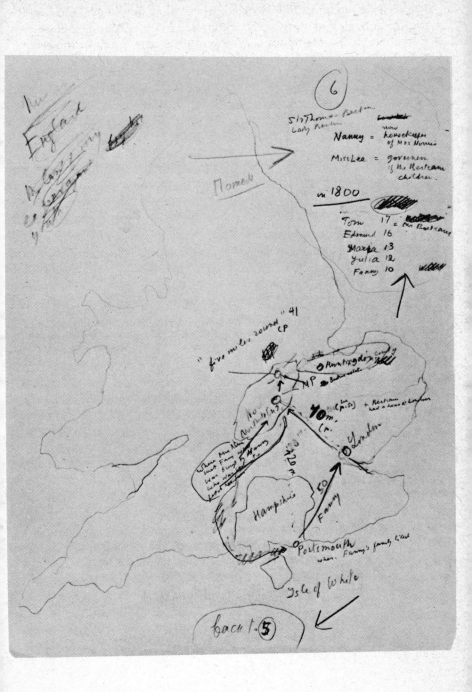

Maria Ward, of Huntingdon, with only seven thousand pounds [as dowry], had the good luck to captivate Sir Thomas Bertram, of Mansfield Park, in the county of Northampton. . . ." The middle-class flutter of the event ("good luck to captivate") is delightfully conveyed here and will give the right tone to the next pages where money affairs predominate over romantic and religious ones with a kind of coy simplicity.* Every sentence in these introductory pages is terse and tapered to a fine point.

But let us get rid of the time-space element first. "About thirty years ago"—let us go back again to that opening sentence. Jane Austen is writing after her main characters, the younger people of the book, have been dismissed, have sunk in the oblivion of hopeful matrimony or hopeless spinsterhood. As we shall see, the main action of the novel takes place in 1808. The ball at Mansfield Park is held on Thursday the twenty-second of December, and if we look through our old calendars, we will see that only in 1808 could 22 December fall on Thursday. Fanny Price, the young heroine of the novel, will be eighteen by that time. She arrived in Mansfield Park in 1800 at the age of ten. King George III, a rather weird figure, was on the throne. He reigned from 1760 to 1820, a longish time, by the end of which the good man was mostly in a state of insanity and the regent, another George, had taken over. In 1808 Napoleon was at the height of his power in France; and Great Britain was at war with him, while Jefferson in this country had just got Congress to pass the Embargo Act, a law prohibiting United States ships from leaving the country for ports covered by the British and French blockade. (If you read *embargo* backwards, you get "O grab me.") But the winds of history are hardly felt in the seclusion of Mansfield Park, although a little trade wind puffs at one point when Sir Thomas has business in the Lesser Antilles.

We have now settled the time element. What about the space element? Mansfield Park is the name of the Bertram estate, a fictitious place located in Northampton (a real place) in the very heart of England.

"About thirty years ago, Miss Maria Ward. . . ." We are still at the first sentence. There are three sisters Ward, and according to the custom of the day the eldest one is called simply and very formally Miss Ward, while the two others have their Christian names prefixed. Maria Ward, the youngest sister, who seems to have been the most attractive one, a languorous, languid, listless lady, she is the one that in 1781 became the wife of a

---

*"No doubt can exist that there is in Jane Austen a slight streak of the philistine. This philistinism is obvious in her preoccupation with incomes and in her rational approach to romance and nature. Only when the philistinism is grotesque, as in Mrs. Norris and her penny-pinching, does Miss Austen really feel it and apply it in her artistic sarcasm." VN note elsewhere in the Austen folder. Ed.

baronet, Sir Thomas Bertram, and is thereafter called Lady Bertram, the mother of four children, two girls and two boys, who are the companions of Fanny Price, their cousin. Fanny's mother, the rather insipid Miss Frances Ward, also called Fanny, in 1781 married, out of spite, an impecunious hard-drinking lieutenant and had in all ten children, of whom Fanny, the heroine of the book, was the second. Finally, the eldest Miss Ward, the ugliest of the Ward sisters, was married also in 1781 to a gouty clergyman and had no children. She is Mrs. Norris, one of the most amusing and grotesque characters in the book.

Having settled these matters, let us glance at Jane Austen's way of presenting them, for the beauty of a book is more enjoyable if one understands its machinery, if one can take it apart. Jane Austen uses four methods of characterization in the beginning of the book. There is, first, the direct description, with little gems of ironic wit on Austen's part. Much of what we hear of Mrs. Norris comes in this category, but the foolish or dull people are constantly characterized. The expedition to the Rushworth country place, Sotherton, is under discussion. "It was hardly possible, indeed, that any thing else should be talked of, for Mrs. Norris was in high spirits about it; and Mrs. Rushworth, a well-meaning, civil, prosing, pompous woman who thought nothing of consequence, but as it related to her own and her son's concerns, had not yet given over pressing Lady Bertram to be of the party. Lady Bertram constantly declined it; but her placid manner of refusal made Mrs. Rushworth still think she wished to come, till Mrs. Norris's more numerous words and louder tone convinced her of the truth."

Another method is characterization through directly quoted speech. The reader discovers for himself the nature of the speaker, not only through the ideas the speaker expresses but through his mode of speech, through his mannerisms. A good example is to be found in Sir Thomas's speech: "Far be it from me to throw any fanciful impediment in the way of a plan which would be so consistent with the relative situations of each." He is speaking of the plan to have his niece, Fanny, come to Mansfield Park. Now, this is a ponderous way of expressing oneself: all he means to say is, "I do not want to invent any obstacles in regard to this plan; it is consistent with the situation." A little further on, says the gentleman going on with his elephantine speech: "To make [this plan] really serviceable to Mrs. Price and creditable to ourselves, we must secure to the child [*comma*] or consider ourselves engaged to secure to her hereafter [*comma*] as circumstances may arise [*comma*] the provision of a gentlewoman [*comma*] if no such establishment should offer as you are so sanguine in expecting." (The *such-as* formula is still with us.) For our purpose here it does not matter what exactly he is trying to say, but it is his manner that interests us, and I give this example to show how well Jane Austen renders the man through his speech. A heavy man (and a heavy father, in terms of the stage).

Yet a third method of characterization is through reported speech. What I mean is that speech is alluded to, and partly quoted, with a description of the character's way. A good example comes when Mrs. Norris is shown finding out the faults of the new parson, Dr. Grant, who has replaced her dead husband. Dr. Grant was very fond of eating, and Mrs. Grant, "instead of contriving to gratify him at little expense, gave her cook as high wages as they did at Mansfield Park." Says Miss Austen, "Mrs. Norris could not speak with any temper of such grievances, nor of the quantity of butter and eggs that were regularly consumed in the house." And now comes the introduction of the oblique speech. "Nobody loved plenty and hospitality more than herself [*says Mrs. Norris—this in itself an ironic characterizing implication, since Mrs. Norris loves it at other people's expense*]—nobody more hated pitiful doings—the parsonage she believed had never been wanting in comforts of any sort, had never borne a bad character in *her time*, but this was a way of going on she could not understand. A fine lady in a country parsonage was quite out of place. *Her* store-room she thought might have been good enough for Mrs. Grant to go into. Enquire where she would, she could not find out that Mrs. Grant had ever had more than five thousand pounds."

A fourth method of characterization is to imitate the character's speech when speaking of him, but this is seldom used except in straight reported conversation, as Edmund telling Fanny the gist of what Miss Crawford has said in her praise.

———

Mrs. Norris is a grotesque character, a rather vicious busybody, a contriving woman. She is not completely heartless, but her heart is a coarse organ. Her nieces Maria and Julia are for her the rich, healthy, big children she does not have, and in a way she dotes upon them while despising Fanny. With subtle wit Miss Austen notes, at the start of the story, that Mrs. Norris "could not possibly keep to herself" the disrespectful things concerning Sir Thomas that her sister, Fanny's mother, had said in a bitter letter. The character of Mrs. Norris is not only a thing of art in itself, it has also a functional quality, for it is because of her meddlesome nature that Fanny is finally adopted by Sir Thomas, a point of characterization that grades into structure. Why was she so eager to have Fanny adopted by the Bertrams? The answer is: "every thing was considered as settled, and the pleasures of so benevolent a scheme were already enjoyed. The division of gratifying sensations ought not, in strict justice, to have been equal; for Sir Thomas was fully resolved to be the real and consistent patron of the selected child, and Mrs. Norris had not the least intention of being at any expense whatever in her maintenance. As far as walking, talking, and contriving reached, she was thoroughly benevolent, and nobody knew better how to dictate liberality to others: but her love of money was equal to her love of directing, and she knew quite as well how to save her own as to spend that of her friends.... Under this infatuating principle, counteracted by no real affection for her sister, it was impossible for her to aim at more than the credit of projecting and arranging so expensive a charity; though perhaps she might so little know herself, as to walk home to the Parsonage after this conversation, in the happy belief of being the most liberal-minded sister and aunt in the world." Thus, though she had no real affection for her sister Mrs. Price, she enjoys the credit of arranging Fanny's future without spending one penny and without doing anything more for the child whom she forces her brother-in-law to adopt.

She calls herself a woman of few words, but torrents of triteness come from the good woman's big mouth. She is a very loud person. Miss Austen devised a way to render this loudness with especial force. Mrs. Norris is having a conversation with the Bertrams concerning the plan to bring Fanny to Mansfield Park: " 'Very true,' cried Mrs. Norris, '[these] are both very important considerations: and it will be just the same to Miss Lee, whether she has three girls to teach, or only two—there can be no difference. I only wish I could be more useful; but you see I do all in my power. I am not one of those that spare their own trouble....' " She goes on a while, then the Bertrams speak, and then again Mrs. Norris: " 'That is exactly what I think,' cried Mrs. Norris, 'and what I was saying to my husband this morning.' " Somewhat earlier, in another bit of conversation with Sir Thomas: " 'I thoroughly understand you,' cried Mrs. Norris; 'you are every thing that is generous and considerate....' " By this repetition of the verb *cried*, Austen suggests the noisy way this unpleasant woman has, and one may note that poor little Fanny when she does come to Mansfield Park is especially distressed by Mrs. Norris's loud voice.

———

By the time the first chapter is over, all the preliminaries have been taken care of. We know talkative, fussy, vulgar Mrs. Norris, stolid Sir Thomas, sulky, needy Mrs. Price, and we know indolent, languorous Lady Bertram and her pug. The decision has been made to fetch Fanny and have her live at Mansfield Park. Characterization in Miss Austen often grades into structure.* For example, it is the indolence of Lady Bertram that keeps her in the country. They had a house in London, and at first, before Fanny appeared, they would spend the spring—the fashionable season—in London; but now "Lady Bertram, in consequence of a little ill-health, and a great deal of indolence, gave up the house in town, which she had been used to occupy every spring, and remained wholly in the country, leaving Sir Thomas to attend his duty in Parliament, with whatever increase or diminution of comfort might arise from her absence." Jane Austen, we must understand, needs this arrangement in order to keep Fanny in the country without complicating the situation by journeys to London.

Fanny's education progresses, so that by the age of fifteen the governess has taught her French and history, but her cousin Edmund Bertram, who takes an interest in her, has "recommended the books which charmed her leisure hours; he encouraged her taste, and corrected her judgment; he made reading useful by talking to her of what she read, and heightened its attraction by judicious praise." Fanny's heart becomes divided between her brother William and Edmund. It is worth noticing what education was given to children in Austen's day and set. When Fanny first arrived the Bertram girls "thought her prodigiously stupid, and for the first two or three weeks were continually bringing some fresh report of it into the drawing-room. 'Dear mamma, only think, my cousin cannot put the map of Europe together—or my cousin cannot tell the principal rivers in Russia— or she never heard of Asia Minor—or she does not know the difference between water-colours and crayons!—How strange!—Did you ever hear anything so stupid?' " One of the points here is that picture puzzles— jigsaw puzzles, maps cut into pieces—were used to learn geography. And that was one hundred and fifty years ago. History was another solid study of the time. The girls continue: " 'How long ago it is, aunt, since we used to repeat the chronological order of the kings of England, with the dates of their accession, and most of the principal events of their reigns!'

" 'Yes,' added the other; 'and of the Roman emperors as low as Severus;

---

*In a note elsewhere in the Austen folder VN defines *plot* as "the supposed story." *Themes, thematic lines* are "images or an idea which is repeated here and there in the novel, as a tune reoccurs in a fugue." *Structure* is "the composition of a book, a development of events, one event causing another, a transition from one theme to another, the cunning way characters are brought in, or a new complex of action is started, or the various themes are linked up or used to move the novel forward." *Style* is "the manner of the author, his special intonations, his vocabulary, and that something which when confronted with a passage makes a reader cry out that's by Austen, not by Dickens." Ed.

besides a great deal of the Heathen Mythology, and all the Metals, Semi-Metals, Planets, and distinguished philosophers.' "

Since the Roman Emperor Severus lived at the beginning of the third century, "as low as Severus" means low in the scale of time, that is, old.

The death of Mr. Norris brings on an important change in that the living falls vacant. It had been reserved for Edmund when he should take orders, but Sir Thomas's affairs are not going well and he is forced to install not a temporary incumbent but a permanent one, an action that will materially reduce Edmund's income since he will be forced to rely on only one living, nearby in Thornton Lacey, that is also in Sir Thomas's gift. A word or two may be useful about the term *living* in connection with the Mansfield Park parsonage. An incumbent is a parson who is in possession of a benefice, of an ecclesiastical *living*, also termed a *spiritual living*. This incumbent clergyman represents a parish; he is a settled pastor. The parsonage is a portion of lands with a house for the maintenance of the incumbent. This clergyman receives an income from his parish, a kind of tax, the *tithe*, due from lands and certain industries within the limits of the parish. In culmination of a long historical development the choice of the clergyman became in some cases the privilege of a lay person, in this case of Sir Thomas Bertram. The choice was subject to the Bishop's approval, but such approval was nothing more than a formality. Sir Thomas, by the usual custom, would expect to receive some profit from the gift of the living. This is the point. Sir Thomas needs a tenant. If the living remained in the family, if Edmund were ready to take over, the income from the Mansfield parish would go to him and would therefore take care of his future. But Edmund is not yet ready to be ordained, to become a clergyman. Had not Tom, the elder son, been guilty of debts and bets, Sir Thomas might have given the living temporarily to some friend to hold until Edmund's ordination, with no profit to himself. But now he cannot afford such an arrangement, and a different disposal of the parsonage is necessary. Tom only hopes that Dr. Grant will soon "pop off," as we learn from a reported speech which characterizes Tom's slangy manner and also his light carelessness for Edmund's future.

As for the actual figures involved, we know that Mrs. Norris upon marrying Mr. Norris wound up with a yearly income very little short of one thousand pounds. If we assume for the sake of the argument that her own property was equal to that of her sister Bertram, or seven thousand pounds, we may assume that her own share of the Norris family income was about two hundred and fifty pounds, and that of Mr. Norris, derived from the parish, about seven hundred a year.

We come to another example of the way a writer introduces certain events in order to have his story move on. Parson Norris dies. The arrival of the Grants to the parsonage is made possible by the death of Mr. Norris, whom Grant replaces. And Grant's arrival in its turn leads to the arrival into the vicinity of Mansfield Park of the young Crawfords, his wife's relatives, who are to play such a large part in the novel. Further, Miss Austen's plan is to remove Sir Thomas from Mansfield Park in order to have the young people of the book overindulge their freedom, and her plan, secondly, is to bring back Sir Thomas to Mansfield Park at the height of the mild orgy that occurs in connection with the rehearsal of a certain play.

So how does she proceed? The eldest son, Tom, who would inherit all the property, has been squandering money. The Bertram affairs are not in good shape. Miss Austen removes Sir Thomas as early as the third chapter. The year is now 1806. Sir Thomas finds it expedient to go to Antigua himself for the better supervision of his affairs and expects to be away nearly a year. Antigua is a far cry from Northampton. It is an island in the West Indies, then belonging to England, one of the Lesser Antilles, about five hundred miles north of Venezuela. The plantations would have been worked by cheap slave labor, the source of the Bertram money.

The Crawfords thereupon make their entrance in Sir Thomas's absence. "Such was the state of affairs in the month of July, and Fanny had just reached her eighteenth year, when the society of the village received an addition in the brother and sister of Mrs. Grant, a Mr. and Miss Crawford, the children of her mother by a second marriage. They were young people of fortune. The son had a good estate in Norfolk, the daughter twenty thousand pounds. As children, their sister had been always very fond of them; but, as her own marriage had been soon followed by the death of their common parent, which left them in the care of a brother of their father, of whom Mrs. Grant knew nothing, she had scarcely seen them since. In their uncle's house they had found a kind home. Admiral and Mrs. Crawford, though agreeing in nothing else, were united in affection for these children, or at least were no farther adverse in their feelings than that each had their favourite, to whom they showed the greatest fondness of the two. The Admiral delighted in the boy, Mrs. Crawford doated on the girl; and it was the lady's death which now obliged her *protégée*, after some months' further trial at her uncle's house, to find another home. Admiral Crawford was a man of vicious conduct, who chose, instead of retaining his niece, to bring his mistress under his own roof; and to this Mrs. Grant was indebted for her sister's proposal of coming to her, a measure quite as welcome on one side as it could be expedient on the other. . . ." One may note the tidy way Miss Austen keeps her monetary accounts in this sequence of events that explain the Crawfords' advent. Practical sense combines with the fairy-tale note, as often happens in fairy tales.

We may now skip to the first actual pain that newly established Mary Crawford caused Fanny. It involves the theme of the horse. A dear old gray pony which Fanny had been riding for her health since she was twelve, now dies in the spring of 1807 when Fanny is seventeen and still needs exercise. This is the second functional death in the book, the first having been that of Mr. Norris. I say *functional* because both deaths affect the development of the novel and are introduced for structural purposes, purposes of development.* Mr. Norris's death had brought in the Grants, and Mrs. Grant brings in Henry and Mary Crawford, who very soon are to provide the novel with a wickedly romantic tinge. The death of the pony in chapter 4 leads, in a charming interplay of characterization involving Mrs. Norris, to Edmund's giving Fanny to ride one of his three horses, a quiet mare, a dear, beautiful, delightful creature as Mary Crawford calls her later. This is all preparation on Austen's part for a wonderful emotional scene that develops in chapter 7. Pretty, small, brown-complexioned, dark-haired Mary Crawford graduates from harp to horse. It is Fanny's new horse that Edmund lends Mary for her first lessons in riding, and he actually volunteers to teach her himself—nay actually touches Mary's small alert hands while doing so. Fanny's emotions while watching the scene from a vantage point are exquisitely depicted. The lesson has extended itself, and the mare has not been returned for her daily ride. Fanny has gone out to look for Edmund. "The houses, though scarcely half a mile apart, were not within sight of each other; but by walking fifty yards from the hall door, she could look down the park, and command a view of the parsonage and all its demesnes, gently rising beyond the village road; and in Dr. Grant's

*Nobody in *Mansfield Park* dies in the arms of the author and reader, as people do in Dickens, Flaubert, Tolstoy. The deaths in *Mansfield Park* happen somewhere behind the scenes and excite little emotion. These dull deaths have, however, a curiously strong influence on the development of plot. They have great structural importance. Thus the death of a pony leads to the *horse theme* which involves an emotional tangle between Edmund, Miss Crawford, and Fanny. The death of the clergyman Mr. Norris leads to the arrival of the Grants, and through the Grants to the Crawfords, the amusing villains of the novel; and the death of the second clergyman at the end of the novel allows the third clergyman, Edmund, to settle in the snug parsonage at Mansfield Park, allows Edmund the 'acquisition' of the Mansfield living, as Austen puts it, by the death of Dr. Grant which, as she goes on, 'occurred just after [Edmund and Fanny] had been married long enough to begin to want an increase of income,' which is a delicate manner of saying that Fanny was in a family way. There is also a dowager who dies—the grandmother of the friends of Yates—and this leads directly to Tom bringing Yates to Mansfield and the *play theme*, which is such a crucial one in the novel. Finally, the death of little Mary Price makes it possible, in the Portsmouth interlude, to have the vivid incident of the little knife take place among the Price children." VN note elsewhere in the Austen folder. Ed.

meadow she immediately saw the group—Edmund and Miss Crawford both on horseback, riding side by side, Dr. and Mrs. Grant, and Mr. Crawford, with two or three grooms, standing about and looking on. A happy party it appeared to her—all interested in one object—cheerful beyond a doubt, for the sound of merriment ascended even to her. It was a sound which did not make *her* cheerful; she wondered that Edmund should forget her, and felt a pang. She could not turn her eyes from the meadow, she could not help watching all that passed. At first Miss Crawford and her companion made the circuit of the field, which was not small, at a foot's pace; then, at *her* apparent suggestion, they rose into a canter; and to Fanny's timid nature it was most astonishing to see how well she sat. After a few minutes, they stopt entirely, Edmund was close to her, he was speaking to her, he was evidently directing her management of the bridle, he had hold of her hand; she saw it, or the imagination supplied what the eye could not reach. She must not wonder at all this; what could be more natural than that Edmund should be making himself useful, and proving his good-nature by any one? She could not but think indeed that Mr. Crawford might as well have saved him the trouble; that it would have been particularly proper and becoming in a brother to have done it himself; but Mr. Crawford, with all his boasted good-nature, and all his coachmanship, probably knew nothing of the matter, and had no active kindness in comparison of Edmund. She began to think it rather hard upon the mare to have such double duty; if she were forgotten the poor mare should be remembered."

But the development does not stop. The theme of the horse leads to another subject. We have already met Mr. Rushworth, who is going to marry Maria Bertram. We have met him, in fact, about the same time as we met the horse. The transition now comes from the horse theme to what we shall call the *Sotherton escapade theme*. In his infatuation with Mary, the little amazon, Edmund has almost completely deprived poor Fanny of that unfortunate mare. Mary on the mare and he on his roadster go for a long ride to Mansfield common. And here is the transition: "A successful scheme of this sort generally brings on another; and the having been to Mansfield common, disposed them all for going somewhere else the day after. There were many other views to be shewn, and though the weather was hot, there were shady lanes wherever they wanted to go. A young party

---

Nabokov's notes on Fanny's horse rides

Mid August 188-

Fanny is deprived of horse-riding, and walks away

E, Seven ⟶ Fanny and the roses in the hot sun (p. 62 - 65 Read)

Her rides recommence the next day.

p. 66-67. Wednesday to Sotherton, ten miles away

p. 68 Open book   chaise and barouche ("convertible")   a. Soon wheeled carriage with a double — seat in front for driver and postn, and two double seats inside, one facing back on the other front, and a folded top.

how was the road to Sotherton?

name of coachman?   Wilcox.

p. 70   Julia hastily leaving the room good.)

Describe how they sat in the barouche

(Henry Crawford driver. Julia on box with next to him. In the Maria Bertram, Mary Crawford, Fanny and Mrs Norris facing back

Fanny beside Mary Crawford

Edmund on horseback   Mrs Norris and Maria Bertram facing front

p. 71   Fanny and Mary

barouche

is always provided with a shady lane." Rushworth's estate, Sotherton, is further than Mansfield common. Theme after theme opens its petals like a domestic rose.

The subject of Sotherton Court has already been raised by Mr. Rushworth's praises of the "improvement" of a friend's estate and his avowed determination to hire the same improver for his own grounds. In the discussion that follows it is gradually decided that Henry Crawford should look over the problem, instead of a professional, and that they all should accompany him in a party. In chapters 8 through 10 the inspection takes place and the Sotherton escapade begins its full cycle, which in turn will prepare for the next escapade, that of the play rehearsal. These themes are gradually developed, are engendered and evolved one from another. This is structure.

Let us return, now, to the beginning of the Sotherton theme. This is the first big conversational piece in the book, one in which Henry Crawford, his sister, young Rushworth, his fiancée Maria Bertram, the Grants, and all the rest are shown in speech. The subject is the improvement of grounds, which means landscaping—the alteration and decoration of houses and grounds on principles more or less "picturesque," which from the age of Pope to the age of Henry Crawford was a chief amusement of cultivated leisure. Mr. Humphrey Repton, then the head of his profession, is introduced by name. Miss Austen must have seen his books on drawing-room tables in the country houses which she visited. Jane Austen misses no opportunity for ironic characterization. Mrs. Norris elaborates all that they would have done in improvements to the parsonage if it had not been for Mr. Norris's poor health. " 'He could hardly ever get out, poor man, to enjoy any thing, and *that* disheartened me from doing several things that Sir Thomas and I used to talk of. If it had not been for *that*, we should have carried on the garden wall, and made the plantation to shut out the churchyard, just as Dr. Grant has done. We were always doing something, as it was. It was only the spring twelvemonth before Mr. Norris's death, that we put in the apricot against the stable wall, which is now grown such a noble tree, and getting to such perfection, sir,' addressing herself then to Dr. Grant.

" 'The tree thrives well, beyond a doubt, madam,' replied Dr. Grant. 'The soil is good; and I never pass it without regretting, that the fruit should be so little worth the trouble of gathering.'

" 'Sir, it is a moor park, we bought it as a moor park, and it cost us—that is, it was a present from Sir Thomas, but I saw the bill, and I know it cost seven shillings, and was charged as a moor park.'

" 'You were imposed on, ma'am,' replied Dr. Grant; 'these potatoes have as much flavour of a moor park apricot, as the fruit from that tree. It is an insipid fruit at the best; but a good apricot is eatable, which none from my garden are.' "

Thus this inedible apricot, nicely corresponding to the late sterile Mr. Norris, this bitter little apricot is all that Mrs. Norris's long voluble speech about her improvement of the grounds and all her late husband's labors are able to produce.

As for Rushworth, the young man becomes puzzled and mixed up in his speech, a point of style rendered obliquely by the author through an ironic description of what he is trying to say. "Mr. Rushworth was eager to assure her ladyship of his acquiescence [about planting shrubbery], and tried to make out something complimentary; but, between his submission to *her* taste, and his having always intended the same himself, with superadded objects of professing attention to the comfort of ladies in general, and of insinuating, that there was one only whom he was anxious to please, he grew puzzled; and Edmund was glad to put an end to his speech by a proposal of wine." This is a device found elsewhere in the novel, as in Lady Bertram's talking of the ball. The author does not give the speech but devotes a descriptive sentence to it. And now comes the point: not only the contents of that sentence but its own rhythm, construction, and intonation convey the special feature of the described speech.

The subject of improving grounds is interrupted by Mary Crawford's arch patter about her harp and her uncle the admiral. Mrs. Grant suggests that Henry Crawford has had some experience as an improver and might assist Rushworth. After some disavowals of his abilities, he accepts Rushworth's proposal and the plan for the party is formulated at Mrs. Norris's instigation. This chapter 6 is a turning point in the structure of the novel. Henry Crawford is flirting with Rushworth's fiancée Maria Bertram. Edmund, who is the conscience of the book, heard all the plans "and said nothing." There is something vaguely sinful, from the point of view of the book, in the whole plan of all these improperly chaperoned young people going for a ramble in the park that belongs to the purblind Rushworth. All the characters have been beautifully brought out in this chapter. The Sotherton escapade is going to precede and prepare for the important chapters 13 to 20, which deal with the play that the young people rehearse.

During the discussion about improving estates, Rushworth observes that he is sure that Repton would cut down the avenue of old oaks that led from the west front of the house in order to provide a more open prospect. "Fanny, who was sitting on the other side of Edmund, exactly opposite Miss Crawford, and who had been attentively listening, now looked at him, and said in a low voice, 'Cut down an avenue! What a pity! Does it not make you think of Cowper? "Ye fallen avenues, once more I mourn your fate unmerited." ' " We must bear in mind that in Fanny's time the reading and knowledge of poetry was much more natural, more usual, more widespread than today. Our cultural, or so-called cultural, outlets are perhaps more various and numerous than in the first decades of the last century, but when I think of the vulgarities of the radio, video, or of the incredible, trite women's magazines of today, I wonder if there is not a lot to be said for Fanny's immersion in poetry, long-winded and often pedestrian though it may have been.

"The Sofa" by William Cowper, which forms part of a long poem called *The Task* (1785), is a good example of the kind of thing that was familiar to the mind of a young lady of Jane's or Fanny's time and set. Cowper combines the didactic tone of an observer of morals with the romantic imagination and nature coloring so characteristic of the following decades. "The Sofa" is a very long poem. It starts with a rather racy account of the history of furniture and then goes on to describe the pleasures of nature. It will be noted that in weighing the comforts, the arts and sciences of city life and the corruption of cities against the moral influence of uncomfortable nature, forest and field, Cowper selects nature. Here is a passage from the first section of "The Sofa" in which he admires the untouched shade trees of a friend's park and deplores the contemporaneous tendency to replace old avenues by open lawns and fancy shrubbery.

> *Not distant far, a length of colonnade*
> *Invites us. Monument of ancient taste,*
> *Now scorn'd, but worthy of a better fate.*
> *Our fathers knew the value of a screen*
> *From sultry suns, and in their shaded walks*
> *And low-protracted bow'rs, enjoy'd at noon*
> *The gloom and coolness of declining day.*
> *We bear our shades about us; self-depriv'd*
> *Of other screen, the thin umbrella spread,*
> *And range an Indian waste without a tree.*

That is, we cut down the trees on our country estates and then have to go about with parasols. This is what Fanny quotes when Rushworth and Crawford discuss landscaping the grounds at Sotherton:

> *Ye fallen avenues! once more I mourn*
> *Your fate unmerited, once more rejoice*
> *That yet a remnant of your race survives.*
> *How airy and how light the graceful arch,*
> *Yet awful as the consecrated roof*
> *Re-echoing pious anthems! while beneath*
> *The chequer'd earth seems restless as a flood*
> *Brush'd by the wind. So sportive is the light*
> *Shot through the boughs, it dances as they dance,*
> *Shadow and sunshine intermingling quick. . . .*

This is a grand passage, with delightful light effects not often met with in eighteenth-century poetry or prose.

At Sotherton Fanny's romantic conception of what a mansion's chapel should be like is disappointed by "a mere, spacious, oblong room, fitted up for the purpose of devotion—with nothing more striking or more solemn than the profusion of mahogany, and the crimson velvet cushions appearing over the ledge of the family gallery above." She is disabused, she says in a low voice to Edmund, "This is not my idea of a chapel. There is nothing awful here, nothing melancholy, nothing grand. Here are no aisles, no arches, no inscriptions, no banners. No banners, cousin, to be 'blown by the night wind of Heaven.' No signs that a 'Scottish monarch sleeps below.' " Here Fanny is quoting, though a little loosely, the description of a church from Sir Walter Scott's *The Lay of the Last Minstrel* (1805), canto 2:

> 10
> *Full many a scutcheon and banner, riven,*
> *Shook to the cold night-wind of heaven. . . .*

And then comes the urn of the wizard:

> 11
> *The moon on the east oriel shone,*
> *Through slender shafts of shapely stone,*
>   *By foliaged tracery combined. . . .*

Various images are painted on the windowpane and

> *The moon-beam kissed the holy pane,*
> *And threw on the pavement a bloody stain.*

12

> *They sate them down on a marble stone*
> *A Scottish monarch slept below. . . .*

Etc. The sunlight pattern of Cowper is nicely balanced by the moonlight pattern of Scott.

More subtle than the direct quotation is the *reminiscence*, which has a special technical meaning when used in discussing literary technique. A literary reminiscence denotes a phrase or image or situation suggestive of an unconscious imitation on the author's part of some earlier author. An author remembers something read somewhere and uses it, recreates it in his own fashion. A good example happens in chapter 10 àt Sotherton. A gate is locked, a key is missing, Rushworth goes to fetch it, Maria and Henry Crawford remain in flirtatious solitude. Maria says, " 'Yes, certainly, the sun shines and the park looks very cheerful. But unluckily that iron gate, that ha-ha, give me a feeling of restraint and hardship. I cannot get out, as the starling said.' As she spoke, and it was with expression, she walked to the gate; he followed her. 'Mr. Rushworth is so long fetching this key!' " Maria's quotation is from a famous passage in Laurence Sterne's *A Sentimental Journey through France and Italy* (1768) in which the narrator, the *I* of the book called Yorick, hears in Paris a caged starling calling to him. The quotation is apt in expressing Maria's tension and unhappiness at her engagement to Rushworth, as she intends it to be. But there is a further point, for the quotation of the starling from *A Sentimental Journey* seems to have a connection with an earlier episode from Sterne, a dim reminiscence of which in the back of Austen's mind seemed to have traveled into her character's bright brain, and there evolved a definite recollection. Journeying from England to France, Yorick lands in Calais and proceeds to look for a carriage to hire or buy that will take him to Paris. The place where carriages were acquired was called a *remise*, and it is at the door of such a *remise* in Calais that the following little scene occurs. The name of the owner of the *remise* is Monsieur Dessein, an actual person of the day, who is also mentioned in a famous French novel of the early eighteenth century, *Adolphe* (1815) by Benjamin Constant de Rebecque. Dessein leads Yorick to his *remise* to view his collection of carriages, post chaises as they were called, four-wheel closed carriages. Yorick is attracted by a fellow traveler, a young lady, who "had a black pair of silk gloves open only at the thumb and the two fore-fingers. . . ." He offers her his arm, and they walk to the door of the *remise*; however, after cursing the key fifty times, Dessein discovers that he has come out with the wrong key in his hand, and, says Yorick, "I continued holding her hand almost without knowing it: so that Monsieur *Dessein* left us together with her hand in mine, and with our faces turned towards the door of the Remise, and said he would be back in five minutes."

So here we have a little theme which is marked by a missing key, giving young love an opportunity to converse.

―――――

The Sotherton escapade provides not only Maria and Henry Crawford but also Mary Crawford and Edmund with the opportunity for conversing in an intimate privacy not ordinarily available to them. Both take advantage of the chance to desert the others: Maria and Henry to slip across an opening beside the locked gate and to wander unseen in the woods on the other side while Rushworth hunts for the key; Mary and Edmund to walk about, ostensibly to measure the grove, while poor Fanny sits deserted on a bench. Miss Austen has neatly landscaped her novel at this point. Moreover, the novel is going to proceed in these chapters like a play. There are three teams, as it were, who start out one after the other:

1. Edmund, Mary Crawford, and Fanny;
2. Henry Crawford, Maria Bertram, and Rushworth;
3. Julia, who outdistances Miss Norris and Mrs. Rushworth in her search for Henry Crawford.

Julia would like to wander about with Henry; Mary would like to stroll with Edmund, who would like that, too; Maria would love to walk with Henry; Henry would love to walk with Maria; at the tender back of Fanny's mind there is, of course, Edmund.

The whole thing can be divided into scenes:

1. Edmund, Mary, and Fanny enter the so-called wilderness, actually a neat little wood, and talk about clergymen. (Mary has had a shock in the chapel when she hears that Edmund expects to be ordained: she had not known that he intended to become a clergyman, a profession she could not contemplate in a future husband.) They reach a bench after Fanny asks to rest at the next opportunity.

2. Fanny remains alone on the bench while Edmund and Mary go to investigate the limits of the wilderness. She will remain on that rustic bench for a whole hour.

3. The next team walks up to her, composed of Henry, Maria, and Rushworth.

4. Rushworth leaves them to go back to fetch the key of the locked gate. Henry and Miss Bertram remain but then leave Fanny in order to explore the farther grove.

5. Miss Bertram and Henry climb around the locked gate and disappear into the park, leaving Fanny alone.

6. Julia—the avant-garde of the third group—arrives on the scene having met Rushworth returning to the house, talks to Fanny, and then climbs through the gate, "looking eagerly into the park." Crawford has been paying attention to her on the drive to Sotherton, and she is jealous of Maria.

7. Fanny is again alone until Rushworth arrives, panting, with the key of the gate, a meeting of the shed ones.

8. Rushworth lets himself into the park, and Fanny is alone again.

9. Fanny decides to go down the path taken by Mary and Edmund and meets them coming from the west side of the park where the famous avenue runs.

10. They go back towards the house and meet the remnant of the third team, Mrs. Norris and Mrs. Rushworth, about to start.

————

November was "the black month," in the view of the Bertram sisters, fixed for the unwelcome father's return. He intended to take the September packet, so that the young people have thirteen weeks—mid-August to mid-November—before his return. (Actually, Sir Thomas returns in October on a private ship.) The father's return will be, as Miss Crawford puts it to Edmund as they stand at the twilit window of Mansfield, while the Misses Bertram, with Rushworth and Crawford, are all busy with candles at the pianoforte, "the fore-runner also of other interesting events; your sister's marriage, and your taking orders," a further introduction of the ordination theme that involves Edmund, Miss Crawford, and Fanny. There is a spirited conversation about the motives of a clergyman and the propriety of his interest in the question of income. At the end of chapter 11 Miss Crawford joins the glee club at the piano; then Edmund leaves admiring the stars with Fanny for the music, and Fanny is left alone shivering at the window, a repetition of the leaving-Fanny theme. Edmund's unconscious hesitation between the bright and elegant beauty of dapper little Mary

Read

Read beginning of Ch. Nine, ~~Read~~ ("the all walked out)
p. 73

The curricle ; a two-wheeled carriage, had
the unique distinction of being the only two-wheeled English
carriage to which a pair of horses (abreast) could be driven
a pole between them took the place
of shafts between which
a single horse is driven

p. 73

The curricle

The young people do not
~~want~~ want to survey the ground
in carriage ~~and~~ : which mean

wonder about
Julia would like to ~~be~~ with ~~Mr~~ Crawford
Mary crawford would like to stroll
with Edmund , who ~~would like that too~~
Maria Bertram would love to walk
with Henry , Henry would love to
walk with Maria

~~Edmund would~~
~~Fanny~~ At the fondly back of Fanny's mind
there is of course Edmund.

p. 74-75 The chapel . The quotation

p. 75-77 The ordination theme . Miss
Mary Craw puts her little foot in

p. 77 " I do not like to see Miss Bertram
so near the altar "

p. 78 The question of surveying the grounds
again. The all walked out.

Crawford and the delicate grace and subdued loveliness of slender Fanny is emblematically demonstrated by the various movements of the young people involved in the music-room scene.

The relaxation of Sir Thomas's standards of conduct, the getting out of hand that took place during the Sotherton expedition, encourages and directly leads to the proposal to act a play before his return. The whole play theme in *Mansfield Park* is an extraordinary achievement. In chapters 12 to 20 the play theme is developed on the lines of fairy-tale magic and of fate. The theme starts with a new character—first to appear and last to vanish in this connection—a young man called Yates, a friend of Tom Bertram. "He came on the wings of disappointment, and with his head full of acting, for it had been a theatrical party [that he had just left]; and the play, in which he had borne a part, was within two days of representation, when the sudden death of one of the nearest connections of the family had destroyed the scheme and dispersed the performers." In his account to the Bertram circle "from the first casting of the parts, to the epilogue, it was all bewitching" (mark the magical note). And Yates bewails the fact that humdrum life or rather casual death prevented the staging. "It is not worth complaining about, but to be sure the poor old dowager could not have died at a worse time; and it is impossible to help wishing, that the news could have been suppressed for just the three days we wanted. It was but three days; and being only a grandmother, and all happening two hundred miles off, I think there would have been no great harm, and it *was* suggested, I know; but Lord Ravenshaw, who I suppose is one of the most correct men in England, would not hear of it."

Tom Bertram remarks that in a way the death of the grandmother is a kind of afterpiece, that is, her funeral which the Ravenshaws will have to perform alone. (At this time it was customary to act a light, often farcical, afterpiece following the main play.) Note that here we find foreshadowed the fatal interruption that Sir Thomas Bertram, the father, will cause later on, for when *Lovers' Vows* is rehearsed at Mansfield, his return will be the dramatic afterpiece.

The magical account by Yates of his theatrical experience fires the imagination of the young people. Henry Crawford declares that he could be fool enough at this moment to act any character that had ever been written from Shylock or Richard III down to the singing hero of a farce, and it is he

Nabokov's map of Sotherton Court

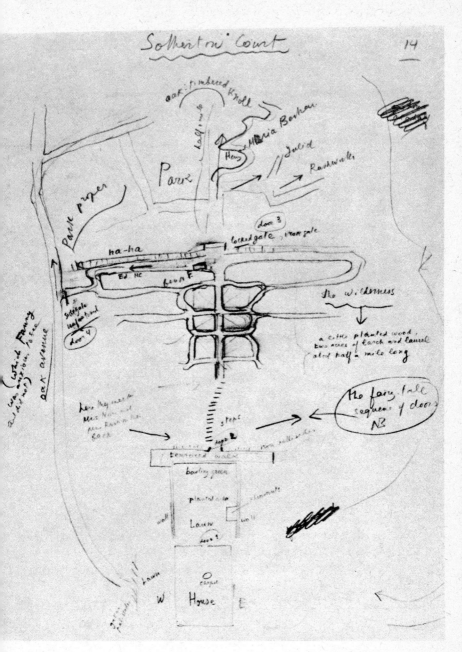

who since "it was yet an untasted pleasure," proposes that they act something, whether a scene, a half a play, anything. Tom remarks that they must have a green baize curtain; Yates casually suggests various pieces of scenery to be built. Edmund takes alarm and tries to splash cold water on the project by elaborate sarcasm: "Nay, . . . Let us do nothing by halves. If we are to act, let it be in a theatre completely fitted up with pit, box, and gallery, and let us have a play entire from beginning to end; so as it be a German play, no matter what, with a good tricking, shifting afterpiece, and a figure-dance, and a hornpipe, and a song between the acts. If we do not out do Ecclesford [the scene of the aborted theatrical party], we do nothing." This allusion to the tricking, shifting afterpiece is a fateful remark, a kind of conjuration, for this is exactly what is going to happen: the father's return will be a kind of tricky sequel, a shifty afterpiece.

They proceed to find a room for the staging, and the billiard room is chosen, but they will have to remove the bookcase in Sir Thomas's study to allow the doors to open at either end. Changing the order of the furniture was a serious thing in those days, and Edmund is more and more frightened. But the indolent mother and the aunt, who dotes upon the two girls, do not object. Indeed, Mrs. Norris takes it upon herself to cut out the curtain and to supervise the props according to her practical mind. But the play is still wanting. Let us note here again a streak of magic, a conjuring trick on the part of artistic fate, for the *Lovers' Vows*, the play mentioned by Yates, is now seemingly forgotten but actually is lying in wait, an unnoticed treasure. They discuss the possibilities of other plays but find either too many or too few parts, and the party is divided between acting a tragedy or a comedy. Then suddenly the charm acts. Tom Bertram, "taking up one of the many volumes of plays that lay on the table, and turning it over, suddenly exclaimed, 'Lovers' Vows! And why should not Lovers' Vows do for *us* as well as for the Ravenshaws? How came it never to be thought of before?' "

Lovers' Vows (1798) was an adaptation made by Mrs. Elisabeth Inchbald of *Das Kind der Liebe* by August Friedrich Ferdinand von Kotzebue. The play is very silly, but no more so perhaps than many modern hits. The plot turns on the fortunes of Frederick, the illegitimate son of Baron Wildenheim, and his mother's waiting maid, Agatha Friburg. The lovers having parted, Agatha leads a strictly virtuous life and brings up her son,

---

VLADIMIR NABOKOV

ch. 13

See p. 109

"Stage"

bookcase

hall

Billiard room

Music room

Fanny's study

used as a "green-room"

curtain

p.112 Breakfast room

Dining room

Drawing rm

carpenter's window by Christoph. Jackson
p. 112

hall

Let me go back to
the beginning of the chapter

Read ch. 13 , p. 106–107

while the young baron marries a wealthy lady from Alsace and goes to live on her estates. When the play opens, the baron's Alsatian wife is dead, and he has returned with his only daughter Amelia to his own castle in Germany. Meanwhile, by one of those coincidences necessary to tragic or comic situations, Agatha has also returned to her native village in the neighborhood of the castle, and there we find her being expelled from the country inn because she cannot pay her bill. By another coincidence she is found by her son Frederick, who has been absent for five years on a campaign but has now returned to seek civil employment. For this purpose a certificate of birth is wanted, and Agatha, aghast at this request, is obliged to tell him of his origin which she has hitherto concealed from him. The confession made, she collapses, and Frederick, having found shelter for her in a cottage, goes out to beg money to buy food. As luck will have it, by still another coincidence he meets in a field the baron and Count Cassel (a rich and foolish suitor of Amelia), and having been given a little but not sufficient money for his purpose, Frederick threatens his unknown father, who sends him to be imprisoned in the castle.

The story of Frederick is interrupted by a scene between Amelia and her tutor, the Reverend Anhalt, who has been commissioned by the baron to plead the cause of Count Cassel; but Amelia loves and is loved by Anhalt and manages, by the forward speeches to which Mary Crawford so coyly objected, to drive him to a declaration. Then hearing of Frederick's imprisonment, they both try to help him: Amelia takes food to him in his dungeon, and Anhalt procures an interview for him with the baron. In his talk with Anhalt Frederick has discovered the identity of his father, and at their meeting the secret of their relationship is revealed. All ends happily. The baron strives to atone for his youthful lapse by marrying his victim and acknowledging Frederick as his son; Count Cassel retires discomfited, and Amelia marries the diffident Anhalt. (The synopsis is mainly drawn from the account in Clara Linklater Thomson, *Jane Austen, a Survey*, 1929.)

This play is selected not because Miss Austen thought it a particularly immoral one in itself but chiefly because it had an extremely convenient complex of parts to distribute among her characters. Nevertheless, it is clear that she disapproves of the Bertram circle's acting this play not only because it is concerned with bastardy, not only because it provided the opportunity for speeches and actions of more overt and frank lovemaking than was suitable for young gentlefolk, but also because the fact that Agatha—no matter how repentant—had loved illicitly and borne a bastard child made the part unsuitable for acting by an unmarried girl. These objections are never specified, but they undoubtedly play a major part in

Fanny's distress when she reads the play, and at least at the start in Edmund's finding the subject and action offensive. "The first use [Fanny] made of her solitude was to take up the volume which had been left on the table, and begin to acquaint herself with the play of which she had heard so much. Her curiosity was all awake, and she ran through it with an eagerness which was suspended only by intervals of astonishment, that it could be chosen in the present instance—that it could be proposed and accepted in a private Theatre! Agatha and Amelia appeared to her in their different ways so totally improper for home representation—the situation of one, and the language of the other, so unfit to be expressed by any woman of modesty, that she could hardly suppose her cousins could be aware of what they were engaging in; and longed to have them roused as soon as possible by the remonstrance which Edmund would certainly make."* There is no reason to suppose that Jane Austen's sentiments do not parallel Fanny's. The point is, however, not that the play itself, as a play, is to be condemned as immoral but that it is suitable only for a professional theatre and actors and most improper for the Bertram circle to act.

Now comes the distribution of the parts. Artistic fate is arranging things so that the true relations between the novel's characters are going to be revealed through the relations of the characters in the play. Henry Crawford shows a devilish cunning in steering himself and Maria into the right parts—that is, into such parts (Frederick and his mother Agatha) that will offer the opportunity of their being constantly together, constantly embracing each other. On the other hand, Yates, who is already attracted by Julia, is angry that Julia gets a minor part, which she rejects. " 'Cottager's wife!' cried Mr. Yates. 'What are you talking of? The most trivial, paltry, insignificant part; the merest common-place—not a tolerable speech in the whole. Your sister do that! It is an insult to propose it. At Ecclesford the governess was to have done it. We all agreed that it could not be offered to any body else.' " But Tom is obdurate. "No, no, Julia must not be Amelia. It is not at all the part for her. She would not like it. She would not do well. She is too tall and robust. Amelia should be a small, light, girlish, skipping figure. It is fit for Miss Crawford, and Miss Crawford only. She looks the part, and I am persuaded will do it admirably." Henry Crawford, who has prevented Julia from being offered the part of Agatha by urging Maria's suitability, tries to repair the damage by urging the part of Amelia, nevertheless, but jealous Julia is suspicious of

*To this paragraph VN adds a note in his annotated copy: "And she is quite right. There is something obscene in Amelia's part." Ed.

his motives. "With hasty indignation therefore, and a tremulous voice," she reproaches him, and when Tom keeps on insisting that Miss Crawford alone is suitable, " 'Do not be afraid of *my* wanting the character,' cried Julia, with angry quickness;—'I am *not* to be Agatha, and I am sure I will do nothing else; and as to Amelia, it is of all parts in the world the most disgusting to me. I quite detest her.' . . . And so saying, she walked hastily out of the room, leaving awkward feelings to more than one, but exciting small compassion in any except Fanny, who had been a quiet auditor of the whole, and who could not think of her as under the agitations of *jealousy*, without great pity."

The discussion of the other parts, particularly Tom's gobbling up the comic roles, gives the reader a better picture of the young people. Rushworth, the dignified numskull, gets the part of Count Cassel, which suits him exquisitely, and he blossoms out as he had never done before in pink and blue satin clothes, proud of his forty-two speeches, which in fact he is never able to memorize. A kind of frenzy is gaining on the young people, much to Fanny's distress. The play is going to be an orgy of liberation, especially for Maria Bertram and Henry Crawford's sinful passion. A critical point is reached—who is going to play Anhalt, the young tutor-clergyman? Fate is obviously pushing Edmund, reluctant Edmund, into this part, in which he will have to be made love to by Amelia, Mary Crawford. The dizzy passion she evokes in him overcomes his scruples. He consents because he cannot endure the idea of a young outside acquaintance, Charles Maddox, being invited to play Anhalt and being made love to by Mary. He says rather lamely to Fanny that he will accept the part to restrain the publicity, to limit the exhibition, to concentrate the folly of the playacting within the family. Having reduced him to their level, his brother and sister greet him joyfully but coolly ignore his stipulations for privacy and begin to invite all of the surrounding county families to be the audience. A kind of curtain raiser is staged when Fanny, the little witness, has to listen first to Mary Crawford rehearsing her part, and then to Edmund rehearsing his. Her room is their meeting place and she is the link between them: Cinderella, polite, dainty, without hope, attending to the needs of others.

One more part must be filled, and then the first three acts of the play can be completely rehearsed. At first Fanny positively declines to engage herself to the part of the Cottager's wife that Julia had spurned; she has no confidence in her acting ability and her instinct warns her away. Mrs. Grant accepts the part, but when on the eve of the rehearsal she cannot attend, Fanny is urged, especially by Edmund, to read the part for her. Fanny's forced consent breaks the spell. Her innocence entering the fray scatters the devils of flirtation and sinful passion. But the rehearsal never finishes. "They *did* begin—and being too much engaged in their own noise, to be struck by an unusual noise in the other part of the house, had proceeded some way, when the door of the room was thrown open, and Julia appearing at it, with a face all aghast, exclaimed, 'My father is come! He is in the hall at this moment.'" So Julia gets the most important part after all, and the first volume of the novel ends.

Under the direction of Miss Austen, two heavy fathers, two ponderous parents, meet in the billiard room—Yates in the part of the heavy Baron Wildenheim and Sir Thomas Bertram in the part of Sir Thomas Bertram. And with a bow and a charming smile, Yates relinquishes the part of the heavy father to Sir Thomas. It is all a kind of an afterplay. "To the Theatre [Tom] went, and reached it just in time to witness the first meeting of his father and his friend. Sir Thomas had been a good deal surprised to find candles burning in his room; and on casting his eye round it, to see other symptoms of recent habitation, and a general air of confusion in the furniture. The removal of the book-case from before the billiard-room door struck him especially, but he had scarcely more than time to feel astonished at all this, before there were sounds from the billiard-room to astonish him still further. Some one was talking there in a very loud accent—he did not know the voice—*more* than talking—almost hallooing. He stept to the door, rejoicing at the last moment in having the means of immediate communication, and opening it, found himself on the stage of a theatre, and opposed to a ranting young man, who appeared likely to knock him down backwards. At the very moment of Yates perceiving Sir Thomas, and giving perhaps the best start he had ever given in the whole course of his rehearsals, Tom Bertram entered at the other end of the room; and never had he found greater difficulty in keeping his countenance. His father's looks of solemnity and amazement on this his first appearance on any stage, and the gradual metamorphosis of the impassioned Baron Wildenheim into the well-bred and easy Mr. Yates, making his bow and apology to Sir Thomas Bertram, was such an exhibition, such a piece of true acting as he would not have lost upon any account. It would be the last—in all probability the last scene on that stage; but he was sure there could not be a finer. The house would close with the greatest éclat."

Without recriminations, Sir Thomas dismisses the scene painter and has the carpenter pull down all that he had put up in the billiard room. "Another day or two, and Mr. Yates was gone likewise. In *his* departure Sir

Thomas felt the chief interest; wanting to be alone with his family.... Sir Thomas had been quite indifferent to Mr. Crawford's going or staying—but his good wishes for Mr. Yates's having a pleasant journey, as he walked with him to the hall door, were given with genuine satisfaction. Mr. Yates had staid to see the destruction of every theatrical preparation at Mansfield, the removal of every thing appertaining to the play; he left the house in all the soberness of its general character; and Sir Thomas hoped, in seeing him out of it, to be rid of the worst object connected with the scheme,* and the last that must be inevitably reminding him of its existence.

"Mrs. Norris contrived to remove one article from his sight that might have distressed him. The curtain over which she had presided with such talent and such success, went off with her to her cottage, where she happened to be particularly in want of green baize."

———

Henry Crawford abruptly breaks off his flirtation with Maria by leaving for Bath before he becomes too deeply involved. Sir Thomas at first approves of Rushworth but is soon disillusioned and offers Maria the opportunity to dismiss the engagement if she wishes. He sees that she treats Rushworth with scorn. She declines, however: "She was in a state of mind to be glad that she had secured her fate beyond recall—that she had pledged herself anew to Sotherton—that she was safe from the possibility of giving Crawford the triumph of governing her actions, and destroying her prospects; and retired in proud resolve, determined only to behave more cautiously to Mr. Rushworth in future, that her father might not be again suspecting her." In due course the marriage takes place and the young couple leave for a honeymoon in Brighton, taking Julia with them.

Fanny meets with Sir Thomas's full approval and becomes his favorite. Taking shelter in the parsonage from a sudden rainstorm, she begins an intimacy, despite some reservations on her part, with Mary Crawford and hears Mary play Edmund's favorite piece on her harp. Her further acquaintance leads to an invitation for her and Edmund to dine at the parsonage, where she encounters Henry Crawford, just returned for a few days' visit. Then a new twist is introduced in the structure of the novel, for Henry is attracted by Fanny's growing beauty and he determines to take up residence for a fortnight and to amuse himself by making Fanny fall in love

*"Yates, the last prop of the play, is removed." VN's note in his annotated copy. Ed.

with him. Brother and sister lightheartedly discuss his project. Henry declares to Mary: "You see her every day, and therefore do not notice it, but I assure you, she is quite a different creature from what she was in the autumn. She was then merely a quiet, modest, not plain looking girl, but she is now absolutely pretty. I used to think she had neither complexion nor countenance; but in that soft skin of hers, so frequently tinged with a blush as it was yesterday, there is decided beauty; and from what I observed of her eyes and mouth, I do not despair of their being capable of expression enough when she has any thing to express. And then—her air, her manner, her tout ensemble, is so indescribably improved! She must be grown two inches, at least, since October."

The sister rails at his fancy, although she admits that Fanny has "a sort of beauty that grows on one." Henry confesses that the challenge Fanny offers is much of the attraction. "I never was so long in company with a girl in my life—trying to entertain her—and succeed so ill! Never met with a girl who looked so grave on me! I must try to get the better of this. Her looks say, 'I will not like you, I am determined not to like you,' and I say, she shall." Mary protests that she does not want Fanny harmed. "I do desire that you will not be making her really unhappy; a *little* love perhaps may animate and do her good, but I will not have you plunge her deep." Henry responds that it will be but a fortnight: " 'No, I will not do her any harm, dear little soul! I only want her to look kindly on me, to give me smiles as well as blushes, to keep a chair for me by herself wherever we are, and be all animation when I take it and talk to her; to think as I think, be interested in all my possessions and pleasures, try to keep me longer at Mansfield, and feel when I go away that she shall never be happy again. I want nothing more.'

" 'Moderation itself!' said Mary. 'I can have no scruples now.' . . .

"And without attempting any further remonstrance, she left Fanny to her fate—a fate which, had not Fanny's heart been guarded in a way unsuspected by Miss Crawford, might have been a little harder than she deserved. . . ."

After years at sea, Fanny's brother William returns, and at Sir Thomas's invitation comes to Mansfield Park for a visit; "Sir Thomas had the pleasure of receiving, in his protégé, certainly a very different person from the one he had equipped seven years ago, but a young man of an open, pleasant countenance, and frank, unstudied, but feeling and respectful manners, and such as confirmed him his friend." Fanny is wonderfully happy with her beloved William, who, on his part, loves his sister dearly.

Henry Crawford sees with admiration "the glow of Fanny's cheek, the brightness of her eye, the deep interest, the absorbed attention, while her brother was describing any of the imminent hazards, or terrific scenes, which such a period, at sea, must supply.

"It was a picture which Henry Crawford had moral taste enough to value. Fanny's attractions increased—increased two-fold—for the sensibility which beautified her complexion and illumined her countenance, was an attraction in itself. He was no longer in doubt of the capabilities of her heart. She had feeling, genuine feeling. It would be something to be loved by such a girl, to excite the first ardours of her young, unsophisticated mind! She interested him more than he had foreseen. A fortnight was not enough. His stay became indefinite."

All of the Bertrams dine at the parsonage. After dinner while their elders play whist, the younger people, with Lady Bertram, play the card game Speculation. Henry has by chance ridden by Edmund's future parsonage at Thornton Lacey and, being much impressed with the house and grounds, presses Edmund to make a number of improvements, just as he had done in the case of the Rushworth estate. It is curious how improvements of grounds go together with Henry Crawford's flirtations. Both are functions of the idea of planning, of scheming. Earlier it was Rushworth's place he was to improve, and he planned to seduce Rushworth's fiancée Maria. But now it is Edmund's future residence, and now he is planning to conquer Edmund's future wife, Fanny Price. He urges that he be allowed to rent the house so that "he might find himself continuing, improving, and *perfecting* that friendship and intimacy with the Mansfield Park family which was increasing in value to him every day." He is rebuffed in a friendly fashion by Sir Thomas, who explains that Edmund will not be living at Mansfield when he has taken orders, now only a few weeks away, but will be looking after his parishioners in residence at Thornton Lacey. (Henry had never conceived that Edmund would not delegate his pastoral duties.) His insistence that the house can be made not into a mere parsonage but into a gentleman's residence interests Mary Crawford. All this talk is artistically interlinked with the game of cards they are playing, Speculation, and Miss Crawford, as she bids, speculates whether or not she should marry Edmund, the clergyman. This reechoing of the game by her thoughts recalls the same interplay between fiction and reality that had been found in the rehearsal chapter when she was playing Amelia to Edmund's Anhalt before Fanny. This theme of planning and scheming, linked up with improvements of grounds, rehearsals, card games, forms a very pretty pattern in the novel.

The ball in chapter 26 is the next structural development. Its preparation involves various emotions and actions and thus helps to shape and develop the story. Impressed by Fanny's improved looks and anxious to give her and William pleasure, Sir Thomas plans a ball in her honor with as much zest as his son Tom had planned the play. Edmund is occupied with two events now at hand which are to fix his fate for life: ordination, which he is to receive in the course of the Christmas week, and matrimony with Mary Crawford, which is only a hope. To engage Miss Crawford early for the first two dances is one of those plans that keep the book rolling and make of the ball a structural event. The same may be said of Fanny's preparations. Miss Austen employs the same sort of connective device we have observed in the Sotherton episode and the play-rehearsal scenes. William has given Fanny the only ornament in her possession, an amber cross brought back from Sicily. But she has only a bit of ribbon to fasten it and is concerned that this will not be suitable, for wear the cross she must. There is also the question of her dress, about which she asks Miss Crawford's advice. When Miss Crawford hears of the problem of the cross, she palms off on Fanny a necklace bought for Fanny by Henry Crawford, insisting that it was an old gift to her from her brother. Despite serious doubts caused by its origin, Fanny is eventually persuaded to accept the necklace. Then she finds that Edmund has purchased a simple gold chain for the cross. She proposes to return the Crawford necklace, but Edmund, delighted by the coincidence and by this fresh evidence of Miss Crawford's kind nature, as he takes it, insists that she must retain the gift. Fanny solves the problem by wearing both at the ball when she discovers to her joy that the necklace is too large to go through the loop of the cross. The necklace theme has succeeded in linking up five people—Fanny, Edmund, Henry, Mary, and William.

The ball is again an event that brings out the characteristic features of the people in the book: coarse and fussy Mrs. Norris whom we glimpse being "entirely taken up in fresh arranging and injuring the noble fire which the butler had prepared." Austen's style is at its best in this word *injure*, incidentally the one really original metaphor in the book. Then there are Lady Bertram, who placidly maintains that Fanny's good looks are due to the fact that her maid, Mrs. Chapman, has helped Fanny to dress (actually Chapman had been sent up too late, for Fanny had already dressed herself); Sir Thomas being his dignified, restrained, slow-speaking self; and the young people all playing their parts. It never occurs to Miss Crawford that Fanny is really in love with Edmund and does not care for Henry. She blunders by archly inquiring if Fanny can imagine why Henry is taking William up to London with him the next day in his carriage, for the time has come for William to return to his ship. Miss Crawford "meant to be giving her little heart a happy flutter, and filling her with sensations of delightful self-consequence"; but when Fanny protests ignorance: " 'Well, then,' replied Miss Crawford, laughing, 'I must suppose it to be purely for the pleasure of conveying your brother and talking of you by the way.' " Instead, Fanny is confused and displeased, "while Miss Crawford wondered she did not smile, and thought her over-anxious, or thought her odd, or thought her any thing rather than insensible of pleasure in Henry's attentions." Edmund receives little pleasure from the ball. He and Miss Crawford have got into another argument about his ordination and "she had absolutely pained him by her manner of speaking of the profession to which he was now on the point of belonging. They had talked—and they had been silent—he had reasoned—she had ridiculed—and they had parted at last with mutual vexation."

Sir Thomas, noticing Henry's attentions to Fanny, begins to think that such a match could be advantageous. Before the journey to London that is to take place the morning after the ball, "After a short consideration, Sir Thomas asked Crawford to join the early breakfast party in that house instead of eating alone; he should himself be of it; and the readiness with which his invitation was accepted, convinced him that the suspicions whence, he must confess to himself, this very ball had in great measure sprung, were well founded. Mr. Crawford was in love with Fanny. He had a pleasing anticipation of what would be. His niece, meanwhile, did not thank him for what he had just done. She had hoped to have William all to herself, the last morning. It would have been an unspeakable indulgence. But though her wishes were overthrown there was no spirit of murmuring within her. On the contrary, she was so totally unused to have her pleasure consulted, or to have any thing take place at all in the way she could desire, that she was more disposed to wonder and rejoice in having carried her point so far [that she would breakfast with them instead of sleeping], than to repine at the counteraction which followed." Sir Thomas sends her to bed, it being three in the morning, although the ball continues with a few determined couples. "In thus sending her away, Sir Thomas perhaps might not be thinking merely of her health. It might occur to him, that Mr. Crawford had been sitting by her long enough, or he might mean to recommend her as a wife by shewing her persuadableness." A nice note to end on!

————

Edmund leaves to visit a friend in Peterborough for a week. His absence provokes Miss Crawford, who regrets her actions at the ball and pumps Fanny for an indication of Edmund's sentiments. Henry returns from London with a surprise for his sister. He has decided that he is firmly in love with Fanny, not trifling with her any longer, and he wants to marry her. He also brings a surprise for Fanny in the shape of letters confirming that his uncle Admiral Crawford's influence, which Henry has engaged, has been felt and William is to receive his long-despaired-of promotion to lieutenant. On top of this he immediately proposes marriage, an action that is so entirely unexpected and unwelcome that Fanny can only retreat in confusion. Miss Crawford sends a note on the subject: "My dear Fanny, for so I may now always call you, to the infinite relief of a tongue that has been stumbling at *Miss Price* for at least the last six weeks—I cannot let my brother go without sending you a few lines of general congratulation, and giving my most joyful consent and approval.—Go on, my dear Fanny, and without fear; there can be no difficulties worth naming. I chuse to suppose that the assurance of *my* consent will be something; so, you may smile upon him with your sweetest smiles this afternoon, and send him back to me even happier than he goes. Yours affectionately, M.C." Miss Crawford's style is superficially elegant but trite and trivial if studied closely. It is full of graceful clichés, like the hope for Fanny's "sweetest smiles," for Fanny was not that type. When Henry calls that evening, he puts pressure on Fanny to respond to his sister; and in haste, "with only one decided feeling, that of wishing not to appear to think any thing really intended, [Fanny] wrote thus, in great trembling both of spirits and hand.

" 'I am very much obliged to you, my dear Miss Crawford, for your kind congratulations, as far as they relate to my dearest William. The rest of your note I know means nothing; but I am so unequal to anything of the sort, that I hope you will excuse my begging you to take no further notice. I have seen too much of Mr. Crawford not to understand his manners; if he understood me as well, he would, I dare say, behave differently. I do not know what I write, but it would be a great favour of you never to mention the subject again. With thanks for the honour of your note, I remain, dear Miss Crawford, &c., &c.' "

In contrast, her general style has elements of force, purity, and precision. With this letter the second volume ends.

A new structural impetus is given to the story at this point by Sir Thomas, the heavy uncle, using all his power and weight to make frail Fanny marry Crawford: "He who had married a daughter to Mr.

Rushworth. Romantic delicacy was certainly not to be expected from him." The whole scene, Sir Thomas's talk with Fanny in the East room, chapter 32, is admirable, one of the best in the novel. Sir Thomas is extremely displeased and shows his displeasure to Fanny's acute distress, but he cannot secure an agreement from her. She is far from certain of the seriousness of Crawford's intentions and tries to cling to the illusion that his proposal is a mere piece of gallantry. Moreover, she is firm that their different characters would make a marriage disastrous. Sir Thomas has a fleeting concern that perhaps a special feeling for Edmund is holding Fanny back, but he dismisses it. Still, Fanny feels the full force of his disapproval. "He ceased. Fanny was by this time crying so bitterly, that angry as he was, he would not press that article farther. Her heart was almost broke by such a picture of what she appeared to him; by such accusations, so heavy, so multiplied, so rising in dreadful gradation! Self-willed, obstinate, selfish, and ungrateful. He thought her all this. She had deceived his expectations; she had lost his good opinion. What was to become of her?"

She continues to be subject to Crawford's pressure and frequent attendance, encouraged by Sir Thomas. When Edmund returns one night there is a kind of continuation and elevation of the play theme when Crawford reads passages from *Henry VIII*, of course one of the poorest of Shakespeare's plays. But in 1808 it would be natural for the average reader to prefer Shakespeare's historical plays to the divine poetry of his fantastically great tragedies like *King Lear* or *Hamlet*. The play theme is nicely linked up with the ordination theme (now that Edmund is ordained) by the discussion between the two men about the art of reading and also the art of delivering sermons. Edmund discusses with Crawford the conduct of his first service and "he had a variety of questions from Crawford as to his feelings and success; questions which being made—though with the vivacity of friendly interest and quick taste—without any touch of that spirit of banter or air of levity which Edmund knew to be most offensive to Fanny, he had true pleasure in satisfying; and when Crawford proceeded to ask his opinion and give his own as to the properest manner in which particular passages in the service should be delivered, shewing it to be a subject on which [Crawford] had thought before, and thought with judgment, Edmund was still more and more pleased. This would be the way to Fanny's heart. She was not to be won by all that gallantry and wit, and good-nature together, could do; or at least, she would not be won by them nearly so soon, without the assistance of sentiment and feeling, and seriousness on serious subjects."*

With his usual volatility, Crawford imagines himself a popular London preacher: "A thoroughly good sermon, thoroughly well delivered, is a capital gratification. I can never hear such a one without the greatest admiration and respect, and more than half a mind to take orders and preach myself. . . . But then, I must have a London audience. I could not preach but to the educated; to those who are capable of estimating my composition. And I do not know that I should be fond of preaching often; now and then, perhaps, once or twice in the spring, after being anxiously expected for half a dozen Sundays together; but not for a constancy; it would not do for a constancy." This theatrical interpretation somehow does not offend Edmund, since Crawford is Mary's brother, but Fanny shakes her head.

Heavy Sir Thomas now has heavyish Edmund talk to Fanny about Henry Crawford. Edmund begins by admitting that Fanny does not now love Crawford, but the theme of his argument is that if she will permit his addresses, she will learn to value and to love him and will gradually loosen the ties that bind her to Mansfield and that prevent her from contemplating a departure. The interview soon lapses into a paean of praise for Mary Crawford from the infatuated Edmund, who fancies being her brother-in-law. It ends with what is to be the theme of watchful waiting: the proposal was too unexpected and therefore unwelcome. " 'I told [the Grants and the Crawfords], that you were of all human creatures the one, over whom habit had most power, and novelty least: and that the very circumstance of the novelty of Crawford's addresses was against him. Their being so new and so recent was all in their disfavour; that you could tolerate nothing that you were not used to; and a great deal more to the same purpose to give them a knowledge of your character. Miss Crawford made us laugh by her plans of encouragement for her brother. She meant to urge him to persevere in the hope of being loved in time, and of having his addresses most kindly received at the end of about ten years' happy marriage.'

"Fanny could with difficulty give the smile that was here asked for. Her

*"Critics like Linklater Thomson are astonished to find that Jane Austen, who in her youth had mocked at the propensities of 'sensibility' that fostered admiration for excessive feeling and sentimentality—for weeping, swooning, quivering, indiscriminate sympathy with anything pathetic or to be assumed morally or practically good—should choose such sensibility to distinguish a heroine whom she preferred above all other of her characters and to whom she had given the name of her favorite niece. . . . But Fanny exhibits those symptoms of fashionable sensibility with such charm, and her emotions are so consistent with the dove-gray sky of the novel, that Thomson's astonishment may be ignored." VN's note elsewhere in the Austen folder. Ed.

feelings were all in revolt. She feared she had been doing wrong, saying too much, overacting the caution which she had been fancying necessary, in guarding against one evil [the revelation of her love for Edmund], laying herself open to another, and to have Miss Crawford's liveliness repeated to her at such a moment, and on such a subject, was a bitter aggravation."

Edmund's conviction that the only reason Fanny has rejected Crawford was the novelty of the whole situation is a matter of structure, for the further development of the novel necessitates one thing, that Crawford remain hanging around, that he be allowed to persevere in his courting. Thus the easy explanation makes it permissible for him to go on with his wooing with the full consent of Sir Thomas and Edmund. Many readers, especially feminine readers, can never forgive subtle and sensitive Fanny for loving such a dull fellow as Edmund, but I can only repeat that the worst way to read a book is childishly to mix with the characters in it as if they were living people. Actually, of course, we often hear of sensitive girls faithfully in love with bores and prigs. Yet it must be said that Edmund, after all, is a good, honest, well-mannered, kind person. So much for the human interest of the thing.

Among those who try to convert poor Fanny, Mary Crawford appeals to her pride. Henry is a most marvelous catch and has been sighed after by many women. Mary's insensibility is such that she does not realize she has given the whole show away when, after confessing that Henry does have a fault in "liking to make girls a little in love with him" she adds: "I do seriously and truly believe that he is attached to you in a way that he never was to any woman before; that he loves you with all his heart, and will love you as nearly for ever as possible. If any man ever loved a woman for ever, I think Henry will do as much for you." Fanny cannot avoid a faint smile and does not respond.

It is not quite clear psychologically why Edmund has not yet made his declaration to Miss Crawford—but there again the structure of the novel requires a certain slowness of progress in Edmund's courtship. At any rate, both Crawfords leave for London on previously arranged visits to friends with no satisfaction from Fanny or Edmund.

———

It occurs to Sir Thomas in one of his "dignified musings" that it might be a good plan to have Fanny visit her family at Portsmouth for a couple of months. We are in February 1809, and she has not seen her parents for almost nine years. The old man is certainly a schemer: "He certainly wished her to go willingly, but he as certainly wished her to be heartily sick of home before her visit ended; and that a little abstinence from the elegancies and luxuries of Mansfield Park, would bring her mind into a sober state, and incline her to a juster estimate of the value of that home of greater permanence, and equal comfort, of which she had the offer." That is, Crawford's place, Everingham in Norfolk. There is an amusing bit about Mrs. Norris, who thinks that the conveyance and the travel expenses that Sir Thomas is defraying might be utilized since she has not seen her sister Price for twenty years. But "it ended to the infinite joy of [William and Fanny], in the recollection that she could not possibly be spared from Mansfield Park at present. . . .

"It had, in fact, occurred to her, that, though taken to Portsmouth for nothing, it would be hardly possible for her to avoid paying her own expenses back again. So her poor dear sister Price was left to all the disappointment of her missing such an opportunity; and another twenty years' absence, perhaps, begun."

A rather lame paragraph treats Edmund: "Edmund's plans were affected by this Portsmouth journey, this absence of Fanny's. He too had a sacrifice to make to Mansfield Park as well as his aunt. He had intended, about this time, to be going to London, but he could not leave his father and mother just when every body else of most importance to their comfort, was leaving them; and with an effort, felt but not boasted of, he delayed for a week or two longer a journey which he was looking forward to, with the hope of its fixing his happiness for ever." So his courtship of Miss Crawford is once more delayed for the purposes of the story.

Jane Austen, after having poor Fanny talked to about Henry by Sir Thomas, then Edmund, then Mary Crawford, wisely eliminates any conversation on the subject during Fanny's trip to Portsmouth with her brother William. Fanny and William leave Mansfield Park on Monday, 6 February 1809, and the next day reach Portsmouth, a naval base in the south of England. Fanny will return to Mansfield not in two months, as planned, but three months later, on Thursday, 4 May 1809, when she is nineteen. Immediately on arrival William is ordered to sea, leaving Fanny alone with her family. "Could Sir Thomas have seen all his niece's feelings, when she wrote her first letter to her aunt, he would not have despaired. . . .

"William was gone;—and the home he had left her in was—Fanny could not conceal it from herself—in almost every respect the very reverse of what she could have wished. It was the abode of noise, disorder, and impropriety. Nobody was in their right place, nothing was done as it ought to be. She could not respect her parents, as she had hoped. On her father, her confidence had not been sanguine, but he was more negligent of his family, his habits were worse, and his manners coarser than she had been prepared for . . . he swore and he drank, he was dirty and gross . . . he scarcely ever noticed her, but to make her the object of a coarse joke.

"Her disappointment in her mother was greater; *there* she had hoped much, and found almost nothing. . . . Mrs. Price was not unkind—but, instead of gaining on her affection and confidence, and becoming more and more dear, her daughter never met with greater kindness from her, than on the first day of her arrival. The instinct of nature was soon satisfied, and Mrs. Price's attachment had no other source. Her heart and her time were already quite full; she had neither leisure nor affection to bestow on Fanny. . . . her days were spent in a kind of slow bustle; always busy without getting on, always behind hand and lamenting it, without altering her ways; wishing to be an economist, without contrivance or regularity; dissatisfied with her servants, without skill to make them better, and whether helping, or reprimanding, or indulging them, without any power of engaging their respect."

Fanny's head aches from the noise and smallness of the house, the dirt, the ill-cooked meals, the slatternly maid, her mother's constant complaints. "The living in incessant noise was to a frame and temper, delicate and nervous like Fanny's, an evil. . . . Here, every body was noisy, every voice was loud, (excepting, perhaps, her mother's, which resembled the soft monotony of Lady Bertram's, only worn into fretfulness.)— Whatever was wanted was halloo'd for, and the servants halloo'd out their excuses from the kitchen. The doors were in constant banging, the stairs were never at rest, nothing was done without a clatter, nobody sat still, and nobody could command attention when they spoke." Only in her sister Susan, aged eleven, does Fanny find any promise for the future, and she devotes herself to teaching Susan manners and the habit of reading. Susan is a quick study and comes to love her.

Fanny's removal to Portsmouth affects the unity of the novel, which up to now, except for a natural and necessary early exchange of messages between Fanny and Mary Crawford, has been pleasantly free from that dismal feature of eighteenth-century English and French novels, information conveyed by letters. But with Fanny isolated in Portsmouth, we are approaching a new change in the structure of the novel in which the action will be developed by correspondence, by the exchange of news. From London Mary Crawford hints to Fanny that Maria Rushworth was much put out of countenance when Fanny's name was mentioned. Yates is still interested in Julia. The Crawfords are going to a party at the Rushworths on 28 February. She remarks that Edmund "moves slowly," perhaps detained in the country by parish duties. "There may be some old woman at Thornton Lacey to be converted. I am unwilling to fancy myself neglected for a *young* one."

Unexpectedly, Crawford turns up in Portsmouth to make a last attempt at winning Fanny. To her relief her family improves under the stimulus and behaves tolerably well to the visitor. Fanny sees a great improvement in Henry. He is taking an interest in his estate: "He had introduced himself to some tenants, whom he had never seen before; he had begun making acquaintance with cottages whose very existence, though on his own estate, had been hitherto unknown to him. This was aimed, and well aimed, at Fanny. It was pleasing to hear him speak so properly; here, he had been acting as he ought to do. To be the friend of the poor and oppressed! Nothing could be more grateful to her, and she was on the point of giving him an approving look when it was all frightened off, by his adding a something too pointed of his hoping soon to have an assistant, a friend, a guide in every plan of utility or charity for Everingham, a somebody that would make Everingham and all about it, a dearer object than it had ever been yet.

"She turned away, and wished he would not say such things. She was willing to allow he might have more good qualities than she had been wont to suppose. She began to feel the possibility of his turning out well at last. . . ." At the end of his visit, "she thought him altogether improved since she had seen him; he was much more gentle, obliging, and attentive to other people's feelings than he had ever been at Mansfield; she had never seen him so agreeable—so *near* being agreeable; his behaviour to her father could not offend, and there was something particularly kind and proper in the notice he took of Susan. He was decidedly improved. . . . it was not so very bad as she would have expected; the pleasure of talking of Mansfield was so very great!" He is much concerned with her health and urges her to inform his sister of any further deterioration so that they can take her back to Mansfield. Here and elsewhere, there is an intimation that if Edmund had married Mary and if Henry had persevered in his tenderness and good behavior, Fanny would have married him after all.

———

The postman's knock replaces more delicate structural devices. The novel, which shows signs of disintegrating, now lapses more and more into the easy epistolary form. This is a sure sign of a certain weariness on the part of the author when she takes recourse in such an easy form. On the other hand, we are approaching the most shocking event of the whole story.

From a chatty letter by Mary, we learn that Edmund has been in London "and that my friends here are very much struck with his gentleman-like appearance. Mrs. Fraser (no bad judge), declares she knows but three men in town who have so good a person, height, and air; and I must confess, when he dined here the other day, there were none to compare with him, and we were a party of sixteen. Luckily there is no distinction of dress now-a-days to tell tales, but—but—but." Henry is to go to Everingham on some business of which Fanny approves, but not until after a party that the Crawfords are giving: "He will see the Rushworths, which I own I am not sorry for—having a little curiosity—and so I think has he, though he will not acknowledge it." It is clear that Edmund has not yet declared himself; his slowness becomes something of a farce. Seven weeks of the two months at Portsmouth were gone before a letter from Edmund at Mansfield arrives. He is upset by Miss Crawford's high spirits in treating serious matters and by the tone of her London friends. "My hopes are very much weaker. . . . When I think of her great attachment to you, indeed, and the whole of her judicious, upright conduct as a sister, she appears a very different creature [than among her London friends], capable of everything noble, and I am ready to blame myself for a too harsh construction of a playful manner. I cannot give her up, Fanny. She is the only woman in the world whom I could ever think of as a wife." He cannot resolve his mind whether he should propose by letter or wait until her return to Mansfield in June. On the whole, a letter would not be satisfactory. At Mrs. Fraser's party he saw Crawford. "I am more and more satisfied with all that I see and hear of him. There is not a shadow of wavering. He thoroughly knows his own mind, and acts up to his resolutions—an inestimable quality. I could not see him, and my eldest sister in the same room, without recollecting what you once told me, and I acknowledge that they did not meet as friends. There was marked coolness on her side. They scarcely spoke. I saw him draw back surprised, and I was sorry that Mrs. Rushworth should resent any former supposed slight to Miss Bertram." The disappointing news is conveyed that Sir Thomas will not fetch Fanny until after Easter, when he has business in town (a delay of a month beyond the original plan).

Fanny's reactions to Edmund's infatuation are conveyed in the intonation of what we now call *stream of consciousness* or *interior monologue*, to be used so wonderfully a hundred and fifty years later by James Joyce. "She was almost vexed into displeasure, and anger, against Edmund. 'There is no good in this delay,' said she. 'Why is not it settled?—

He is blinded, and nothing will open his eyes, nothing can, after having had truths before him so long in vain.—He will marry her, and be poor and miserable. God grant that her influence do not make him cease to be respectable!'—She looked over the letter again. ' "So very fond of me!" 'tis nonsense all. She loves nobody but her self and her brother. Her friends leading her astray for years! She is quite as likely to have led *them* astray. They have all, perhaps, been corrupting one another; but if they are so much fonder of her than she is of them, she is the less likely to have been hurt, except by their flattery. "The only woman in the world whom he could ever think of as a wife." I firmly believe it. It is an attachment to govern his whole life. Accepted or refused, his heart is wedded to her for ever. "The loss of Mary I must consider as comprehending the loss of Crawford and Fanny." Edmund, you do not know *me*. The families would never be connected, if you did not connect them! Oh! write, write. Finish it at once. Let there be an end of this suspense. Fix, commit, condemn yourself.'

"Such sensations, however, were too near a kin to resentment to be long guiding Fanny's soliloquies. She was soon more softened and sorrowful."

From Lady Bertram she learns that Tom has been very sick in London and, although in serious condition, from the neglect of his friends, has been moved to Mansfield. Tom's illness prevents Edmund from writing a letter of declaration to Miss Crawford; nothing but obstacles, which he seems to keep in his own path, cross their relationship. A letter from Miss Crawford suggests that the Bertram property would be in better hands if it were Sir Edmund's instead of Sir Thomas's. Henry has been seeing quite a bit of Maria Rushworth but Fanny is not to be alarmed. Fanny is disgusted at the greater part of the letter. But letters continue to pour in on her about Tom and also about Maria. Then Miss Crawford writes a warning letter about an awful rumor: "A most scandalous, ill-natured rumour has just reached me, and I write, dear Fanny, to warn you against giving the least credit to it, should it spread into the country. Depend upon it there is some mistake, and that a day or two will clear it up—at any rate, that Henry is blameless, and in spite of a moment's *etourderie* thinks of nobody but you. Say not a word of it—hear nothing, surmise nothing, whisper nothing, till I write again. I am sure it will be all hushed up, and nothing proved but Rushworth's folly. If they are gone, I would lay my life they are only gone to Mansfield Park, and Julia with them. But why would not you let us come for you? I wish you may not repent it. Yours &c."

Fanny stands aghast, not quite understanding what has happened. Two days later she is sitting in the parlor, where the sun's rays "instead of cheering, made her still more melancholy; for sun-shine appeared to her a totally different thing in a town and in the country. Here, its power was only a glare, a stifling, sickly glare, serving but to bring forward stains and dirt that might otherwise have slept. There was neither health nor gaiety in sun-shine in a town. She sat in a blaze of oppressive heat, in a cloud of moving dust; and her eyes could only wander from the walls, marked by her father's head, to the table cut and notched by her brothers, where stood the tea-board never thoroughly cleaned, the cups and saucers wiped in streaks, the milk a mixture of motes floating in thin blue, and the bread and butter growing every minute more greasy than even Rebecca's hands had first produced it." In this dirty room she hears the dirty news. Her father reads a newspaper report that Henry and Maria Rushworth have eloped. One should note that being informed of this by a newspaper article is essentially the same as being informed by letter. It is still the epistolary formula.

The action is now fast and furious. A letter from Edmund in London informs Fanny that the adulterous pair cannot be traced but that a new blow has fallen: Julia has eloped for Scotland with Yates. Edmund is coming to fetch Fanny from Portsmouth on the morrow and, with Susan, they will go to Mansfield Park. He arrives and is "particularly struck by the alteration in Fanny's looks, and from his ignorance of the daily evils of her father's house, attributing an undue share of the change, attributing *all* to the recent event, took her hand, and said in a low, but very expressive tone, 'No wonder—you must feel it—you must suffer. How a man who had once loved, could desert you! But *your's*—your regard was new compared with— —Fanny, think of *me!*' " It is clear that he feels he must give up Mary Crawford because of the scandal. The moment he arrived in Portsmouth "she found herself pressed to his heart with only these words, just articulate, 'My Fanny—my only sister—my only comfort now.' "

The Portsmouth interlude—three months in the life of Fanny—is now over, and the epistolary form of the novel is also ended. We are back where we were, so to speak, but the Crawfords are now eliminated. Miss Austen would have had to write practically another volume of five hundred pages if she had wished to narrate those elopements in the same direct and detailed form as she had done in relating the games and flirtations at Mansfield Park before Fanny left for Portsmouth. The epistolary form has helped to prop up the structure of the novel at this point, but there is no doubt that too much has happened behind the scenes and that this letter-writing business is a shortcut of no very great artistic merit.

We have now only two chapters left, and what is left is no more than a mopping-up process. Shattered by her favorite Maria's action and the divorce that shortly brings an end to a marriage that she has prided herself on having instigated, Mrs. Norris is, indirectly, said to have become an altered creature, quiet, indifferent to everything that passes, and she departs to share a remote house with Maria. We are not shown this change directly; hence we remember her only as the constantly grotesque creature of the main part of the book. Edmund is at last disillusioned by Miss Crawford. She gives no sign of understanding the moral issues involved and can speak no more than of the "folly" of her brother and Maria. He is horrified. "To hear the woman whom—no harsher name than folly given!—So voluntarily, so freely, so coolly to canvass it!—No reluctance, no horror, no feminine—shall I say? no modest loathings!—This is what the world does. For where, Fanny, shall we find a woman whom nature had so richly endowed?—Spoilt, spoilt!—"

"It was the detection, not the offence which she reprobated," says Edmund with a muffled sob. He describes to Fanny Miss Crawford's exclamation: "Why would [Fanny] not have him? It is all her fault. Simple girl!—I shall never forgive her. Had she accepted him as she ought, they might now have been on the point of marriage, and Henry would have been too happy and too busy to want any other object. He would have taken no pains to be on terms with Mrs. Rushworth again. It would have all ended in a regular standing flirtation, in yearly meetings at Sotherton and Everingham." Edmund adds, "But the charm is broken. My eyes are opened." He tells Miss Crawford of his astonishment at her attitude, and especially at her hoping that if Sir Thomas will not interfere, it is possible that Henry may marry Maria. Her reply brings the ordination conflict to a close: "She turned extremely red. . . . She would have laughed if she could. It was a sort of laugh, as she answered, 'A pretty good lecture, upon my word. Was it part of your last sermon? At this rate you will soon reform every body at Mansfield and Thornton Lacey; and when I hear of you next, it may be as a celebrated preacher in some great society of Methodists, or as a missionary into foreign parts.'" He bids her farewell and turns to go. "I had gone a few steps, Fanny, when I heard the door open behind me. 'Mr. Bertram,' said she. I looked back. 'Mr. Bertram,' said she, with a smile—but it was a smile ill-suited to the conversation that had passed, a saucy playful smile, seeming to invite, in order to subdue me; at least, it appeared so to me. I resisted; it was the impulse of the moment to resist, and still walked on. I have since—sometimes—for a moment—regretted that I did not go back; but I know I was right; and such has been the end of our

JANE AUSTEN 53

acquaintance!" At the end of the chapter Edmund thinks that he will never marry—but the reader knows better.

In the last chapter crime is punished, virtue receives its just reward, and sinners change their ways.

Yates has more money and fewer debts than Sir Thomas had expected, and is received into the fold.

Tom's health and morals improve. He has suffered. He has learned to think. There is a last allusion to the play theme here. He felt himself accessory to the affair between his sister and Crawford "by all the dangerous intimacy of his unjustifiable theatre, [this] made an impression on his mind which, at the age of six-and-twenty, with no want of sense, or good companions, was durable in its happy effects. He became what he ought to be, useful to his father, steady and quiet, and not living merely for himself."

Sir Thomas sees how his judgment has failed in many things, especially in his plan of education for his children: "principle, active principle, had been wanting."

Mr. Rushworth is punished for his stupidity and may be duped again if he remarries.

Maria and Henry, the adulterers, separate, both wretched.

Mrs. Norris quits Mansfield to "devote herself to her unfortunate Maria, and in an establishment being formed for them in another country [i.e., county]—remote and private, where, shut up together with little society, on one side no affection, on the other, no judgment, it may be reasonably supposed that their tempers became their mutual punishment."

Julia has only been copying Maria and is forgiven.

Henry Crawford "ruined by early independence and bad domestic example, indulged in the freaks of a cold-blooded vanity a little too long.... Would he have persevered, and uprightly, Fanny must have been his reward—and a reward very voluntarily bestowed—within a reasonable period from Edmund's marrying Mary." But Maria's apparent indifference when they met in London mortified him. "He could not bear to be thrown off by the woman whose smiles had been so wholly at his command; he must exert himself to subdue so proud a display of resentment; it was anger on Fanny's account; he must get the better of it, and make Mrs. Rushworth Maria Bertram again in her treatment of himself." The world treats the man of such a scandal more lightly than the woman, but "we may fairly consider a man of sense like Henry Crawford, to be providing for himself no small portion of vexation and regret—vexation that must rise sometimes to self-reproach, and regret to wretchedness—in having so requited hospitality, so injured family peace, so forfeited his best, most estimable and endeared acquaintance, and so lost the woman whom he had rationally, as well as passionately loved."

Miss Crawford lives with the Grants, who have moved to London. "Mary had had enough of her own friends, enough of vanity, ambition, love, and disappointment in the course of the last half year, to be in need of the true kindness of her sister's heart, and the rational tranquillity of her ways.— They lived together; and when Dr. Grant had brought on apoplexy and death, by three great institutionary dinners in one week, they still lived together; for Mary, though perfectly resolved against ever attaching herself to a younger brother again, was long in finding among the dashing representatives, or idle heir apparents, who were at the command of her beauty, and her 20,000*l.* any one who could satisfy the better taste she had acquired at Mansfield, whose character and manners could authorise a hope of the domestic happiness she had there learnt to estimate, or put Edmund Bertram sufficiently out of her head."

Edmund finds in Fanny the ideal wife, with a slight suggestion of incest: "Scarcely had he done regretting Mary Crawford, and observing to Fanny how impossible it was that he should ever meet with such another woman, before it began to strike him whether a very different kind of woman might not do just as well—or a great deal better; whether Fanny herself was not growing as dear, as important to him in all her smiles, and all her ways, as Mary Crawford had ever been; and whether it might not be a possible, an hopeful undertaking to persuade her that her warm and sisterly regard for him would be foundation enough for wedded love. . . . Let no one presume to give the feelings of a young woman on receiving the assurance of that affection of which she has scarcely allowed herself to entertain a hope."

Lady Bertram now has Susan to replace Fanny as "the stationary niece," and the Cinderella theme continues. "With so much true merit and true love, and no want of fortune and friends, the happiness of the married cousins must appear as secure as earthly happiness can be.—Equally formed for domestic life, and attached to country pleasures, their home was the home of affection and comfort; and to complete the picture of good, the acquisition of Mansfield living by the death of Dr. Grant, occurred just after they had been married long enough to begin to want an increase of income, and feel their distance from the paternal abode an inconvenience.

"On that event they removed to Mansfield, and the Parsonage there, which under each of its two former owners, Fanny had never been able to approach but with some painful sensation of restraint or alarm, soon grew as dear to her heart, and as thoroughly perfect in her eyes, as every thing else, within the view and patronage of Mansfield Park, had long been."

It is a curious contention that beyond and after the story told in detail by the author, life for all the characters runs a smooth course. God, so to speak, takes over.

––––––––

To consider a question of method in Miss Austen's book, we should note that there are some features about *Mansfield Park* (and discoverable in her other novels) that we shall find greatly expanded in *Bleak House* (and discoverable in other novels by Dickens). This can hardly be called a direct influence of Austen upon Dickens. These features in both belong to the domain of comedy—the comedy of manners, to be exact—and are typical of the sentimental novel of the eighteenth and nineteenth centuries.

The first feature common to both Jane Austen and Dickens is the choice of a young girl as the sifting agent—the Cinderella type, a ward, an orphan, a governess, and the like—through whom or by whom the other characters are seen.

In the second point the connection is rather peculiar and striking: Jane Austen's method of giving her dislikable, or less likable, characters some grotesque little trick of demeanor, or manner, or attitude and bringing it up every time the character appears. Two obvious examples are Mrs. Norris and monetary matters, or Lady Bertram and her pug. Miss Austen artistically introduces some variety in this approach by changes of light, so to speak, by having the changing action of the book lend some new color to this or that person's usual attitude, but on the whole these comedy characters carry their droll defects from scene to scene throughout the novel as they would in a play. We shall see that Dickens uses the same method.

The third point I wish to raise is in reference to the Portsmouth scenes. Had Dickens come before Austen, we should have said that the Price family is positively Dickensian and that the Price children tie up nicely with the child theme that runs through *Bleak House*.

––––––––

A few of the more prominent elements of Jane Austen's style are worth mention. Her imagery is subdued. Although here and there she paints graceful word pictures with her delicate brush on a little bit of ivory (as she said herself), the imagery in relation to landscapes, gestures, colors, and so on, is very restrained. It is quite a shock to come to loud-speaking, flushed, robust Dickens after meeting delicate, dainty, pale Jane. She seldom uses comparisons by similes and metaphors. At Portsmouth the sea "dancing in its glee and dashing against the ramparts" is unusual. Infrequent, too, are such conventional or hackneyed metaphors as the drop of water in comparing the Price household with the Bertram: "and as to the little irritations, sometimes introduced by aunt Norris, they were short, they were trifling, they were as a drop of water to the ocean, compared with the ceaseless tumult of her present abode." She makes apt use of participles (such as *smiling*, *looking*, etc.) in descriptions of attitudes and gestures, or of phrases like *with an arch smile*, but introducing them in a parenthetical way, without *he* or *she said*, as if they were stage directions. This trick she learned from Samuel Johnson, but in *Mansfield Park* it is a very apt device since the whole novel resembles a play. Possibly also due to the Johnson influence is the oblique rendering of the construction and intonation of a speech in descriptive form, as in the report of Rushworth's words to Lady Bertram in chapter 6. Action and characterization proceed through dialogue or monologue. An excellent example comes in Maria's proprietorial speech as the party nears Sotherton, her future home: "Now we shall have no more rough road, Miss Crawford, our difficulties are over. The rest of the way is such as it ought to be. Mr. Rushworth has made it since he succeeded to the estate. Here begins the village. Those cottages are really a disgrace. The church spire is reckoned remarkably handsome. I am glad the church is not so close to the Great House as often happens in old places. The annoyance of the bells must be terrible. There is the parsonage; a tidy looking house, and I understand the clergyman and his wife are very decent people. Those are alms-houses, built by some of the family. To the right is the steward's house; he is a very respectable man. Now we are coming to the lodge gates; but we have nearly a mile through the park still."

Especially in dealing with Fanny's reactions, Austen uses a device that I call the *knight's move*, a term from chess to describe a sudden swerve to one or the other side on the board of Fanny's chequered emotions. At Sir Thomas's departure for Antigua, "Fanny's relief, and her consciousness of it, were quite equal to her cousins', but a more tender nature suggested that her feelings were ungrateful, and [*knight's move*:] she really grieved because she could not grieve." Before she has been invited to accompany the party to Sotherton, she keenly desires to see the avenue of trees at Sotherton before it is altered, but since it is too far for her to go, she says, "Oh! it does not signify. Whenever I do see it, [*now comes the knight's swerve*] you [Edmund] will tell me how it has been altered" by the discussed improvements. She will see the unaltered avenue, in short, through his recollection. When Mary Crawford remarks that her brother Henry writes very short letters from Bath, Fanny says that " 'When they are at a distance from all their family,' said Fanny [*knight's move:*], colouring for William's sake, 'they can write long letters.' " She is not conscious of being jealous when Edmund courts Mary, and she does not indulge in self-pity, but when Julia departs from the assignment of roles in a huff because of Henry's preference for Maria, Fanny "could not think of her as under the agitations of *jealousy*, [*knight's move:*] without great pity." When hesitating to participate in the play for considerations of truth and purity, she is "inclined to suspect [*knight's move:*] the truth and purity of her own scruples." She is "*so* glad" to accept an invitation to dine with the Grants, but at once asks herself (*knight's move:*) "And yet why should I be glad? for am I not certain of seeing or hearing something there to pain me?" When choosing a necklace she fancies that "there was one necklace more frequently placed before her eyes than the rest," and "she hoped in fixing on this, to be chusing [*knight's move:*] what Miss Crawford least wished to keep."

Prominent among the elements of Austen's style is what I like to call the *special dimple* achieved by furtively introducing into the sentence a bit of delicate irony between the components of a plain informative statement. I shall put in italics what I consider to be the key phrases. "Mrs. Price in her turn was injured and angry; and an answer which comprehended each sister in its bitterness, and bestowed such very disrespectful reflections on the pride of Sir Thomas, *as Mrs. Norris could not possibly keep to herself*, put an end to all intercourse between them for a considerable period." The narrative of the sisters continues: "Their homes were so distant, and the circles in which they moved so distinct, as almost to preclude the means of ever hearing of each other's existence during the eleven following years, *or at least to make it very wonderful to Sir Thomas, that Mrs. Norris should ever have it in her power to tell them, as she now and then did in an angry voice*, that Fanny had got another child." When the younger Fanny is introduced to the Bertram children, "they were too much used to company and praise, to have anything like natural shyness, *and their confidence increasing from their cousin's total want of it*, they were soon able to take a full survey of her face and her frock in easy indifference." The next day the two daughters "could not but hold her cheap on finding that she had but two sashes, and had never learned French; and when they perceived her to be little struck with the duet *they were so good as to play*, they could do no more than make her a *generous present of some of their least valued toys*, and leave her to herself. . . ." Lady Bertram "was a woman who spent her days in sitting nicely dressed on a sofa, doing some long piece of needle-work, *of little use and no beauty*, thinking more of her pug than her children. . . ." We may call this kind of sentence the *dimpled* sentence, a delicately ironic dimple in the author's pale virgin cheek.

Another element is what I call the *epigrammatic intonation*, a certain terse rhythm in the witty expression of a slightly paradoxical thought. This tone of voice is terse and tender, dry and yet musical, pithy but limpid and light. An example is her description of ten-year-old Fanny as she arrived at Mansfield. "She was small of her age, with no glow of complexion, nor any other striking beauty; exceedingly timid and shy, and shrinking from notice; but her air, though awkward, was not vulgar, her voice was sweet, and when she spoke, her countenance was pretty." In the early days of her arrival Fanny "had nothing worse to endure on the part of Tom, than that sort of merriment which a young man of seventeen will always think fair with a child of ten. He was just entering into life, full of spirits, and with all the liberal dispositions of an eldest son. . . . His kindness to his little cousin was consistent with his situation and rights: he made her some very pretty presents, and laughed at her." Although when she comes, Miss Crawford has in mind the attractions of an elder son, "to the credit of the lady it may be added, that without [Edmund] being a man of the world or an elder brother, without any of the arts of flattery or the gaieties of small talk, he began to be agreeable to her. She felt it to be so, though she had not foreseen and could hardly understand it; for he was not pleasant by any common rule, he talked no nonsense, he paid no compliments, his opinions were unbending, his attentions tranquil and simple. There was a charm, perhaps, in his sincerity, his steadiness, his integrity, which Miss Crawford might be equal to feel, though not equal to discuss with herself. She did not think very much about it, however; he pleased her for the present; she liked to have him near her; it was enough."

Style like this is not Austen's invention, nor is it even an English invention: I suspect it really comes from French literature where it is profusely represented in the eighteenth and early nineteenth centuries. Austen did not read French but got the epigrammatic rhythm from the pert, precise, and polished kind of style which was the fashion. Nevertheless, she handles it to perfection.

———

Style is not a tool, it is not a method, it is not a choice of words alone. Being much more than all this, style constitutes an intrinsic component or characteristic of the author's personality. Thus when we speak of style we mean an individual artist's peculiar nature, and the way it expresses itself in his artistic output. It is essential to remember that though every living person may have his or her style, it is the style peculiar to this or that individual writer of genius that is alone worth discussion. And this genius cannot express itself in a writer's literary style unless it is present in his soul. A mode of expression can be perfected by an author. It is not unusual that in the course of his literary career a writer's style becomes ever more precise and impressive, as indeed Jane Austen's did. But a writer devoid of talent cannot develop a literary style of any worth; at best it will be an artificial mechanism deliberately set together and devoid of the divine spark.

This is why I do not believe that anybody can be taught to write fiction unless he already possesses literary talent. Only in the latter case can a young author be helped to find himself, to free his language from clichés, to eliminate clumsiness, to form a habit of searching with unflinching patience for the right word, the only right word which will convey with the utmost precision the exact shade and intensity of thought. In such matters there are worse teachers than Jane Austen.

Nabokov's chronology for *Mansfield Park*

Recapitulation   **Structure**

Chronology of Mansfield Park

In the reign of George III (1760-1820)

p.1 "About thirty years ago": 1811 (the year "Mansfield Park" was begun) – 30 = 1781

1781   Miss Maria Ward marr. Sir Thomas Bertram, member of Parliament, a stiff, stern baronet.

between 1783, 1784, 1787, 1788   Tom, Edmund, Maria and Julia are born in this order

1787   Miss Ward (eldest) and Frances marry the Rev. Norris, a the eldest marr. gouty clergyman and Lieutenant Price a tippling naval officer

between 1789, 1790 1798   William Price, Fanny (1790) and seven other children are born

1800   Fanny, aged 10, comes from Portsmouth (Hampshire) to live with the Bertrams at Mansfield Park (Northampton)   draw map

1805 spring   The Rev. Norris dies and Dr Grant takes his place at Mansfield parsonage. p.47

1806   Sir Thomas Bertram with his son Tom sails for Antigua in the (a voyage of about two months) Lesser Antilles

miss her canary 1807   spring, Fanny's grey pony dies (she had been riding since spring 1803) p.61 — Sept, Tom returns to England (see p.44)

The pace of novel slows down p.34 ch 4   1808   July, Henry and Mary Crawford, brother and sister of Mrs Grant come to Mansfield parsonage. (children of her mother by a second marriage) early August, a Wednesday Both families visit Sotherton, the place of Rushworth, 10 mi. away End of Sept.   Fanny first ball and the Hon. John Yates arrives and suggests staying a play. first End of october Beginning of November   Sir Thomas returns from the West Indies just as the play is about to be rehearsed. on the third, November 10th   Maria Bertram marries Rushworth

¶ December   Henry Crawford falls in love with Fanny William, her brother, arrives

p. ch. 28 (ch I of II vol.) [p.237 - p245]   — December 22nd, Thursday, ball at Mansfield Park. Fanny is 18 1809 February   Fanny leaves for Portsmouth 1809 May 10th   Henry C. and Maria Rushw. elope her marriage to Rushworth has lasted exactly six months   **structure**

p.404   1809 Dr. Summer   Edmund opens his heart to Fanny 1781 - 1808 = 27 yrs = 34 pp. 1808 - 1809 = 1 year = 370 pp.

Read first pages to Prof. Mchild "

Scotland

Ireland

Mr and Mrs Woodcourt residence

The dedlock county seat "Chesney wold"

Yorkshire

Lincolnshire

Norfolk

Northampton
MP

Rutland
Cambridge
shire

Suffolk

John yarndyce house
(" Bleak House)

Bedford

Hertfordshire
Vaughan

Essex

Herts

London

Middlesex

London
Thames

Hants
Wincheste
museum

Surrey

Kent

IWall
heights

Sussex

Isle of Wight

Bleak House
(1852-1853)

We are now ready to tackle Dickens. We are now ready to embrace Dickens. We are now ready to bask in Dickens. In our dealings with Jane Austen we had to make a certain effort in order to join the ladies in the drawing room. In the case of Dickens we remain at table with our tawny port. We had to find an approach to Jane Austen and her *Mansfield Park*. I think we did find it and did have some degree of fun with her delicate patterns, with her collection of eggshells in cotton wool. But the fun was forced. We had to slip into a certain mood; we had to focus our eyes in a certain way. Personally I dislike porcelain and the minor arts, but I have often forced myself to see some bit of precious translucent china through the eyes of an expert and have discovered a vicarious bliss in the process. Let us not forget that there are people who have devoted to Jane all their lives, their ivy-clad lives. I am sure that some readers have a better ear for Miss Austen than I have. However, I have tried to be very objective. My objective method was, among other ways, an approach through the prism of the culture that her young ladies and gentlemen had imbibed from the cool fountainhead of the eighteenth and young nineteenth centuries. We also followed Jane in her somewhat spidery manner of composition: I want to remind the reader of the central part that a rehearsal plays in the web of *Mansfield Park*.

With Dickens we expand. It seems to me that Jane Austen's fiction had been a charming rearrangement of old-fashioned values. In the case of Dickens the values are new. Modern authors still get drunk on his vintage. Here there is no problem of approach as with Jane Austen, no courtship, no dillydallying. We just surrender ourselves to Dickens's voice—that is

Nabokov's map of Great Britain locating the action of *Bleak House*

all. If it were possible I would like to devote the fifty minutes of every class meeting to mute meditation, concentration, and admiration of Dickens. However, my job is to direct and rationalize those meditations, that admiration. All we have to do when reading *Bleak House* is to relax and let our spines take over. Although we read with our minds, the seat of artistic delight is between the shoulder blades. That little shiver behind is quite certainly the highest form of emotion that humanity has attained when evolving pure art and pure science. Let us worship the spine and its tingle. Let us be proud of our being vertebrates, for we are vertebrates tipped at the head with a divine flame. The brain only continues the spine: the wick really goes through the whole length of the candle. If we are not capable of enjoying that shiver, if we cannot enjoy literature, then let us give up the whole thing and concentrate on our comics, our videos, our books-of-the-week. But I think Dickens will prove stronger.

In discussing *Bleak House* we shall soon notice that the romantic plot of the novel is an illusion and is not of much artistic importance. There are better things in the book than the sad case of Lady Dedlock. We shall need some information about lawsuits in England, but otherwise it is going to be all play.

———

At first blush it might seem that *Bleak House* is a satire. Let us see. If a satire is of little aesthetic value, it does not attain its object, however worthy that object may be. On the other hand, if a satire is permeated by artistic genius, then its object is of little importance and vanishes with its times while the dazzling satire remains, for all time, as a work of art. So why speak of satire at all?

The study of the sociological or political impact of literature has to be devised mainly for those who are by temperament or education immune to the aesthetic vibrancy of authentic literature, for those who do not experience the telltale tingle between the shoulder blades. (I repeat again and again it is no use reading a book at all if you do not read it with your back.) It may be all right to contend that Dickens was eager to castigate the iniquities of Chancery. Such cases as that of Jarndyce did occur now and then in the middle of the last century although, as legal historians have shown, the bulk of our author's information on legal matters goes back to the 1820s and 1830s so that many of his targets had ceased to exist by the time *Bleak House* was written. But if the target is gone, let us enjoy the carved beauty of his weapon. Again, as an indictment of the aristocracy the description of the Dedlocks and their set is of no interest or importance whatsoever since our author's knowledge and notions of that set are extremely meager and crude, and as artistic achievements the Dedlocks, I am sorry to say, are as dead as doornails or door locks (the Dead locks are dead). So let us be thankful for the web and ignore the spider; let us admire the structural qualities of the crime theme and ignore the weakness of the satire and its theatrical gestures.

Finally, the sociologist may write a whole book, if he please, on the abuses that children underwent at a period of time that the historian will call the murky dawn of the industrial age—child labor and all that. But to be quite frank, the link of these poor children in *Bleak House* is not so much with social circumstances of the 1850s as with earlier times and mirrors of time. From the point of view of literary technique the connection is, rather, with the children of previous novels, the sentimental novel of the late eighteenth and early nineteenth centuries. One should read again the pages of *Mansfield Park* on the Price family in Portsmouth and see for oneself the quite definite artistic pedigree, the quite definite connection between Miss Austen's poor children and the poor children of *Bleak House*, and there are other literary sources, of course. So much for the technique. Now from the emotional point of view, here again we are hardly in the 1850s at all—we are with Dickens in his own childhood—and so once more the historical frame breaks down.

As is quite clear, the enchanter interests me more than the yarn spinner or the teacher. In the case of Dickens, this attitude seems to me to be the only way of keeping Dickens alive, above the reformer, above the penny novelette, above the sentimental trash, above the theatrical nonsense. There he shines forever on the heights of which we know the exact elevation, the outlines and the formation, and the mountain trails to get there through the fog. It is in his imagery that he is great.

———

Here are some of the things to notice while reading the book:

1. One of the novel's most striking themes refers to children—their troubles, insecurity, humble joys, and the joy they give, but mainly their misery. "I, a stranger and afraid in a world I never made," to quote

———

Overleaf: Nabokov's notes on the characters in his teaching copy of *Bleak House*

good-good bad-bad good father-bad man
Bagnet, Skimpole, Vholes (all three have three children)
Turveydrop
Rouncewell - fair
L. Dedlock and Hawdon: Esther
And another friend of Bucket has 19 children
Mrs Jellyby, Mrs Pardiggle - bad mother.
Bricklayer's wives
good
Caddy - good mother
Mrs Rouncewell
Smallweed
Neckett - good father

CHARACTERS

MR. BAYHAM BADGER, a medical practitioner in London. Zero

MATTHEW BAGNET ("Lignum Vitae"), an ex-artilleryman and bassoon-player. good

WOOLWICH BAGNET, his son.

LAWRENCE BOYTHORN, the impetuous, hearty friend of Mr. Jarndyce. Good

MR. INSPECTOR BUCKET, a sagacious, indefatigable detective officer. Fair

RIGHT HON. WILLIAM BUFFY, M.P., a friend of Sir Leicester Dedlock's.

RICHARD CARSTONE, a ward of Mr. Jarndyce, and a suitor in Chancery. Good

THE REV. MR. CHADBAND, a large, greasy, self-satisfied man, of no particular denomination. Fraud

SIR LEICESTER DEDLOCK, a representative of one of the great county families. Fair

MR. GRIDLEY ("The Man from Shropshire"), a ruined suitor in Chancery. Miserable

WILLIAM GUPPY, a lawyer's clerk, in the employ of Kenge and Carboy. Evil

CAPTAIN HAWDON ("Nemo"), a military officer; afterwards a law-writer. Good

JOHN JARNDYCE, a handsome, upright, unmarried man of about sixty; the guardian of Richard Carstone and Ada Clare. Very Good

MR. JELLYBY, the mild, quiet husband of Mrs. Jellyby. Zero

"PEEPY" JELLYBY, the neglected and unfortunate son of the preceding. Miserable

JO ("Toughey"), a street-crossing sweeper. Miserable

TONY JOBLING ("Weevle"), a law-writer, and a friend of Mr. Guppy's. Zero

MR. KENGE ("Conversation Kenge"), a portly, important-looking person; senior member of Kenge and Carboy, solicitors. Zero

MR. KROOK, a marine-store dealer; an old and eccentric man. Evil

MERCURY, a footman in the service of Sir Leicester Dedlock. Zero

MR. ROUNCEWELL, an ironmaster; the son of Sir Leicester Dedlock's housekeeper. Good

GEORGE ROUNCEWELL ("Mr. George"), another son; a wild young lad, who enlists; afterwards keeper of a shooting-gallery. Good 281

WATT ROUNCEWELL, the grandson of Mrs. Rouncewell. Good

HAROLD SKIMPOLE, a brilliant, vivacious, sentimental, but thoroughly selfish man. Fraud

BARTHOLOMEW SMALLWEED, grandson of Mr. and Mrs. Smallweed. Evil

GRANDFATHER SMALLWEED, a superannuated old man. Evil

MR. SNAGSBY, a law-stationer; a mild, timid man. Good

PHIL SQUOD, a man employed in Mr. George's shooting-gallery. 288 Good

LITTLE SWILLS, a red-faced comic vocalist. Zero

MR. TULKINGHORN, a solicitor of the Court of Chancery, and legal adviser to Sir Leicester Dedlock. *Evil*

MR. TURVEYDROP, a very gentlemanly man, celebrated for deportment. *Fra...*

PRINCE TURVEYDROP, his son; a fair man, of youthful appearance. *Zero*

MR. VHOLES, solicitor to Richard Carstone. *508 evil*

ALLAN WOODCOURT, a young surgeon. *good*

MRS. BAYHAM BADGER, a middle-aged lady, who dresses youthfully. *Frau...* *(164) 3 d lady*

MRS. BAGNET, a soldierly-looking woman; wife of Matthew Bagnet.

MALTA and QUEBEC BAGNET, her daughters.

MRS. BUCKET, the acute wife of Mr. Inspector Bucket. *Good*

MRS. CHADBAND, a stern, silent woman; wife of the Rev. Mr. Chadband.

ADA CLARE, a ward of Mr. John Jarndyce. *Good*

LADY HONORIA DEDLOCK, a proud and ambitious woman; the wife of Sir Leicester Dedlock. *Misery*

VOLUMNIA DEDLOCK, a lady of sixty; a cousin of Sir Leicester Dedlock's.

MISS FLITE, a little, half-crazed old woman, a suitor in Chancery. *Misery*

GUSTER, a maidservant of the Snagsbys. *Misery*

MADEMOISELLE HORTENSE, Lady Dedlock's waiting-woman. *Evil* *(35)*

MRS. JELLYBY, a lady devoted to public duties, to the neglect of her home.

CAROLINE JELLYBY ("Caddy"), her eldest daughter and amanuensis. *Mise...*

JENNY and LIZ, brickmakers' wives. *Misery*

CHARLOTTE NECKETT ("Charley"), a womanly, self-reliant girl, elder daughter of a sheriff's officer. *Misery* *2d lady*

MRS. PARDIGGLE, an active member of many general committees. *Fraud* *(95)*

ROSA, Lady Dedlock's maid; a dark-haired village beauty.

MRS. ROUNCEWELL, the handsome, stately old housekeeper to Sir Leicester Dedlock.

GRANDMOTHER SMALLWEED, an old woman, fallen into a childish state.

JUDY SMALLWEED, her granddaughter.

MRS. SNAGSBY, a short, shrewish woman. *Evil*

ESTHER SUMMERSON, the protégée of Mr. Jarndyce; a prudent and wise woman, and a self-denying friend. *Very good*

MRS. WOODCOURT, a handsome old lady; mother of Allan Woodcourt. *mild Fraud*

1. Charlotte Neckett (=Charley) (Esther-maid) as rosy + pretty as one of Flora's attend...

2. Ada "my darling, my beauty"

3. Rosa (2 d maid) " the timid little beauty   Greenwich —

4. Caroline Jellyby ("Caddy") " with her so pretty face on fire"

all flushing + prettiness of gentle little nymphs all belong to one genus attend to wants of other people

Housman. Also, parent-child relations are of interest, involving as they do the theme of "orphans": either the parent or the child is lost. The good mother nurses a dead child or dies herself. And children who are the attendants of other children. I have a sneaking fondness for the story about Dickens in his difficult London youth one day walking behind a workingman who was carrying a big-headed child across his shoulder. As the man walked on, without turning, with Dickens behind him, the child across the man's shoulders looked at Dickens, and Dickens, who was eating cherries out of a paper bag as he walked, silently popped one cherry after another into the silent child's mouth without anybody being the wiser.

2. Chancery—fog—madness: this is another theme.

3. Every character has his attribute, a kind of colored shadow that appears whenever the person appears.

4. Things participate—pictures, houses, carriages.

5. The sociological side, brilliantly stressed for example by Edmund Wilson in his collection of essays *The Wound and the Bow*, is neither interesting nor important.

6. The whodunit plot (with a kind of pre-Sherlock sleuth) of the second part of the book.

7. The dualism permeating the whole work, evil almost as strong as the good, embodied in Chancery, as a kind of Hell, with its emissary devils Tulkinghorn and Vholes, and a host of smaller devils, even to their clothes, black and shabby. On the good side we have Jarndyce, Esther, Woodcourt, Ada, Mrs. Bagnet; in between are the tempted ones, sometimes redeemed by love as in Sir Leicester, where love conquers rather artificially his vanity and prejudices. Richard, too, is saved, for though he has erred he is essentially good. Lady Dedlock is redeemed by suffering, and Dostoevski is wildly gesticulating in the background. Even the smallest act of goodness may bring salvation. Skimpole and, of course, the Smallweeds and Krook are completely the devil's allies. And so are the philanthropists, Mrs. Jellyby for instance, who spread misery around them while deceiving themselves that they are doing good though actually indulging their selfish instincts. The whole idea is that these people—Mrs. Jellyby, Mrs. Pardiggle, etc.—are giving their time and energy to all kinds of fanciful affairs (paralleling the Chancery theme of uselessness, perfect for the lawyers but misery for the victims) when their children are abandoned and miserable. There may be hope for Bucket and "Coavinses" (doing their duty without unnecessary cruelty) but none for the false missionaries, the Chadbands, etc. The "good" ones are often victims of the "evil" ones, but

therein lies salvation for the former, perdition for the latter. All these forces and people in conflict (often wrapped up in the Chancery theme) are symbols of greater, more universal forces, even to the death of Krook by fire (self-generated), the devil's natural medium. Such conflicts are the "skeleton" of the book, but Dickens was too much of an artist to make all this obtrusive or obvious. His people are alive, not merely clothed ideas or symbols.

_____

Bleak House consists of three main themes:

1. The Court of Chancery theme revolving around the dreary suit of Jarndyce and Jarndyce, emblemized by London's foul fog and Miss Flite's caged birds. Lawyers and mad suitors are its representatives.

2. The theme of miserable children and their relationships with those they help and with their parents, most of whom are frauds or freaks. The most unhappy child of all is the homeless Jo, who vegetates in the foul shadow of Chancery and is an unconscious agent in the mystery plot.

3. The mystery theme, a romantic tangle of trails followed in turn by three sleuths, Guppy, Tulkinghorn, Bucket, and their helpers, and leading to the unfortunate Lady Dedlock, mother of Esther born out of wedlock.

The magic trick Dickens is out to perform implies balancing these three globes, juggling with them, keeping them in a state of coherent unity, maintaining these three balloons in the air without getting their strings snarled.

I have tried to show by means of connecting lines in my diagram the variety of ways in which these three themes and their agents are linked up in the meandering course of the story. Only a few of the characters are noticed here, but their list is huge: of the children alone there are about thirty specimens. I should perhaps have connected Rachael, Esther's former nurse who knows the secret of her birth, with one of the frauds, the Reverend Chadband whom Rachael married. Hawdon is Lady Dedlock's former lover (also called Nemo in the book), Esther's father. Tulkinghorn, Sir Leicester Dedlock's solicitor, and Bucket the detective are the sleuths who try, not unsuccessfully, to unravel that little mystery, driving, incidentally, Lady Dedlock to her death. These sleuths find various helps such as my lady's French maid Hortense and the old scoundrel Smallweed, who is the brother-in-law of the weirdest, most foglike character in the book, Krook.

My plan is to follow each of these three themes, starting with the

Chancery—fog—bird—mad-suitor one; and among other things and creatures a little mad woman, Miss Flite, and the eerie Krook will be discussed as representatives of that theme. I shall then pick up the child theme in all its details and show poor Jo at his best, and also a very repulsive fraud, the false child Mr. Skimpole. The mystery theme will be treated next. Please mark that Dickens is an enchanter, an artist, in his dealings with the Chancery fog, a crusader combined with an artist in the child theme, and a very clever storyteller in the mystery theme that propels and directs the story. It is the artist that attracts us; so, after outlining the three main themes and the personalities of some of their agents, I shall analyze the form of the book, its structure, its style, its imagery, its verbal magic. We shall have a good deal of fun with Esther and her lovers, the impossibly good Woodcourt and the very convincing quixotic John Jarndyce, as well as with such worthies as Sir Leicester Dedlock and others.

The basic situation in *Bleak House* in regard to the Chancery theme is quite simple. A lawsuit, Jarndyce and Jarndyce, is dragging on for years. Numerous suitors expect fortunes that never come. One of the Jarndyces—John Jarndyce—is a good man who takes the whole affair calmly and does not expect anything from the suit, which he believes will scarcely be terminated in his lifetime. He has a young ward Esther Summerson, who is not directly concerned with the Chancery business but is the sifting agent of the book. John Jarndyce is also the guardian of Ada and Richard, who are cousins and on the opposite side of the suit. Richard gets tremendously involved psychologically in the lawsuit and goes crazy. Two other suitors, old Miss Flite and a Mr. Gridley, are mad already.

The Chancery theme is the one with which the book opens, but before looking into it let me draw attention to one of the niceties of the Dickensian method. The interminable suit and the Lord Chancellor are described: "How many people out of the suit, Jarndyce and Jarndyce has stretched forth its unwholesome hand to spoil and corrupt, would be a very wide question. From the master, upon whose impaling files reams of dusty warrants in Jarndyce and Jarndyce have grimly writhed into many shapes; down to the copying-clerk in the Six Clerks' Office, who has copied his tens of thousands of Chancery-folio-pages under that eternal heading; no man's nature has been made the better by it. In trickery, evasion, procrastination,

---

Nabokov's diagram of the main themes in *Bleak House*

Mention my self humm...

p. 337-388   Lecture 2   BH²

Open your books
at the list of chapters

Mrs Pon is wonderful character
there... Mis... a Mother... the children
never seen a ... of someone... and we can see
what came in...

chart of main themes (or Formula of
the Book)
in "Bleak House"   in form of themes

1

Chancery theme
(Fog, Caged Birds)

2

Child theme
(Misery, little helpers)

parents, frauds,

Lawyers,

jo

(Hawdon)

Esther

Rachael

Lady D.

Hortense

Guppy

Bucket

Tulkinghorn

Krook

old Smallweed

Mystery theme

3

spoliation, botheration, under false pretences of all sorts, there are influences that can never come to good. . . .

"Thus in the midst of the mud and at the heart of the fog, sits the Lord High Chancellor in his High Court of Chancery."

Now let us go back to the very first paragraph in the book: "London. Michaelmas Term lately over, and the Lord Chancellor sitting in Lincoln's Inn Hall. Implacable November weather. As much mud in the streets, as if the waters had but newly retired from the face of the earth. . . . Dogs, undistinguishable in mire. Horses, scarcely better; splashed to their very blinkers. Foot passengers, jostling one another's umbrellas, in a general infection of ill-temper, and losing their foot-hold at street-corners, where tens of thousands of other foot passengers have been slipping and sliding since the day broke (if this day ever broke), adding new deposits to the crust upon crust of mud, sticking at those points tenaciously to the pavement, and accumulating at compound interest." Accumulating at compound interest, a metaphor which links the real mud and mist to the mud and muddle of Chancery. Sitting in the midst of the mist and the mud and the muddle, the Lord Chancellor is addressed by Mr. Tangle as "Mlud." At the heart of the mud and fog, "My Lord" is himself reduced to "Mud" if we remove the lawyer's slight lisp. My Lord, Mlud, Mud. We shall mark at once, at the very beginning of our inquiry, that this is a typical Dickensian device: wordplay, making inanimate words not only live but perform tricks transcending their immediate sense.

There is another example of a verbal link in these first pages. In the initial paragraph, the smoke lowering down from the chimney pots is compared to "a soft black drizzle." Much later in the book the man Krook will dissolve in this black drizzle. But more immediately, in the paragraph about Chancery and the suit of Jarndyce and Jarndyce one finds the emblematic names of solicitors in Chancery "Chizzle, Mizzle, and otherwise [who] have lapsed into a habit of vaguely promising themselves that they will look into that outstanding little matter, and see what can be done for Drizzle—who was not well used—when Jarndyce and Jarndyce shall be got out of office." Chizzle, Mizzle, Drizzle, a dismal alliteration. And then, right after, "Shirking and sharking, in all their many varieties, have been sown broadcast by the ill-fated cause. . . ." *Shirking and sharking* means to live by stratagems as those lawyers live in the mud and drizzle of Chancery, and, if we go back to the first paragraph again, we find that shirking and sharking is a companion alliteration and an echo of the slipping and sliding of the pedestrians in the mud.

Let us now follow in the footsteps of the mad little woman Miss Flite, who appears as a fantastic suitor at the very beginning and marches off when the empty court is closed up for the day. Very shortly the three young people of the book, Richard (whose destiny is going to be linked up in a singular way with the mad woman's), his Ada (the cousin whom he will marry), and Esther—these three young people visit the Lord Chancellor and under the colonnade meet Miss Flite: "a curious little old woman in a squeezed bonnet, and carrying a reticule, came curtseying and smiling up to us, with an air of great ceremony.

" 'Oh!' said she. 'The wards in Jarndyce! Ve-ry happy, I am sure, to have the honour! It is a good omen for youth, and hope, and beauty, when they find themselves in this place, and don't know what's to come of it.'

" 'Mad!' whispered Richard, not thinking she could hear him.

" 'Right! Mad, young gentleman,' she returned so quickly that he was quite abashed. 'I was a ward myself. I was not mad at that time,' curtseying low, and smiling between every little sentence. 'I had youth and hope. I believe, beauty. It matters very little now. Neither of the three served, or saved me. I have the honour to attend Court regularly. With my documents. I expect a judgment. Shortly. On the Day of Judgment. . . . Pray accept my blessing.'

"As Ada was a little frightened, I said to humour the poor old lady, that we were much obliged to her.

" 'Ye-es!' she said mincingly. 'I imagine so. And here is Conversation Kenge. With *his* documents! How does your honourable worship do?'

" 'Quite well, quite well! Now don't be troublesome, that's a good soul!' said Mr. Kenge, leading the way back.

" 'By no means,' said the poor old lady, keeping up with Ada and me. 'Anything but troublesome. I shall confer estates on both,—which is not being troublesome, I trust? I expect a judgment. Shortly. On the Day of Judgment. This is a good omen for you. Accept my blessing!'

"She stopped at the bottom of the steep, broad flight of stairs; but we looked back as we went up, and she was still there, saying, still with a curtsey and a smile between every little sentence, 'Youth. And hope. And beauty. And Chancery. And Conversation Kenge! Ha! Pray accept my blessing!' "

The words—*youth, hope, beauty*—that she keeps repeating are important words, as we shall see farther on. The next day during their walk in London the three young people, and a fourth young person, come again across Miss Flite. Here a new theme is gradually introduced into her speech—this is the bird theme—song, wings, flight. Miss Flite is interested in flight and song, in the melodious birds of the garden of

Lincoln's Inn. We then visit her lodgings, above those of Krook. There is also another lodger, Nemo, of whom more later, also one of the most important figures in the book. Miss Flite shows off some twenty cages of birds. " 'I began to keep the little creatures,' she said, 'with an object that the wards will readily comprehend. With the intention of restoring them to liberty. When my judgment should be given. Ye-es! They die in prison, though. Their lives, poor silly things, are so short in comparison with Chancery proceedings, that, one by one, the whole collection has died over and over again. I doubt, do you know, whether one of these, though they are all young, will live to be free! Ve-ry mortifying, is it not?' "

She lets in the light so that the birds will sing for her visitors, but she will not tell their names. The sentence "Another time, I'll tell you their names" is very significant: there is a pathetic mystery here. She again repeats the words *youth, hope, beauty*. These words are now linked with the birds, and the bars of their cages seem to throw their shadow, seem already to bar with their shadows the symbols of youth, beauty, hope. To see still better how nicely Miss Flite is connected with Esther, you may mark when Esther in her early teens is leaving home for school with her only companion a bird in a cage. I want to remind you very forcibly at this point of another caged bird that I mentioned in connection with *Mansfield Park* when I referred to a passage from Sterne's *Sentimental Journey* about a starling—and about liberty and about captivity. Here we are again following the same thematic line. Cages, bird cages, their bars, the shadow of their bars striking out, as it were, all happiness. Miss Flite's birds, we should notice finally, are larks, linnets, and goldfinches, which correspond to lark-youth, linnet-hope, goldfinch-beauty.

When her visitors passed the door of the strange lodger Nemo, Miss Flite had warned them, hush, hush. Then this strange lodger is hushed, is dead, and by his own hand, and Miss Flite is sent for a doctor, and later stands trembling inside his door. This dead lodger, we shall learn, was connected with Esther, whose father he was, and with Lady Dedlock, whose lover he was. Such thematic lines as the Miss Flite one are very fascinating and instructive. A little later another poor child, another captive child, one of the many poor captive children of the book, the girl Caddy Jellyby, is mentioned as meeting her lover, Prince, in Miss Flite's room. Still later, on a visit by the young people, accompanied by Mr. Jarndyce, we learn from Krook's mouth the names of the birds: Hope, Joy, Youth, Peace, Rest, Life, Dust, Ashes, Waste, Want, Ruin, Despair, Madness, Death, Cunning, Folly, Words, Wigs, Rags, Sheepskin, Plunder, Precedent, Jargon, Gammon, and Spinach. But old Krook leaves out

Beauty—beauty which, incidentally, Esther loses in the course of the novel when she falls ill.

The thematic link between Richard and Miss Flite, between his madness and hers, is started when he becomes infatuated with the suit. This is a very important passage: "He had got at the core of that mystery now, he told us; and nothing could be plainer than that the will under which he and Ada were to take, I don't know how many thousands of pounds, must be finally established, if there were any sense or justice in the Court of Chancery . . . and that this happy conclusion could not be much longer delayed. He proved this to himself by all the weary arguments on that side he had read, and every one of them sunk him deeper in the infatuation. He had even begun to haunt the Court. He told us how he saw Miss Flite there daily; how they talked together, and how he did her little kindnesses; and how, while he laughed at her, he pitied her from his heart. But he never thought—never, my poor, dear, sanguine Richard, capable of so much happiness then, and with such better things before him!—what a fatal link was riveting between his fresh youth and her faded age; between his free hopes and her caged birds, and her hungry garret, and her wandering mind."

Miss Flite is acquainted with another mad suitor, Mr. Gridley, who is also introduced at the very start: "Another ruined suitor, who periodically appears from Shropshire, and breaks out into efforts to address the Chancellor at the close of the day's business, and who can by no means be made to understand that the Chancellor is legally ignorant of his existence after making it desolate for a quarter of a century, plants himself in a good place and keeps an eye on the Judge, ready to call out 'My Lord!' in a voice of sonorous complaint on the instant of his rising. A few lawyers' clerks and others who know this suitor by sight, linger, on the chance of his furnishing some fun, and enlivening the dismal weather a little." Later on this Mr. Gridley has a lengthy tirade about his situation addressed to Mr. Jarndyce. He has been ruined by a suit about a legacy in which the costs have eaten up three times the whole amount, and the suit is as yet unsettled. His sense of injury has been elevated to a principle which he will not abandon: " 'I have been in prison for contempt of Court. I have been in prison for threatening the solicitor. I have been in this trouble, and that trouble, and shall be again. I am the man from Shropshire, and I sometimes go beyond amusing them—though they have found it amusing, too, to see me committed into custody, and brought up in custody, and all that. It would be better for me, they tell me, if I restrained myself. I tell them, that if I did restrain myself, I should become imbecile. I was a good-enough-tempered man once, I believe. People in my part of the country say they remember me so; but, now, I must have this vent under my sense of injury, or nothing could hold my wits together. . . . Besides,' he added, breaking fiercely out, 'I'll shame them. To the last, I'll show myself in that Court to its shame.' " As Esther remarks, "His passion was fearful. I could not have believed in such rage without seeing it." But he dies in Mr. George's place, attended by the trooper, by Bucket, Esther and Richard, and by Miss Flite. As he dies, " 'O no, Gridley!' she cried, as he fell heavily and calmly back from before her, 'not without my blessing. After so many years!' "

In a very weak passage the author uses Miss Flite to tell Esther of the noble conduct of Dr. Woodcourt during a shipwreck in the East Indian seas. This does not come off well, although it is a brave attempt on the author's part to link up the mad little woman not only with Richard's tragic sickness but also with Esther's future happiness. The relation between Miss Flite and Richard becomes increasingly stressed until, at the last when Richard dies, Esther writes that "When all was still, at a late hour, poor crazed Miss Flite came weeping to me, and told me she had given her birds their liberty."

Another Chancery-theme character is introduced when Esther and her friends on a visit to Miss Flite stop for a moment in front of Krook's shop, above which Miss Flite roomed: "a shop, over which was written KROOK, RAG AND BOTTLE WAREHOUSE. Also, in long thin letters, KROOK, DEALER IN MARINE STORES. In one part of the window was a picture of a red paper mill, at which a cart was unloading a quantity of sacks of old rags. In another, was the inscription, BONES BOUGHT. In another, KITCHEN-STUFF BOUGHT. In another, OLD IRON BOUGHT. In another, WASTE PAPER BOUGHT. In another, LADIES' AND GENTLEMEN'S WARDROBES BOUGHT. Everything seemed to be bought, and nothing to be sold there. In all parts of the window were quantities of dirty bottles: blacking bottles, medicine bottles, ginger-beer and soda-water bottles, pickle bottles, wine bottles, ink bottles: I am reminded by mentioning the latter, that the shop had, in several little particulars, the air of being in a legal neighbourhood, and of being, as it were, a dirty hanger-on and disowned relation of the law. There were a great many ink bottles. There was a little tottering bench of shabby old volumes, outside the door, labelled 'Law Books, all at 9d.' "

Here the connection between Krook and the Chancery theme with its legal symbols and rotting laws is established. Please hold in juxtaposition the terms BONES BOUGHT and LADIES' AND GENTLEMEN'S WARDROBES BOUGHT. For what is a suitor in a Chancery case but bones and ragged clothes, and the rags of the robes of law—the rags of law—and the wastepaper that Krook also buys. This, indeed, is pointed out by Esther herself, with some assistance from Richard Carstone and Charles Dickens: "The litter of rags tumbled partly into and partly out of a one-legged wooden scale, hanging without any counterpoise from a beam, might have been counsellors' bands and gowns torn up. One had only to fancy, as Richard whispered to Ada and me while we all stood looking in, that yonder bones in a corner, piled together and picked very clean, were the bones of clients, to make the picture complete." Richard, who whispers this, is destined to be a victim of Chancery himself when a temperamental flaw in his nature leads him to drop one after another of the various professions he dabbles in before becoming entangled in the mad muddle and poisonous visions of the Chancery inheritance that will never come.

Krook himself appears, emerging, as it were, from the very heart of the fog (remember his trick of calling the Lord Chancellor his brother—his brother in rust and dust, in madness and mud): "He was short, cadaverous, and withered; with his head sunk sideways between his shoulders, and the breath issuing in visible smoke from his mouth, as if he were on fire within. His throat, chin, and eyebrows were so frosted with white hairs, and so gnarled with veins and puckered skin, that he looked from his breast upward, like some old root in a fall of snow." There is Krook—crooked Krook. The gnarled-root-in-snow simile should be added to the growing collection of Dickensian comparisons to be discussed later. Another little theme which emerges here, and is going to breed, is the allusion to fire: "as if he were on fire within." *As if*—an ominous note.

A later passage where Krook rattles off the names of Miss Flite's birds—symbols of Chancery and misery—has already been mentioned. Now his horrible cat is introduced, ripping at a bundle of rags with his tigerish claws, with a sound that sets Esther's pretty teeth on edge. Incidentally, old Smallweed, in the mystery-theme group, with his green eyes and sharp claws, is not only a brother-in-law of Krook's but also a kind of human representative of Krook's cat. The bird theme and the cat theme gradually meet—both Krook and his green-eyed, gray tiger are waiting for the birds to leave their cages. Here the symbolic slant depends on the idea that only death can liberate a Chancery suitor. Thus, Gridley dies and is free. Thus, Richard dies and is free. Krook horrifies his audience with an account of the suicide of a certain Tom Jarndyce, a Chancery suitor whom he quotes: "it's being ground to bits in a slow mill, it's being roasted at a slow fire." Mark this "slow fire." Krook himself in his crooked, cranky way is also a victim of Chancery—and he too will burn. Indeed, we get a definite hint of what is going to be his doom. The man was perpetually full of gin, which as dictionaries tell us is a strong liquor made by distilling grain mash, especially rye mash. Krook seems to carry with him wherever he goes a kind of portable hell. Portable hell—this is Mr. Nabokov, not Mr. Dickens.

Krook is not only linked with the Chancery theme, but is also connected with the mystery theme. After Nemo's death, in order to get from Krook certain letters relating to Lady Dedlock's former love affair, Guppy, a lawyer's clerk in a dither of romance and blackmail, and his friend Tony Jobling (also called Weevle) visit Krook. They have his gin bottle refilled, which he receives "in his arms like a beloved grandchild." Alas, the grandchild might have been more aptly described as an internal parasite. Now we come to the marvelous pages in chapter 32 dealing with Krook's marvelous death, a tangible symbol of the slow fire and fog of Chancery. Recall the imagery in the first pages of the book—smog, the soft black drizzle, the flakes of soot—this is the keynote, the breeding spot of the gruesome theme which is now going to be developed to its logical end, with the addition of the gin.

Guppy and Weevle are on their way to Weevle's room (the room in which Lady Dedlock's lover Hawdon had committed suicide, in the same house where Miss Flite and Krook dwell) to await midnight when Krook is to hand over the letters. On their way they run into a Mr. Snagsby, a law stationer. There is a curious smell and flavor about the thick foggy air. " 'Airing yourself, as I am doing, before you go to bed?' the stationer inquires.

" 'Why, there's not much air to be got here; and what there is is not very refreshing,' Weevle answers, glancing up and down the court.

" 'Very true, sir. Don't you observe,' says Mr. Snagsby, pausing to sniff and taste the air a little; 'don't you observe, Mr. Weevle, that you're—not to put too fine a point upon it—that you're rather greasy here, sir?'

" 'Why, I have noticed myself that there is a queer kind of flavour in the place to-night,' Mr. Weevle rejoins. 'I suppose it's chops at the Sol's Arms.'

" 'Chops, do you think? Oh!—Chops, eh?' Mr. Snagsby sniffs and tastes again. 'Well, sir, I suppose it is. But I should say their cook at the Sol wanted a little looking after. She has been burning 'em, sir? And I don't think,' Mr. Snagsby sniffs and tastes again, and then spits and wipes his mouth; 'I don't think—not to put too fine a point upon it—that they were quite fresh, when they were shown the gridiron.' "

The two friends go up to Weevle's room and have a discussion of the mysterious Krook and the horrors that Weevle feels living in this room and in this house. Weevle complains to Guppy about the atmosphere—mental and physical—in that room. Mark the candle heavily burning with "a great cabbage head and a long winding-sheet." No use reading Dickens if one cannot visualize that.

Guppy happens to look at his coat sleeve. " 'Why, Tony, what on earth is going on in this house to-night? Is there a chimney on fire?'

" 'Chimney on fire!'

" 'Ah!' returns Mr. Guppy. 'See how the soot's falling. See here, on my arm! See again on the table here! Confound the stuff, it won't blow off—smears, like black fat!' "

Weevle investigates down the staircase but all seems quiet, and he "quotes the remark he lately made to Mr. Snagsby, about their cooking chops at the Sol's Arms.

" 'And it was then,' resumes Mr. Guppy, still glancing with remarkable aversion at the coat-sleeve, as they pursue their conversation before the fire, leaning on opposite sides of the table, with their heads very near together, 'that he told you of his having taken the bundle of letters from his lodger's portmanteau?' "

The talk goes on a while, but when Weevle stirs the fire, it makes Guppy start. " 'Fah! Here's more of this hateful soot hanging about,' says he. 'Let us open the window a bit, and get a mouthful of air. It's too close.' " They continue the conversation, leaning on the windowsill, Guppy tapping his hand on the sill until he hastily draws his hand away. " 'What in the Devil's name,' he says, 'is this! Look at my fingers!'

"A thick yellow liquor defiles them, which is offensive to the touch and sight and more offensive to the smell. A stagnant, sickening oil, with some natural repulsion in it that makes them both shudder.

" 'What have you been doing here? What have you been pouring out of window?'

" 'I pouring out of window? Nothing, I swear. Never, since I have been here!' cries the lodger.

"And yet look here—and look here! When he brings the candle, here, from the corner of the window-sill, it slowly drips, and creeps away down the bricks; here, lies in a little thick nauseous pool.

" 'This is a horrible house,' says Mr. Guppy, shutting down the window. 'Give me some water, or I shall cut my hand off.'

"He so washes, and rubs, and scrubs, and smells and washes, that he has not long restored himself with a glass of brandy, and stood silently before the fire, when Saint Paul's bell strikes twelve, and all those other bells strike twelve from their towers of various heights in the dark air, and in many tones."

Weevle goes down the stairs to keep the appointment and to secure the bundle of Nemo's papers promised him, but returns in terror. " 'I couldn't make him hear, and I softly opened the door and looked in. And the burning smell is there—and the soot is there, and the oil is there—and he is not there!'—Tony ends this with a groan.

"Mr. Guppy takes the light. They go down, more dead than alive, and holding one another, push open the door of the back shop. The cat has retreated close to it, and stands snarling—not at them; at something on the ground, before the fire. There is a very little fire left in the grate, but there is a smouldering suffocating vapour in the room, and a dark greasy coating on the walls and ceiling." The old man's coat and cap hang on a chair. The red string that had tied the papers is on the floor, but no papers are to be seen: only a crumbled black thing on the floor. " 'What's the matter with the cat?' says Mr. Guppy. 'Look at her!'

" 'Mad, I think. And no wonder in this evil place.'

"They advance slowly, looking at all these things. The cat remains where they found her, still snarling at the something on the ground, before the fire and between the two chairs. What is it? Hold up the light.

"Here is a small burnt patch of flooring; here is the tinder from a little bundle of burnt paper, but not so light as usual, seeming to be steeped in something; and here it is—is it the cinder of a small charred and broken log of wood sprinked with white ashes, or is it coal? O Horror, he is here! and this from which we run away, striking out the light and overturning one another into the street, is all that represents him.

"Help, help, help! come into this house for Heaven's sake!

"Plenty will come in, but none can help. The Lord Chancellor of that Court, true to his title in his last act, has died the death of all Lord Chancellors in all Courts, and of all authorities in all places under all names soever, where false pretences are made, and where injustice is done. Call the death by any name Your Highness will, attribute it to whom you will, or say it might have been prevented how you will, it is the same death eternally—inborn, inbred, engendered in the corrupted humours of the vicious body itself, and that only—Spontaneous Combustion, and none other of all the deaths that can be died."

And so the metaphor becomes a physical fact, and the evil within a man has destroyed the man. Old Krook is diffused and merged in the fog from which he emerged—fog to fog, mud to mud, madness to madness, black drizzle and greasy ointments of witchcraft. We feel it all physically, and it does not, of course, matter a jot whether or not a man burning down that way from the saturated gin inside him is a scientific possibility. Dickens with his eloquent tongue in his bearded cheek, Dickens, when introducing his book and also within the text, refers to what he lists as actual cases of spontaneous combustion, the gin and the sin catching fire and the man burning to the ground.

There is something else here more important than the question, is this possible? Namely, we should contrast two styles here in this extended passage: the rapid, colloquial style of Guppy and Weevle, full of jerky movement, and the eloquent apostrophic tolling style of the end. The term *apostrophic* is from *apostrophe*, which in rhetoric means "a feigned turning from one's audience to address directly a person or thing, or an imaginary object." Now the question is: what author's style does this apostrophic, booming accent in Dickens recall? The answer is, Thomas Carlyle, (1795-1881), and I am especially thinking of his *History of the French Revolution* which appeared in 1837. It is fun to dip into that magnificent work and find therein that apostrophic accent, rolling and tolling around the idea of destiny, futility, and nemesis. Two examples may suffice: "Serene Highnesses, who sit there protocolling and manifestoing, and consoling mankind! how were it if, for once in the thousand years, your parchments, formularies and reasons of state were blown to the four winds . . . and Mankind said for itself what the thing was that would console it" (chapter 4, "The Marseillaise").

"Unhappy France; unhappy in King, Queen and Constitution; one knows not in which unhappiest. Was the meaning of our so glorious French Revolution this, and no other, that when Shams and Delusions, long soul-killing, had become body-killing . . . a great People rose," etc. (chapter 9, "Varenne").

We are now in a position to sum up our Chancery theme. It started with an account of the mental and natural fog attending the Chancery business. In the early pages "My Lord" was reduced to mud, and we heard the very sound of the mud, slippery and sly, in the trickery of Chancery. We discovered the symbolic meaning, the symbolic plight, the symbolic names. Crazy Miss Flite and her birds are linked with the plight of two other Chancery suitors, both of whom die in the course of the book. Then we came to Krook, a symbol of Chancery's slow fog and slow fire, mud and madness, which acquire a tangible quality in the horror of his prodigious fate. But what is the fate of the suit itself, of this Jarndyce and Jarndyce case that has been rolling on for years and years, breeding devils and destroying angels? Well, just as Krook's end was sound logic in the magic world of Dickens, so the Chancery case also has a logical end within the grotesque logic of that grotesque world.

One day when the suit was to come up again, Esther and her friends were delayed so that "when we came to Westminster Hall, we found that the day's business was begun. Worse than that, we found such an unusual crowd in the Court of Chancery that it was full to the door, and we could neither see nor hear what was passing within. It appeared to be something droll, for occasionally there was a laugh, and a cry of 'Silence!' It appeared to be something interesting, for every one was pushing and striving to get nearer. It appeared to be something that made the professional gentlemen very merry, for there were several young counsellors in wigs and whiskers on the outside of the crowd, and when one of them told the others about it, they put their hands in their pockets, and quite doubled themselves up with laughter, and went stamping about the pavement of the hall.

"We asked a gentleman by us, if he knew what cause was on? He told us Jarndyce and Jarndyce. We asked him if he knew what was doing in it? He said, really no he did not, nobody ever did; but as well as he could make out, it was over. Over for the day? we asked him. No, he said; over for good.

"Over for good!

"When we heard this unaccountable answer, we looked at one another quite lost in amazement. Could it be possible that the Will had set things right at last, and that Richard and Ada were going to be rich?* It seemed too good to be true. Alas, it was!

"Our suspense was short; for a break up soon took place in the crowd, and the people came streaming out looking flushed and hot, and bringing a quantity of bad air with them. Still they were all exceedingly amused, and were more like people coming out from a Farce or a Juggler than from a court of Justice. We stood aside, watching for any countenance we knew; and presently great bundles of paper began to be carried out—bundles in bags, bundles too large to be got into any bags, immense masses of papers of all shapes and no shapes, which the bearers staggered under, and threw down for the time being, anyhow, on the Hall pavement, while they went back to bring out more. Even these clerks were laughing. We glanced at the papers, and seeing Jarndyce and Jarndyce everywhere, asked an official-looking person who was standing in the midst of them, whether the cause was over. 'Yes,' he said; 'it was all up with it at last!' and burst out laughing too."

*Shortly before, under the propulsion of Mr. Bucket, old Smallweed had disgorged a copy of a Jarndyce will, which he had found among the accumulation of Krook's old wastepapers. This will was later than those in contest and gave the major share of the estate to Ada and Richard. It had seemed at the time that this new will would end the suit with some promptness. Ed.

The costs had absorbed the whole case, all the fortunes involved. And so the fantastic fog of Chancery is dispersed—and only the dead do not laugh.

————

Before one comes to the real children in Dickens's important children's theme, the fraud Harold Skimpole must be looked at. Skimpole, a falsely brilliant fellow, is introduced to us by Jarndyce, in chapter 6, who says, "There's no one here [in my house] but the finest creature upon earth—a child." This definition of a child is important for the understanding of the novel, which deals in its inner essential part mainly with the misery of little ones, with the pathos of childhood—and Dickens is at his best in these matters. So the definition found by good and kind John Jarndyce is quite correct as it stands: a child *was* from the point of view of Dickens the finest creature upon earth. But now comes an interesting point: the definition "a child" cannot be really applied to the man Skimpole. Skimpole deceives the world, and he deceives Mr. Jarndyce into thinking that he, Skimpole, is as innocent, as naive, as carefree as a child. Actually he is nothing of the sort; but this false childishness of his throws into splendid relief the virtues of authentic childhood in other parts of the book.

Jarndyce explains to Richard that Skimpole is grown up, at least as old as he, Jarndyce, is, " 'but in simplicity, and freshness, and enthusiasm, and a fine guileless inaptitude for all worldly affairs, he is a perfect child.

" '. . . He is a musical man; an Amateur, but might have been a Professional. He is an Artist, too; an Amateur, but might have been a Professional. He is a man of attainments and of captivating manners. He has been unfortunate in his affairs, and unfortunate in his pursuits, and unfortunate in his family; but he don't care—he's a child!'

" 'Did you imply that he has children of his own, sir?' inquired Richard.

" 'Yes, Rick! Half-a-dozen. More! Nearer a dozen, I should think. But he has never looked after them. How could he? He wanted somebody to look after *him*. He is a child, you know!' "

We are presented to Mr. Skimpole through Esther's eyes: "He was a little bright creature, with a rather large head; but a delicate face, and a sweet voice, and there was a perfect charm in him. All he said was so free from effort and spontaneous, and was said with such a captivating gaiety, that it was fascinating to hear him talk. Being of a more slender figure than Mr. Jarndyce, and having a richer complexion, with browner hair, he looked younger. Indeed, he had more the appearance, in all respects, of a damaged young man, than a well-preserved elderly one. There was an easy negligence in his manner, and even in his dress (his hair carelessly disposed, and his neckerchief loose and flowing, as I have seen artists paint their own portraits), which I could not separate from the idea of a romantic youth who had undergone some unique process of depreciation. It struck me as being not at all like the manner or appearance of a man who had advanced in life by the usual road of years, cares, and experiences." He had failed as a doctor in the household of a German prince since "he had always been a mere child in point of weights and measures, and had never known anything about them (except that they disgusted him)." When called on to perform any duty, such as ministering to the prince or his people, "he was generally found lying on his back, in bed, reading the newspapers, or making fancy sketches in pencil, and couldn't come. The prince, at last, objecting to this, 'in which,' said Mr. Skimpole, in the frankest manner, 'he was perfectly right,' the engagement terminated, and Mr. Skimpole having (as he added with delightful gaiety) 'nothing to live upon but love, fell in love, and married, and surrounded himself with rosy cheeks.' His good friend Jarndyce and some other of his good friends then helped him, in quicker or slower succession, to several openings in life; but to no purpose, for he must confess to two of the oldest infirmities in the world: one was, that he had no idea of time; the other, that he had no idea of money. In consequence of which he never kept an appointment, never could transact any business, and never knew the value of anything! . . . All he asked of society was, to let him live. *That* wasn't much. His wants were few. Give him the papers, conversation, music, mutton, coffee, landscape, fruit in the season, a few sheets of Bristol-board, and a little claret, and he asked no more. He was a mere child in the world, but he didn't cry for the moon. He said to the world, 'Go your several ways in peace! Wear red coats, blue coats, lawn sleeves, put pens behind your ears, wear aprons; go after glory, holiness, commerce, trade, any object you prefer; only—let Harold Skimpole live!'

"All this, and a great deal more, he told us, not only with the utmost brilliancy and enjoyment, but with a certain vivacious candour—speaking of himself as if he were not at all his own affair, as if Skimpole were a third person, as if he knew that Skimpole had his singularities, but still had his claims too, which were the general business of the community and must not be slighted. He was quite enchanting," although Esther remains somewhat confused as to *why* he was free of all duties and accountabilities of life.

The next morning at breakfast Skimpole discourses engagingly on Bees and Drones and frankly expresses the thought that the Drone is the embodiment of a wiser and pleasanter idea than the Bee. But Skimpole is not really a stingless drone, and this is the secret point of his personality: he has a sting which remains concealed for a long time. His offhand professions of childishness and carelessness afforded much pleasure to Mr. Jarndyce, who was relieved to find what he thought was a candid man in a world of deceit. But the candid Mr. Skimpole used good Jarndyce's kind heart for his own ends. A little later, in London, the presence of something hard and evil behind Skimpole's childish banter becomes more and more evident. A sheriff's officer named Neckett, from the firm of Coavins, who had come one day to arrest Skimpole for his debts, dies, and Skimpole refers to it in a manner that shocks Esther: " 'Coavinses has been arrested by the great Bailiff,' said Mr. Skimpole. 'He will never do violence to the sunshine any more.' " The man has left a motherless family, which Skimpole jokes about as he lightly touches the piano by which he is seated. " 'And he told me,' he said, playing little chords where [*says the narrator*] I shall put full stops, 'That Coavinses had left [*period*] Three children [*period*] No mother [*period*] And that Coavinses' profession [*period*] Being unpopular [*period*] The rising Coavinses [*period*] Were at a considerable disadvantage.' " Mark the device here—the cheerful rogue idly touching these musical chords in between his trite banter.

Now Dickens is going to do a very clever thing. He is going to take us to the motherless household of the dead man and show us the plight of the children there; and in the light of this plight, Mr. Skimpole's so-called childishness will reveal its falsity. Esther is the narrator: "I tapped at the door, and a little shrill voice inside said, 'We are locked in. Mrs. Blinder's got the key!'

"I applied the key on hearing this, and opened the door. In a poor room, with a sloping ceiling, and containing very little furniture, was a mite of a boy, some five or six years old, nursing and hushing a heavy child of eighteen months. [*I like the 'heavy,' which weighs down the sentence at the necessary point.*] There was no fire, though the weather was cold; both children were wrapped in some poor shawls and tippets, as a substitute. Their clothing was not so warm, however, but that their noses looked red and pinched, and their small figures shrunken, as the boy walked up and down, nursing and hushing the child with its head on his shoulder.

" 'Who has locked you up here alone?' we naturally asked.

" 'Charley,' said the boy, standing still to gaze at us.

" 'Is Charley your brother?'

" 'No. She's my sister, Charlotte. Father called her Charley.' . . .

" 'Where is Charley now?'

" 'Out a-washing,' said the boy. . . .

"We were looking at one another, and at these two children, when there came into the room a very little girl, childish in figure but shrewd and older-looking in the face—pretty-faced too—wearing a womanly sort of bonnet much too large for her, and drying her bare arms on a womanly sort of apron. Her fingers were white and wrinkled with washing, and the soap-suds were yet smoking which she wiped off her arms. But for this, she might have been a child, playing at washing, and imitating a poor working-woman with a quick observation of the truth." So Skimpole is a vile parody of a child, whereas this little girl is a pathetic imitator of an adult woman. "The child [the boy] was nursing, stretched forth its arms, and cried out to be taken by Charley. The little girl took it, in a womanly sort of manner belonging to the apron and the bonnet, and stood looking at us over the burden that clung to her most affectionately.

" 'Is it possible,' whispered [Mr. Jarndyce] . . . 'that this child works for the rest? Look at this! For God's sake look at this!'

"It was a thing to look at. The three children close together, and two of them relying solely on the third, and the third so young and yet with an air of age and steadiness that sat so strangely on the childish figure."

Now, please, note the intonation of pity and of a kind of tender awe in Mr. Jarndyce's speech: " 'Charley, Charley!' said my guardian. 'How old are you?'

" 'Over thirteen, sir,' replied the child.

" 'O! What a great age!' said my guardian. 'What a great age, Charley!'

"I cannot describe the tenderness with which he spoke to her; half playfully, yet all the more compassionately and mournfully.

" 'And do you live alone here with these babies, Charley?' said my guardian.

" 'Yes, sir,' returned the child, looking up into his face with perfect confidence, 'since father died.'

" 'And how do you live, Charley? O! Charley,' said my guardian, turning his face away for a moment, 'how do you live?' "

I should not like to hear the charge of sentimentality made against this strain that runs through *Bleak House*. I want to submit that people who denounce the sentimental are generally unaware of what sentiment is. There is no doubt that, say, a story of a student turned shepherd for the sake of a maiden is sentimental and silly and flat and stale. But let us ask ourselves, is not there some difference between Dickens's technique and the old writers. For instance, how different is this world of Dickens from the world of Homer or from the world of Cervantes. Does a hero of

Homer's really feel the divine throb of pity? Horror, yes—and a kind of generalized routine compassion—but is the keen sense of specialized pity as we understand it today, as it were, in the dactyllic past? For let us nurse no doubt about it: despite all our hideous reversions to the wild state, modern man is on the whole a better man than Homer's man, *homo homericus*, or than medieval man. In the imaginary battle of *americus* versus *homericus*, the first wins humanity's prize. Of course, I am aware that dim throbs of pathos do occur in the *Odyssey*, that Odysseus and his old father do, suddenly, when they meet again after many years, and after a few casual remarks, suddenly raise their heads and lament in a kind of elemental ululation, a vague howl against fate, as if they were not quite conscious of their own woe. Yes, this compassion is not quite conscious of itself; it is, I repeat, generalized emotion in that old world with its blood puddles and dung heaps on marble, whose only redemption, after all, is that it left us a handful of magnificent epics, an immortal horizon of verse. Well, you have sufficiently heard from me about the thorns and fangs of that world. Don Quixote does interfere in the flogging of a child, but Don Quixote is a madman. Cervantes takes the cruel world in his stride, and there is always a belly laugh just around the corner of the least pity.

Now here, in the passage about the little Necketts, Dickens's great art should not be mistaken for a cockney version of the seat of emotion—it is the real thing, keen, subtle, specialized compassion, with a grading and merging of melting shades, with the very accent of profound pity in the words uttered, and with an artist's choice of the most visible, most audible, most tangible epithets.

And now the Skimpole theme is going to meet, head-on, one of the most tragic themes in the book, that of the poor boy Jo. This orphan, this very sick little Jo, is brought by Esther and the girl Charley, now her maid,* to the Jarndyce house for shelter on a cold, wild night. Jo is shown shrunk into the corner of a window seat in the hall of the Jarndyce house, staring with an indifference that scarcely could be called wonder at the comfort and brightness about him. Esther is again the narrator. " 'This is a sorrowful case,' said my guardian, after asking him a question or two, and touching him, and examining his eyes. 'What do you say, Harold?'

" 'You had better turn him out,' said Mr. Skimpole.

" 'What do you mean?' inquired my guardian, almost sternly.

---

*Elsewhere among the papers, VN has a note that "Charley coming to Esther as a maid is the 'sweet little shadow' instead of the dark shadow of Hortense" who had offered her services to Esther after she had been discharged by Lady Dedlock but had not been accepted. Ed.

" 'My dear Jarndyce,' said Mr. Skimpole, 'you know what I am: I am a child. Be cross to me, if I deserve it. But I have a constitutional objection to this sort of thing. I always had, when I was a medical man. He's not safe, you know. There's a very bad sort of fever about him.'

"Mr. Skimpole had retreated from the hall to the drawing-room again, and said this in his airy way, seated on the music-stool as we stood by.

" 'You'll say it's childish,' observed Mr. Skimpole, looking gaily at us. 'Well, I dare say it may be; but I *am* a child, and I never pretend to be anything else. If you put him out in the road, you only put him where he was before. He will be no worse off than he was, you know. Even make him better off, if you like. Give him sixpence, or five shillings, or five pound ten—you are arithmeticians, and I am not—and get rid of him!'

" 'And what is he to do then?' asked my guardian.

" 'Upon my life,' said Mr. Skimpole, shrugging his shoulders with his engaging smile, 'I have not the least idea what he is to do then. But I have no doubt he'll do it.' "

This is of course to imply that all poor Jo has to do is just to die like a sick animal in a ditch. However, Jo is put to bed in a wholesome loft room. And as the reader learns much later, Skimpole is easily bribed by a detective to show the room where Jo is, and Jo is taken away and disappears for a long time.

The Skimpole theme is then related to Richard. Skimpole begins to sponge on him and even, after a bribe, produces a new lawyer for him to pursue the fruitless suit. Mr. Jarndyce takes Esther with him on a visit to Skimpole's lodgings to caution him, still believing in his naive innocence. "It was dingy enough, and not at all clean; but furnished with an odd kind of shabby luxury, with a large footstool, a sofa, and plenty of cushions, an easy-chair, and plenty of pillows, a piano, books, drawing materials, music, newspapers, and a few sketches and pictures. A broken pane of glass in one of the dirty windows was papered and wafered over; but there was a little plate of hothouse nectarines on the table, and there was another of grapes, and another of sponge-cakes, and there was a bottle of light wine. Mr. Skimpole himself reclined upon the sofa, in a dressing-gown, drinking some fragrant coffee from an old china cup—it was then about mid-day—and looking at a collection of wallflowers in the balcony.

"He was not in the least disconcerted by our appearance, but rose and received us in his usual airy manner.

" 'Here I am, you see!' he said, when we were seated: not without some difficulty, the greater part of the chairs being broken. 'Here I am! This is my frugal breakfast. Some men want legs of beef and mutton for breakfast;

I don't. Give me my peach, my cup of coffee, and my claret; I am content. I don't want them for themselves, but they remind me of the sun. There's nothing solar about legs of beef and mutton. Mere animal satisfaction!'

" 'This is our friend's consulting room (or would be, if he ever prescribed), his sanctum, his studio,' said my guardian to us. [*The prescribing is a parody of the doctor theme in Dr. Woodcourt.*]

" 'Yes,' said Mr. Skimpole, turning his bright face about, 'this is the bird's cage. This is where the bird lives and sings. They pluck his feathers now and then, and clip his wings; but he sings, he sings.'

"He handed us the grapes, repeating in his radiant way, 'He sings! Not an ambitious note, but still he sings.' . . .

" 'This is a day,' said Mr. Skimpole, gaily taking a little claret in a tumbler, 'that will ever be remembered here. We shall call it Saint Clare and Saint Summerson day. You must see my daughters. I have a blue-eyed daughter who is my Beauty daughter [Arethusa], I have a Sentiment daughter [Laura], and I have a Comedy daughter [Kitty]. You must see them all. They'll be enchanted.' "

Something rather significant is happening here from the thematic point of view. Just as in a musical fugue one theme can be imitated in parody of another, we have here a parody of the caged-bird theme in connection with Miss Flite, the crazy little woman. Skimpole is not really caged. He is a painted bird with a clockwork arrangement for mechanical song. His cage is an imitation, just as his childishness is an imitation. There is also a thematic parody in the names he gives to his daughters, compared to the names of the birds in Miss Flite's theme. Skimpole the child is really Skimpole the fraud, and in this extremely artistic way Dickens reveals Skimpole's real nature. If you have completely understood what I have been driving at, then we have made a very definite step towards understanding the mystery of literary art, for it should be clear that my course, among other things, is a kind of detective investigation of the mystery of literary structures. But remember that what I can manage to discuss is by no means exhaustive. There are many things—themes and facets of themes—that you should find by yourselves. A book is like a trunk tightly packed with things. At the customs an official's hand plunges perfunctorily into it, but he who seeks treasures examines every thread.

Towards the end of the book Esther is concerned that Skimpole is draining Richard dry and calls on him to ask him to break off his connection, which he blithely agrees to do when he learns that Richard has no money left. In the course of the conversation it is disclosed that it was he who had assisted in removing Jo after he had been put to bed at Jarndyce's orders, a disappearance that had remained a complete mystery. He defends himself in characteristic fashion: "Observe the case, my dear Miss Summerson. Here is a boy received into the house and put to bed, in a state that I strongly object to. The boy being in bed, a man arrives—like the house that Jack built. Here is the man who demands the boy who is received into the house and put to bed in a state that I strongly object to. Here is a bank-note produced by the man who demands the boy who is received into the house and put to bed in a state that I strongly object to. Here is the Skimpole who accepts the bank-note produced by the man who demands the boy who is received into the house and put to bed in a state that I strongly object to. Those are the facts. Very well. Should the Skimpole have refused the note? *Why* should the Skimpole have refused the note? Skimpole protests to Bucket; 'what's this for? I don't understand it, it is of no use to me, take it away.' Bucket still entreats Skimpole to accept it. Are there reasons why Skimpole, not being warped by prejudices, should accept it? Yes. Skimpole perceives them. What are they?"

The reasons boil down to the fact that as a police officer, charged with the execution of justice, Bucket has a strong faith in money which Skimpole would shake by rejecting the offered bank note with the result that Bucket would be of no further use as a detective. Moreover, if it is blameable in Skimpole to accept, it was more blameable in Bucket to offer the money: "Now, Skimpole wishes to think well of Bucket; Skimpole deems it essential, in its little place, to the general cohesion of things, that he *should* think well of Bucket. The State expressly asks him to trust to Bucket. And he does. And that's all he does!"

Skimpole, at the last, is neatly summed up by Esther: "A coolness arose between him and my guardian, based principally on the foregoing grounds, and on his having heartlessly disregarded my guardian's entreaties (as we afterwards learned from Ada) in reference to Richard. His being heavily in my guardian's debt, had nothing to do with their separation. He died some five years afterwards, and left a diary behind him, with letters and other materials towards his Life; which was published, and which showed him to have been the victim of a combination on the part of mankind against an amiable child. It was considered very pleasant reading, but I never read more of it myself than the sentence on which I chanced to light on opening the book. It was this. 'Jarndyce, in common with most other men I have known, is the Incarnation of Selfishness.'" Actually Jarndyce is one of the best and kindest human beings ever described in a novel.

So to sum up. In the counterpoint arrangement of our book, Mr. Skimpole is shown first as a gay, lighthearted, childish person, a delightful infant, a candid and innocent child. Good John Jarndyce, being in some ways the real child of the book, is completely taken in and taken up with the pseudochild Skimpole. Dickens has Esther describe Skimpole so as to bring out his shallow but pleasing wit and his cheap but amusing charm; and soon, through this charm, we begin to perceive the essential cruelty and coarseness and utter dishonesty of the man. As a parody of a child, he serves, moreover, the purpose of bringing out in beautiful relief the real children in the book who are little helpers, who assume the responsibilities of grown-up people, children who are pathetic imitations of guardians and providers. Of the utmost importance for the inner development of the story is the meeting between Skimpole and Jo; Skimpole betrays Jo, the false child betraying the real one. There is within the Skimpole theme a parody of the caged-bird theme. Richard, the unfortunate suitor, is really the caged bird. Skimpole who preys upon him is at best a painted fowl, at worst a vulture. Finally, though almost entirely undeveloped, there is the contrast between the real doctor, Woodcourt, who uses his knowledge to help mankind, and Skimpole, who refuses to practice medicine and, on the only occasion in which he is consulted, correctly diagnoses Jo's fever as dangerous but recommends that he be thrown out of the house, undoubtedly to die.

The most touching pages in the book are devoted to the child theme. You will note the stoic account of Esther's childhood, her godmother (actually aunt) Barbary continually impressing on her consciousness a sense of guilt. We have the neglected children of the philanthropist Mrs. Jellyby, the orphaned Neckett children as little helpers, the "dirty little limp girls in gauze dresses" (and the little boy who dances alone in the kitchen) who take dancing lessons at the Turveydrop school to learn the trade. With the coldly philanthropic Mrs. Pardiggle we visit the family of a brickmaker and look at a dead baby. But among all these poor children, dead or alive or half-alive, among these "poor dull children in pain" the most unfortunate little creature is the boy Jo, who is so closely and blindly mixed up with the mystery theme.

At the coroner's inquest on the dead lodger Nemo it is recalled that he had been seen talking with the boy who swept the crossing down the lane, and the boy is brought in. "O! Here's the boy, gentlemen!

"Here he is, very muddy, very hoarse, very ragged. Now, boy!—But stop a minute. Caution. This boy must be put through a few preliminary paces.

"Name, Jo. Nothing else that he knows on. Don't know that everybody has two names. Never heerd of sich a think. Don't know that Jo is short for a longer name. Thinks it long enough for *him*. *He* don't find no fault with it. Spell it? No. *He* can't spell it. No father, no mother, no friends. Never been to school. What's home? Knows a broom's a broom, and knows it's wicked to tell a lie. Don't recollect who told him about the broom, or about the lie, but knows both. Can't exactly say what'll be done to him arter he's dead if he tells a lie to the gentlemen here, but believes it'll be something wery bad to punish him, and serve him right—and so he'll tell the truth."

After the inquest, at which Jo is not allowed to testify, he is privately questioned by Mr. Tulkinghorn, the solicitor. Jo knows only: "That one cold winter night, when he, the boy, was shivering in a doorway near his crossing, the man turned to look at him, and came back, and, having questioned him and found that he had not a friend in the world, said, 'Neither have I. Not one!' and gave him the price of a supper and a night's lodging. That the man had often spoken to him since; and asked him whether he slept sound at night, and how he bore cold and hunger, and whether he ever wished to die; and similar strange questions. . . .

" 'He wos wery good to me,' says the boy, wiping his eyes with his wretched sleeve. 'Wen I see him a-layin' so stritched out just now, I wished he could have heerd me tell him so. He wos wery good to me, he wos!' "

Dickens then writes in his Carlylean mode, with tolling repetitions. The lodger's body, "the body of our dear brother here departed [is borne off] to a hemmed-in churchyard, pestiferous and obscene, whence malignant diseases are communicated to the bodies of our dear brothers and sisters who have not departed. . . . Into a beastly scrap of ground which a Turk would reject as a savage abomination, and a Caffre would shudder at, they bring our dear brother here departed, to receive Christian burial.

"With houses looking on, on every side, save where a reeking little tunnel of a court gives access to the iron gate—with every villainy of life in action close on death, and every poisonous element of death in action close on life—here, they lower our dear brother down a foot or two: here, sow him in corruption, to be raised in corruption: an avenging ghost at many a sick bedside: a shameful testimony to future ages, how civilisation and barbarism walked this boastful island together."

And here is the blurred silhouette of Jo in the fog and the night. "With the night comes a slouching figure through the tunnel-court, to the outside of the iron gate. It holds the gate with its hands, and looks in between the bars; stands looking in for a little while.

"It then, with an old broom it carries, softly sweeps the step, and makes the archway clean. It does so very busily and trimly; looks in again, a little while; and so departs.

VLADIMIR NABOKOV

"Jo, is it thou? [*Again the Carlylean eloquence*] Well, well! Though a rejected witness, who 'can't exactly say' what will be done to him in greater hands than men's, thou art not quite in outer darkness. There is something like a distant ray of light in thy muttered reason for this:

" 'He wos wery good to me, he wos!' "

Constantly "moved on" by the police, Jo sets out from London and, in the first stages of smallpox, is sheltered by Esther and Charley, to whom he transmits the disease, and then, mysteriously disappearing, is not heard from until he reappears in London, worn down by his illness and privations, and lies dying in the shooting gallery that belongs to Mr. George. His heart is compared to a heavy cart. "For the cart so hard to draw, is near its journey's end, and drags over stony ground. All round the clock it labours up the broken steps, shattered and worn. Not many times can the sun rise, and behold it still upon its weary road. . . . There, too, is Mr. Jarndyce many a time, and Allan Woodcourt almost always; both thinking much, how strangely Fate [*with the genial help of Charles Dickens*] has entangled this rough outcast in the web of very different lives. . . . Jo is in a sleep or in a stupor to-day, and Allan Woodcourt, newly arrived, stands by him, looking down upon his wasted form. After a while, he softly seats himself upon the bedside with his face towards him . . . and touches his chest and heart. The cart had very nearly given up, but labours on a little more. . . .

" 'Well, Jo! What is the matter? Don't be frightened.'

" 'I thought,' says Jo, who has started, and is looking round, 'I thought I wos in Tom-all-Alone's [*the frightful slum where he lived*] agin. Ain't there nobody but you, Mr. Woodcot?' [*Mark the symbolism in the special twist Jo gives the doctor's name, turned into* Woodcot, *that is, a little cottage of wood, a coffin.*]

" 'Nobody.'

" 'And I ain't took back to Tom-all-Alone's. Am I, sir?'

" 'No.' Jo closes his eyes, muttering, 'I'm wery thankful.'

"After watching him closely a little while, Allan puts his mouth very near his ear, and says to him in a low, distinct voice:

" 'Jo! Did you ever know a prayer?'

" 'Never knowd nothink, sir.'

" 'Not so much as one short prayer?'

" 'No, sir. Nothink at all. . . . *I* never knowd what it wos all about.' . . . After a short relapse into sleep or stupor, he makes, of a sudden, a strong effort to get out of bed.

" 'Stay, Jo! What now?'

" 'It's time for me to go to that there berryin-ground, sir,' he returns, with a wild look.

" 'Lie down, and tell me. What burying-ground, Jo?'

" 'Where they laid him as wos wery good to me, wery good to me indeed, he wos. It's time fur me to go down to that there berryin-ground, sir, and ask to be put along with him. I wants to go there and be berried. . . .'

" 'Bye-and-bye, Jo. By-and-bye.' . . .

" 'Thank'ee, sir. Thank'ee, sir. They'll have to get the key of the gate afore they can take me in, for it's allus locked. And there's a step there, as I used fur to clean with my broom.—It's turned wery dark, sir. Is there any light a-comin?'

" 'It is coming fast, Jo.'

"Fast. The cart is shaken all to pieces, and the rugged road is very near its end.

" 'Jo, my poor fellow!'

" 'I hear you, sir, in the dark, but I'm a-gropin—a-gropin—let me catch hold of your hand.'

" 'Jo, can you say what I say?'

" 'I'll say anythink as you say, sir, fur I know it's good.'

" 'OUR FATHER.'

" 'Our Father!—yes, that's wery good, sir.' [Father, *a word he had never used*.]

" 'WHICH ART IN HEAVEN.'

" 'Art in Heaven—is the light a-comin, sir?'

" 'It is close at hand. HALLOWED BE THY NAME!'

" 'Hallowed be—thy——' "

And now listen to the booming bell of Carlyle's apostrophic style: "The light is come upon the dark benighted way. Dead!

"Dead, your Majesty. Dead, my lords and gentlemen. Dead, Right Reverends and Wrong Reverends of every order. Dead, men and women, born with Heavenly compassion in your hearts. And dying thus around us every day."

This is a lesson in style, not in participative emotion.

———

The crime-mystery theme provides the main action of the novel and is its backbone, its binding force. Structurally, it is the most important of the novel's themes of mystery and misery, Chancery and chance.

One of the branches of the Jarndyce family consisted of two sisters. One of these sisters, the elder, had been engaged to Boythorn, John Jarndyce's eccentric friend. The other sister had an affair with a Captain Hawdon and bore an illegitimate daughter. The elder sister deceived the young mother into believing that her child had died at birth. Then, breaking all connection with her fiance, Boythorn, her family and her friends, this elder sister retired with the little girl to a small town and reared the child in austerity and harshness that were deserved, in her opinion, by the sinful way it had taken to arrive into this world. The young mother, later, married Sir Leicester Dedlock. After many years of comfortable though deadish wedlock, she, now Lady Dedlock, is being shown some new insignificant affidavits connected with the Jarndyce case by the family lawyer Tulkinghorn and is singularly affected by the handwriting in which one of the documents has been copied. She tries to ascribe her own questions about it to mere curiosity, but almost the next moment she faints. This is enough for Mr. Tulkinghorn to start an investigation of his own. He tracks down the scribe, a man going by the name of Nemo (Latin for "no one"), only to find him dead in a squalid room at Krook's of an overdose of opium, which was much easier to get then than it is now. Not a scrap of paper is found in the room, but a package of most important letters has already been whisked away by Krook even before he brought Tulkinghorn into the lodger's room. At the inquest held over the body of the dead Nemo it is found that no one knows anything about him. The only witness with whom Nemo used to exchange some personal, friendly words, the little streetsweeper Jo, is rejected by the authorities. But Mr. Tulkinghorn questions him in private.

From newspaper reports Lady Dedlock learns about Jo and comes to see him in disguise, dressed in her French maid's clothes. She gives him money when he shows her localities, etc., associated with Nemo, for she knows from his handwriting that he was Captain Hawdon, and, especially, Jo takes her to see the pestilent graveyard with the iron gate where Nemo has been buried. Jo's story spreads and reaches Tulkinghorn, who confronts Jo with Hortense, the French maid, who wears the clothes that Lady Dedlock had borrowed on her secret visit to Jo. Jo recognizes the clothes but is emphatically certain that the voice, the hand, and the rings on the hand of the woman now before him are not those belonging to the other. Thus Tulkinghorn's idea that Jo's mysterious visitor was Lady Dedlock is confirmed. Tulkinghorn then continues his investigation, but he also sees to it that Jo is made "to move on" by the police, since he does not want others to learn too much from him. (This is why Jo happens to be in Hertfordshire when he is taken ill and why Bucket, with Skimpole's help, removes him from Jarndyce's house.) Tulkinghorn gradually discovers the identity of Nemo, Captain Hawdon. Getting the trooper George to deliver to him a letter in the Captain's hand is part of this process. When Tulkinghorn is ready with his story, he tells it in front of Lady Dedlock as if referring to other persons. Seeing herself discovered and at Tulkinghorn's mercy, Lady Dedlock comes to his room in her country mansion, Chesney Wold, to discuss his intentions. She is ready to leave her house, her husband, and to disappear. Tulkinghorn decides that she is to stay and continue in her role as a fashionable woman in society and Sir Leicester's wife until he makes his decision and chooses his time. When at a later date he tells her that he is about to disclose her past to her husband, she goes out at night for a long walk, and that very night Tulkinghorn is murdered in his rooms. Did she murder him?

The detective Bucket is hired by Sir Leicester to track down his solicitor's unknown murderer. Bucket first suspects George, the trooper, who has been heard threatening Tulkinghorn, and has George arrested. Later many things seem to point to Lady Dedlock, but all these are false clues. The real murderer is Hortense, the French maid, who has willingly helped Mr. Tulkinghorn to ferret out the secret of her former mistress, Lady Dedlock, but who turns against Tulkinghorn when the latter fails to recompense her sufficiently for her services and, moreover, offends her when he threatens her with jail and practically throws her out of his rooms.

But a Mr. Guppy, a law clerk, had also followed his own line of investigation. For personal reasons (he was in love with Esther), he tried to get from Krook some letters he suspected had fallen into the old man's hands after Captain Hawdon's death. He nearly succeeded, when Krook unexpectedly and weirdly dies. Thus, the letters, and with them the secret of the Captain's love affair with Lady Dedlock and of Esther's birth, fell in the hands of a pack of blackmailers headed by old Smallweed. Though Tulkinghorn had then bought the letters from them, the Smallweeds after his death try to extort money from Sir Leicester. Detective Bucket, our third pursuer, an experienced man, seeks to settle the matter to the Dedlocks' advantage but in doing so has to tell Sir Leicester his wife's secret. Sir Leicester loves his wife too much not to forgive her. But Lady Dedlock, warned by Guppy of the fate of her letters, sees in it the hand of vengeful Fate and leaves her home forever, ignorant of her husband's reaction to the "secret."

Sir Leicester sends Bucket in hot pursuit. Bucket takes along Esther, whom he knows to be her daughter. In the midst of a freezing ice storm, together they trace Lady Dedlock to the brickmaker's cottage in

Hertfordshire, not far from Bleak House, to which Lady Dedlock had gone to seek Esther, who unknown to her had been all the time in London. Bucket finds out that two women had left the cottage shortly before his arrival, one bound for the north but the other southward for London. Bucket and Esther follow the northbound one for a long while until the astute Mr. Bucket suddenly decides to go back through the storm and to pick up the other woman's trail. The northbound woman had worn Lady Dedlock's clothes, the London-bound one was dressed as the poor brickmaker's wife, but it suddenly dawns on Bucket that the two had exchanged their clothes. He is right, but he and Esther come too late. Lady Dedlock, dressed as a poor woman, has reached London and has gone to Captain Hawdon's grave. She dies of exhaustion and exposure, clutching the bars of the iron gate, after walking a hundred miles through a dreadful storm, practically without rest.

As one can see from this bare resumé, the plot of the mystery theme does not quite live up to the poetry of the book.

———

Gustave Flaubert's ideal of a writer of fiction was vividly expressed when he remarked that, like God in His world, so the author in his book should be nowhere and everywhere, invisible and omnipresent. There do exist several major works of fiction where the presence of the author is as unobtrusive as Flaubert wished it to be, although he himself did not attain that ideal in *Madame Bovary*. But even in such works where the author is ideally unobtrusive, he remains diffused through the book so that his very absence becomes a kind of radiant presence. As the French say, *il brille par son absence*—"he shines by his absence." In connection with *Bleak House* we are concerned with one of those authors who are so to speak not supreme deities, diffuse and aloof, but puttering, amiable, sympathetic demigods, who descend into their books under various disguises or send therein various middlemen, representatives, agents, minions, spies, and stooges.

Roughly speaking, there are three types of such representatives. Let us inspect them.

First, the narrator insofar as he speaks in the first person, the capital *I* of the story, its moving pillar. The narrator can appear in various forms: he may be the author himself or a first-person protagonist; or the writer may invent an author whom he quotes, as Cervantes does with his Arabic historian; or one of the third-person characters in the book may be a part-time narrator, after which the master's voice takes over again. The main point is that, whatever the method, there is a certain capital *I* who tells a certain story.

Second, a type of author's representative, what I call the *sifting agent*. This sifting agent may or may not be coincident with the narrator. In fact, the most typical sifting agents I know, such as Fanny Price in *Mansfield Park* or Emma Bovary in the scene of the ball, are not first-person narrators but third-person characters. Again, they may or may not be representative of the author's own ideas; but their main feature is that whatever happens in the book, every event and every image and every landscape and every character is seen through the eyes, is perceived through the senses, of a main character, a he or she who is the sifting agent, who sifts the story through his-her own emotions and notions.

The third type is the so-called *perry*, possibly derived from *periscope*, despite the double *r*, or perhaps from *parry* in vague connection with foil as in fencing. But this does not matter much since anyway I invented the term myself many years ago. It denotes the lowest kind of author's minion: the character or characters who, throughout the book, or at least in certain parts of the book, are so to speak on duty; whose only purpose, whose only reason for being, is that they visit the places which the author wishes the reader to visit and meet the characters whom the author wishes the reader to meet. In such chapters the perry has hardly an identity of his own. He has no will, no soul, no heart, nothing—he is a mere peregrinating perry although of course he can regain his identity in some other part of the book. The perry visits some household only because the author wants to describe the characters in that household. He is very helpful, the perry. Without the perry a story is sometimes difficult to direct and propel; but better kill the story than have a perry drag its thread about like a lame insect dragging a dusty bit of cobweb.

Now in *Bleak House* Esther is all things: she is a part-time narrator, a kind of baby-sitter replacing the author, as I shall presently explain. She is also, in some chapters at least, a sifting agent, seeing things for herself, in her own way, although the master's voice is prone to drown hers even when she speaks in the first person; and, thirdly, the author often uses her,

---

Nabokov's outline of the main structural features of *Bleak House*

Bleak House   *Structure*

Main Structural Features of the Book

Nr. 1   Esther's Book.

Nr. 2   Esther's Looks.

~~Nr. 3   John Jarndyce's Curious Courtship.~~

Nr. **3**   The Coincidental Allan Woodcourt.
N₂ 4   *John Jarndyce's Curious Courtship*

Nr. 5   Impersonations and Disguises [Lady Dedlock,--
                    Hortense, Jenny -- Bucket as a doctor,
                                    as a "tradesman"]

Nr. 6   False Clues and True [("Bleak" House, the three
                                    possible Murderers))]

Nr. **7**   Sudden Relationships *Secret* and *sudden* *reunions*

Nr. 8   The Improvement of the Bad, or Not So Good,
                    Characters [Sir Leicester, Guppy,
                        Mrs. Woodcourt, Bucket]

Nr. 9   The Mark of a Great Writer.

alas, as a perry to move to this or that place while this or that character or event has to be described.

Eight particular structural features are to be noticed in *Bleak House.*

1. ESTHER'S BOOK

In chapter 3 Esther, brought up by a godmother (Lady Dedlock's sister), for the first time appears as the narrator, and here Dickens commits a little mistake for which he will have to pay dearly. He begins Esther's story in a kind of would-be girlish style, in bubbling baby talk (the "my dear old doll" is an easy trick), but he will see very soon that it is an impossible medium for telling a robust story and *we* shall see very soon his own vigorous and colorful style breaking through artificial baby talk, as is represented by: "My dear old doll! I was such a shy little thing that I seldom dared to open my lips, and never dared to open my heart, to anybody else. It almost makes me cry to think what a relief it used to be to me, when I came home from school of a day, to run upstairs to my room, and say, 'O you dear faithful Dolly, I knew you would be expecting me!' and then to sit down on the floor, leaning on the elbow of her great chair, and tell her all I had noticed since we parted. I had always rather a noticing way—not a quick way, O no!—a silent way of noticing what passed before me, and thinking I should like to understand it better. I have not by any means a quick understanding. When I love a person very tenderly indeed, it seems to brighten. But even that may be my vanity." Note that in these first pages of Esther's story there are practically no figures of speech, no vivid comparisons, etc. Yet certain features of the baby style begin to break down, as in the Dickensian alliteration "the clock ticked, the fire clicked," when Esther and her godmother are sitting before the fire, which is not in keeping with the schoolgirl style of Esther.

But when her godmother, Miss Barbary (really her aunt), dies and the lawyer Kenge takes matters into his hands, the style of Esther's narrative reverts to a general Dickensian style. For instance, Kenge petting his glasses: " 'Not of Jarndyce and Jarndyce?' said Mr. Kenge, looking over his glasses at me, and softly turning the case about and about, as if he were petting something." One can see what is happening. Dickens starts painting the delightful picture of Kenge, smooth round Kenge, Conversation Kenge (as he is nicknamed), and quite forgets it is a naive girl who is supposed to be writing all this. And within a few pages we already find samples of Dickensian imagery creeping into her narrative, rich comparisons and the like. "When [Mrs. Rachael] gave me one cold parting kiss upon my forehead, like a thaw-drop from the stone porch—it was a very frosty day—I felt so miserable" or "I sat . . . watching the frosty trees, that were like beautiful pieces of spar; and the fields all smooth and white with last night's snow; and the sun, so red but yielding so little heat; and the ice, dark like metal, where the skaters and sliders had brushed the snow away." Or Esther's description of Mrs. Jellyby's slovenly attire: "we could not help noticing that her dress didn't nearly meet up the back, and that the open space was railed across with a lattice-work of stay-lace—like a summer-house." The intonation and irony of her description of Peepy Jellyby's head caught between the bars is thoroughly Dickensian: "I made my way to the poor child, who was one of the dirtiest little unfortunates I ever saw, and found him very hot and frightened, and crying loudly, fixed by the neck between two iron railings, while a milkman and a beadle, with the kindest intentions possible, were endeavouring to drag him back by the legs, under a general impression that his skull was compressible by those means. As I found (after pacifying him), that he was a little boy, with a naturally large head, I thought that, perhaps, where his head could go, his body could follow, and mentioned that the best mode of extrication might be to push him forward. This was so favourably received by the milkman and beadle, that he would immediately have been pushed into the area, if I had not held his pinafore, while Richard and Mr. Guppy ran down through the kitchen, to catch him when he should be released."

Dickensian incantatory eloquence is prominent in such passages as Esther's description of her meeting with Lady Dedlock, her mother: "I explained, as nearly as I could then, or can recall now—for my agitation and distress throughout were so great that I scarcely understood myself, though every word that was uttered in the mother's voice, so unfamiliar and so melancholy to me; which in my childhood I had never learned to love and recognise, had never been sung to sleep with, had never heard a blessing from, had never had a hope inspired by; made an enduring impression on my memory—I say I explained, or tried to do it, how I had only hoped that Mr. Jarndyce, who had been the best of fathers to me, might be able to afford some counsel and support to her. But my mother answered no, it was impossible; no one could help her. Through the desert that lay before her, she must go alone."

By midstream, Dickens, writing through Esther, can take up the narration in a more fluent, supple, and conventional style than he did under his own name. This and the absence of vividly listed descriptive details in the beginnings of chapters are the only true points of difference between their respective styles. Esther and the author more or less grow accustomed to their different points of view as reflected in their styles: Dickens with all kinds of musical, humorous, metaphorical, oratorical, booming effects and breaks in style on the one hand; and Esther, on the other, starting chapters with flowing conservative phrases. But in the description at Westminster Hall of the close of the Jarndyce suit, already quoted, when the whole estate is found to have been absorbed by the costs, Dickens at last merges almost completely with Esther. Stylistically, the whole book is a gradual sliding into the matrimonial state between the two. And when they insert word pictures or render conversations, there is no difference between them.

Seven years after the event, as we learn in chapter 64, Esther writes her book, which amounts to thirty-three of the chapters, or a half of the whole novel, composed of sixty-seven chapters. A wonderful memory! I must say that despite the superb planning of the novel, the main mistake was to let Esther tell part of the story. I would not have let the girl near!

2. ESTHER'S LOOKS

Esther had so strong a resemblance to her mother that Mr. Guppy is much struck by a familiarity that he cannot at first place, when on a country jaunt he tours Chesney Wold, in Lincolnshire, and sees Lady Dedlock's portrait. Mr. George is also disturbed about her looks, without realizing that he sees a resemblance to his dead friend Captain Hawdon, who was Esther's father. And Jo, when he is "moved on" and trudges through the storm to be rescued at Bleak House, can scarcely be persuaded in his fear that Esther is not the unknown lady to whom he showed Nemo's house and the graveyard. But a tragedy strikes her. In retrospect, as she writes chapter 31, Esther mentions that she had a foreboding the day Jo fell sick, an omen that is all too well justified, for Charley catches smallpox from Jo and when Esther nurses her back to health (her looks spared), it is passed on to Esther, who is not so fortunate, for she at length recovers with her face disfigured by ugly scars that completely destroy her looks. As she recovers, she realizes that all mirrors have been removed from her room, and she knows the reason why. But when she goes to Mr. Boythorn's country place in Lincolnshire, next to Chesney Wold, she finally looks at herself. "For I had not yet looked in the glass, and had never asked to have my own restored to me. I knew this to be a weakness which must be overcome; but I had always said to myself that I would begin afresh, when I got to where I now was. Therefore I had wanted to be alone, and therefore I said, now alone, in my own room, 'Esther, if you are to be happy, if you are to have any right to pray to be true-hearted, you must keep your word, my dear.' I was quite resolved to keep it; but I sat down for a little while first, to reflect upon all my blessings. And then I said my prayers, and thought a little more.

"My hair had not been cut off, though it had been in danger more than once. It was long and thick: I let it down, and shook it out, and went up to the glass upon the dressing-table. There was a little muslin curtain drawn across it. I drew it back: and stood for a moment looking through such a veil of my own hair, that I could see nothing else. Then I put my hair aside, and looked at the reflection in the mirror; encouraged by seeing how placidly it looked at me. I was very much changed—O very, very much. At first, my face was so strange to me, that I think I should have put my hands before it and started back, but for the encouragement I have mentioned. Very soon it became more familiar, and then I knew the extent of the alteration in it better than I had done at first. It was not like what I had expected; but I had expected nothing definite, and I dare say anything definite would have surprised me.

"I had never been a beauty, and had never thought myself one; but I had been very different from this. It was all gone now. Heaven was so good to me, that I could let it go with a few not bitter tears, and could stand there arranging my hair for the night quite thankfully."

She confesses to herself that she could have loved Allan Woodcourt and been devoted to him, but that it must now be over. Worrying about some flowers he had given her and which she had dried, "At last I came to the conclusion that I might keep them; if I treasured them only as a remembrance of what was irrevocably past and gone, never to be looked back on any more, in any other light. I hope this may not seem trivial. I was very much in earnest." This prepares the reader for her accepting Jarndyce's proposal at a later time. She had firmly given up all dreams of Woodcourt.

Dickens has handled the problem shrewdly in this scene, for a certain vagueness must be left veiling her altered features so that the reader's imagination may not be embarrassed when at the end of the book she becomes Woodcourt's bride, and when in the very last pages a doubt, charmingly phrased, is cast on the question whether her good looks have gone after all. So it is that though Esther sees her face in the mirror, the reader does not, nor are details provided at any later time. When at the inevitable reunion of mother and daughter Lady Dedlock catches her to her breast, kisses her, weeps, etc., the resemblance theme culminates in the curious reflection Esther makes, "I felt . . . a burst of gratitude to the providence of God that I was so changed as that I never could disgrace her by any trace of likeness; so that nobody could ever now look at me, and look at her, and remotely think of any near tie between us." All this is very unreal (within the limits of the novel), and one wonders was it really necessary to disfigure the poor girl for this rather abstract purpose; indeed, *can* smallpox kill a family resemblance? But the closest a reader can come to any view of the changed Esther is when Ada holds to her lovely cheek Esther's "scarred [pockmarked] face."

It may seem that the author becomes a little fed up with his invention of her changed looks, since Esther soon says, for him, that she will not mention them anymore. Thus when she meets her friends again her appearance is not mentioned except for a few references to its effect on other people, ranging from the astonishment of a village child at the change to Richard's thoughtful, "Always the same dear girl!" when she raises her veil, which at first she wears in public. Later on the theme plays a structural part in connection with Mr. Guppy's renouncing his love after seeing her, so she may seem after all to be strikingly ugly. But perhaps her looks will improve? Perhaps the scars will vanish? We wonder and wonder. Still later when she and Ada visit Richard in the scene that leads to Ada's revelation of her secret marriage, Richard says of Esther that her compassionate face is so like the face of old days, and when she smiles and shakes her head, and he repeats, "——So exactly like the face of old days," we wonder whether the beauty of her soul is not concealing her scars. It is here, I think, that her looks in one way or another, begin to improve—at least in the reader's mind. Towards the end of this scene she remarks on her "plain old face"; plain, after all, is not disfigured. Moreover, I still think that at the very end of the novel, after seven years have elapsed and she is twenty-eight, the scars have quietly vanished. Esther is bustling about preparing for a visit from Ada, her little son Richard, and Mr. Jarndyce, and then she sits quietly on the porch. When Allan returns and asks what she is doing there, she replies that she has been thinking: " 'I am almost ashamed to tell you, but I will. I have been thinking about my old looks—such as they were.'

" 'And what have you been thinking about *them*, my busy bee?' said Allan.

" 'I have been thinking, that I thought it was impossible that you *could* have loved me any better, even if I had retained them.'

" '——Such as they were?' said Allan, laughing.

" 'Such as they were, of course.'

" 'My dear Dame Durden,' said Allan, drawing my arm through his, 'do you ever look in the glass?'

" 'You know I do; you see me do it.'

" 'And don't you know that you are prettier than you ever were?'

"I did not know that; I am not certain that I know it now. But I know that my dearest little pets are very pretty, and that my darling [Ada] is very beautiful, and that my husband is very handsome, and that my guardian has the brightest and most benevolent face that ever was seen; and that they can very well do without much beauty in me—even supposing——"

3. THE COINCIDENTAL ALLAN WOODCOURT

In chapter 11 "a dark young man," the surgeon, appears, for the first time, at the deathbed of Nemo (Captain Hawdon, Esther's father). Two chapters later there is a very tender and serious scene in which Richard and Ada have fallen in love with each other. And at the same point—so to link things up nicely—the dark young surgeon Woodcourt appears at the chapter's end as a guest at a dinner party, and Esther, when asked if she had not thought him "sensible and agreeable," answers yes, rather wistfully perhaps. Later, just when a hint is given that Jarndyce, gray-haired Jarndyce, is in love with Esther but is silent about it, at this point Woodcourt reappears before going to China. He will be away a long, long time. He leaves some flowers for Esther. Later, Miss Flite shows Esther a newspaper cutting of Woodcourt's heroism during a shipwreck. After Esther's face has been disfigured by smallpox, she renounces her love for Woodcourt. When Esther and Charley travel to the seaport Deal to convey Ada's offer to Richard of her little inheritance, Esther runs into Woodcourt, who has come back from India. The meeting is preceded by a delightful description of the sea, a piece of artistic imagery which, I think, makes one condone the terrific coincidence. Says Esther of the nondescript face: "He was so very sorry for me that he could scarcely speak," and, at the end of the chapter, "in his last look as we drove away, I saw that he was very sorry for me. I was glad to see it. I felt for my old self as the dead may feel if they ever revisit these scenes. I was glad to be tenderly remembered, to be gently pitied, not to be quite forgotten."—A nice lyrical strain here, a little remindful of Fanny Price.

By a second remarkable coincidence, Woodcourt comes upon the brickmaker's wife sleeping in Tom-all-Alone's, and by yet another coincidence he meets Jo there, in the presence of this woman who has also been wondering about Jo's whereabouts. Woodcourt takes the sick Jo to George's shooting gallery. There the wonderful scene of Jo's death again makes the reader condone the rather artificial means of bringing us to Jo's bedside through Woodcourt, the perry. In chapter 51 Woodcourt visits the lawyer Vholes, and then Richard. There is a curious trick here: it is Esther who is writing the chapter but she is not present at the interview between Woodcourt and Vholes or Woodcourt and Richard, both of which are reported in detail. The question is, how does she know what happened in both places? The bright reader must inevitably conclude that she got all these details from Woodcourt after she became his wife: she could not have known all these past events so circumstantially if Woodcourt had not been on terms of sufficient intimacy to tell her about them. In other words, the good reader should suspect that she will marry Woodcourt after all and hear these details from him.

4. JOHN JARNDYCE'S CURIOUS COURTSHIP

When Esther is in the coach being taken to London after Miss Barbary's death, an anonymous gentleman tries to cheer her up. He seems to know about Mrs. Rachael, the nurse hired by Miss Barbary, who had seen Esther off with so little affection, and to disapprove of her. When he offers Esther a piece of thickly sugared plum cake and a pie made out of the livers of fat geese, and she declines, saying they are too rich for her, he mutters, "Floored again!" and throws them out the window as lightly as he will later cast away his own happiness. Afterwards we learn this has been the good, kindhearted, and fairly wealthy John Jarndyce, who serves as a magnet for all kinds of people—miserable children and rogues, and shams, and fools, falsely philanthropic women, and crazy people. If Don Quixote had come to Dickensian London, I suggest that his kind and noble heart might have attracted people in the same way.

As early as chapter 17 we get the first hint that Jarndyce, gray-haired Jarndyce, is in love with twenty-one-year-old Esther but is silent about it. The Don Quixote theme is mentioned by name when Lady Dedlock meets the party, who are visiting nearby Mr. Boythorn, and the young people are presented to her. Gracefully, when the lovely Ada is introduced, " 'You will lose the disinterested part of your Don Quixote character,' said Lady Dedlock to Mr. Jarndyce over her shoulder again, 'if you only redress the wrongs of beauty like this.' " She is referring to the fact that at Jarndyce's request the Lord Chancellor has appointed him to be the guardian of Richard and Ada even though the main contention of the suit was over the respective shares of the estate between them. Thus he was being quixotic, Lady Dedlock implies in a compliment, to harbor and to support two young people who were legally his antagonists. His guardianship of Esther was a personal decision he made after a letter from Miss Barbary, Lady Dedlock's sister and Esther's real aunt.

John Jarndyce, some time after Esther's illness, comes to the decision of writing her a letter of proposal. But, and here comes the point, it seems to be suggested that he, a man at least thirty years Esther's senior, suggests marriage to protect her from the cruel world and is not going to change towards her, will remain her friend and will not become her lover. Not only is this attitude quixotic if what I suspect is true, but also the whole plan of preparing her to receive a letter, the contents of which she is able to guess, only upon her sending Charley for it after a week's pondering: " 'You have wrought changes in me, little woman, since the winter day in the stage-coach. First and last you have done me a world of good, since that time.'

" 'Ah, Guardian, what have you done for me since that time!'

" 'But,' said he, 'that is not to be remembered now.'

" 'It can never be forgotten.'

" 'Yes, Esther,' said he, with a gentle seriousness, 'it is to be forgotten now; to be forgotten for a while. You are only to remember now, that nothing can change me as you know me. Can you feel assured of that, my dear?'

" 'I can, and I do,' I said.

" 'That's much,' he answered. 'That's everything. But I must not take that, at a word. I will not write this something in my thoughts, until you have quite resolved within yourself that nothing can change me as you know me. If you doubt that in the least degree, I will never write it. If you are sure of that, on good consideration, send Charley to me this night week—"for the letter." But if you are not quite certain, never send. Mind, I trust to your truth, in this thing as in everything. If you are not quite certain on that one point, never send.'

" 'Guardian,' said I, 'I am already certain. I can no more be changed in that conviction, than you can be changed towards me. I shall send Charley for the letter.'

"He shook my hand and said no more."

For an elderly man, deeply in love with a young woman, a proposal on such terms is of course a great act of renunciation, self-control, and tragic temptation. Esther, on the other hand, accepts it under the innocent impression, "That his generosity rose above my disfigurement, and my inheritance of shame," a disfigurement that Dickens is going to play down thoroughly in the last chapters. Actually, of course, and this does not seem to have entered the mind of any of the three parties concerned—Esther Summerson, John Jarndyce, and Charles Dickens—the marriage would not be quite as fair towards Esther as it seems, since owing to its white-marriage implications it would deprive Esther of her normal motherhood while, on the other hand, making it unlawful and immoral for her to love any other man. Just possibly there is an echo of the caged-bird theme when Esther, weeping although happy and thankful, addresses herself in the glass, "When you are mistress of Bleak House, you are to be as cheerful as a bird. In fact, you are always to be cheerful; so let us begin for once and for all."

The interplay between Jarndyce and Woodcourt starts when Caddy Turveydrop is sick: " 'Well, you know,' returned my guardian quickly, 'there's Woodcourt.' " I like the skimming way he does it: some kind of vague intuition on his part? At this point Woodcourt is planning to go to America, where in French and British books rejected lovers so often go. Some ten chapters later we learn that Mrs. Woodcourt, our young doctor's mother who early on had suspected her son's attachment to Esther and had tried to break it up, has changed for the better, is less grotesque, and talks less about her pedigree. Dickens is preparing an acceptable mother-in-law for his feminine readers. Mark the nobility of Jarndyce, who suggests that if Mrs. Woodcourt comes to stay with Esther, Woodcourt can visit them both. We also hear that Woodcourt is not going to America, after all, but will be a country doctor in England working among the poor.

Esther then learns from Woodcourt that he loves her, that her "scarred face" is all unchanged to him. Too late! She is engaged to Jarndyce and supposes that the marriage has not yet taken place only because she is in mourning for her mother. But Dickens and Jarndyce have a delightful trick up their Siamese sleeve. The whole scene is rather poor but may please sentimental readers. It is not quite clear to the reader whether Woodcourt at this point knows of Esther's engagement, for if he does he hardly ought to have cut in, no matter how elegantly he does it. However, Dickens and Esther (as an after-the-event narrator) are cheating—they know all along that Jarndyce will stage a noble fade out. So Esther and Dickens are now going to have a little mild fun at the expense of the reader. She tells Jarndyce that she is ready to become the "mistress of Bleak House." "Next month," says Jarndyce. Now Esther and Dickens are ready to spring their little surprise on the little reader. Jarndyce goes to Yorkshire to assist Woodcourt in finding a house there for himself. Then he has Esther come to inspect his find. The bomb explodes. The name of the house is again

Bleak House, and she will be its mistress since noble Jarndyce is abandoning Esther to Woodcourt. This has been efficiently prepared for, and there is even a belated tribute to Mrs. Woodcourt who knew everything and now approves the match. Finally, we learn that when Woodcourt was opening his heart to Esther he was doing so with Jarndyce's consent. After Richard's death there is just perhaps the slightest hint that possibly John Jarndyce may still find a young wife in Ada, Richard's widow. But at the least, he is the symbolic guardian of all the unfortunate people in the novel.

5. IMPERSONATIONS AND DISGUISES

In order to discover whether it was Lady Dedlock who asked Jo about Nemo, Tulkinghorn arranges it so that Jo is shown Hortense, her discharged French maid, veiled, and he recognizes the clothes. But it is not same jewelled hand nor is it the same voice. Later, Dickens will have some trouble in plausibly arranging Tulkinghorn's murder by Hortense, but the connection, anyway, is established at this point. Now the sleuths know it was Lady Dedlock who tried to find out things about Nemo from Jo. Another masquerade occurs when Miss Flite, visiting Esther at Bleak House when she is recovering from smallpox, informs her that a veiled lady (Lady Dedlock) has inquired about Esther's health at the brickmaker's cottage. (We know that Lady Dedlock now knows that Esther is her daughter—knowledge breeds tenderness.) The veiled lady has taken, as a little keepsake, the handkerchief that Esther had left there when she had covered the dead baby with it, a symbolic action. This is not the first time that Dickens uses Miss Flite in order to kill two birds with one rock: first, to amuse the reader, and second, as a source of information, a lucidity which is not in keeping with her character.

Detective Bucket has several disguises, not least of which is his playing the fool at the Bagnets (his disguise being his extreme friendliness) while all the time keeping a wary eye on George and then taking him into custody after the two leave. Bucket, being an expert in disguise himself, is capable of penetrating the disguises of others. When Bucket and Esther reach the dead Lady Dedlock at the gate to the burying-ground, in his best Sherlock Holmes manner he describes how he came to suspect that Lady Dedlock had exchanged clothes with Jenny, the brickmaker's wife, and returned to London. Esther does not understand until she lifts "the heavy head": "And it was my mother, cold and dead." Melodramatic, but effectively staged.

It might seem, in view of the growing movement of the fog theme in the preceding chapters, that Bleak House, John Jarndyce's house, would be the height of dismal bleakness. But no—in a structural move which is extremely artistic, we swerve into the sunshine, and the fog is left behind for a while. Bleak House is a beautiful, sunny house. The good reader will recall a clue to this effect that had earlier been given at the Chancery: " 'The Jarndyce in question,' said the Lord Chancellor, still turning over leaves, 'is Jarndyce of Bleak House.'

" 'Jarndyce of Bleak House, my lord,' said Mr. Kenge.

" 'A dreary name,' said the Lord Chancellor.

" 'But not a dreary place at present, my lord,' said Mr. Kenge."

While the wards are waiting in London before being taken to Bleak House, Richard tells Ada that he vaguely recalls Jarndyce as "a bluff, rosy fellow." But still, the sunshine and the cheerfulness of the house come as a splendid surprise.

The clues to the person who killed Tulkinghorn are mixed in a masterly way. Very nicely, Dickens makes Mr. George casually remark that a Frenchwoman comes to his shooting gallery. (Hortense will need these shooting lessons, but most readers will overlook the connection.) And what about Lady Dedlock? "I would he were!" thinks Lady Dedlock after her cousin Volumnia has gushed that Tulkinghorn has neglected her so that "I had almost made up my mind that he was dead." This is what Lady Dedlock is made to say to herself to prepare suspense and suspicion when Tulkinghorn is murdered. It may deceive the reader into thinking that Lady Dedlock will kill him, but the reader of detective stories loves to be deceived. After Tulkinghorn's interview with Lady Dedlock, he goes to sleep while she paces her room, distraught, for hours. There is a hint that he may soon die ("And truly when the stars go out and the wan day peeps into the turret-chamber, finding him at his oldest, he looks as if the digger and the spade were both commissioned, and would soon be digging"), and his death should now be firmly linked up in the deceived reader's mind with Lady Dedlock; while Hortense, the real murderess, has not been heard of for some time.

Hortense now visits Tulkinghorn and airs her grievances. She has not been rewarded enough for her impersonation of Lady Dedlock in front of Jo; she hates Lady Dedlock; she wants employment in a similar position. This is a little weak, and Dickens's attempts to make her speak English like a Frenchwoman are ridiculous. She is a she-tiger, nevertheless, even though her reactions to Tulkinghorn's threats to have her locked up in jail if she continues to pester him are unknown at that time.

After warning Lady Dedlock that her release of the servant Rosa has violated their agreement to preserve the status quo and that he must now reveal her secret to Sir Leicester, Tulkinghorn goes home—to his death as Dickens hints. Lady Dedlock leaves her house for a stroll in the moonlight, as if following him. The reader may think: Aha! This is too pat. The author is deceiving me; the real murderer is someone else. Perhaps Mr. George? Although a good man he has a violent temper. Moreover, at a rather tedious Bagnet family birthday party, their friend Mr. George arrives very white in the face. (Aha, says the reader.) He explains his pallor by the fact that Jo has died, but the reader wonders. Then he is arrested, and Esther, Jarndyce, and the Bagnets visit him in jail. A nice twist occurs here: George describes the woman he met on Tulkinghorn's stairs about the time Tulkinghorn was murdered. She looked—in figure and in height—like . . . Esther. She wore a loose black mantle with a fringe. Now the dull reader will immediately think: George is too good to have done it. It was, of course, Lady Dedlock strikingly resembling her daughter. But the bright reader will retort: we have had already another woman impersonating Lady Dedlock rather efficiently.

One minor mystery is about to be solved. Mrs. Bagnet knows who George's mother is and sets out to fetch her, walking to Chesney Wold. (Two mothers are in the same place—a parallel between Esther's and George's situation.)

Tulkinghorn's funeral is a great chapter, a rising wave after some rather flat chapters that have preceded it. Bucket the detective is in a closed carriage, watching his wife and his lodger (who is his lodger? Hortense!) at Tulkinghorn's funeral. Bucket is growing in structural size. He is amusing to follow to the end of the mystery theme. Sir Leicester is still a pompous noodle, although a stroke will change him. There is an amusing Sherlock Holmesian talk Bucket has with a tall footman in which it transpires that Lady Dedlock, on the night of the crime, when she left the house for a couple of hours, wore the same cloak that Mr. George had described on the lady he met coming down Tulkinghorn's stairs just when the crime was committed. (Since Bucket knows that Hortense and not Lady Dedlock killed Tulkinghorn, this scene is a piece of deliberate cheating in relation to the reader.) Whether or not the reader believes at this point that Lady Dedlock is the murderess is another question—depending upon the reader. However, no mystery writer would have anybody point at the real murderer by means of the anonymous letters that are received (sent by

Hortense, as it turns out) accusing Lady Dedlock of the crime. Bucket's net finally ensnares Hortense. His wife, who at his orders has been spying on her, finds in her room a printed description of Chesney Wold with a piece missing that matches the paper wadding of the pistol, and the pistol itself is recovered by dragging a pond to which Hortense and Mrs. Bucket had gone on a holiday expedition. There is another piece of deliberate cheating when in the interview with Sir Leicester, after Bucket has got rid of the blackmailing Smallweeds, he declares dramatically, "The party to be apprehended is now in this house ... and I'm about to take her into custody in your presence." The only woman the reader thinks is in the house is Lady Dedlock; but Bucket means Hortense who, unknown to the reader, has come with him and who is awaiting his summons, thinking she is to receive some reward. Lady Dedlock remains unaware of the solution of the crime, and she flees on a route followed by Esther and Bucket until she is found dead back in London, clutching the bars of the gate behind which Captain Hawdon lies buried.

7. SUDDEN RELATIONSHIPS

A curious point that reoccurs throughout the novel—and is a feature of many mystery novels—is that of "sudden relationships." Thus:

a. Miss Barbary, who brought up Esther, turns out to be Lady Dedlock's sister, and, later on, the woman Boythorn had loved.

b. Esther turns out to be Lady Dedlock's daughter.

c. Nemo (Captain Hawdon) turns out to be her father.

d. Mr. George turns out to be the son of Mrs. Rouncewell, the Dedlock's housekeeper. George, also, it develops, was Hawdon's friend.

e. Mrs. Chadband turns out to be Mrs. Rachael, Esther's former nurse.

f. Hortense turns out to be Bucket's mysterious lodger.

g. Krook turns out to be Mrs. Smallweed's brother.

8. THE IMPROVEMENT OF THE BAD OR NOT SO GOOD CHARACTERS

It is a structural point when Esther asks Guppy to lay aside "advancing my interests, and promoting my fortunes, making discoveries of which I should be the subject. . . . I am acquainted with my personal history," she says. I think the author's intention is to eliminate the Guppy line (half-eliminated already by the loss of the letters) so as not to interfere with the Tulkinghorn theme. He "looked ashamed"—not in keeping with Guppy's character. Dickens at this point makes him a better man than the rascal he was. It is curious that although his shock and retreat at seeing Esther's disfigured face show he had no real love for her (loss of a point), his not wishing to marry an ugly girl even if she proved to be aristocratic and rich is a point in his favor. Nevertheless, it is a weak passage.

When he learns the awful truth from Bucket: "Sir Leicester, who has covered his face with his hands, uttering a single groan, requests him to pause for a moment. By-and-bye he takes his hands away; and so preserves his dignity and outward calmness, though there is no more colour in his face than in his white hair, that Mr. Bucket is a little awed by him." Here is a turning point for Sir Leicester, where for better or worse in the artistic sense he stops being a dummy and becomes a human being in distress. Actually, he has undergone a stroke in the process. After his shock, Sir Leicester's forgiveness of Lady Dedlock shows him to be a lovable human being who is holding up nobly, and his scene with George is very moving, as is his waiting for his wife's return. "His formal array of words" as he speaks of there being no change in his attitude toward her is now "serious and affecting." He is almost on the point of turning into another John Jarndyce. By now the nobleman is as good as a good commoner!

———

What do we mean when we speak of the form of a story? One thing is its structure, which means the development of a given story, why this or that line is followed; the choice of characters, the use that the author makes of his characters; their interplay, their various themes, the thematic lines and their intersection; the various moves of the story introduced by the author to produce this or that direct or indirect effect; the preparation of effects and impressions. In a word, we mean the planned pattern of a work of art. This is structure.

Another aspect of form is style, which means how does the structure work; it means the manner of the author, his mannerisms, various special tricks; and if his style is vivid what kind of imagery, of description, does he use, how does he proceed; and if he uses comparisons, how does he employ and vary the rhetorical devices of metaphor and simile and their combinations. The effect of style is the key to literature, a magic key to Dickens, Gogol, Flaubert, Tolstoy, to all great masters.

Form (structure and style) = Subject Matter: the why and the how = the what.

The first thing that we notice about the style of Dickens is his intensely sensuous imagery, his art of vivid sensuous evocation.

1. VIVID EVOCATION, WITH OR WITHOUT
THE USE OF FIGURES OF SPEECH

The bursts of vivid imagery are spaced—they do not occur for stretches—and then there is again an accumulation of fine descriptive details. When Dickens has some information to impart to his reader through conversation or meditation, the imagery is generally not conspicuous. But there are magnificent passages, as for example the apotheosis of the fog theme in the description of the High Court of Chancery: "On such an afternoon, if ever, the Lord High Chancellor ought to be sitting here—as here he is—with a foggy glory round his head, softly fenced in with crimson cloth and curtains, addressed by a large advocate with great whiskers, a little voice, and an interminable brief, and outwardly directing his contemplation to the lantern in the roof, where he can see nothing but fog."

"The little plaintiff, or defendant, who was promised a new rocking-horse when Jarndyce and Jarndyce should be settled, has grown up, possessed himself of a real horse, and trotted away into the other world." The two wards are ordered by the Court to reside with their uncle. This is the fully inflated summary or result of the marvelous agglomeration of natural and human fog in this first chapter. Thus the main characters (the two wards and Jarndyce) are introduced, still anonymous and abstract at this point. They seem to rise out of the fog, the author plucks them out before they are submerged again, and the chapter ends.

The first description of Chesney Wold and of its mistress, Lady Dedlock, is a passage of sheer genius: "The waters are out in Lincolnshire. An arch of the bridge in the park has been sapped and sopped away. The adjacent low-lying ground, for half a mile in breadth, is a stagnant river, with melancholy trees for islands in it, and a surface punctured all over, all day long, with falling rain. My Lady Dedlock's 'place' has been extremely dreary. The weather, for many a day and night, has been so wet that the trees seem wet through, and the soft loppings and prunings of the woodman's axe can make no crash or crackle as they fall. The deer, looking soaked, leave quagmires, where they pass. The shot of a rifle loses its sharpness in the moist air, and its smoke moves in a tardy little cloud towards the green rise, coppice-topped, that makes a background for the falling rain. The view from my Lady Dedlock's own windows is alternately a lead-coloured view, and a view in Indian ink. The vases on the stone terrace in the foreground catch the rain all day; and the heavy drops fall, drip, drip, drip, upon the broad flagged pavement, called, from old time, the Ghost's Walk, all night. On Sundays, the little church in the park is mouldy; the oaken pulpit breaks out into a cold sweat; and there is a general smell and taste as of the ancient Dedlocks in their graves. My Lady Dedlock (who is childless), looking out in the early twilight from her boudoir at a keeper's lodge, and seeing the light of a fire upon the latticed panes, and smoke rising from the chimney, and a child, chased by a woman, running out into the rain to meet the shining figure of a wrapped-up man coming through the gate, has been put quite out of temper. My Lady Dedlock says she has been 'bored to death.' " This rain at Chesney Wold is the countryside counterpart of the London fog; and the keeper's child is part of the children theme.

We have an admirable image of a sleepy, sunny little town where Mr. Boythorn meets Esther and her companions: "Late in the afternoon we came to the market-town where we were to alight from the coach—a dull little town, with a church-spire, and a market-place, and a market-cross, and one intensely sunny street, and a pond with an old horse cooling his legs in it, and a very few men sleepily lying and standing about in narrow little bits of shade. After the rustling of the leaves and the waving of the corn all along the road, it looked as still, as hot, as motionless a little town as England could produce."

Esther has a terrifying experience when she is sick with the smallpox: "Dare I hint at that worse time when, strung together somewhere in great black space, there was a flaming necklace, or ring, or starry circle of some kind, of which I was one of the beads! And when my only prayer was to be taken off from the rest, and when it was such inexplicable agony and misery to be a part of the dreadful thing?"

When Esther sends Charley for Mr. Jarndyce's letter, the description of the house has a functional result; the house *acts*, as it were: "When the appointed night came, I said to Charley as soon as I was alone, 'Go and knock at Mr. Jarndyce's door, Charley, and say you have come from me— "for the letter." ' Charley went up the stairs, and down the stairs, and along the passages—the zigzag way about the old-fashioned house seemed very long in my listening ears that night—and so came back, along the passages, and down the stairs, and up the stairs, and brought the letter. 'Lay it on the table, Charley,' said I. So Charley laid it on the table and went to bed, and I sat looking at it without taking it up, thinking of many things."

When Esther visits the seaport Deal to see Richard, we have a description of the harbor: "Then the fog began to rise like a curtain; and numbers of ships, that we had had no idea were near, appeared. I don't know how many sail the waiter told us were then lying in the Downs. Some of these vessels were of grand size: one was a large Indiaman just come home: and when the sun shone through the clouds, making silvery pools in the dark sea, the way in which these ships brightened, and shadowed, and changed, amid a bustle of boats pulling off from the shore to them and from them to the shore, and a general life and motion in themselves and everything around them, was most beautiful."*

Some readers may suppose that such things as these evocations are trifles not worth stopping at; but literature consists of such trifles. Literature consists, in fact, not of general ideas but of particular revelations, not of schools of thought but of individuals of genius. Literature is not about something: it is the thing itself, the quiddity. Without the masterpiece, literature does not exist. The passage describing the harbor at Deal occurs at a point when Esther travels to the town in order to see Richard, whose attitude towards life, the strain of freakishness in his otherwise noble nature, and the dark destiny that hangs over him, trouble her and make her want to help him. Over her shoulder Dickens shows us the harbor. There are many vessels there, a multitude of boats that appear with a kind of quiet magic as the fog begins to rise. Among them, as mentioned, there is a large Indiaman, that is, a merchant ship just home from India: "when the sun shone through the clouds, making silvery pools in the dark sea. . . ." Let us pause: can we visualize that? Of course we can, and we do so with a greater thrill of recognition because in comparison to the conventional blue sea of literary tradition these silvery pools in the dark sea offer something that Dickens noted for the very first time with the innocent and sensuous eye of the true artist, saw and immediately put into words. Or more exactly, without the words there would have been no vision; and if one follows the soft, swishing, slightly blurred sound of the sibilants in the description, one will find that the image had to have a voice too in order to live. And then Dickens goes on to indicate the way "these ships brightened, and shadowed, and changed"—and I think it is quite impossible to choose and combine any better words than he did here to render the delicate quality of shadow and silver sheen in that delightful sea view. And for those who would think that all magic is just play—pretty play—but something that can be deleted without impairing the story, let

*On an inserted leaf VN compares, unfavorably to her, Jane Austen's description of the sea at Portsmouth Harbor when Fanny Price is visiting her family: " 'The day was uncommonly lovely. It was really March; but it was April in its mild air, brisk soft wind, and bright sun, occasionally clouded for a minute; and every thing looked so beautiful [*and a little repetitious*] under the influence of such a sky, the effects of the shadows pursuing each other on the ships at Spithead and the island beyond, with the ever-varying hues of the sea now at high water, dancing in its glee and dashing against the ramparts,' etc. The hues are not rendered; *glee* is borrowed from minor poetry; the whole thing is conventional and limp." Ed.

me point out that this *is* the story: the ship from India there, in that unique setting, is bringing, has brought, young Dr. Woodcourt back to Esther, and in fact they will meet in a moment. So that the shadowy silver view, with those tremulous pools of light and that bustle of shimmering boats, acquires in retrospect a flutter of marvelous excitement, a glorious note of welcome, a kind of distant ovation. And this is how Dickens meant his book to be appreciated.

2. ABRUPT LISTING OF DESCRIPTIVE DETAILS

This listing has the intonation of an author's notebook, of notes jotted down but some of them later expanded. There is also a rudimentary touch of stream of consciousness here, which is the disconnected notation of passing thoughts.

The novel opens thus, in a passage already quoted: "London. Michaelmas Term lately over. . . . Implacable November weather. . . . Dogs, undistinguishable in mire. Horses scarcely better; splashed to their very blinkers. . . . Fog everywhere." When Nemo has been found dead: "Beadle goes into various shops and parlours, examining the inhabitants. . . . Policeman seen to smile to potboy. Public loses interest, and undergoes reaction. Taunts the beadle in shrill youthful voices. . . . Policeman at last finds it necessary to support the law." (Carlyle also used this kind of abrupt account.)

"Snagsby appears: greasy, warm, herbaceous, and chewing. Bolts a bit of bread and butter. Says, 'Bless my soul, sir! Mr. Tulkinghorn!' " (This combines an abrupt, efficient style with vivid epithets, again as Carlyle did.)

3. FIGURES OF SPEECH: SIMILES AND METAPHORS

Similes are direct comparisons, using the words *like* or *as*. "Eighteen of Mr. Tangle's [the lawyer's] learned friends, each armed with a little summary of eighteen hundred sheets, bob up like eighteen hammers in a pianoforte, make eighteen bows, and drop into their eighteen places of obscurity."

The carriage taking the young people to stay the night at Mrs. Jellyby's turns up "a narrow street of high houses, like an oblong cistern to hold the fog."

At Caddy's wedding, Mrs. Jellyby's untidy hair looks "like the mane of a dustman's horse."

At dawn, the lamplighter "going his rounds, like an executioner to a despotic king, strikes off the little heads of fire that have aspired to lessen the darkness."

"Mr. Vholes, quiet and unmoved, as a man of so much respectability ought to be, takes off his close black gloves as if he were skinning his hands, lifts off his tight hat as if he were scalping himself, and sits down at his desk."

A metaphor animates one thing to be described by evoking another without the link of a *like*; sometimes Dickens combines it with a simile.

The solicitor Tulkinghorn's dress is respectable and in a general way suitable for a retainer. "It expresses, as it were, the steward of the legal mysteries, the butler of the legal cellar, of the Dedlocks."

"The [Jellyby] children tumbled about, and notched memoranda of their accidents in their legs, which were perfect little calendars of distress."

"Solitude, with dusky wings, sits brooding upon Chesney Wold."

When Esther, with Mr. Jarndyce, visits the house where the suitor Tom Jarndyce had shot his brains out, she writes, "It is a street of perishing blind houses, with their eyes stoned out; without a pane of glass, without so much as a window-frame. . . ."

Snagsby, having taken over the business of Peffer, puts up a newly painted sign "displacing the time-honoured and not easily to be deciphered legend, PEFFER, only. For smoke, which is the London ivy, had so wreathed itself round Peffer's name, and clung to his dwelling-place, that the affectionate parasite quite overpowered the parent tree."

4. REPETITION

Dickens enjoys a kind of incantation, a verbal formula repetitively recited with growing emphasis; an oratorical, forensic device. "On such an afternoon, if ever, the Lord High Chancellor ought to be sitting here. . . . On such an afternoon, some score of members of the High Court of Chancery bar ought to be—as here they are—mistily engaged in one of the ten thousand stages of an endless cause, tripping one another up on slippery precedents, groping knee-deep in technicalities, running their goat-hair and horse-hair warded heads against walls of words, and making a pretence of equity with serious faces, as players might. On such an afternoon, the various solicitors in the cause . . . ought to be—as are they not?—ranged in a line, in a long matted well (but you might look in vain for Truth at the bottom of it), between the registrar's red table and the silk gowns . . .

mountains of costly nonsense, piled before them. Well may the court be dim, with wasting candles here and there; well may the fog hang heavy in it, as if it would never get out; well may the stained glass windows lose their colour, and admit no light of day into the place; well may the uninitiated from the streets, who peep in through the glass panes in the door, be deterred from entrance by its owlish aspect, and by the drawl languidly echoing to the roof from the padded dais where the Lord High Chancellor looks into the lantern that has no light in it, and where the attendant wigs are all stuck in a fog-bank!" One should notice here the effect of the three booming *on such an afternoon*'s, and the four wailing *well may*'s as well as the frequent concorded repetition of sound that constitutes assonance, "engaged . . . stages . . . tripping . . . slippery"; and the marked alliteration, "warded . . . walls of words . . . door . . . deterred . . . drawl . . . languidly . . . Lord . . . looks . . . lantern . . . light."

Just before Sir Leicester and his relatives gather at Chesney Wold at the election, the musical, sonorous *so*'s reverberate: "Dreary and solemn the old house looks, with so many appliances of habitation, and with no inhabitants except the pictured forms upon the walls. So did these come and go, a Dedlock in possession might have ruminated passing along; so did they see this gallery hushed and quiet, as I see it now; so think, as I think, of the gap that they would make in this domain when they were gone; so find it, as I find it, difficult to believe that it could be, without them; so pass from my world, as I pass from theirs, now closing the reverberating door; so leave no blank to miss them, and so die."

5. ORATORICAL QUESTION AND ANSWER

This device is often combined with repetition. "Who happen to be in the Lord Chancellor's court this murky afternoon besides the Lord Chancellor, the counsel in the cause, two or three counsel who are never in any cause, and the well of solicitors before mentioned? There is the registrar below the Judge, in wig and gown; and there are two or three maces, or petty-bags, or privy purses, or whatever they may be, in legal court suits."

As Bucket awaits Jarndyce to bring Esther to accompany him in search of the fleeing Lady Dedlock, Dickens imagines himself inside Bucket's mind: "Where is she? Living or dead, where is she? If, as he folds the handkerchief and carefully puts it up, it were able, with an enchanted power, to bring before him the place where she found it, and the night landscape near the cottage where it covered the little child, would he descry her there? On the waste, where the brick-kilns are burning . . . traversing this deserted blighted spot, there is a lonely figure with the sad world to itself, pelted by the snow and driven by the wind, and cast out, it would seem, from all companionship. It is the figure of a woman, too; but it is miserably dressed, and no such clothes ever came through the hall, and out at the great door, of the Dedlock mansion."

In the answer Dickens gives here to the questions, he provides the reader with a hint of the exchange of clothes between Lady Dedlock and Jenny that will for some time puzzle Bucket until he guesses the truth.

6. THE CARLYLEAN APOSTROPHIC MANNER

Apostrophes may be directed, as it were, at a stunned audience, or at a sculptural group of great sinners, or towards some force of elemental nature, or to the victim of injustice. As Jo slouches towards the burying ground to visit the grave of Nemo, Dickens apostrophizes: "Come night, come darkness, for you cannot come too soon, or stay too long, by such a place as this! Come, straggling lights into the windows of the ugly houses; and you who do iniquity therein, do it at least with this dread scene shut out! Come, flame of gas, burning so sullenly above the iron gate, on which the poisoned air deposits its witch-ointment slimy to the touch!" The apostrophe, already quoted, at Jo's death should also be noted, and before that, the apostrophe when Guppy and Weevle rush for help after discovering Krook's extraordinary end.

7. EPITHETS

Dickens nurtures the rich adjective, or verb, or noun, as an epithet, a basic prerequisite in the case of vivid imagery: the plump seed from which the blossoming and branching metaphor grows. In the opening we have people leaning over the parapet of the Thames, peeping down at the river "into a nether sky of fog." The clerks in Chancery "flesh their wit" on a ridiculous case. Ada describes Mrs. Pardiggle's prominent eyes as "choking eyes." As Guppy tries to persuade Weevle to remain in his lodgings in Krook's house, he is "biting his thumb with the appetite of vexation." As Sir Leicester waits for Lady Dedlock's return, in the midnight streets no late sounds are heard unless a man "so very nomadically drunk" as to stray there goes along bellowing.

As happens to all great writers who have a keen visual perception of things, a commonplace epithet can sometimes acquire unusual life and freshness because of the background against which it is set. "The welcome light soon shines upon the wall, as Krook [who had gone down for a lighted candle and now comes up again] comes slowly up, with his green-eyed cat following at his heels." All cats have green eyes—but notice how green these eyes are owing to the lighted candle slowly ascending the stairs. It is often the position of an epithet, and the reflection cast upon it by neighboring words, that give the epithet its vivid charm.

8. EVOCATIVE NAMES

We have Krook, of course, and then there are Blaze and Sparkle, Jewellers; Mr. Blower and Mr. Tangle are lawyers; Boodle and Coodle and Doodle, etc., are politicians. This is a device of old comedy.

9. ALLITERATION AND ASSONANCE

The device has already been remarked in connection with repetition. But we may enjoy Mr. Smallweed to his wife: "You dancing, prancing, shambling, scrambling, poll-parrott" as an example of assonance; or the alliteration of the arch of the bridge that has been "sapped and sopped away" in Lincolnshire, where Lady Dedlock lives in a "deadened" world. *Jarndyce and Jarndyce* is, in a way, an absolute alliteration reduced to the absurd.

10. THE *AND-AND-AND* DEVICE

This is made a characteristic of Esther's emotional manner, as when she describes her companionship at Bleak House with Ada and Richard: "I am sure that I, sitting with them, and walking with them, and talking with them, and noticing from day to day how they went on, falling deeper and deeper in love, and saying nothing about it, and each shyly thinking that this love was the greatest of secrets. . . ." And in another example, when Esther accepts Jarndyce: "I put my two arms round his neck and kissed him; and he said was this the mistress of Bleak House; and I said yes; and it made no difference presently, and we all went out together, and I said nothing to my precious pet [Ada] about it."

11. THE HUMOROUS, QUAINT, ALLUSIVE, WHIMSICAL NOTE

"His family is as old as the hills, and infinitely more respectable"; or, "The turkey in the poultry-yard, always troubled with a class-grievance (probably Christmas)"; or, "the crowing of the sanguine cock in the cellar at the little dairy in Cursitor Street, whose ideas of daylight it would be curious to ascertain, since he knows from his personal observation next to nothing about it"; or, "a short, shrewd niece, something too violently compressed about the waist, and with a sharp nose like a sharp autumn evening, inclining to be frosty towards the end."

12. PLAY ON WORDS

Some examples are "Inquest-Inkwhich" (tied up with fog); or "Hospital-Horsepittle"; or the law-stationer relates his "Joful and woful experience"; or " 'Ill fo manger, you know,' pursues Jobling, pronouncing that word as if he meant a necessary fixture in an English stable." There is still a long way from here to Joyce's *Finnegans Wake*, that petrified superpun, but it is the right direction.

13. OBLIQUE DESCRIPTION OF SPEECH

This is a further development of Samuel Johnson and Jane Austen's manner, with a greater number of samples of speech within the description. Mrs. Piper testifies at the inquest on the death of Nemo by indirect report: "Why, Mrs. Piper has a good deal to say, chiefly in parentheses and without punctuation, but not much to tell. Mrs. Piper lives in the court (which her husband is a cabinet-maker), and it has long been well beknown among the neighbours (counting from the day next but one before the half-baptising of Alexander James Piper aged eighteen months and four days old on accounts of not being expected to live such was the sufferings gentlemen of that child in his gums) as the Plaintive—so Mrs. Piper insists on calling the deceased—was reported to have sold himself. Thinks it was the Plaintive's air in which that report originatinin. See the Plaintive often and considered as his air was feariocious and not to be allowed to go about some children being timid (and if doubted hoping Mrs. Perkins may be brought forard for she is here and will do credit to her husband and herself and family). Has seen the Plaintive wexed and worrited by the children (for children they will ever be and you cannot expect them specially if of playful dispositions to be Methoozellers which you was not yourself)," etc., etc.

Oblique rendering of speech is frequently used, in less eccentric characters, to speed up or to concentrate a mood, sometimes accompanied, as here, by lyrical repetition: Esther is persuading the secretly married Ada to go with her to visit Richard: " 'My dear,' said I, 'you have not had any difference with Richard since I have been so much away?'

" 'No, Esther.'

" 'Not heard of him, perhaps?' said I.

" 'Yes, I have heard of him,' said Ada.

"Such tears in her eyes and such love in her face. I could not make my darling out. Should I go to Richard's by myself? I said. No, Ada thought I had better not go by myself. Would she go with me? Yes, Ada thought she had better go with me. Should we go now? Yes, let us go now. Well, I could not understand my darling, with the tears in her eyes and the love in her face!"

———

A writer might be a good storyteller or a good moralist, but unless he be an enchanter, an artist, he is not a great writer. Dickens is a good moralist, a good storyteller, and a superb enchanter, but as a storyteller he lags somewhat behind his other virtues. In other words, he is supremely good at picturing his characters and their habitats in any given situation, but there are flaws in his work when he tries to establish various links between these characters in a pattern of action.

What is the joint impression that a great work of art produces upon us? (By us, I mean the good reader.) The Precision of Poetry and the Excitement of Science. And this is the impact of *Bleak House* at its best. At his best Dickens the enchanter, Dickens the artist, comes to the fore. At his second best, in *Bleak House* the moralist teacher is much in evidence, often not without art. At its worst, *Bleak House* reveals the storyteller stumbling now and then, although the general structure still remains excellent.

Despite certain faults in the telling of his story, Dickens remains, nevertheless, a great writer. Control over a considerable constellation of characters and themes, the technique of holding people and events bunched together, or of evoking absent characters through dialogue—in other words, the art of not only creating people but keeping created people alive within the reader's mind throughout a long novel—this, of course, is the obvious sign of greatness. When Grandfather Smallweed is carried in his chair into George's shooting gallery in an endeavor to get a sample of Captain Hawdon's handwriting, the driver of the cab and another person act as bearers. " 'This person,' [the other bearer, he says] 'we engaged in the street outside for a pint of beer. Which is twopence. . . . Judy, my child [he goes on, to his daughter], give the person his twopence. It's a great deal for what he has done.'

"The person, who is one of those extraordinary specimens of human fungus that spring up spontaneously in the western streets of London, ready dressed in an old red jacket, with a 'Mission' for holding horses and calling coaches, receives his twopence with anything but transport, tosses the money into the air, catches it over-handed, and retires." This gesture, this one gesture, with its epithet "over-handed"—a trifle—but the man is alive forever in a good reader's mind.

A great writer's world is indeed a magic democracy where even some very minor character, even the most incidental character like the person who tosses the twopence, has the right to live and breed.

VLADIMIR NABOKOV

GUSTAVE FLAUBERT (1821-1880)

Madame Bovary
(1856)

We now start to enjoy yet another masterpiece, yet another fairy tale. Of all the fairy tales in this series, Flaubert's novel *Madame Bovary* is the most romantic. Stylistically it is prose doing what poetry is supposed to do.*

A child to whom you read a story may ask you, is the story true? And if not, the child demands a true one. Let us not persevere in this juvenile attitude towards the books we read. Of course, if somebody tells you that Mr. Smith has seen a blue saucer with a green operator whiz by, you *do* ask, is it true? because in one way or another the fact of its being true would affect your whole life, would be of infinite practical consequence to you. But do not ask whether a poem or a novel is true. Let us not kid ourselves; let us remember that literature is of no practical value whatsoever, except in the very special case of somebody's wishing to become, of all things, a professor of literature. The girl Emma Bovary never existed: the book *Madame Bovary* shall exist forever and ever. A book lives longer than a girl.

The book is concerned with adultery and contains situations and allusions that shocked the prudish philistine government of Napoleon III. Indeed, the novel was actually tried in a court of justice for obscenity. Just imagine that. As if the work of an artist could ever be obscene. I am glad to say that Flaubert won his case. That was exactly a hundred years ago. In our days, our times. . . . But let me keep to my subject.

*For some features of Flaubert's style, see VN's Notes at the end of the essay. Ed.

We shall discuss *Madame Bovary* as Flaubert intended it to be discussed: in terms of structures (*mouvements* as he termed them), thematic lines, style, poetry, and characters. The novel consists of thirty-five chapters, each about ten pages long, and is divided into three parts set respectively in Rouen and Tostes, in Yonville, and in Yonville, Rouen, and Yonville, all of these places invented except Rouen, a cathedral city in northern France.

The main action is supposed to take place in the 1830s and 1840s, under King Louis Philippe (1830-1848). Chapter 1 begins in the winter of 1827, and in a kind of afterword the lives of some of the characters are followed up till 1856 into the reign of Napoleon III and indeed up to the date of Flaubert's completing the book. *Madame Bovary* was begun at Croisset, near Rouen, on the nineteenth of September 1851, finished in April 1856, sent out in June, and published serially at the end of the same year in the *Revue de Paris*. A hundred miles to the north of Rouen, Charles Dickens in Boulogne was finishing *Bleak House* in the summer of 1853 when Flaubert had reached part two of his novel; one year before that, in Russia, Gogol had died and Tolstoy had published his first important work, *Childhood*.

Three forces make and mold a human being: heredity, environment, and the unknown agent X. Of these the second, environment, is by far the least important, while the last, agent X, is by far the most influential. In the case of characters living in books, it is of course the author who controls, directs, and applies the three forces. The society around Madame Bovary has been manufactured by Flaubert as deliberately as Madame Bovary herself has been made by him, and to say that this Flaubertian society acted upon that Flaubertian character is to talk in circles. Everything that happens in the book happens exclusively in Flaubert's mind, no matter what the initial trivial impulse may have been, and no matter what conditions in the France of his time existed or seemed to him to exist. This is why I am opposed to those who insist upon the influence of objective social conditions upon the heroine Emma Bovary. Flaubert's novel deals with the delicate calculus of human fate, not with the arithmetic of social conditioning.

We are told that most of the characters in *Madame Bovary* are bourgeois. But one thing that we should clear up once and for all is the meaning that Flaubert gives to the term *bourgeois*. Unless it simply means *townsman*, as it often does in French, the term *bourgeois* as used by Flaubert means "philistine," people preoccupied with the material side of life and believing only in conventional values. He never uses the word *bourgeois* with any politico-economic Marxist connotation. Flaubert's bourgeois is a state of mind, not a state of pocket. In a famous scene of our book when a hardworking old woman, getting a medal for having slaved for her farmer-boss, is confronted with a committee of relaxed bourgeois beaming at her—mind you, in that scene both parties are philistines, the beaming politicians and the superstitious old peasant woman—both sides are bourgeois in Flaubert's sense. I shall clear up the term completely if I say that, for instance, today in communist Russia, Soviet literature, Soviet art, Soviet music, Soviet aspirations are fundamentally and smugly bourgeois. It is the lace curtain behind the iron one. A Soviet official, small or big, is the perfect type of bourgeois mind, of a philistine. The key to Flaubert's term is the philistinism of his Monsieur Homais. Let me add for double clarity that Marx would have called Flaubert a bourgeois in the politico-economic sense and Flaubert would have called Marx a bourgeois in the spiritual sense; and both would have been right, since Flaubert was a well-to-do gentleman in physical life and Marx was a philistine in his attitude towards the arts.

———

The reign of Louis Philippe, the citizen king (*le roi bourgeois*), from 1830 to 1848, was a pleasantly dingy era in comparison to Napoleon's fireworks in the beginning of the century and to our own variegated times. In the 1840s "the annals of France were tranquil under the cold administration of Guizot." But "1847 opened with gloomy aspects for the French Government: irritation, want, the desire for a more popular and perhaps more brilliant rule. . . . Trickery and subterfuge seemed to reign in high places." A revolution broke out in February 1848. Louis Philippe, "assuming the name of Mr. William Smith, closed an inglorious reign by an inglorious flight in a hackney cab" (*Encyclopaedia Britannica*, 9th edition, 1879). I have mentioned this bit of history because good Louis Philippe with his cab and umbrella was such a Flaubertian character. Now another character, Charles Bovary, was born according to my computations in 1815; entered school in 1828; became an "officer of health" (which is one degree below doctor) in 1835; married his first wife, the widow Dubuc, in the same year, at Tostes, where he started practicing medicine. After losing her, he married Emma Rouault (the heroine of the book) in 1838; moved to another town, Yonville, in 1840; and after losing his second wife in 1846, he died in 1847, aged thirty-two.

This is the chronology of the book in a capsule.

———

In the first chapter we pick up our initial thematic line: the *layers* or *layer-cake theme*. This is the fall of 1828; Charles is thirteen and on his first day in school he is still holding his cap on his knees in the classroom. "It was one of those headgears of a composite type in which one may trace elements of the bearskin and otterskin cap, the Lancers' *shapska* [*a flat sort of helmet*], the round hat of felt, and the housecap of cotton; in fine, one of those pathetic things that are as deeply expressive in their mute ugliness as the face of an imbecile. Ovoid, splayed with whalebone, it began with a kind of circular sausage repeated three times; then, higher up, there followed two rows of lozenges, one of velvet, the other of rabbit fur, separated by a red band; next came a kind of bag ending in a polygon of cardboard with intricate braiding upon it; and from this there hung, at the end of a long, too slender cord, a twisted tassel of gold threads. The cap was new; its visor shone."* (We may compare this to Gogol's description in *Dead Souls* of Chichikov's traveling case and Korobochka's carriage—also a layers theme!)

In this, and in the three other examples to be discussed, the image is developed layer by layer, tier by tier, room by room, coffin by coffin. The cap is a pathetic and tasteless affair: it symbolizes the whole of poor Charles's future life—equally pathetic and tasteless.

Charles loses his first wife. In June 1838, when he is twenty-three, Charles and Emma are married in a grand farmhouse wedding. A set dish, a tiered cake—also a pathetic affair in poor taste—is provided by a pastry cook who is new to the district and so has taken great pains. "It started off at the base with a square of blue cardboard [*taking off, as it were, where the cap had finished; the cap ended in a polygon of cardboard*]; this square held a temple with porticoes and colonnades and stucco statuettes in niches studded with gilt-paper stars; there came next on the second layer a castle in meringue surrounded by minute fortifications in candied angelica, almonds, raisins, and quarters of orange; and, finally, on the uppermost platform, which represented a green meadow with rocks, lakes of jam, and nutshell boats, a little cupid sat in a chocolate swing whose two uprights had two real rosebuds for knobs at the top."

*Quotations in this essay are taken from the Rinehart edition of 1948 but greatly revised by VN in his preserved heavily annotated copy. Ed.

The opening pages from Nabokov's teaching copy of *Madame Bovary*

Part One

I

WE WERE in class when the head-master came in, followed by a "new fellow," not wearing the school uniform, and a school servant carrying a large desk. Those who had been asleep woke up, and every one rose as if just surprised at his work.

The head-master made a sign to us to sit down. Then, turning to the class-master, he said to him in a low voice—

"Monsieur Roger, here is a pupil whom I recommend to your care; he'll be in the second. If his work and conduct are satisfactory, he will go into one of the upper classes, as becomes his age."

The "new fellow," standing in the corner behind the door so that he could hardly be seen, was a country boy of about fifteen, and taller than any of us. His hair was cut square on his forehead, like a village chorister's; he looked reliable, but very ill at ease. Although he was not broad-shouldered, his short jacket of green cloth with black buttons must have been tight about the arm-holes, and showed at the opening of the cuffs red wrists accustomed to being bare. His legs, in blue stockings, looked out from beneath yellow trousers, drawn tight by braces. He wore stout, ill-cleaned, hob-nailed shoes.

We began repeating the lesson. He listened with all his ears, as attentive as if at a sermon, not daring even to cross his legs or lean on his elbow; and when at two o'clock the bell rang,

19.IX.51

The lake of jam here is a kind of premonitory emblem of the romantic Swiss lakes upon which, to the sound of Lamartine's fashionable lyrical verse, Emma Bovary, the budding adulteress, will drift in her dreams; and we shall meet again the little cupid on the bronze clock in the squalid splendor of the Rouen hotel room where Emma has her assignations with Léon, her second lover.

We are still in June 1838 but at Tostes. Charles had been living in this house since the winter of 1835-1836, with his first wife until she died, in February 1837, then alone. He and his new wife Emma will spend two years in Tostes (till March 1840) before moving on to Yonville. *First layer*: "The brick front ran flush with the street, or rather highway. [*Second layer*:] Behind the door hung a cloak with a small cape, a bridle, and a black leather cap, and on the floor, in a corner, there was a pair of leggings still caked with dry mud. [*Third layer*:] On the right was the parlor, which served also as dining room. Canary yellow wallpaper, relieved at the top by a garland of pale flowers, quivered throughout its length on its loose canvas; the windows were hung crosswise with white calico curtains, and on the narrow mantelpiece a clock with a head of Hippocrates shone resplendent between two silver-plated candlesticks under oval shades. [*Fourth layer*:] On the other side of the passage was Charles's consulting room, a little place about six paces wide, with a table, three chairs, and an office armchair. Volumes of the *Dictionary of Medical Science*, the leaves unopened (that is, not yet cut open) but the binding rather the worse for the successive sales through which they had gone, occupied almost alone the six shelves of a deal bookcase. [*Fifth layer*:] The smell of frying butter could be felt seeping through the walls during office hours, just as in the kitchen one could hear the patients coughing in the consultation room and recounting all their woes. [*Sixth layer*:] Next came [*"venait ensuite," which exactly copies the formula of the cap*] a large dilapidated room with an oven. It opened straight onto the stable yard and was now used as a woodshed, cellar, and storeroom."

In March 1846 after eight years of married life, including two tempestuous love affairs of which her husband knew nothing, Emma Bovary contracts a nightmare heap of debts she cannot meet and commits suicide. In his only moment of romanticist fantasy, poor Charles makes the following plan for her funeral: "He shut himself up in his consulting room,

---

Nabokov's notes on the layers theme in *Madame Bovary* with his drawing of Charles's cap

our first thematic line
the first one is **The Layers Theme** or Layers cake theme

~~DeLeCbtOfBSGLthen~~

your page 16. first paragr.

p. 2
PK

This is the fall of 1828:
Charles is 13

1. The Cap
~~revision~~

I transl. from the french It was one of those headgears of a composite type in which one
may trace ~~~~ elements of the ~~and a~~ otterskin cap, the Lancers'
(a flat wart of helmet) shapska ~~(~~ ~~)~~ , the ~~coans hat of felt~~ ~~~~ widebrow ~~~~ and the
~~nightcap~~ house cap of cotton; in fine, one of those pathetic things, that are as
deeply expressive in their mute ugliness as the face of an imbecile. It has ten edges
Ōvoid, ~~~~ (splayed) with whalebone it began with a kind of
(elle commençait)
circular sausage (not pompon - delete pompon) repeated three times; then, higher up, there followed in
two rows of ~~velvet~~ lozenges, ~~~~ 1 2 3 years
one of velvet, the other of rabbit fur separated by a red band;
next came (venait ensuite) a kind of bag ~~~~
ending in a polygon of cardboard with intricate braiding upon
it; and from this, there hung, at the end of a long, too
slender cord, a cross-shaped twisted tassel of gold threads. The
cap was new; its visor shone.

Cp. to Gogol's description in "Dead Souls" hmused the
of Chichikov's traveling case and Korobocka's
carriage - also a "Layers" theme!

I shall discuss four examples of what I call the
"Layers" theme. This cap is the first example. In all
four examples you shall note that the image is developed up tier
layer by layer, tier by tier, room by room, coffin by coffin.
The cap is a ~~completed affair~~ pathetic and tasteless
affair; ~~also~~ its symbolizes the whole of poor Charles future
life. - pathetic and tasteless

took a pen, and after a spell of sobbing, wrote: " 'I want her to be buri   in her wedding dress, with white shoes, and a wreath. Her hair is to be spread out over her shoulders. [*Now come the layers.*] Three coffins, one of oak, one of mahogany, and one of lead. . . . Over all, there is to be laid a large piece of green velvet.' "

All the layers themes in the book come together here. With the utmost lucidity we recall the list of parts that made up Charles's pathetic cap on his first day of school, and the wedding layer cake.

————

Madame Bovary the first is the widow of a bailiff. This is the first and false Madame Bovary, so to speak. In chapter 2 while the first wife is still alive, the second one looms. Just as Charles installed himself opposite the old doctor as his successor, so the future Madame Bovary appears before the old one is dead. Flaubert could not describe her wedding to Charles since that would have spoiled the wedding feast of the next Madame Bovary. This is how Flaubert calls the first wife: Madame Dubuc (the name of her first husband), then Madame Bovary, Madame Bovary Junior (in relation to Charles's mother), then Héloïse, but the widow Dubuc when her notary absconds with her money in his keeping; and finally Madame Dubuc.

In other words, as seen through the simple mind of Charles, she starts to revert to her initial condition when Charles falls in love with Emma Rouault, passing through the same stages but backward. After her death, when Charles Bovary marries Emma, poor dead Héloïse reverts completely to the initial Madame Dubuc. It is Charles who becomes a widower, but his widowhood is somehow transferred to the betrayed and then dead Héloïse. Emma never seems to have pitied the pathetic fate of Héloïse Bovary. Incidentally, a financial shock assists in causing the death of both ladies.

————

The term *romantic* has several meanings. When discussing *Madame Bovary*—the book and the lady herself—I shall use *romantic* in the following sense: "characterized by a dreamy, imaginative habit of mind tending to dwell on picturesque possibilities derived mainly from literature." (*Romanesque* rather than romanticist.) A romantic person, mentally and emotionally living in the unreal, is profound or shallow depending on the quality of his or her mind. Emma Bovary is intelligent, sensitive, comparatively well educated, but she has a shallow mind: her charm, beauty, and refinement do not preclude a fatal streak of philistinism in her. Her exotic daydreams do not prevent her from being small-town bourgeois at heart, clinging to conventional ideas or committing this or that conventional violation of the conventional, adultery being a most conventional way to rise above the conventional; and her passion for luxury does not prevent her from revealing once or twice what Flaubert terms a peasant hardness, a strain of rustic practicality. However, her extraordinary physical charm, her unusual grace, her birdlike, hummingbirdlike vivacity—all this is irresistibly attractive and enchanting to three men in the book, her husband and her two successive lovers, both of them heels: Rodolphe, who finds in her a dreamy childish tenderness in welcome contrast to the harlots he has been consorting with; and Léon, an ambitious mediocrity, who is flattered by having a real lady for his mistress.

Now what about the husband, Charles Bovary? He is a dull, heavy, plodding fellow, with no charm, no brains, no culture, and with a complete set of conventional notions and habits. He is a philistine, but he also is a pathetic human being. The two following points are of the utmost importance. What seduces him in Emma and what he finds in her is exactly what Emma herself is looking for and not finding in her romantic daydreams. Charles dimly, but deeply, perceives in her personality an iridescent loveliness, luxury, a dreamy remoteness, poetry, romance. This is one point, and I shall offer some samples in a moment. The second point is that the love Charles almost unwittingly develops for Emma is a real feeling, deep and true, in absolute contrast to the brutal or frivolous emotions experienced by Rodolphe and Léon, her smug and vulgar lovers. So here is the pleasing paradox of Flaubert's fairy tale: the dullest and most inept person in the book is the only one who is redeemed by a divine something in the all-powerful, forgiving, and unswerving love that he bears Emma, alive or dead. There is yet a fourth character in the book who is in love with Emma but that fourth is merely a Dickensian child, Justin. Nevertheless, I recommend him for sympathetic attention.

Let us go back to the time when Charles was still married to Héloïse Dubuc. In chapter 2 Bovary's horse—horses play a tremendous part in this book, forming a little theme of their own*—takes him at a dreamy trot to Emma, the daughter of a patient of his, a farmer. Emma, however, is no ordinary farmer's daughter: she is a graceful young lady, a "demoiselle," brought up in a good boarding school with young ladies of the gentry. So here is

*For data on the horse theme, see the Notes at the end of the essay. Ed.

Charles Bovary, shaken out from his clammy connubial bed (he never loved that unfortunate first wife of his, oldish, flat-chested and with as many pimples as the spring has buds—the widow of another man, as Flaubert has Charles consider her in his mind), so here is Charles, the young country doctor, shaken out of his dull bed by a messenger and then proceeding to the farm of Les Bertaux to reset the leg of a farmer. As he approaches the farm, his gentle horse all of a sudden shies violently, a subtle premonition that the young man's quiet life will be shattered.

We see the farm and then Emma through his eyes as he comes there for the first time, still married to that unfortunate widow. The half a dozen peacocks in the yard seem a vague promise, a lesson in iridescence. We may follow the little theme of Emma's sunshade towards the end of the chapter. Some days later, during a day of thaw when the bark of the trees was glossy with dampness and the snow on the roofs of the outbuildings was melting, Emma stood on the threshold; then she went to fetch her sunshade and opened it. The sunshade of prismatic silk through which the sun shone illumed the white skin of her face with shifting reflected colors. She smiled under the tender warmth, and drops of water could be heard falling with a precise drumming note, one by one, on the taut moiré, the stretched silk.

Various items of Emma's sensuous grace are shown through Bovary's eyes: her blue dress with the three flounces, her elegant fingernails, and her hairdo. This hairdo has been so dreadfully translated in all versions that the correct description must be given else one cannot visualize her correctly: "Her hair in two black bandeaux, or folds, which seemed each of a single piece, so sleek were they, her hair was parted in the middle by a delicate line that dipped slightly as it followed the incurvation of her skull [*this is a young doctor looking*]; and the bandeaux just revealed the lobes of her ears [*lobes, not upper "tips" as all translators have it: the upper part of the ears was of course covered by those sleek black folds*], her hair knotted behind in a thick chignon. Her cheekbones were rosy."

The sensual impression that she makes on our young man is further stressed by the description of a summer day seen from the inside, from the parlor: "the outside shutters were closed. Through the chinks of the wood the sun sent across the stone floor long fine rays that broke at the angles of the furniture and played upon the ceiling. On the table flies were walking up the glasses that had been used, and buzzing as they drowned themselves in the dregs of the cider. The daylight that came in by the chimney made velvet of the soot at the back of the fireplace, and touched with livid blue the cold cinders. Between the window and the hearth Emma sat sewing; she wore no fichu; he could see droplets of sweat on her bare shoulders."

Note the long fine sun rays through the chinks in the closed shutters, and the flies walking up the glasses (not "crawling" as translators have it: flies do not crawl, they walk, they rub their hands), walking up the glasses and drowning in the dregs of the cider. And mark the insidious daylight that made velvet of the soot at the back of the fireplace and touched with livid blue the cold cinders. The droplets of sweat on Emma's shoulders (she wore an open dress), mark them too. This is imagery at its best.

The wedding procession winding its way through the fields should be compared with the funeral procession, with dead Emma, winding its way through other fields at the end of the book. In the wedding: "The procession, at first united like one long colored scarf that undulated across the fields, along the narrow path winding amid the green wheat, soon lengthened out, and broke up into different groups that loitered to talk. The fiddler walked in front with his violin, gay with ribbons at its scroll. Then came the married pair, the relations, the friends, all following pell-mell; the children stayed behind amusing themselves plucking the fruiting bells from the oak-stems, or playing amongst themselves unseen. Emma's dress, too long, trailed a little on the ground; from time to time she stopped to lift its hem, and then delicately, with her gloved fingers, she picked off bits of coarse grass and small spikes of thistles, while Charles, his hand unoccupied, waited until she had finished. Old Rouault, with a new silk hat and the cuffs of his black coat covering his hands down to the nails, gave his arm to Madame Bovary senior. As to Monsieur Bovary senior, who, really despising all these folk, had come simply in a frock-coat of military cut with one row of buttons—he was passing bar-room compliments to a young peasant girl with fair hair. She bowed, blushed, and did not know what to say. The other wedding guests talked of their business or played the fool behind each other's backs, tuning themselves up for the coming fun. If one listened closely one could always catch the squeaking [cricket's note] of the fiddler, who went on playing across the fields."

Emma is being buried. "The six men, three on either side, walked slowly, panting a little. The priests, the choristers, and the two choir-boys recited the *De profundis*, and their voices echoed over the fields, rising and falling. Sometimes they disappeared in the windings of the path; but the great silver cross rose always between the trees. [*Compare the fiddler at the wedding*.]

"The women followed in black cloaks with turned-down hoods; each of them carried in her hands a large lighted candle, and Charles felt himself weakening at this continual repetition of prayers and torches, beneath this oppressive odor of wax and of cassocks. A fresh breeze was blowing; the rye and colza ["cabbage seed"] were green, dew-droplets trembled at the roadsides and on the hawthorn hedges. All sorts of joyous sounds filled the air; the jolting of a cart rolling afar off in the ruts, the crowing of a cock, repeated again and again, or the gamboling of a foal running away under the apple trees. The pure sky was fretted with luminous clouds; a bluish haze rested upon the huts covered with iris. Charles as he passed recognized each courtyard. He remembered mornings like this, when, after visiting some patient, he came out from one and returned to her. [*Curiously enough, he does not remember the wedding; the reader is in a better position than he.*]

"The black cloth bestrewn with white beads blew up from time to time, laying bare the coffin. The tired bearers walked more slowly, and it advanced with constant jerks, like a boat that pitches with every wave."

After the wedding our young man's bliss in his daily life is pictured in another subtly sensuous paragraph. And here again we are forced to improve on the poor translations: "In bed, in the morning, by her side, his elbow on the pillow, he watched the sunlight as it touched the golden bloom on her cheeks half hidden by the scallops of her nightcap. At close range her eyes looked strangely large, especially when on waking up she opened and shut them. Black in the shade, dark blue in broad daylight, they had, as it were, layers of successive colors, which, denser at the bottom, grew lighter toward the surface of the cornea." (A little echo of the layers theme.)

In chapter 6 Emma's childhood is shown in retrospect in terms of shallow romanesque culture, in terms of the books she read and what she got from those books. Emma is a great reader of romances, of more or less exotic novels, of romantic verse. Some of the authors she knows are first-rate, such as Walter Scott or Victor Hugo; others not quite first-rate, such as Bernardin de Saint-Pierre or Lamartine. But good or bad this is not the point. The point is that she is a bad reader. She reads books emotionally, in a shallow juvenile manner, putting herself in this or that female character's

---

Nabokov's annotations on Emma's reading in his teaching copy of *Madame Bovary*

in the study. On week-nights it was some abstract of sacred history or the Lectures of the Abbé Frayssinous, and on Sundays passages from the "Génie du Christianisme," as a recreation. How she listened at first to the sonorous lamentations of its romantic melancholies re-echoing through the world and eternity! If her childhood had been spent in the shop-parlor of some business quarter, she might perhaps have opened her heart to those lyrical invasions of Nature, which usually come to us only through translation in books. But she knew the country too well; she knew the lowing of cattle, the milking, the plows. Accustomed to calm aspects of life, she turned, on the contrary, to those of excitement. She loved the sea only for the sake of its storms, and the green fields only when broken up by ruins. She wanted to get some personal profit out of things, and she rejected as useless all that did not contribute to the immediate desires of her heart, being of a temperament more sentimental than artistic, looking for emotions, not landscapes.

At the convent there was an old maid who came for a week each month to mend the linen. Patronized by the clergy, because she belonged to an ancient family of noblemen ruined by the Revolution, she dined in the refectory at the table of the good sisters, and after the meal had a bit of chat with them before going back to her work. The girls often slipped out from the study to go and see her. She knew by heart the love-songs of the last century, and sang them in a low voice as she stitched away. She told stories, gave them news, went errands in the town, and on the sly lent the big girls some novel, that she always carried in the pockets of her apron, and of which the good lady herself swallowed long chapters in the intervals of her work. They were all love, lovers, sweethearts, persecuted ladies fainting in lonely pavilions, postilions killed at every stage, horses ridden to death on every page, somber forests, heart-aches, vows, sobs, tears and kisses, little skiffs by moonlight, nightingales in shady

groves, "gentlemen" brave as lions, gentle as lambs, virtuous as no one ever was, always well dressed, and weeping like fountains.

For six months, then, Emma, at fifteen years of age, soiled her hands with books from old lending libraries. With Walter Scott, later on, she fell in love with historical events, dreamed of old chests, guard-rooms and minstrels. She would have liked to live in some old manor-house, like those long-waisted chatelaines who, under the shade of pointed arches, spent their days leaning on the stone, chin in hand, watching a cavalier with white plume galloping on his black horse from the distant fields. At this time she had a cult for Mary Stuart and enthusiastic veneration for illustrious or unhappy women. Joan of Arc, Héloïse, Agnès Sorel, the beautiful Ferronière, and Clémence Isaure stood out to her like comets in the dark immensity of history, where also were seen, more lost in shadow, and unconnected, St. Louis with his oak, the dying Bayard, some cruelties of Louis XI, a little of St. Bartholomew's, the plume of the Bearnais, and always the remembrance of the plates painted in honor of Louis XIV.

In the music-class, in the ballads she sang, there was nothing but little angels with golden wings, madonnas, lagunes, gondoliers; mild compositions that allowed her to catch a glimpse across the silliness of style and the imprudences of the music, of the attractive phantasmagoria of sentimental realities. Some of her companions brought "keepsakes" given them as new year's gifts to the convent. These had to be hidden; it was quite an undertaking; they were read in the dormitory. Delicately handling the beautiful satin bindings, Emma looked with dazzled eyes at the names of the unknown authors, who had signed their verses for the most part counts or viscounts.

She trembled as she blew back the tissue paper over the engraving and saw it fold in two and fall gently against the page. Here behind the balustrade of a balcony was a young man in a

place. Flaubert does a very subtle thing. In several passages he lists all the romantic clichés dear to Emma's heart; but his cunning choice of these cheap images and their cadenced arrangement along the curving phrase produce an effect of harmony and art. In the convent, the novels she read "were all love, lovers, paramours, persecuted ladies fainting in lonely pavilions, postilions killed at every relay, horses ridden to death on every page, somber forests, heart-aches, vows, sobs, tears and kisses, little skiffs by moonlight, nightingales in shady groves, 'gentlemen' brave as lions, gentle as lambs, virtuous as no one ever was, always well dressed and weeping like tombstone urns. For six months, then, Emma, at fifteen years of age, sleeked her hands over with the dust of books from old lending libraries. With Walter Scott, later on, she fell in love with historical events, dreamed of old chests, guardrooms and minstrels. She would have liked to live in some old manor-house, like those long-waisted chatelaines who, under the foils of ogives, pointed arches, spent their days leaning on the stone, chin in hand, watching the approach of a cavalier with white plume galloping on his black horse from the distant fields."

He uses the same artistic trick when listing Homais's vulgarities. The subject may be crude and repulsive. Its expression is artistically modulated and balanced. This is style. This is art. This is the only thing that really matters in books.

The theme of Emma's daydreaming has some connections with the whippet, the gift of a gamekeeper, which she took "out walking [in Tostes], for she went out sometimes in order to be alone for a moment, and not to see before her eyes the eternal garden and the dusty road. . . . Her thoughts, aimless at first, would wander at random, like her whippet, who ran round and round in the open country, yelping after the yellow butterflies, chasing the shrew-mice, or nibbling the poppies on the edge of some acres of wheat. Then gradually her ideas took definite shape, and sitting on the grass that she dug up with little prods of her sunshade, Emma repeated to herself, 'Good heavens! why did I marry?'

"She asked herself if by some other chance combination it would not have been possible to meet another man; and she tried to imagine what would have been those unrealized events, that different life, that unknown husband. All, surely, could not be like this one. He might have been handsome, witty, distinguished, attractive, such as, no doubt, her old schoolmates had married. What were they doing now? In town, with the noise of the streets, the buzz of the theaters, and the lights of the ballroom, they were living lives where the heart expands, the senses blossom. But her life was as cold as a garret whose dormer-window looks on the north, and boredom, the silent spider, was darkly weaving its web in every nook of her heart."

The loss of this whippet on the journey from Tostes to Yonville symbolizes the end of her mildly romantic, elegiac daydreaming at Tostes and the beginning of more passionate experiences at fateful Yonville.

But even before Yonville, Emma's daydreaming romantic image of Paris emerges from the silk cigar case she picked up on that empty country road returning from Vaubyessard,* much as in Proust's *In Search of Lost Time*, the greatest novel of the first half of our century, the little town of Combray with all its gardens (a memory) emerges from a cup of tea. This vision of Paris is one of a succession of Emma's daydreams that appear throughout the book. One daydream, shortly destroyed, is that she can make the name of Bovary famous through Charles: "Why, at least, was not her husband one of those men of grim and passionate pursuits who work all night deep in their books, and finally at sixty, when the age of rheumatism sets in, wear a cross of honor stitched on their ill-fitting black coat? She wished the name of Bovary, which was hers, had been illustrious, to see it displayed at the booksellers', repeated in the newspapers, known to all France. But Charles had no ambition."

The daydream theme joins quite naturally with the theme of deceit. She hides the cigar case over which she dreams; she deceives Charles from the very first in order to have him take her elsewhere. By faking an illness, she is responsible for the removal to Yonville, supposedly a better climate: "Would this misery last for ever? Would she never issue from it? Yet she was as good as all the women who were living happily. She had seen duchesses at Vaubyessard with clumsier waists and commoner ways, and she execrated the injustice of God. She leant her head against the walls to weep; she envied the lives of stir; longed for masked balls, for violent pleasures with all the wildness that she did not know, but that these must surely yield.

"She grew pale and suffered from palpitations of the heart. Charles prescribed valerian and camphor baths. Everything that was tried only seemed to irritate her more. . . .

"As she was constantly complaining about Tostes, Charles fancied that her illness was no doubt due to some local cause, and fixing on this idea, began to think seriously of setting up elsewhere.

*VN notes that Emma found the cigar case, which becomes to her the symbol of fashionable romantic Parisian life, when Charles had stopped to mend the horse's harness. Later, Rodolphe will also fix a broken bridle after the seduction that begins her romantic association with him. Ed.

"From that moment she drank vinegar to make herself thin, contracted a sharp little cough, and completely lost her appetite."

It is in Yonville that fate will overtake her. The fate of her bridal bouquet is a kind of premonition or emblem of her taking her own life a few years later. She had wondered when she found Bovary's first wife's bridal flowers what would be done to her bouquet. Now on leaving Tostes she burns it herself in a wonderful passage: "One day when, in view of her departure, she was tidying a drawer, something pricked her finger. It was a wire of her wedding-bouquet. The orange blossoms were yellow with dust and the silver-bordered satin ribbons frayed at the edges. She threw it into the fire. It flared up more quickly than dry straw. Then it was like a red bush in the cinders. She watched it burn. The little pasteboard berries burst, the wire twisted, the gold lace melted; and the shriveled paper petals, fluttering like black butterflies at the back of the stove, at last flew up the chimney." In a letter of about 22 July 1852, Flaubert wrote what could be applicable to this passage, "A really good sentence in prose should be like a good line in poetry, something you cannot change, and just as rhythmic and sonorous."

The theme of daydreaming surfaces again in the romantic names she thinks of bestowing on her daughter. "First she went over all those that have Italian endings, such as Clara, Louisa, Amanda, Atala; she liked Galsuinde pretty well, and Yseult or Léocadie still better." The other characters are faithful to themselves in the names they propose. "Charles wanted the child to be named after her mother; Emma opposed this." Monsieur Léon, says Homais, " 'wonders why you do not choose Madeleine. It is very much in fashion now.'

"But Madame Bovary senior cried out loudly against this name of a sinner. As to Monsieur Homais, he had a preference for names that recalled some great man, an illustrious fact, or a humane idea. . . ." One should note why Emma finally chooses Berthe. "At last Emma remembered that at the château of Vaubyessard she had heard the Marchioness call a young lady Berthe; from that moment this name was chosen. . . ."

The romantic considerations in naming the child contrast with the conditions under which she had been farmed out to nurse, an extraordinary custom of those days. Emma strolls with Léon to visit the child. "They recognized the house by an old walnut-tree which shaded it. Low and

---

Nabokov's notes on the daydream theme in his teaching copy of *Madame Bovary*

leant her head against the walls to weep; she envied lives of stir; longed for masked balls, for violent pleasures with all the wildness that she did not know, but that these must surely yield.

She grew pale and suffered from palpitations of the heart. Charles prescribed valerian and camphor baths. Everything that was tried only seemed to irritate her the more.

On certain days she chattered with feverish rapidity, and this over-excitement was suddenly followed by a state of torpor, in which she remained without speaking, without moving. What then revived her was pouring a bottle of eau-de-cologne over her arms.

As she was constantly complaining about Tostes, Charles fancied that her illness was no doubt due to some local cause, and fixing on this idea, began to think seriously of setting up elsewhere.

From that moment she drank vinegar to make herself thin, contracted a sharp little cough, and completely lost her appetite.

It cost Charles much to give up Tostes after living there four years and "when he was beginning to get on there." Yet if it must be! He took her to Rouen to see his old master. It was a nervous complaint; change of air was needed.

After looking about him on this side and on that, Charles learnt that in the Neufchâtel arrondissement there was a considerable market-town called Yonville-l'Abbaye, whose doctor, a Polish refugee, had decamped a week before. Then he wrote to the druggist of the place to ask the population, the distance from the nearest doctor, what his predecessor had made a year, and so forth; and the answer being satisfactory, he made up his mind to move about spring, if Emma's health did not improve.

One day when, in view of her departure, she was tidying a drawer, something pricked her finger. It was a wire of her wedding-bouquet. The orange blossoms were yellow with dust and the silver-bordered satin ribbons frayed at the edges. She

threw it into the fire. It flared up more quickly than dry straw. Then it was like a red bush in the cinders, slowly devoured. She watched it burn. The little pasteboard berries burst, the wire twisted, the gold lace melted; and the shrivelled paper petals, fluttering like black butterflies at the back of the stove, at last flew up the chimney.

When they left Tostes in the month of March, Madame Bovary was pregnant.

covered with brown tiles, there hung outside it, beneath the dormer-window of the garret, a string of onions. Faggots upright against a thorn fence surrounded a bed of lettuces, a few square feet of lavender, and sweet peas strung on sticks. Dirty water was running here and there on the grass, and all round were several nondescript rags, knitted stockings, a red calico jacket, and a large sheet of coarse linen spread over the hedge. At the noise of the gate the nurse appeared with a baby she was suckling on one arm. With her other hand she was pulling along a poor puny little fellow, his face covered with scrofula, the son of a Rouen hosier, whom his parents, too taken up with their business, left in the country."

The ups and downs of Emma's emotions—the longings, the passion, the frustration, the loves, the disappointments—a chequered sequence, end in a violent self-inflicted and very messy death. Yet before we part with Emma, we shall mark the essential hardness of her nature, somehow symbolized by a slight physical flaw, by the hard dry angularities of her hands; her hands were fondly groomed, delicate and white, pretty, perhaps, but not beautiful.

She is false, she is deceitful by nature: she deceives Charles from the very start before actually committing adultery. She lives among philistines, and she is a philistine herself. Her mental vulgarity is not so obvious as that of Homais. It might be too hard on her to say that the trite, ready-made pseudoprogressive aspects of Homais's nature are duplicated in a feminine pseudoromantic way in Emma; but one cannot help feeling that Homais and Emma not only phonetically echo each other but do have something in common—and that something is the vulgar cruelty of their natures. In Emma the vulgarity, the philistinism, is veiled by her grace, her cunning, her beauty, her meandering intelligence, her power of idealization, her moments of tenderness and understanding, and by the fact that her brief bird life ends in human tragedy.

Not so Homais. He is the successful philistine. And to the last, as she lies dead, poor Emma is attended by him, the busybody Homais, and the prosaic priest Bournisien. There is a delightful scene when these two—the believer in drugs and the believer in God—go to sleep in two armchairs near her dead body, facing each other, snoring in front of each other with bulging bellies and fallen jaws, twinned in sleep, united at last in the same human weakness of sleep. And what an insult to poor Emma's destiny—the epitaph Homais finds for her grave! His mind is crammed with trite Latin tags but at first he is stumped by not being able to find anything better than *sta viator*; pause, traveler (or stay, passenger). Pause where?

The end of this Latin tag is *heroam calcas*—you tread on a hero's dust. But finally Homais with his usual temerity substituted for hero's dust, your beloved wife's dust. Stay, passenger, you tread upon your beloved wife— the last thing that could be said about poor Charles who, despite all his stupidity, loved Emma with a deep, pathetic adoration, a fact that she *did* realize for one brief moment before she died. And where does he die? In the very arbor where Rodolphe and Emma used to make love.

(Incidentally, in that last page of his life, not bumblebees are visiting the lilacs in that garden but bright green beetles. Oh those ignoble, treacherous, and philistine translators! One would think that Monsieur Homais, who knew a little English, was Flaubert's English translator.)

Homais has various chinks in his armor:

1. His science comes from pamphlets, his general culture from newspapers; his taste in literature is appalling, especially in the combination of authors he cites. In his ignorance, he remarks at one point " 'That is the question,' as I lately read in a newspaper," not knowing that he is quoting Shakespeare and not a Rouen journalist—nor perhaps had the author of the political article in that newspaper known it either.

2. He still feels now and then that dreadful fright he got when he was almost jailed for practicing medicine.

3. He is a traitor, a cad, a toad, and does not mind sacrificing his dignity to the more serious interests of his business or to obtain a decoration.

4. He is a coward, and notwithstanding his brave words he is afraid of blood, death, dead bodies.

5. He is without mercy and poisonously vindictive.

6. He is a pompous ass, a smug humbug, a gorgeous philistine, a pillar of society as are so many philistines.

7. He does get his decoration at the end of the novel in 1856. Flaubert considered that his age was the age of philistinism, which he called *muflisme*. However, this kind of thing is not peculiar to any special government or regime; if anything, philistinism is more in evidence during revolutions and in police states than under more traditional regimes. The philistine in violent action is always more dangerous than the philistine who quietly sits before his television set.

Let us recapitulate for a moment Emma's loves, platonic and otherwise:

1. As a schoolgirl she may have had a crush on her music teacher, who passes with his encased violin in one of the retrospective paragraphs of the book.

2. As a young woman married to Charles (with whom at the beginning

she is not in love), she first has an amorous friendship, a perfectly platonic one technically, with Léon Dupuis, a notary clerk.

3. Her first "affair" is with Rodolphe Boulanger, the local squire.

4. In the middle of this affair, since Rodolphe turns out to be more brutal than the romantic ideal she longed for, Emma attempts to discover an ideal in her husband; she tries seeing him as a great physician and begins a brief phase of tenderness and tentative pride.

5. After poor Charles has completely botched the operation on the poor stableboy's clubfoot—one of the greatest episodes in the book—she goes back to Rodolphe with more passion than before.

6. When Rodolphe abolishes her last romantic dream of elopement and a dream life in Italy, after a serious illness she finds a subject of romantic adoration in God.

7. She has a few minutes of daydreaming about the opera singer Lagardy.

8. Her affair with vapid, cowardly Léon after she meets him again is a grotesque and pathetic materialization of all her romantic dreams.

9. In Charles, just before she dies, she discovers his human and divine side, his perfect love for her—all that she had missed.

10. The ivory body of Jesus Christ on the cross that she kisses a few minutes before her death, this love can be said to end in something like her previous tragic disappointment since all the misery of her life takes over again when she hears the awful song of the hideous vagabond as she dies.

Who are the "good" people of the book? Obviously, the villain is Lheureux, but who, besides poor Charles, are the good characters? Somewhat obviously, Emma's father, old Rouault; somewhat unconvincingly, the boy Justin, whom we glimpse crying on Emma's grave, a bleak note; and speaking of Dickensian notes let us not forget two other unfortunate children, Emma's little daughter, and of course that other little Dickensian girl, that girl of thirteen, hunchbacked, a little bleak housemaid, a dingy nymphet, who serves Lheureux as clerk, a glimpse to ponder. Who else in the book do we have as good people? The best person is the third doctor, the great Lariviere, although I have always hated the transparent tear he sheds over the dying Emma. Some might even say: Flaubert's father had

at this point let us sum up some things   for a few minutes

So let us list —   Who Emma's loves platonic and otherwise

Great Medium   Mordereaux

Whether any of those loves were platonic or otherwise?

I have ten points

1) As a school girl she had a crush for a music teacher (who passes with
his encased violin in one of the retrospective paragraphs of the book)
   Shall in cond.
   the Vicomte?

2) as a young woman married to Charles (with whom she at the beginning
as a young married woman was not in love), she had an amorous friendship, a perfectly
technically   platonic one, with Leon Dupuis, a notary clerk.

3) Her first affair is with Rodolphe Boulanger, a local squire
the romantic tag of Rodolf and the matter of fact

4) In the middle of it since Rodolphe turned out to be more brutal
than the romantic ideal she longed for, Emma tries to discover
an ideal in her husband (seeing him as a great physician,
and a bit of tender phase of tenderness and pride.

Ch. XI
p 179 5) After poor Charles had completely botched the operation on
   the stableboys   One of the greatest episodes in the book
   a poor fellow's clubfoot she back to Rodolphe with more
198 present   passion than before
202 dreams
letter

6) When Rodolphe dealt abolished her last romantic dream (of elopement
of a dream-life in Italy) after a severe illness
She finds a subject of romantic adoration in God

7) a few minutes of daydreaming about the singer Lagardy
as

8) Her affair with Leon when the husband is a grotesque and pathetic material diddl
all   rapid, cowardly   discov
of her romantic dreams   sees   and divine (— all that she had missed

9) In Charles just before her death she can his human and side, his perfect love for her)

10) The irony body of Jesus Christ on the cross (she kisses
   a few minutes before her death   can be said
   to end in something like previous   tragic disappointment, since
   compensation fell her former   since
   all the misery of her life takes over again when she hears
the awful song of her vagabond as she dies.

Why are good people in the book?
   very comparatively Mme Homais   Roualt
   something unconvincingly — Bovary Justin
   most subjectively — the kind doctor, the great Larivière.

been a doctor, and so this is Flaubert senior shedding a tear over the misfortunes of the character that his son has created.

————

A question: can we call *Madame Bovary realistic* or *naturalistic*? I wonder.

A novel in which a young and healthy husband night after night never wakes to find the better half of his bed empty; never hears the sand and pebbles thrown at the shutters by a lover; never receives an anonymous letter from some local busybody;

A novel in which the biggest busybody of them all, Homais—Monsieur Homais, whom we might have expected to have kept a statistical eye upon all the cuckolds of his beloved Yonville, actually never notices, never learns anything about Emma's affairs;

A novel in which little Justin—a nervous young boy of fourteen who faints at the sight of blood and smashes crockery out of sheer nervousness—should go to weep in the dead of night (where?) in a cemetery on the grave of a woman whose ghost might come to reproach him for not having refused to give her the key to death;

A novel in which a young woman who has not been riding for several years—if indeed she ever did ride when she lived on her father's farm— now gallops away to the woods with perfect poise, and never feels any stiffness in the joints afterwards;

A novel in which many other implausible details abound—such as the very implausible naiveté of a certain cabdriver—such a novel has been called a landmark of so-called realism, whatever that is.

In point of fact, all fiction is fiction. All art is deception. Flaubert's world, as all worlds of major writers, is a world of fancy with its own logic, its own conventions, its own coincidences. The curious impossibilities I have listed do not clash with the pattern of the book—and indeed are only discovered by dull college professors or bright students. And you will bear in mind that all the fairy tales we have lovingly examined after *Mansfield Park* are loosely fitted by their authors into certain historical frames. All reality is comparative reality since any given reality, the window you see, the smells you perceive, the sounds you hear, are not only dependent on a crude give-and-take of the senses but also depend upon various levels of information. Flaubert may have seemed realistic or naturalistic a hundred years ago to readers brought up on the writings of those sentimental ladies and gentlemen that Emma admired. But realism, naturalism, are only comparative notions. What a given generation feels as naturalism in a writer seems to an older generation to be exaggeration of drab detail, and to a younger generation not enough drab detail. The *isms* go; the *ist* dies; art remains.

Ponder most carefully the following fact: a master of Flaubert's artistic power manages to transform what he has conceived as a sordid world inhabited by frauds and philistines and mediocrities and brutes and wayward ladies into one of the most perfect pieces of poetical fiction known, and this he achieves by bringing all the parts into harmony, by the inner force of style, by all such devices of form as the counterpoint of transition from one theme to another, of foreshadowing and echoes. Without Flaubert there would have been no Marcel Proust in France, no James Joyce in Ireland. Chekhov in Russia would not have been quite Chekhov. So much for Flaubert's literary influence.

Flaubert had a special device which may be called the *counterpoint method*, or the method of parallel interlinings and interruptions of two or more conversations or trains of thought. The first example comes after Léon Dupuis has been introduced. Léon, a young man, a notary's clerk, is brought in by the device of describing Emma as he sees her, in the red glow of the fireplace at the inn which seems to shine through her. Farther on, when another man, Rodolphe Boulanger, comes into her presence, she is also shown through his eyes, but Emma as seen through Rodolphe's eyes is of a more sensual quality than the on the whole pure image that Léon perceives. Incidentally, Léon's hair is described later as brown (*chatain*); here, he is blond, or looks so to Flaubert, by the light of the fire especially kindled to illume Emma.

Now comes the contrapuntal theme in the conversation at the inn on the first arrival in Yonville of Emma and Charles. Exactly one year after his starting to compose the book (eighty to ninety pages in one year—that is a fellow after my heart), Flaubert wrote to his mistress Louise Colet on 19 September 1852: "What a nuisance my Bovary is. . . . This scene at the inn may take me three months for all I know. At times I am on the brink of tears—so keenly do I feel my helplessness. But I prefer my brain to burst rather than to skip that scene. I have to place simultaneously, in the same conversation, five or six people (who talk), several others (who are talked about), the whole region, descriptions of persons and things—and amid all this I have to show a gentleman and a lady who begin to fall in love with each other because they have tastes in common. And if I only had enough room! But the fact is that the scene should be rapid and yet not dry, ample without being lumpy."

So in the large parlor of the inn a conversation starts. Four people are involved. On the one hand, a dialogue between Emma and Léon, whom she has just met, which is interrupted by monologues and sundry remarks on Homais's part, who is conversing mainly with Charles Bovary, for Homais is eager to get on good terms with the new doctor.

In this scene the first movement consists of a brisk interchange among all four: "Homais asked to be allowed to keep on his cap, for fear of catching a cold in the head; then, turning to his neighbor—

" 'Madame is no doubt a little fatigued; one gets jolted so abominably in our "Hirondelle." '

" 'That is true,' replied Emma; 'but moving about always amuses me. I like change of place.'

" 'It is so dreary,' sighed the clerk, 'to be always riveted to the same places.'

" 'If you were like me,' said Charles, 'constantly obliged to be in the saddle—'

" 'But,' Léon went on, addressing himself to Madame Bovary, 'nothing, it seems to me, is more pleasant [than to ride]—when one can,' he added." (The horse theme slips in and out here.)

The second movement consists of a long speech by Homais, ending in his giving some tips to Charles about a house to buy. " 'Moreover,' said the druggist, 'the practice of medicine is not very hard work in our part of the world . . . for people still have recourse to novenas, to relics, to the priest, rather than come straight to the doctor or druggist. The climate, however, is not, truth to tell, bad, and we even have a few men of ninety in our parish. The thermometer (I have made some observations) falls in winter to 4 degrees, and in the hottest season rises to 25 or 30 degrees Centigrade at the outside, which gives us 24 degrees Réaumur as the maximum, or otherwise 54 degrees Fahrenheit (English scale), not more. And, as a matter of fact, we are sheltered from the north winds by the forest of Argueil on the one side, from the west winds by the Saint-Jean hills on the other; and this heat, moreover, which, on account of the aqueous vapors given off by the river and the considerable number of cattle in the fields, which, as you know, exhale much ammonia, that is to say, nitrogen, hydrogen, and oxygen (no, nitrogen and hydrogen alone), and which pumping up the humus from the soil, mixing together all those different emanations, unites them into a bundle, so to say, and combining with the electricity diffused through the atmosphere, when there is any, might in the long-run, as in tropical countries, engender insalubrious miasmata,— this heat, I say, finds itself perfectly tempered on the side whence it comes, or rather whence it should come—that is to say, the southern side—by the southeastern winds, which, having cooled themselves passing over the Seine, reach us sometimes all at once like breezes from Russia.' "

In the middle of the speech he makes a mistake: there is always a little chink in the philistine armor. His thermometer should read 86 Fahrenheit, not 54; he forgot to add 32 when switching from one system to the other. He almost makes another fumble in speaking of exhaled air but he recovers the ball. He tries to cram all his knowledge of physics and chemistry into one elephantine sentence; he has a good memory for odds and ends derived from newspapers and pamphlets, but that is all.

Just as Homais's speech is a jumble of pseudoscience and journalese, so in the third movement the conversation between Emma and Léon is a trickle of stale poetization. " 'At any rate, you have some walks in the neighborhood?' continued Madame Bovary, speaking to the young man.

" 'Oh, very few,' he answered. 'There is a place they call La Pâture, on the top of the hill, on the edge of the forest. Sometimes, on Sundays, I go and stay there with a book, watching the sunset.'

" 'I think there is nothing so admirable as sunsets,' she resumed, 'but especially by the side of the sea.'

" 'Oh, I adore the sea!' said Monsieur Léon.

" 'And then, does it not seem to you,' continued Madame Bovary, 'that the mind travels more freely on this limitless expanse, the contemplation of which elevates the soul, gives ideas of the infinite, the ideal?'

" 'It is the same with mountainous landscapes,' continued Léon."

It is very important to mark that the Léon-Emma team is as trivial, trite, and platitudinous in their pseudoartistic emotions as the pompous and fundamentally ignorant Homais is in regard to science. False art and false science meet here. In a letter to his mistress (9 October 1852) Flaubert indicates the subtle point of this scene. "I am in the act of composing a conversation between a young man and a young woman about literature, the sea, mountains, music, and all other so-called poetic subjects. It may all seem to be seriously meant to the average reader, but in point of fact the grotesque is my real intention. It will be the first time, I think, that a novel appears where fun is made of the leading lady and her young man. But irony does not impair pathos—on the contrary, irony enhances the pathetic side."

Léon reveals his ineptitude, the chink in *his* armor, when he mentions the pianist: "A cousin of mine who traveled in Switzerland last year told me that one could not picture to oneself the poetry of the lakes, the charm of the waterfalls, the gigantic effect of the glaciers. One sees pines of incredible size across torrents, log cabins suspended over precipices, and, a thousand feet below one, whole valleys when the clouds open. Such spectacles must stir to enthusiasm, incline to prayer, to ecstasy; and I no longer marvel at that celebrated musician who, the better to inspire his imagination, was in the habit of playing the piano before some imposing site." How the sights of Switzerland must move you to prayer, to ecstasy! No wonder a famous musician used to play his piano in front of some magnificent landscape in order to stimulate his imagination. This is superb!

Shortly we find the whole bible of the bad reader—all a good reader does not do. " 'My wife doesn't care about [gardening],' said Charles; 'although she has been advised to take exercise, she prefers always sitting in her room reading.'

" 'Like me,' replied Léon. 'And indeed, what is better than to sit by one's fireside in the evening with a book, while the wind beats against the window and the lamp is burning?'

" 'What, indeed?' she said, fixing her large black eyes wide upon him.

" 'One thinks of nothing,' he continued; 'the hours slip by. Motionless we traverse countries we fancy we see, and your thought, blending with the fiction, toys with details, or follows the outline of the adventures. It mingles with the characters, and it seems as if it were yourself palpitating beneath their costumes.'

" 'That is true! that is true!' she said."

Books are not written for those who are fond of poems that make one weep or those who like noble characters in prose as Léon and Emma think. Only children can be excused for identifying themselves with the characters in a book, or enjoying badly written adventure stories; but this is what Emma and Léon do. " 'Has it ever happened to you,' Léon went on, 'to come across some vague idea of your own in a book, some dim image that comes back to you from afar, and as the completest expression of your own slightest sentiment?'

" 'I have experienced it,' she replied.

" 'That is why,' he said, 'I especially love the poets. I think verse more tender than prose, and that it moves far more easily to tears.'

" 'Still in the long-run it is tiring,' continued Emma. 'Now I, on the contrary, adore stories that rush breathlessly along, that frighten one. I detest commonplace heroes and moderate sentiments, such as there are in nature.'

" 'Yes, indeed,' observed the clerk, 'works, not touching the heart, miss, it seems to me, the true end of art. It is so sweet, amid all the disenchantments of life, to be able to dwell in thought upon noble characters, pure affections, and pictures of happiness.' "

_____

Flaubert set himself the task of giving his book a highly artistic structure. In addition to the counterpoint, one of his tricks was to make his transitions from one subject to another within the chapters as elegant and smooth as possible. In *Bleak House* the transition from subject to subject moves, on the whole, from chapter to chapter—say from Chancery to the Dedlocks, and so on. But in *Madame Bovary* there is a continual movement *within* the chapters. I call this device *structural transition*. We shall inspect certain examples of it. If the transitions in *Bleak House* can be compared to steps, with the pattern proceeding *en escalier*, here in *Madame Bovary* the pattern is a fluid system of waves.

The first transition, a fairly simple one, occurs at the very beginning of the book. The story starts with the assumption that the author, aged seven, and a certain Charles Bovary, aged thirteen, were schoolmates in Rouen in 1828. It is in the manner of a subjective account, in the first person *we*, but of course this is merely a literary device since Flaubert invented Charles from top to toe. This pseudosubjective account runs for about three pages and then changes from the subjective to an objective narrative, a shift from the direct impression of the present to an account in ordinary novelistic narrative of Bovary's past. The transition is governed by the sentence: "It was the curé of his village who had taught him his first Latin." We go back to be informed of his parents, and of his birth, and we then work our way up again through early boyhood and back to the present in school where two paragraphs, in a return to the first person, take him through his third year. After this the narrator is heard no more and we float on to Bovary's college days and medical studies.

In Yonville just before Léon leaves for Paris, a more complex structural transition takes place from Emma and her mood to Léon and his, and then to his departure. While making this transition Flaubert, as he does several times in the book, takes advantage of the structural meanderings of the transition to review a few of his characters, picking up and rapidly checking, as it were, some of their traits. We start with Emma returning home after her frustrating interview with the priest (seeking to calm the fever that Léon has aroused), annoyed that all is calm in the house while within she is in tumult. Irritably, she pushes away the advances of her young daughter Berthe, who falls and cuts her cheek. Charles hastens to Homais, the druggist, for some sticking plaster which he affixes to Berthe's cheek. He assures Emma that the cut is not serious but she chooses not to come down to dinner and, instead, remains with Berthe until the child falls asleep. After dinner Charles returns the sticking plaster and stays at the pharmacy where Homais and his wife discuss with him the dangers of childhood. Taking Léon aside, Charles asks him to price in Rouen the making of a daguerreotype of himself that in his pathetic smugness he proposes to give to Emma. Homais suspects that Léon is having some love affair in Rouen, and the innkeeper Madame Lefrançois questions the tax collector Binet about him. Léon's talk with Binet helps, perhaps, to crystallize his weariness at loving Emma with no result. His cowardice at changing his place is reviewed, and then he makes up his mind to go to Paris. Flaubert has attained what he wanted, and the flawless transition is established from Emma's mood to Leon's mood and his decision to leave Yonville. Later, we shall find another careful transition when Rodolphe Boulanger is introduced.

On 15 January 1853, as he was about to begin part two, Flaubert wrote to Louise Colet: "It has taken me five days to write one page.... What troubles me in my book is the insufficiency of the so-called amusing element. There is little action. But I maintain that images are action. It is harder to sustain a book's interest by this means, but if one fails it is the fault of style. I have now lined up five chapters of my second part in which nothing happens. It is a continuous picture of small-town life and of an inactive romance, a romance that is especially difficult to paint because it is simultaneously timid and deep, but alas without any inner wild passion. Léon, my young lover, is of a temperate nature. Already in the first part of the book I had something of this kind: my husband loves his wife somewhat in the same way as my lover does. Both are mediocrities in the same environment, but still they have to be differentiated. If I succeed, it will be a marvelous bit, because it means painting color upon color and without well-defined tones." Everything, says Flaubert, is a matter of style, or more exactly of the particular turn and aspect one gives to things.

Emma's vague promise of happiness coming from her feelings for Léon innocently leads to Lheureux (ironically a well-chosen name, "the happy

7

Structure Transition

1

Открыв книгу

parents   lesson of latin at home

October 1828
school
p.1-4
"We" (= Fels)

birth 1815   charles is 13

baby   We are 7

child   boy   school boy   medical student | medical man

end of Ch. 1

explain
Quos... 3 23
Analysis 7 24   p.1-4   15 - top p 13   contain a direct impression (of course, deliberately falsified, since Flaubert never knew "Charles" whom he invented — repeat — the semblance of a direct impression based on the assumption that the author (aged 7) and Charles Bovary (aged 13) were schoolmates at Rouen, in 1828. I repeat they never were.
14 top p.13   the beginning of a (from direct impression to an objective account on ..... the structural transition begins): the village priest, we are told, had prepared him for school, had taught him charles some Latin, and his parent had sent him to school as late as possible — when he was 13. So we switch further back to his parents, and his birth, in 1815 and watch him grow this babyhood, childhood, boyhood and (on p.7) then we see he is a schoolboy and the "we is repeated" for the last time in the book

one," for the diabolical engine of fate.) Lheureux, the draper and moneylender, arrives with the trappings of happiness. In the same breath he tells Emma confidentially that he lends money; asks after the health of a café keeper, Tellier, whom he presumes her husband is treating; and says that he, too, will have to consult the doctor one day about a pain in his back. All these are premonitions, artistically speaking. Flaubert will plan it in such a way that Lheureux will lend money to Emma, as he had lent money to Tellier, and will ruin her as he ruins Tellier before the old fellow dies; moreover, he will take his own ailments to the famous doctor who in a hopeless attempt is called to treat Emma after she takes poison. This is the planning of a work of art.

Desperate with her love for Léon, "Domestic mediocrity drove her to luxurious fancies, connubial tenderness to adulterous desires." Daydreaming of her school days in the convent, "she felt herself soft and quite deserted, like the down of a bird whirled by the tempest, and it was unconsciously that she went towards the church, inclined to no matter what devotions, so that her soul was absorbed and all existence lost in it." About the scene with the curé Flaubert wrote to Louise Colet in mid-April 1853: "At last I am beginning to see a glimmer of light in that damned dialogue of the parish priest scene. . . . I want to express the following situation: my little woman in a fit of religious emotion goes to the village church; at its door she finds the parish priest. Although stupid, vulgar, this priest of mine is a good, even an excellent fellow; but his mind dwells entirely on physical things (the troubles of the poor, lack of food or firewood), and he does not perceive moral torments, vague mystic aspirations; he is very chaste and practices all his duties. The episode is to have at most six or seven pages without a single reflection or explanation coming from the author (all in direct dialogue)." We shall note that this episode is composed after the counterpoint method: the curé answering what he thinks Emma is saying, or rather answering imaginary stock questions in a routine conversation with a parishioner, and she voicing a kind of complaining inner note that he does not heed—and all the time the children are fooling in the church and distracting the good priest's attention from the little he has to say to her.

Emma's apparent virtue frightens off Léon so that when he leaves for Paris the way is clear for a more forward lover. The transition is going to be from Emma's illness following Léon's departure to her meeting with Rodolphe and then the scene of the county fair. The meeting is a first-class illustration of structural transition which took Flaubert many days to compose. His intention is to introduce Rodolphe Boulanger, a local country gentleman, at heart exactly the same kind of cheap vulgarian as his predecessor, but with a dashing, brutal charm about him. The transition goes as follows: Charles had invited his mother to come to Yonville in order to decide what to do about Emma's condition, for she is pining away. The mother comes, decides that Emma reads too many books, evil novels, and undertakes to discontinue Emma's subscription at the lending library when she passes through Rouen on her way home. The mother leaves on a Wednesday, which is the market day at Yonville. Leaning out of the window to watch the Wednesday crowds, Emma sees a gentleman in a green velvet coat (green velvet is what Charles picks for her pall) coming to Bovary's house with a farm boy who wants to be bled. In the study downstairs when the patient faints Charles shouts for Emma to come down. (It should be noted that Charles is consistently instrumental, in a really fateful way, in introducing Emma to her lovers or helping her in continuing to see them.) It is Rodolphe who watches (with the reader) the following lovely scene: "Madame Bovary began taking off his tie. The strings of his shirt had got into a knot, and for a few minutes her light fingers kept running about the young fellow's neck. Then she poured some vinegar on her cambric handkerchief; she moistened his temples with little dabs, and then blew upon them softly. The yokel revived. . . .

"Madame Bovary took the basin to put it under the table. With the movement she made in sinking to a squatting position, her dress (it was a summer dress with four flounces, yellow, long in the waist and wide in the skirt) ballooned out around her on the stone floor of the room; and as Emma, stooping, swayed a little on her haunches as she stretched out her arms, the ballooning stuff of her skirt dimpled with the inflections of her body."

The county fair episode is instrumental in bringing Rodolphe and Emma together. On 15 July 1853, Flaubert wrote: "Tonight I have made a preliminary sketch of my great scene of the county fair. It will be huge— about thirty manuscript pages. This is what I want to do. While describing that rural show (where all the secondary characters of the book appear, speak, and act) I shall pursue . . . between its details and on the front of the stage a continuous dialogue between a lady and a gentleman who is turning his charm on her. Moreover, I have in the middle of the solemn speech of a councilor and at the end something I have quite finished writing, namely a newspaper article by Homais, who gives an account of the festivities in his best philosophic, poetic, and progressive style." The thirty pages of the episode took three months to write. In another letter, of 7 September,

Flaubert noted: "How difficult it is.... A tough chapter. I have therein all the characters of my book intermingled in action and in dialogue, and ... a big landscape that envelops them. If I succeed it will be most symphonic." On 12 October: "If ever the values of a symphony have been transferred to literature, it will be in this chapter of my book. It must be a vibrating totality of sounds. One should hear simultaneously the bellowing of the bulls, the murmur of love, and the phrases of the politicians. The sun shines on it, and there are gusts of wind that set big white bonnets astir.... I obtain dramatic movement merely through dialogue interplay and character contrast."

As if this were a show in young love's honor, Flaubert brings all the characters together in the marketplace for a demonstration of style: this is what the chapter really is about. The couple, Rodolphe (symbol of bogus passion) and Emma (the victim), are linked up with Homais (the bogus guardian of the poison of which she will die), Lheureux (who stands for the financial ruin and shame that will rush her to the jar of arsenic), and there is Charles (connubial comfort).

In grouping the characters at the beginning of the county fair, Flaubert does something especially significant in regard to the moneylending draper Lheureux and Emma. Some time before, it will be recalled, Lheureux when offering Emma his services—articles of wear and if need be, money—was curiously concerned with the illness of Tellier, the proprietor of the café opposite the inn. Now the landlady of the inn tells Homais, not without satisfaction, that the café opposite is going to close. It is clear that Lheureux has discovered that the proprietor's health is getting steadily worse and that it is high time to get back from him the swollen sums he has loaned him, and as a result poor Tellier is now bankrupt. "What an appalling disaster!" exclaims Homais, who, says Flaubert ironically, finds expressions suitable to all circumstances. But there is something behind this irony. For just as Homais exclaims "What an appalling disaster!" in his fatuous, exaggerated, pompous way, at the same time the landlady points across the square, saying, "And there goes Lheureux, he is bowing to Madame Bovary, she's taking Monsieur Boulanger's arm." The beauty of this structural line is that Lheureux, who has ruined the café owner, is thematically linked here with Emma, who will perish because of Lheureux as much as because of her lovers—and her death really will be an "appalling disaster." The ironic and the pathetic are beautifully intertwined in Flaubert's novel.

At the county fair the *parallel interruption* or *counterpoint method* is utilized once more. Rodolphe finds three stools, puts them together to form a bench, and he and Emma sit down on the balcony of the town hall to watch the show on the platform, listen to the speakers, and indulge in a flirtatious conversation. Technically, they are not lovers yet. In the first movement of the counterpoint, the councilor speaks, horribly mixing his metaphors and, through sheer verbal automatism, contradicting himself: "Gentlemen! May I be permitted first of all (before addressing you on the object of our meeting to-day, and this sentiment will, I am sure, be shared by you all), may I be permitted, I say, to pay a tribute to the higher administration, to the government, to the monarch, gentlemen, our sovereign, to that beloved king, to whom no branch of public or private prosperity is a matter of indifference, and who directs with a hand at once so firm and wise the chariot of the state amid the incessant perils of a stormy sea, knowing, moreover, how to make peace respected as well as war, industry, commerce, agriculture, and the fine arts."

In the first stage the conversation of Rodolphe and Emma alternates with chunks of official oratory. " 'I ought,' said Rodolphe, 'to get back a little further.'

" 'Why?' said Emma.

"But at this moment the voice of the councilor rose to an extraordinary pitch. He declaimed—

" 'This is no longer the time, gentlemen, when civil discord shed blood in our public places, when the landed gentry, the business-man, the working-man himself, peacefully going to sleep at night, trembled lest he should be awakened suddenly by the disasters of fire and warning church bells, when the most subversive doctrines audaciously undermined foundations.'

" 'Well, some one down there might see me,' Rodolphe resumed, 'then I should have to invent excuses for a fortnight; and with my bad reputation—'

" 'Oh, you are slandering yourself,' said Emma.

" 'No! It is dreadful, I assure you.'

" 'But, gentlemen,' continued the councilor, 'if, banishing from my memory the remembrance of these sad pictures, I carry my eyes back to the actual situation of our dear country, what do I see there?' "

Flaubert collects all the possible clichés of journalistic and political speech; but it is very important to note that, if the official speeches are stale "journalese," the romantic conversation between Rodolphe and Emma is stale "romantese." The whole beauty of the thing is that it is not good and evil interrupting each other, but one kind of evil intermingled with another kind of evil. As Flaubert remarked, he paints color on color.

The second movement starts when Councilor Lieuvain sits down and

Monsieur Derozerays speaks. "His was not perhaps so florid as that of the councilor, but it recommended itself by a more direct style, that is to say, by more special knowledge and more elevated considerations. Thus the praise of the Government took up less space in it; religion and agriculture more. He showed in it the relations of these two, and how they had always contributed to civilization. Rodolphe with Madame Bovary was talking dreams, presentiments, magnetism." In contrast to the preceding movement, at the start the conversation between the two and the speech from the platform are rendered descriptively until in the third movement the direct quotation resumes and the snatches of prize-giving exclamations borne on the wind from the platform alternate rapidly without comment or description: "From magnetism little by little Rodolphe had come to affinities, and while the president was citing Cincinnatus and his plow, Diocletian planting his cabbages, and the Emperors of China inaugurating the year by the sowing of seed, the young man was explaining to the young woman that these irresistible attractions find their cause in some previous state of existence.

" 'Thus we,' he said, 'why did we come to know one another? What chance willed it? It was because across the infinite, like two streams that flow but to unite, our special bents of mind had driven us towards each other.'

"And he seized her hand; she did not withdraw it.

" 'For good farming generally!' cried the president.

" 'Just now, for example, when I went to your house—'

" 'To Monsieur Bizet of Quincampoix.'

" '—did I know I should accompany you?'

" 'Seventy francs.'

" 'A hundred times I wished to go; and I followed you—I remained.'

" 'Manures!'

" 'And I shall remain to-night, to-morrow, all other days, all my life!'

" 'To Monsieur Caron of Argueil, a gold medal!'

" 'For I have never in the society of any other person found so complete a charm.'

" 'To Monsieur Bain of Givry-Saint-Martin.'

" 'And I shall carry away with me the remembrance of you.'

" 'For a merino ram!'

" 'But you will forget me; I shall pass away like a shadow.'

" 'To Monsieur Belot of Notre-Dame.'

" 'Oh, do say no! I shall be something in your thought, in your life, shall I not?'

" 'Porcine race; prizes—equal, to Messrs. Lehérissé and Cullembourg, sixty francs!'

"Rodolphe was pressing her hand, and he felt it all warm and quivering like a captive dove that wants to continue its flight; but, whether she was trying to take it away or whether she was answering his pressure, she made a movement with her fingers. He exclaimed—

" 'Oh, I thank you! You do not repulse me! You are good! You understand that I am yours! Let me look at you; let me contemplate you!'

"A gust of wind that blew in at the window ruffled the cloth on the table, and in the square below all the great caps of the peasant women were uplifted by it like the wings of white butterflies fluttering.

" 'Use of oil-cakes,' continued the president. He was hurrying on: 'Flemish manure—flax-growing—drainage—long leases—domestic service.' "

The fourth movement begins here when both fall silent and the words from the platform where a special prize is now being awarded are heard in full, with commentary: "Rodolphe was no longer speaking. They looked at one another. A supreme desire made their dry lips tremble, and softly, without an effort, their fingers intertwined.

" 'Catherine Nicaise Elizabeth Leroux, of Sassetot-la-Guerrière, for fifty-four years of service at the same farm, a silver medal—value, twenty-five francs!' . . .

"Then there came forward on the platform a little old woman with timid bearing, who seemed to shrink within her poor clothes. . . . Something of monastic rigidity dignified her face. Nothing of sadness or of emotion weakened that pale look. In her constant proximity to cattle she had caught their dumbness and their calm. . . . Thus stood before these beaming bourgeois this half-century of servitude. . . .

" 'Approach! approach!'

" 'Are you deaf?' said Tuvache, jumping up in his armchair; and he began shouting in her ear, 'Fifty-four years in service. A silver medal! Twenty-five francs! For you!'

"Then, when she had her medal, she looked at it, and a smile of beatitude spread over her face; and as she walked away they could hear her muttering—

" 'I'll give it to our cure up home, to say some masses for me!'

" 'What fanaticism!' exclaimed the druggist, leaning across to the notary."

The apotheosis to this splendid contrapuntal chapter is Homais's account in the Rouen paper of the show and banquet: " 'Why these festoons, these flowers, these garlands? Whither hurries this crowd like the waves of a furious sea under the torrents of a tropical sun pouring its heat upon our meads?' . . .

"He cited himself among the first of the members of the jury, and he even called attention in a note to the fact that Monsieur Homais, druggist, had sent a memoir on cider to the agricultural society. When he came to the distribution of the prizes, he painted the joy of the prize-winners in dithyrambic strophes. 'The father embraced the son, the brother the brother, the husband his consort. More than one showed his humble medal with pride, and no doubt when he got home to his good housewife, he hung it up weeping on the modest walls of his cot.

" 'About six o'clock a banquet prepared in the grass-plot of Monsieur Liegeard brought together the principal personages of the festivity. The greatest cordiality reigned here. Divers toasts were proposed: Monsieur Lieuvain, the King; Monsieur Tuvache, the Prefect; Monsieur Derozerays, Agriculture; Monsieur Homais, Industry and the Fine Arts, those twin sisters; Monsieur Leplichey, Ameliorations. In the evening some brilliant fireworks on a sudden illumined the air. One would have called it a veritable kaleidoscope, a real operatic scene; and for a moment our little locality might have thought itself transported into the midst of a dream of the "Thousand and One Nights." ' "

In a way, Industry and the Fine Arts, those twin sisters, symbolize the hog breeders and the tender couple in a kind of farcical synthesis. This is a wonderful chapter. It has had an enormous influence on James Joyce; and I do not think that, despite superficial innovations, Joyce has gone any further than Flaubert.

—

"Today . . . a man and a woman, lover and mistress in one [in thought], I have been riding on horseback through a wood, on an autumn afternoon, under yellow leaves, and I was the horses, the leaves, the wind, the words that were exchanged and the crimson sun . . . and my two lovers." So Flaubert on 23 December 1853, to Louise Colet, about the famous chapter 9 of the second part, Rodolphe's seduction of Emma.

Within the general frame and scheme of the nineteenth-century novel, this kind of scene was technically known as a woman's fall, the fall of

---

Nabokov's list of mistranslated words in the Aveling translation of *Madame Bovary*

Last batch of mistranslated words

B   open
    ask

|||||||||||||||||||||||||||||||||||

198 25   Brown collar   damn Newgate frill   (Hadocks)
209 12   insensate   insane
          [crossed out line]
223 8   good for nothings Guns
227 7   dances kickergabout girls wiggling
230 9   Bent forward   held her head high
233 (cont.) pealed   boomed   [chandoya]
235 5   cries like a peacon shary cries
          [crossed out line]
240 1   driving his carriage owning a carriage
255 32   Capharnaum   storeroom   (or house of confusion)
          [Capernaum]   ↑ in honored sense

          derived from the name of a derelict
          city in Palestine

272 23   oblique in shape oblong
273 31   pavement   sidewalk
286 5   wanted to smoke   smoked
283 26   I must irrigate my mind I need some relaxation   *
290 10   a young girl   a plump woman
293 10   whistled   no whistled
303 4   fainted   almost fainted
          [scratch]   clozgard

          [crossed out line]

345 11   benzine   benzoin   oddddd leddting.
          [during pm petroleum]   [balsamic gum]
349 6   spurs to his boot a spur to one shoe
364 1   spanish flies   green beetles   dddd

Cache on collier
Newgate frill

the green boonet ose one
the feile and
weren't Were emblems
of philistinism for Flaube
and in his sense
You could be to have
progressive ideas and
still be a philistin

amor nel cor   p.196, l. 25 is Italian and of the poetic
              variety and means love within the heart

On p.198, l. 7, Read. Who was this Clarence?

On p. 201, Nesler had Emma Bovary. (Read)

p 302   doctors and sailors   explain

virtue. In the course of this delightfully written scene the behavior of Emma's long blue veil—a character in its own serpentine right—is especially to be marked.* After dismounting from their horses, they walk. "Then some hundred paces farther on she again stopped, and through her veil, that fell slantingly from her man's hat over her hips, her face appeared in a bluish transparency as if she were floating under azure waves." So, when she is daydreaming about the event in her room on their return: "Then she saw herself in the glass and wondered at her face. Never had her eyes been so large, so black, of so profound a depth. Something subtle about her being transfigured her. She repeated, 'I have a lover! a lover!' delighting at the idea as if a second puberty had come to her. So at last she was to know those joys of love, that fever of happiness of which she had despaired! She was entering upon marvels where all would be passion, ecstasy, delirium. An azure infinity encompassed her, the heights of sentiment sparkled under her thought, and ordinary existence appeared only afar off, down below in the darkness in the interspaces of these heights." And one should not forget that, later, the poisonous arsenic was in a blue jar—and the blue haze that hung about the countryside at her funeral.

The event itself that gave rise to her daydreaming is briefly described but with one most significant detail: "The cloth of her habit caught against the velvet of his coat. She threw back her white neck, swelling with a sigh, and faltering, in tears, with a long shudder and hiding her face, she gave herself up to him.

"The shades of night were falling; the horizontal sun passing between the branches dazzled her eyes. Here and there around her, in the leaves or on the ground, trembled luminous patches, as if humming-birds in flight** had scattered their feathers. Silence was everywhere; a mild something seemed to come forth from the trees; she felt her heart, whose beating had begun again, and the blood coursing through her flesh like a stream of milk. Then far away, beyond the wood, on the other hills, she heard a vague prolonged cry, a voice which lingered, and in silence she heard it mingling like music with the last pulsations of her throbbing nerves. Rodolphe, a cigar in his teeth, was mending with his penknife one of the bridles that had broken."

When Emma has returned from love's swoon, you will please mark the

---

*In listing the details of the horse theme (for which see the Notes at the end of this essay), VN writes, that "the scene can be said to be seen through the long blue veil of her amazon dress." Ed.
**"This is a simile that must be supposed to have occurred to Emma. Hummingbirds do not occur in Europe. May have found it in Chateaubriand." VN in his annotated copy. Ed.

remote note that reaches her from somewhere beyond the quiet woods—a musical moan in the distance—for all its enchantment is nothing but the glorified echo of a hideous vagabond's raucous song. And presently Emma and Rodolphe come back from their ride—with a smile on the face of the author. For that raucous song here and in Rouen will hideously mingle with Emma's death rattle less than five years later.

Following the end of Emma's affair with Rodolphe in which he jilts her at the very moment she expected him to elope with her into the blue mist of her romantic dreams, two associated scenes are written in Flaubert's favorite contrapuntal structure. The first is the night at the opera *Lucia di Lammermoor* when Emma meets Léon again after his return from Paris. The elegant young men she notices parading in the pit of the opera house, leaning with the palms of their gloved hands on the glossy knob of their canes, form an introduction to the preliminary hubbub of various instruments getting ready to play.

In the first movement of the scene Emma is intoxicated with the tenor's melodious lamentations, which remind her of her love for Rodolphe long gone. Charles interrupts the music of her mood by his matter-of-fact remarks. He sees the opera as a jumble of idiotic gestures, but she understands the plot because she has read the novel in French. In the second, she follows the fate of Lucy on the stage while her thoughts dwell upon her own fate. She identifies herself with the girl on the stage and is ready to be made love to by anybody whom she may identify with the tenor. But in the third movement the roles are reversed. It is the opera, the singing, that creates the unwelcome interruptions, and it is her conversation with Léon that is the real thing. Charles was beginning to enjoy himself when he is dragged away to a café. Fourthly, Léon suggests that she come back on Sunday to see the last scene they had missed. The equations are truly schematic: for Emma the opera at first equals reality; the singer initially is Rodolphe, and then he is himself, Lagardy, a possible lover; the possible lover becomes Léon; and finally Léon is equated with reality and she loses interest in the opera in order to go with him to a café to escape the heat of the opera house.

Another example of the counterpoint theme is the cathedral episode. We have some preliminary sparring when Léon calls upon Emma at the inn before we come to their assignation in the cathedral. This preliminary conversation echoes that with Rodolphe at the county fair but this time Emma is far more sophisticated. In the first movement of the cathedral scene Léon enters the church to wait for Emma. The interplay is now between the beadle in his janitor's uniform (the permanent guide in wait for sightseers) on the one hand and Léon who does not want to see the sights. What he does see of the cathedral—the iridescent light dappling the floor and so on—is in keeping with his concentration upon Emma, whom he visualizes as the jealously guarded Spanish ladies sung by the French poet Musset who go to church and there pass love messages to their cavaliers. The beadle is boiling with anger at seeing a potential sightseer taking the liberty of admiring the church by himself.

The second movement is inaugurated when Emma enters, abruptly thrusts a paper at Léon (a letter of renunciation), and goes into the chapel of the Virgin to pray. "She rose, and they were about to leave, when the beadle came forward, hurriedly saying—

" 'Madame, no doubt, does not belong to these parts? Madame would like to see the curiosities of the church?'

" 'Oh, no!' cried the clerk.

" 'Why not?' said she. For she clung with her expiring virtue to the Virgin, the sculptures, the tombs—anything."

Now the torrent of the beadle's descriptive eloquence runs parallel to the impatient storm in Léon's mood. The beadle is about to show them, of all things, the steeple when Léon rushes Emma out of the church. But, thirdly, when they have already reached the outside, the beadle manages again to interfere by bringing out a pile of large bound volumes for sale, all about the cathedral. Finally, the frantic Léon tries to find a cab and then tries to get Emma into the cab. It is done in Paris, he responds when she demurs—to her the Paris of the green-silk cigar case—and this, as an irresistible argument, decides her. "Still the cab did not come. Léon was afraid she might go back into the church. At last the cab appeared.

" 'At least go out by the north porch,' cried the beadle, who was left alone on the threshold, 'so as to see the Resurrection, the Last Judgment, Paradise, King David, and the Condemned in Hell-flames.'

" 'Where to, sir?' asked the coachman.

" 'Where you like,' said Léon, forcing Emma into the cab.

"And the lumbering contraption set out."

Just as the agricultural subjects (the hogs and the manure) at the fair foreshadowed the mud that the boy Justin cleans off Emma's shoes after her walks to the house of her lover Rodolphe, so the last gust of the beadle's parrotlike eloquence foreshadows the hell flames which Emma might still have escaped had she not stepped into that cab with Léon.

This ends the cathedral part of the counterpoint. It is echoed in the next scene of the closed cab.* Here again the first idea on the coachman's part is to show the couple, whom in the simplicity of his uninformed mind he takes for tourists, the sights of Rouen, a poet's statue for instance. Then there is an automatic attempt on the cabby's part to drive jauntily up to the station, and there are other attempts of the same nature. But every time he is told by a voice from the mysterious inside of his cab to drive on. There is no need to go into the details of this remarkably amusing carriage drive, for a quotation will speak for itself. Yet one must remark that a grotesque hackney cab, with its window shades drawn, circulating in the full sight of the Rouen citizens is a far cry from that ride in the tawny woods over the purple heather with Rodolphe. Emma's adultery is cheapening. "And the lumbering contraption set out. It went down the Rue Grand-Pont, crossed the Place des Arts, the Quai Napoléon, the Pont Neuf, and stopped short before the statue of Pierre Corneille.

" 'Go on,' cried a voice that came from within.

"The cab went on again, and as soon as it reached the Carrefour Lafayette, set off down-hill, and entered the station at a gallop.

" 'No, straight on!' cried the same voice.

"The cab came out by the gate, and soon having reached the Cours, trotted quietly beneath the elm trees. The coachman wiped his brow, put his leather hat between his knees, and drove his carriage beyond the side alley by the turfy margin of the waters. . . .

"But suddenly it turned with a dash across Quatremares, Sotteville, La Grande-Chausée, the Rue d'Elbeuf, and made its third halt in front of the Jardin des Plantes.

" 'Get on, will you?' cried the voice more furiously.

"And at once resuming its course, it passed by Saint-Sever. . . . It went up the Boulevard Bouvreuil, along the Boulevard Cauchoise, then the whole of Mont-Riboudet to the Deville hills.

"It came back; and then, without any fixed plan or direction, wandered about at hazard. The cab was seen at Saint-Pol, at Lescure, at Mont Gargan, at La Rougue-Marc and Place du Gaillardbois; in the Rue Maladrerie, Rue Dinanderie, before Saint-Romain, Saint-Vivien, Saint-Maclou, Saint-Nicaise—in front of the Customs, at the 'Veille Tour,' the 'Trois Pipes,' and the Monumental Cemetery. From time to time the coachman on his box cast despairing eyes at the public-houses. He could not understand

*The entire passage of the cab, from the words of the coachman "Where to?" to the end of the chapter was suppressed by the editors of the magazine *Revue de Paris* where *Madame Bovary* was appearing serially. In the issue of 1 December 1856, where this passage was to appear, there is a footnote informing the reader of the omission. VN.

what furious desire for locomotion urged these individuals never to wish to stop. He tried to now and then, and at once exclamations of anger burst forth from behind him. Then he lashed his perspiring jades afresh, and drove on, indifferent to the jolting, scraping against things here and there, not caring if he did, demoralized, and almost weeping with thirst, fatigue, and depression.

"And on the harbor, in the midst of the drays and casks, and in the streets, at the corners, the good folk opened large wonder-stricken eyes at this sight, so extraordinary in the provinces, a cab with blinds drawn, and which reappeared thus constantly, shut more closely than a tomb, and tossing about like a ship.

"Once in the middle of the day, in the open country, just as the sun beat most fiercely against the old plated lanterns, an ungloved hand passed beneath the small blinds of yellow canvas, and threw out some scraps of torn paper that scattered in the wind, and farther off alighted, like white butterflies, on a field of red clover all in bloom. [*This was the negative letter Emma had given to Léon in the cathedral.*]

"At about six o'clock the carriage stopped in a back street of the Beauvoisine Quarter, and a woman got out, who walked with her veil down, and without turning her head."

———

On her return to Yonville Emma is met by her maid, who brings a message that she is required at once at the house of Monsieur Homais. There is a curious atmosphere of disaster as she enters the pharmacy—for instance the first thing she sees is the great armchair lying on its back, overturned— however, the disorder is only due to the fact that the Homais family is furiously making jam. Emma is vaguely worried about the message; Homais, however, has completely forgotten what he wants to tell her. It later transpires that he had been asked by Charles to inform Emma, with all sorts of precautions, of her father-in-law's death, a piece of news she receives with the utmost indifference when Homais does blurt it out at the end of his furious monologue directed against little Justin, who having been told to fetch an additional pan for the jam, took one from the lumber room in the dangerous neighborhood of a blue jar with arsenic. The subtle part of this wonderful scene is that the real message, the real information given to Emma and impressed on her mind is the fact of the existence of that jar of poison, of the place where it is, of the key to the room that little Justin has; and although at this moment she is in a delicious daze of adultery and does not think of death, that piece of information, intermingled with the news of old Bovary's death, will remain in her retentive memory.

———

There is no need to follow in detail the tricks Emma practices to make her poor husband consent to her going to Rouen for her meetings with Léon in their favorite hotel bedroom that soon seems to them to be like home. At this point Emma reaches the highest degree of happiness with Léon: her sentimental lake dreams, her girlish mooning among the modulations of Lamartine, all this is fulfilled—there is water, a boat, a lover, and a boatman. A ribbon of silk turns up in the boat. The boatman mentions someone—Adolphe, Dodolphe—a gay dog who had recently been in that boat with companions and girls. Emma shivers.

But gradually, like old pieces of scenery, her life begins to shake and fall apart. Beginning with chapter 4 of the third part, fate, abetted by Flaubert, proceeds to destroy her with beautiful precision. From the technical point of composition, this is the tapering point where art and science meet. Emma somehow manages to prop up the toppling falsehood of her piano lessons in Rouen; for a while, also, she props up Lheureux's tumbling bills with other bills. In what may be termed yet another counterpoint scene Homais butts in by insisting that Léon entertain him in Rouen at the exact time that Emma is waiting for Léon at the hotel, a grotesque and very amusing scene that recalls the cathedral episode, with Homais in the beadle's part. A rakish fancy-dress ball in Rouen is not a success for poor Emma, who realizes what sleazy company she is in. Finally, her own house starts to crumble down. One day on returning from town she finds a notice of the sale of her furniture unless her debt, now 8,000 francs, is paid within twenty-four hours. Here begins her last journey, from one person to another in search of money. All the characters join in this tragic climax.

Her first attempt is to secure more time. " 'I implore you, Monsieur Lheureux, just a few days more!'

"She was sobbing.

" 'There! tears now!'

" 'You are driving me to despair!'

" ' I do not give a damn if I do,' said he, shutting the door."

From Lheureux she goes to Rouen, but Léon by now is anxious to get rid of her. She even suggests that he steal the money from his office: "An infernal boldness looked out from her burning eyes, and their lids drew close together with a lascivious and encouraging look,' so that the young man felt himself growing weak beneath the mute will of this woman who was urging him to a crime." His promises prove worthless and he does not keep their appointment that afternoon. "He pressed her hand, but it felt quite lifeless. Emma had no strength left for any sentiment.

"Four o'clock struck, and she rose to return to Yonville, mechanically obeying the force of old habits."

Leaving Rouen, she is forced to make way for the Viscount Vaubyessard—or was it someone else—driving a prancing black horse. She travels back in the same coach as Homais after a searing encounter with the loathsome blind beggar. In Yonville she approaches the notary Monsieur Guillaumin who tries to make love to her. "He dragged himself toward her on his knees, regardless of his dressing-gown.

" 'For pity's sake, stay! I love you!'

"He seized her by her waist. Madame Bovary's face flushed a bright red. She recoiled with a terrible look, crying—'You are taking a shameless advantage of my distress, sir! I am to be pitied—not to be sold.'

"And she went out."

Then she goes to Binet, and Flaubert shifts his angle of view: we and two women watch the scene through a window although nothing can be heard. "The tax-collector seemed to be listening with wide-open eyes, as if he did not understand. She went on in a tender, suppliant manner. She came nearer to him, her breast heaving; they no longer spoke.

" 'Is she making him advances?' said Madame Tuvache.

"Binet was scarlet to his very ears. She took hold of his hands.

" 'Oh, it's too much!'

"And no doubt she was suggesting something abominable to him; for the tax-collector—yet he was brave, had fought at Bautzen and at Lutzen, had been through the French campaign, and had even been recommended for the cross—suddenly, as at the sight of a serpent, recoiled as far as he could from her, crying—

" 'Madame! what do you mean?'

" 'Women like that ought to be whipped,' said Madame Tuvache."

Next she goes to the old nurse Rollet for a few minutes' rest, and after a daydream that Leon had come with the money, "Suddenly she struck her brow and uttered a cry; for the thought of Rodolphe, like a flash of lightning in a dark night, had passed into her soul. He was so good, so delicate, so generous! And besides, should he hesitate to do her this service, she would know well enough how to constrain him to it by re-waking, in a single moment, their lost love. So she set out toward La Huchette, not seeing that she was hastening to offer herself to that which but a while ago had so angered her, not in the least conscious of her prostitution." The false tale she tells vain and vulgar Rodolphe dovetails with the real episode at the beginning of the book where a real notary runs away and causes the death of the first Madame Bovary, Emma's predecessor. Rodolphe's caresses stop abruptly at her plea for 3,000 francs. " 'Ah!' thought Rodolphe, turning suddenly very pale, 'that was what she came for.' At last he said with a calm air—

" 'Dear madame, I do not have them.'

"He did not lie. If he had them, he would, no doubt, have given them, although it is generally disagreeable to do such fine things: a demand for money being, of all the winds that blow upon love, the coldest and most destructive.

"First she looked at him for some moments.

" 'You do not have them!' she repeated several times. 'You do not have them! I ought to have spared myself this last shame. You never loved me. You are no better than the others.' . . .

" 'I haven't got them,' replied Rodolphe, with that perfect calm with which resigned rage covers itself as with a shield.

"She went out. . . . The earth beneath her feet was more yielding than the sea, and the furrows seemed to her immense brown waves breaking into foam. Everything in her head, of memories, ideas, went off at once like a thousand pieces of fireworks. She saw her father, Lheureux's office, their room at home, another landscape. Madness was coming upon her; she grew afraid, and managed to recover herself, in a confused way, it is true, for she did not in the least remember the cause of her terrible condition, that is to say, the question of money. She suffered only in her love, and felt her soul passing from her in this memory, as wounded men, dying, feel their life ebb from their bleeding wounds."

"Then in an ecstasy of heroism, that made her almost joyous, she ran down the hill, crossed the cow-plank, the footpath, the alley, the market, and reached the druggist's shop." There she wheedled the key to the lumber room from Justin. "The key turned in the lock, and she went straight to the third shelf, so well did her memory guide her, seized the blue jar, tore out the cork, plunged in her hand, and withdrawing it full of a white powder, she began eating it.

" 'Stop!' [Justin] cried, rushing at her.

" 'Hush! some one will come.'

"He was in despair, was calling out.

" 'Say nothing, or all the blame will fall on your master.'

"Then she went home, suddenly calmed, and with something of the serenity of one that had performed a duty."

The progressive agony of Emma's death is described in remorseless clinical detail until at the end: "Her chest soon began panting rapidly; the whole of her tongue protruded from her mouth; her eyes, as they rolled, grew paler, like the two globes of a lamp that is going out, so that one might have thought her already dead but for the fearful laboring of her ribs, shaken by violent breathing, as if the soul were leaping to free itself. . . . Bournisien had again begun to pray, his face bowed against the edge of the bed, his long black cassock trailing behind him on the floor. Charles was on the other side, on his knees, his arms outstretched towards Emma. He had taken her hands and pressed them, shuddering at every beat of her heart, as at the shaking of a falling ruin. As the death-rattle became stronger the priest prayed faster; his prayers mingled with the stifled sobs of Bovary, and sometimes all seemed lost in the muffled murmur of the Latin syllables that rang like a tolling bell.

"Suddenly there came a noise from the sidewalk, the loud sound of clogs and the tap of a stick; and a voice rose—a raucous voice—that sang—

'When summer skies shine hot above
A little maiden dreams of love.'

"Emma raised herself like a galvanized corpse, her hair undone, her eyes fixed, staring.

'To gather carefully
The fallen ears of corn.
Nanette goes bending down
To the earth where they were born.'

" 'The blind man!' she cried. And Emma began to laugh, an atrocious, frantic, despairing laugh, thinking she saw the hideous face of the poor wretch standing out against the eternal night like a dreadful threat.

'The wind was strong that summer day,
Her skirt was short and flew away.'

She fell back upon the mattress in a convulsion. They all drew near. She was no more."

Notes

Gogol called his *Dead Souls* a prose poem; Flaubert's novel is also a prose poem but one that is composed better, with a closer, finer texture. In order to plunge at once into the matter, I want to draw attention first of all to Flaubert's use of the word *and* preceded by a semicolon. (The semicolon is sometimes replaced by a lame comma in the English translations, but we will put the semicolon back.) This *semicolon-and* comes after an enumeration of actions or states or objects; then the semicolon creates a pause and the *and* proceeds to round up the paragraph, to introduce a culminating image, or a vivid detail, descriptive, poetic, melancholy, or amusing. This is a peculiar feature of Flaubert's style.

At the beginning of the marriage: "[Charles] could not refrain from constantly touching her comb, her rings, her fichu; sometimes he gave her big smacking kisses on her cheeks, or else tiny kisses in Indian file all along her bare arm from the tips of her fingers up to her shoulder; and she would push him away, half-smiling, half-vexed, as you do a child who hangs about you."

Emma bored with her marriage at the end of the first part: "She listened in a kind of dazed concentration to each cracked sound of the church bell. On some roof a cat would walk arching its back in the pale sun. The wind on the highway blew up strands of dust. Now and then a distant dog howled; and the bell, keeping time, continued its monotonous ringing over the fields."

After Léon's departure for Paris Emma opens her window and watches the clouds: "They were accumulating in the west, on the side of Rouen, and swiftly rolled their black convolutions from behind which the long sun rays stretched out like the golden arrows of a suspended trophy, while the rest of the empty sky was as white as porcelain. But a blast of wind bowed the poplars, and suddenly the rain fell; it pattered against the green leaves. Then the sun reappeared, the hens clucked, sparrows beat their wings in the drenched bushes; and streams of rainwater on the gravel carried away the pink petals of an acacia."

Emma lies dead: "Emma's head was turned towards her right shoulder, the corner of her mouth, which was open, seemed like a black hole at the lower part of her face; her two thumbs were bent into the palms of her hands; a kind of white dust besprinkled her lashes, and her eyes were beginning to disappear in a viscous pallor that looked like a thin web, as if spiders had been at work there. The sheet sunk in from her breast to her knees, and then rose at the tips of the toes; and it seemed to Charles that an infinite mass, an enormous load, were weighing upon her."

Another aspect of his style, rudiments of which may have been noticed in some examples of his use of *and*, is Flaubert's fondness for what may be termed the unfolding method, the successive development of visual details, one thing after another thing, with an accumulation of this or that emotion. A good example comes at the beginning of part two where a camera seems to be moving along and taking us to Yonville through a gradually revealed unfolded landscape: "We leave the highroad at La Boissiere and keep straight on to the top of the Leux hill, from which the valley is seen. The river that runs through it makes of it, as it were, two regions with distinct physiognomies,—all on the left is pasture land, all on the right arable. The meadow stretches under a bulge of low hills to join at the back with the pasture land of the Bray country, while on the eastern side, the plain, gently rising, broadens out, showing as far as eye can follow its blond wheat fields. The white stripe of the river separates the tint of the meadows from that of the ploughed land, and the country is like a great unfolded mantle with a green velvet cape fringed with silver.

"Before us, on the verge of the horizon, stand the oaks of the forest of Argeuil, with the steeps of the Saint-Jean hills that bear from top to bottom red irregular scars; these are rain-tracks, and the brick-tones standing out in narrow streaks against the gray color of the mountainside are due to the quantity of iron springs that flow beyond in the adjoining country."

A third feature—one pertaining more to poetry than to prose—is Flaubert's method of rendering emotions or states of mind through an exchange of meaningless words. Charles has just lost his wife, and Homais is keeping him company. "Homais, to do something, took a decanter on one of the shelves in order to water the geraniums.

" 'Ah! thanks,' said Charles; 'you are so—'

"He did not finish, choking as he was under the profusion of memories that Homais' action recalled to him. [*Emma had used to water these flowers.*]

"Then to distract him, Homais thought fit to talk a little horticulture: plants, he said, needed humidity. Charles bowed his head in assent.

" 'Besides,' Homais continued, 'the fine days will soon be here again.'

" 'Oh,' said Bovary.

"Homais having exhausted his supply of topics, gently draws the small window curtains aside.

" 'Hm! There's Monsieur Tuvache passing.'

"Charles repeated after him mechanically, '. . . Monsieur Tuvache passing.' "

Meaningless words, but how suggestive.

Another point in analyzing Flaubert's style concerns the use of the French imperfect form of the past tense, expressive of an action or state in continuance, something that has been happening in an habitual way. In English this is best rendered by *would* or *used to*: on rainy days she used to do this or that; then the church bells would sound; the rain would stop, etc. Proust says somewhere that Flaubert's mastery of time, of flowing time, is expressed by his use of the imperfect, of the *imparfait*. This imperfect, says Proust, enables Flaubert to express the continuity of time and its unity.

Translators have not bothered about this matter at all. In numerous passages the sense of repetition, of dreariness in Emma's life, for instance in the chapter relating to her life at Tostes, is not adequately rendered in English because the translator did not trouble to insert here and there a *would* or a *used to*, or a sequence of *woulds*.

In Tostes, Emma walks out with her whippet: "She would begin [*not "began"*] by looking around her to see if nothing had changed since last she had been there. She would find [*not "found"*] again in the same places the foxgloves and wallflowers, the beds of nettles growing round the big stones, and the patches of lichen along the three windows, whose shutters, always closed, were rotting away on their rusty iron bars. Her thoughts, aimless at first, would wander [*not "wandered"*] at random. . . ."

Flaubert does not use many metaphors, but when he does they render emotions in terms which are in keeping with the characters' personalities:

Emma, after Léon's departure: "and sorrow rushed into her hollow soul with gentle ululations such as the winter wind makes in abandoned mansions." (Of course this is the way Emma would have described her own sorrow if she had had artistic genius.)

Rodolphe tires of Emma's passionate protestations: "Because lips libertine and venal had murmured such words to him, he believed but little in the candor of hers; he thought that exaggerated speeches hiding mediocre affections must be discounted;—as if the fulness of the soul did not sometimes overflow into the emptiest metaphors, since no one can ever give the exact measure of his needs, nor of his conceptions, nor of his sorrows; for human speech is like a cracked kettle, on which we hammer out tunes to make bears dance when we long to touch the stars to tears." (I hear Flaubert complaining about the difficulties of composition.)

Rodolphe turns over old love letters before writing to Emma in farewell on the eve of their elopement: "At last, bored and weary, Rodolphe took back the box to the cupboard, saying to himself, 'What a lot of rubbish!' Which summed up his opinion; for pleasures, like schoolboys in a school-yard, had so trampled upon his heart that no green thing grew there and that which passed through it, more heedless than children, did not even, like them, leave a name carved upon the wall." (I see Flaubert revisiting his old school in Rouen.)

IMAGERY

Here are a few descriptive passages that show Flaubert at his best in dealing with sense data selected, permeated, and grouped by an artist's eye.

A wintry landscape through which Charles rides to set old Rouault's broken leg: "The flat country stretched as far as eye could see, and clumps of trees placed at long intervals around farms made purplish-black blotches on the vast gray surface that faded, at the horizon, into the dismal tint of the sky."

Emma and Rodolphe meet to make love: "The stars glistened through the leafless jasmine branches. Behind them they heard the river flowing, and now and again on the bank the clacking sound of the dry reeds. Masses of shadow here and there loomed out in the darkness, and sometimes quivering with one movement, they rose up and swayed like immense black waves pressing forward to engulf them. The cold of the night made them clasp closer; the sighs of their lips seemed to them deeper; their eyes, that they could hardly see, larger; and in the midst of the silence low words were spoken that fell on their souls sonorous, crystalline, and that reverberated in multiplied repetitions."

Emma as she appeared to Léon in her room at the inn the day after the opera: "Emma in a dimity negligée leaned her chignon against the back of the old armchair; the tawny wallpaper formed as it were a golden background behind her, and the mirror reflected her uncovered head with its white parting in the middle and the lobes of her ears just visible beneath the folds of her hair."

THE EQUINE THEME

To pick out the appearances of the horse theme amounts to giving a synopsis of the whole of *Madame Bovary*. Horses play a curiously important part in the book's romance.

The theme begins with "one night [Charles and his first wife] were awakened by the sound of a horse pulling up outside the door." A messenger has come from old Rouault, who has broken his leg.

As Charles approaches the farm where, in a minute he will meet Emma, his horse shies violently, as if at the shadow of his and her fate.

As he looks for his riding crop, he bends over Emma in a stumbling movement to help her pick it up from behind a sack of flour. (Freud, that medieval quack, might have made a lot of this scene. [Horses are a symbol of sexuality in Freud. Ed.])

As the drunken guests return from the wedding in the light of the moon, runaway carriages at full gallop plunge into irrigation ditches.

Her old father, as he sees the young pair off, recalls how he carried off his own young wife years ago, on horseback, on a cushion behind his saddle.

Mark the flower Emma lets fall from her mouth while leaning out of a window, the petal falling on the mane of her husband's horse.

The good nuns, in one of Emma's memories of the convent, had given so much good advice as to the modesty of the body and the salvation of the soul, that she did "as tightly reined horses do—she pulled up short and the bit slid from her teeth."

Her host at Vaubyessard shows her his horses.

As she and her husband leave the château, they see the viscount and other horsemen galloping by.

Charles settles down to the trot of his old horse taking him to his patients.

Emma's first conversation with Léon at the Yonville inn starts with the horse topic. "If you were like me," says Charles, "constantly obliged to be in the saddle—" "But," says Léon, addressing himself to Emma, "how nice to ride for pleasure. . . ." How nice indeed.

Rodolphe suggests to Charles that riding might do Emma a world of good.

The famous scene of Rodolphe and Emma's amorous ride in the wood can be said to be seen through the long blue veil of her amazon dress. Note the riding crop she raises to answer the blown kiss that her windowed child sends her before the ride.

Later, as she reads her father's letter from the farm, she remembers the farm—the colts that neighed and galloped, galloped.

We can find a grotesque twist to the same theme in the special *equinus* (horse-hoof-like) variety of the stableboy's clubfoot that Bovary tries to cure.

Emma gives Rodolphe a handsome riding crop as a present. (Old Freud chuckles in the dark.)

Emma's dream of a new life with Rodolphe begins with a daydream: "to the gallop of four horses she was carried away" to Italy.

A blue tilbury carriage takes Rodolphe away at a rapid trot, out of her life.

Another famous scene—Emma and Léon in that closed carriage. The equine theme has become considerably more vulgar.

In the last chapters the *Hirondelle*, the stagecoach between Yonville and Rouen, begins to play a considerable part in her life.

In Rouen, she catches a glimpse of the viscount's black horse, a memory.

During her last tragic visit to Rodolphe, who answers her plea for money that he has none to give her, she points with sarcastic remarks at the expensive ornaments on his riding crop. (The chuckle in the dark is now diabolical.)

After her death, one day when Charles has gone to sell his old horse—his last resource—he meets Rodolphe. He knows now that Rodolphe has been his wife's lover. This is the end of the equine theme. As symbolism goes it is perhaps not more symbolic than a convertible would be today.

Nabokov's chronology for *Madame Bovary*

Chronology of MADAME BOVARY

First Part

1815   Charles born   (1815 - 1847)

1821   Gustave born   (1821 - 1880)

1827   Charles begins lessons with village priest   (spring)

1828   (spring) confirmation

1828   (fall)   enters school

1831   (spring) is removed from school

1834   (spring) fails in exam medical (father hears of it five years later)

1835   (spring) passes exam, becomes "officier de santé" he may practice but

1835   (fall?) goes to Tostes to practice

1836   (Jan.) marries first wife Heloise Dubuc

1837   (6th or 7th Jan.) goes to Les Bertaux first time

1837   (early spring) first wife dies

  "   (later in the spring) goes to Les Bertaux again

  "   (Michaelmas, Sept.) makes proposal to Emma Rouault

1838   (June) wedding

  "   (Sept.) ball   at the local politician

1839   (Sept.) no ball (all winter at Tostes)

1840   (Feb.) turkey from Rouault

Second Part

1840   (March) Tostes to Yonville, Emma pregnant

  "   (summer) Bertha born (she will be 15" at end of early

  "   (summer) walk to the nurse's house

  "   (winter) at Yonville

1841   (Feb) walk to cotton mill

  "   (March) Bertha taken home

  "   (early April) visit to priest

  "   (early May) Léon leaves for Paris

1841-42
Winter

1842   (spring) (   ) Rodolphe brings farmboy to be bled

1842   (locally) county fair

  "   (early Oct) ? ride; Emma becomes Rodolphe's mistress

  "   (winter)   affair with Rodolphe

1843   (spring)   operation

  "   (summer)   affair with Rodolphe refuses

1843   (3rd Sep) Rodolphe leaves Emma

  "   (4th Sep) Monday (the date fixed for their elopement, see chap.12; no other 4th of Sep. falls on Monday in the early forties) Emma falls sick - brain fever.

  "   (17 Oct)   recovery

1844   (June) opera, Léon

Third Part

1844   (all year) affair with Léon

1845   (summer) roses

  "   (autumn) Charles with Bertha in garden

1846   (mid-Lent, early March) fancy dress ball

  "   (March) Emma asks Léon for money

  "   (Whitsuntide, around end May) (March) Emma dies, aged 26-28

  "   (Whitsuntide, around end May) Felicite runs off with Theodore, taking all Emma's clothes; Léon marries

  "   (early summer) Charles finds Rodolphe's last letter

  "   (winter) Homais getting rid of beggar

1847   (around March) mausoleum

  "   (summer, Aug) Charles finds all letters; goes to cemetery; sells horse; meets Rodolphe; dies next day. aged 33.

1847   Homais' call: Louis-Philippe (1830-1848) 'our good king', Ch. 71

1848   (Feb) revolution

1856   (April, Napoleon III is now Emperor) Bertha, aged 15, works in a cotton mill. Three doctors have succeeded one another at Yonville between 1847 and 1856; Homais has just received the Cross of the Legion.

"The Strange Case of Dr. Jekyll and Mr. Hyde" (1885)

"D r. Jekyll and Mr. Hyde" was written in bed, at Bournemouth on the English Channel, in 1885 in between hemorrhages from the lungs. It was published in January 1886. Dr. Jekyll is a fat, benevolent physician, not without human frailties, who at times by means of a potion projects himself into, or concentrates or precipitates, an evil person of brutal and animal nature taking the name of Hyde, in which character he leads a patchy criminal life of sorts. For a time he is able to revert to his Jekyll personality—there is a down-to-Hyde drug and a back-to-Jekyll drug—but gradually his better nature weakens and finally the back-to-Jekyll potion fails, and he poisons himself when on the verge of exposure. This is the bald plot of the story.

First of all, if you have the Pocket Books edition I have, you will veil the monstrous, abominable, atrocious, criminal, foul, vile, youth-depraving jacket—or better say straitjacket. You will ignore the fact that ham actors under the direction of pork packers have acted in a parody of the book, which parody was then photographed on a film and showed in places called theatres; it seems to me that to call a movie house a theatre is the same as to call an undertaker a mortician.

And now comes my main injunction. Please completely forget, disremember, obliterate, unlearn, consign to oblivion any notion you may have had that "Jekyll and Hyde" is some kind of a mystery story, a detective story, or movie. It is of course quite true that Stevenson's short novel, written in 1885, is one of the ancestors of the modern mystery story. But today's mystery story is the very negation of style, being, at the best, conventional literature. Frankly, I am not one of those college professors

Nabokov's handmade cover for "Dr. Jekyll and Mr. Hyde"

who coyly boasts of enjoying detective stories—they are too badly written for my taste and bore me to death. Whereas Stevenson's story is—God bless his pure soul—lame as a detective story. Neither is it a parable nor an allegory, for it would be tasteless as either. It has, however, its own special enchantment if we regard it as a phenomenon of style. It is not only a good "bogey story," as Stevenson exclaimed when awakening from a dream in which he had visualized it much in the same way I suppose as magic cerebration had granted Coleridge the vision of the most famous of unfinished poems. It is also, and more importantly, "a fable that lies nearer to poetry than to ordinary prose fiction"* and therefore belongs to the same order of art as, for instance, *Madame Bovary* or *Dead Souls*.

There is a delightful winey taste about this book; in fact, a good deal of old mellow wine is drunk in the story: one recalls the wine that Utterson so comfortably sips. This sparkling and comforting draft is very different from the icy pangs caused by the chameleon liquor, the magic reagent that Jekyll brews in his dusty laboratory. Everything is very appetizingly put. Gabriel John Utterson of Gaunt Street mouths his words most roundly; there is an appetizing tang about the chill morning in London, and there is even a certain richness of tone in the description of the horrible sensations Jekyll undergoes during his *hydizations*. Stevenson had to rely on style very much in order to perform the trick, in order to master the two main difficulties confronting him: (1) to make the magic potion a plausible drug based on a chemist's ingredients and (2) to make Jekyll's evil side before and after the hydization a believable evil.** "I was so far in my reflections

---

*VN states that critical quotations in this essay are drawn from Stephen Gwynn, *Robert Louis Stevenson* (London: Macmillan, 1939). Ed.

**In VN's Stevenson folder there are four pages of typed quotations from Stevenson's *Essays in the Art of Writing* (London: Chatto & Windus, 1920), which he read to his students. Among these pages is the following quotation, which seems apt here: "In the change from the successive shallow statements of the old chronicler to the dense and luminous flow of highly synthetic narrative, there is implied a vast amount of both philosophy and wit. The philosophy we clearly see, recognising in the synthetic writer a far more deep and stimulating view of life, and a far keener sense of the generation and affinity of events. The wit we might imagine to be lost; but it is not so, for it is just that wit, these perpetual nice contrivances, these difficulties overcome, this double purpose attained, these two oranges kept simultaneously dancing in the air that, consciously or not, afford the reader his delight. Nay, and this wit, so little recognised, is the necessary organ of that philosophy which we so much admire. That style is therefore the most perfect, not, as fools say, which is the most natural, for the most natural is the disjointed babble of the chronicler; but which attains the highest degree of elegant and pregnant implication unobtrusively; or if obtrusively, then with the greatest gain to sense and vigour. Even the derangement of the phrases from their (so-called) natural order is luminous for the mind; and it is by the means of such designed reversal that the elements of a judgment may be most pertinently marshalled, or the stages of a complicated action most perspicuously bound into one.

"The web, then, or the pattern: a web at once sensuous and logical, an elegant and pregnant texture: that is style, that is the foundation of the art of literature." Ed.

when, as I have said, a side light began to shine upon the subject from the laboratory table. I began to perceive more deeply than it has ever yet been stated, the trembling immateriality, the mist-like transience, of this seemingly so solid body in which we walk attired. Certain agents I found to have the power to shake and pluck back that fleshly vestment, even as a wind might toss the curtains of a pavilion. . . . I not only recognised my natural body for the mere aura and effulgence of certain of the powers that made up my spirit, but managed to compound a drug by which these powers should be dethroned from their supremacy, and a second form and countenance substituted, none the less natural to me because they were the expression, and bore the stamp of lower elements in my soul.*

"I hesitated long before I put this theory to the test of practice. I knew well that I risked death; for any drug that so potently controlled and shook the very fortress of identity, might by the least scruple of an overdose or at the least inopportunity in the moment of exhibition, utterly blot out that immaterial tabernacle which I looked to it to change. But the temptation of a discovery so singular and profound, at last overcame the suggestions of alarm. I had long since prepared my tincture; I purchased at once, from a firm of wholesale chemists, a large quantity of a particular salt which I knew, from my experiments, to be the last ingredient required; and late one accursed night, I compounded the elements, watched them boil and smoke together in the glass, and when the ebullition had subsided, with a strong glow of courage, drank off the potion.

"The most racking pangs succeeded: a grinding in the bones, deadly nausea, and a horror of the spirit that cannot be exceeded at the hour of birth or death. Then these agonies began swiftly to subside, and I came to myself as if out of a great sickness. There was something strange in my sensations, something indescribably new and, from its very novelty, incredibly sweet. I felt younger, lighter, happier in body; within I was conscious of a heady recklessness, a current of disordered sensual images running like a mill race in my fancy, a solution of the bonds of obligation, an unknown but not an innocent freedom of the soul. I knew myself, at the first breath of this new life, to be more wicked, tenfold more wicked, sold a slave to my original evil; and the thought, in that moment, braced and delighted me like wine. I stretched out my hands, exulting in the freshness of these sensations; and in the act, I was suddenly aware that I had lost in stature. . . . Even as good shone upon the countenance of the one, evil was

*"The dualism, thus, is not 'body and soul' but 'good and evil.' " VN note in his annotated copy. Ed.

written broadly and plainly on the face of the other. Evil, besides (which I must still believe to be the lethal side of man) had left on that body an imprint of deformity and decay. And yet when I looked upon that ugly idol in the glass, I was conscious of no repugnance, rather of a leap of welcome. This, too, was myself. It seemed natural and human. In my eyes it bore a livelier image of the spirit, it seemed more express and single, than the imperfect and divided countenance I had been hitherto accustomed to call mine. And in so far I was doubtless right. I have observed that when I wore the semblance of Edward Hyde, none could come near to me at first without a visible misgiving of the flesh. This, as I take it, was because all human beings, as we meet them, are commingled out of good and evil: and Edward Hyde, alone in the ranks of mankind, was pure evil."

The names Jekyll and Hyde are of Scandinavian origin, and I suspect that Stevenson chose them from the same page of an old book on surnames where I looked them up myself. Hyde comes from the Anglo-Saxon *hyd*, which is the Danish *hide*, "a haven." And Jekyll comes from the Danish name *Jökulle*, which means "an icicle." Not knowing these simple derivations one would be apt to find all kinds of symbolic meanings, especially in Hyde, the most obvious being that Hyde is a kind of hiding place for Dr. Jekyll, in whom the jocular doctor and the killer are combined.

Three important points are completely obliterated by the popular notions about this seldom read book:

1. Is Jekyll good? No, he is a composite being, a mixture of good and bad, a preparation consisting of a ninety-nine percent solution of Jekyllite and one percent of Hyde (or *hydatid* from the Greek "water" which in zoology is a tiny pouch within the body of man and other animals, a pouch containing a limpid fluid with larval tapeworms in it—a delightful arrangement, for the little tapeworms at least. Thus in a sense, Mr. Hyde is Dr. Jekyll's parasite—but I must warn that Stevenson knew nothing of this when he chose the name.) Jekyll's morals are poor from the Victorian point of view. He is a hypocritical creature carefully concealing his little sins. He is vindictive, never forgiving Dr. Lanyon with whom he disagrees in scientific matters. He is foolhardy. Hyde is mingled with him, within him. In this mixture of good and bad in Dr. Jekyll, the bad can be separated as Hyde, who is a precipitate of pure evil, a precipitation in the chemical sense since something of the composite Jekyll remains behind to wonder in horror at Hyde while Hyde is in action.

2. Jekyll is not really transformed into Hyde but projects a concentrate of pure evil that becomes Hyde, who is smaller than Jekyll, a big man, to

indicate the larger amount of good that Jekyll possesses.

3. There are really three personalities—Jekyll, Hyde, and a third, the Jekyll residue when Hyde takes over.

The situation may be represented visually.

Henry Jekyll
(large)

Edward Hyde
(small)

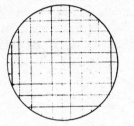

But if you look closely you see that within this big, luminous, pleasantly tweedy Jekyll there are scattered rudiments of evil.

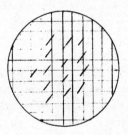

When the magic drug starts to work, a dark concentration of this evil begins forming

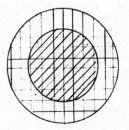

and is projected or ejected as

Still, if you look closely at Hyde, you will notice that above him floats aghast, but dominating, a residue of Jekyll, a kind of smoke ring, or halo, as if this black concentrated evil had fallen out of the remaining ring of good, but this ring of good still remains: Hyde still wants to change back to Jekyll. This is the significant point.

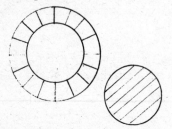

It follows that Jekyll's transformation implies a concentration of evil that already inhabited him rather than a complete metamorphosis. Jekyll is not pure good, and Hyde (Jekyll's statement to the contrary) is not pure evil, for just as parts of unacceptable Hyde dwell within acceptable Jekyll, so over Hyde hovers a halo of Jekyll, horrified at his worser half's iniquity.

The relations of the two are typified by Jekyll's house, which is half Jekyll and half Hyde. As Utterson and his friend Enfield were taking a ramble one Sunday they came to a bystreet in a busy quarter of London which, though small and what is called quiet, drove a thriving trade on weekdays. "Even on Sunday, when it veiled its more florid charms and lay comparatively empty of passage, the street shone out in contrast to its dingy neighbourhood, like a fire in a forest; and with its freshly painted shutters, well-polished brasses, and general cleanliness and gaiety of note, instantly caught and pleased the eye of the passenger.

"Two doors from one corner, on the left hand going east, the line was

Nabokov's diagrams of the relationship between Jekyll and Hyde

Henry Jekyll (Remember p 8) ⟶ Edward Hyde
(Hans)

Big ~~Jeckly~~ Jekyll   Small Hyde

ноtoM

But if you look close you see that within
this big luminous, pleasantly tweedy Jekyll that
are scattered rudiments of evil

When the magic drug starts to work   a (concentration
                                              dark
of this evil begins forming ~~H~~ ~~clear~~ thing :

                 and this is ~~projected~~ as   or ejected

But if you look closely at Hyde you will
notice that above him float aghast, but
dominating, a residue of Jekyll, a kind of
                                       smoke ring
                                       or halo

Combined
in head ⟶

as if this black concentrated evil
had fallen out of the remaining ring of good
but it still remains: Hyde still revolts, is horror-laden
~~round~~ to Jekyll — this is the significant point

broken by the entry of a court; and just at that point, a certain sinister block of building thrust forward its gable on the street. It was two storeys high; showed no window, nothing but a door on the lower storey and a blind forehead of discoloured wall on the upper; and bore in every feature, the marks of prolonged and sordid negligence. The door, which was equipped with neither bell nor knocker, was blistered and distained. Tramps slouched into the recess and struck matches on the panels; children kept shop upon the steps; the schoolboy had tried his knife on the mouldings; and for close on a generation, no one had appeared to drive away these random visitors or repair their ravages."

This is the door that Enfield points out to Utterson with his cane, which was used by a repugnantly evil man who had deliberately trampled over a running young girl and, being collared by Enfield, had agreed to recompense the child's parents with a hundred pounds. Opening the door with a key, he had returned with ten pounds in gold and a cheque for the remainder signed by Dr. Jekyll, which proves to be valid. Blackmail, thinks Enfield. He continues to Utterson: "It seems scarcely a house. There is no other door, and nobody goes in or out of that one but, once in a great while, the gentleman of my adventure. There are three windows looking on the court on the first floor; none below; the windows are always shut but they're clean. And then there is a chimney which is generally smoking; so somebody must live there. And yet it's not so sure; for the buildings are so packed together about that court, that it's hard to say where one ends and another begins."

Around the corner from the bystreet there is a square of ancient, handsome houses, somewhat run to seed and cut up into flats and chambers. "One house, however, second from the corner, was still occupied entire; and at the door of this, which wore a great air of wealth and comfort," Utterson was to knock and inquire for his friend, Dr. Jekyll. Utterson knows that the door of the building through which Mr. Hyde had passed is the door to the old dissecting room of the surgeon who had owned the house before Dr. Jekyll bought it and that it is a part of the elegant house fronting on the square. The dissecting room Dr. Jekyll had altered for his chemical experiments, and it was there (we learn much later) that he made his transformations into Mr. Hyde, at which times Hyde lived in that wing.

A student drawing of the layout of Dr. Jekyll's house, with Nabokov's alterations

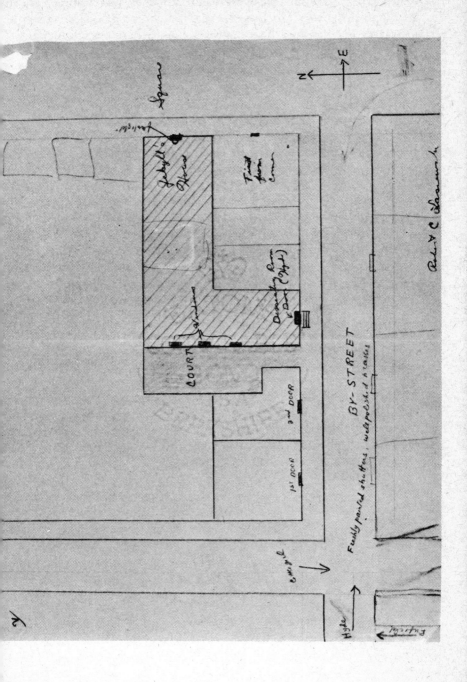

Just as Jekyll is a mixture of good and bad, so Jekyll's dwelling place is also a mixture, a very neat symbol, a very neat representation of the Jekyll and Hyde relationship. The drawing shows where the distant, east-directed and dignified front door of the Jekyll residence opens on the square. But in a bystreet, corresponding to another side of the same block of houses, its geography curiously distorted and concealed by an agglomeration of various buildings and courts in that particular spot, is the mysterious Hyde side door. Thus in the composite Jekyll building with its mellow and grand front hall there are corridors leading to Hyde, to the old surgery theatre, now Jekyll's laboratory, where not so much dissection as chemical experiments were conducted by the doctor. Stevenson musters all possible devices, images, intonations, word patterns, and also false scents, to build up gradually a world in which the strange transformation to be described in Jekyll's own words will have the impact of satisfactory and artistic reality upon the reader—or rather will lead to such a state of mind in which the reader will not ask himself whether this transformation is possible or not. Something of the same sort is managed by Dickens in *Bleak House* when by a miracle of subtle approach and variegated prose he manages to make real and satisfying the case of the gin-loaded old man who literally catches fire inside and is burnt to the ground.

————

Stevenson's artistic purpose was to make "a fantastic drama pass in the presence of plain sensible men" in an atmosphere familiar to the readers of Dickens, in the setting of London's bleak fog, of solemn elderly gentlemen drinking old port, of ugly faced houses, of family lawyers and devoted butlers, of anonymous vices thriving somewhere behind the solemn square on which Jekyll lives, and of cold mornings and of hansom cabs. Mr. Utterson, Jekyll's lawyer, is "a decent, reticent, likeable, trustworthy, courageous and crusty gentleman; and what such people can accept as 'real,' the readers are supposed also to accept as real." Utterson's friend Enfield is called "unimpressionable," a sturdy young businessman definitely on the dull side (in fact it is this sturdy dullness that brings him and Utterson together). It is this dull Enfield, a man of little imagination and not good at observing things, whom Stevenson selects to tell the beginning of the story. Enfield does not realize that the door on the bystreet which Hyde uses to bring the cheque signed by Jekyll is the door of the laboratory in Jekyll's house. However, Utterson realizes the connection immediately, and the story has started.

Although to Utterson the fanciful was the immodest, Enfield's story leads him, at home, to take from his safe Jekyll's will in his own handwriting (for Utterson had refused to lend the least assistance in the making of it) and to read again its provision: "not only that, in the case of the decease of Henry Jekyll, M.D., D.C.L., L.L.D., F.R.S., etc., all his possessions were to pass into the hands of his 'friend and benefactor Edward Hyde,' but that in case of Dr. Jekyll's 'disappearance or unexplained absence for any period exceeding three calendar months,' the said Edward Hyde should step into the said Henry Jekyll's shoes without further delay and free from any burthen or obligation, beyond the payment of a few small sums to the members of the doctor's household." Utterson had long detested this will, his indignation swelled by his ignorance of Mr. Hyde: "now, by a sudden turn, it was his knowledge [from Enfield's story of the evil small man and the child]. It was already bad enough when the name was but a name of which he could learn no more. It was worse when it began to be clothed upon with detestable attributes; and out of the shifting, insubstantial mists that had so long baffled his eye, there leaped up the sudden, definite presentment of a fiend.

" 'I thought it was madness,' he said, as he replaced the obnoxious paper in the safe, 'and now I begin to fear it is disgrace.' "

Enfield's story about the accident starts to breed in Utterson's mind when he goes to bed. Enfield had begun: "I was coming home from some place at the end of the world, about three o'clock of a black winter morning, and my way lay through a part of town where there was literally nothing to be seen but lamps. Street after street, and all the folks asleep—street after street, all lighted up as if for a procession and all as empty as a church...." (Enfield was a stolid matter-of-fact young man, but Stevenson, the artist, just could not help lending him that phrase about the streets all lighted up, with the folks asleep, and all as empty as a church.) This phrase starts to grow and reecho and mirror and remirror itself in dozing Utterson's head: "Mr. Enfield's tale went by before his mind in a scroll of lighted pictures. He would be aware of the great field of lamps of a nocturnal city; then of the figure of a man walking swiftly; then of a child running from the doctor's; and then these met, and that human Juggernaut trod the child down and passed on regardless of her screams. Or else he would see a room in a rich house, where his friend lay asleep, dreaming and smiling at his dreams; and then the door of that room would be opened, the curtains of the bed plucked apart, the sleeper recalled, and lo! there would stand by his side a figure to whom power was given, and even at that dead hour, he must rise and do its bidding. The figure in these two phases haunted the lawyer all night; and if at any time he dozed over, it was but to see it glide more stealthily through sleeping houses, or move the more swiftly and still the more swiftly, even to dizziness, through wider labyrinths of lamplighted city, and at every street corner crush a child and leave her screaming. And still the figure had no face by which he might know it; even in his dreams, it had no face."

Utterson determines to search him out; at various hours when he is free, he posts himself by the door, and at last he sees Mr. Hyde. "He was small and very plainly dressed, and the look of him, even at that distance, went somehow strongly against the watcher's inclination." (Enfield had remarked: "But there was one curious circumstance. I had taken a loathing to my gentleman at first sight.") Utterson accosts him and after some pretexts he asks to see Hyde's face, which Stevenson carefully does not describe. Utterson does tell the reader other things, however: "Mr. Hyde was pale and dwarfish, he gave an impression of deformity without any nameable malformation, he had a displeasing smile, he had borne himself to the lawyer with a sort of murderous mixture of timidity and boldness, and he spoke with a husky, whispering and somewhat broken voice; all these were points against him, but not all of these together could explain the hitherto unknown disgust, loathing and fear with which Mr. Utterson regarded him. . . . O my poor old Harry Jekyll, if ever I read Satan's signature upon a face, it is on that of your new friend."

Utterson goes around to the square, rings the bell, and inquires of Poole the butler whether Dr. Jekyll is in, but Poole reports that he has gone out. Utterson asks whether it is right that Hyde should let himself in by the old dissecting-room door when the doctor is out, but the butler reassures him that Hyde has a key by the doctor's permission and that the servants have all been ordered to obey him. " 'I do not think I ever met Mr. Hyde?' asked Utterson.

" 'O, dear no, sir. He never *dines* here,' replied the butler. 'Indeed we see very little of him on this side of the house; he mostly comes and goes by the laboratory.' "

Utterson suspects blackmail, and determines to help Jekyll if he will be permitted. Shortly the opportunity comes but Jekyll will not be helped. " 'You do not understand my position,' returned the doctor, with a certain incoherency of manner. 'I am painfully situated, Utterson; my position is a very strange—a very strange one. It is one of those affairs that cannot be mended by talking.' " He adds, however, "just to put your good heart at rest, I will tell you one thing: the moment I choose, I can be rid of Mr. Hyde. I give you my hand upon that," and the interview closes with Utterson reluctantly agreeing to Jekyll's plea to see that Hyde gets his rights "when I am no longer here."

The Carew murder is the event that begins to bring the story into focus. A servant girl, romantically given, is musing in the moonlight when she perceives a mild and beautiful old gentleman inquiring the way of a certain Mr. Hyde, who had once visited her master and for whom she had conceived a dislike. "He had in his hand a heavy cane, with which he was trifling; but he answered never a word, and seemed to listen with an ill-contained impatience. And then all of a sudden he broke out in a great flame of anger, stamping with his foot, brandishing the cane, and carrying on (as the maid described it) like a madman. The old gentleman took a step back, with the air of one very much surprised and a trifle hurt; and at that Mr. Hyde broke out of all bounds and clubbed him to the earth. And next moment, with ape-like fury, he was trampling his victim under foot and hailing down a storm of blows, under which the bones were audibly shattered and the body jumped upon the roadway. At the horror of these sights and sounds, the maid fainted."

The old man had been carrying a letter addressed to Utterson, who is therefore called upon by a police inspector and identifies the body as that of Sir Danvers Carew. He recognizes the remains of the stick as a cane he had presented to Dr. Jekyll many years before, and he offers to lead the officer to Mr. Hyde's address in Soho, one of the worst parts of London. There are some pretty verbal effects, particularly of alliteration,* in the paragraph: "It was by this time about nine in the morning, and the first fog of the season. A great chocolate-coloured pall lowered over heaven, but the wind was continually charging and routing these embattled vapours; so that as the cab crawled from street to street, Mr. Utterson beheld a marvelous number of degrees and hues of twilight; for here it would be dark like the back-end of evening; and light of some strange conflagration; and here, for a moment, the fog would be broken up, and a haggard shaft of daylight

---

*Among the typed quotations from Stevenson's *Essays in the Art of Writing* in VN's folder is the following: "It used to be a piece of good advice to all young writers to avoid alliteration; and the advice was sound, in so far as it prevented daubing. None the less for that, was it abominable nonsense, and the mere raving of those blindest of the blind who will not see. The beauty of the contents of a phrase, or of a sentence, depends implicitly upon alliteration and upon assonance. The vowel demands to be repeated; the consonant demands to be repeated; and both cry aloud to be perpetually varied. You may follow the adventures of a letter through any passage that has particularly pleased you; find it, perhaps, denied a while, to tantalise the ear; find it fired again at you in a whole broadside; or find it pass into congenerous sounds, one liquid or labial melting away into another. And you will find another and much stranger circumstance. Literature is written by and for two senses: a sort of internal ear, quick to perceive 'unheard melodies'; and the eye, which directs the pen and deciphers the printed phrase." To this, VN adds the note, "and let me add as a reader, the internal eye visualizes its color and its meaning." Ed.

would glance in between the swirling wreaths. The dismal quarter of Soho seen under these changing glimpses, with its muddy ways, and slatternly passengers, and its lamps, which had never been extinguished or had been kindled afresh to combat this mournful reinvasion of darkness, seemed, in the lawyer's eyes, like a district of some city in a nightmare."

Hyde is not at home, the flat has been ransacked in great disorder, and it is clear that the murderer has fled. That afternoon Utterson calls on Jekyll and is received in the laboratory: "The fire burned in the grate; a lamp was set lighted on the chimney shelf, for even in the houses the fog began to lie thickly; and there, close up to the warmth, sat Dr. Jekyll, looking deadly sick. He did not rise to meet his visitor, but held out a cold hand and bade him welcome in a changed voice." In response to Utterson's question whether Hyde is in concealment there, " 'Utterson, I swear to God,' cried the doctor, 'I swear to God I will never set eyes on him again. I bind my honour to you that I am done with him in this world. It is all at an end. And indeed he does not want my help; you do not know him as I do; he is safe, he is quite safe; mark my words, he will never more be heard of.' " He shows Utterson a letter signed "Edward Hyde" which signifies that his benefactor need not be concerned since he has means of escape on which he places a sure dependence. Under Utterson's questioning, Jekyll admits that it was Hyde who had dictated the terms of the will and Utterson congratulates him on his escape from being murdered himself. " 'I have had what is far more to the purpose,' returned the doctor solemnly: 'I have had a lesson—O God, Utterson, what a lesson I have had!' And he covered his face for a moment with his hands." From his chief clerk Utterson learns that the hand of the Hyde letter, though sloping in the opposite direction, is very like that of Jekyll. " 'What!' he thought. 'Henry Jekyll forge for a murderer!' And his blood ran cold in his veins."

Stevenson has set himself a difficult artistic problem, and we wonder very much if he is strong enough to solve it. Let us break it up into the following points:

1. In order to make the fantasy plausible he wishes to have it pass through the minds of matter-of-fact persons, Utterson and Enfield, who even for all their commonplace logic must be affected by something bizarre and nightmarish in Hyde.

2. These two stolid souls must convey to the reader something of the horror of Hyde, but at the same time they, being neither artists nor scientists, unlike Dr. Lanyon, cannot be allowed by the author to notice details.

3. Now if Stevenson makes Enfield and Utterson too commonplace and too plain, they will not be able to express even the vague discomfort Hyde causes them. On the other hand, the reader is curious not only about their reactions but he wishes also to see Hyde's face for himself.

4. But the author himself does not see Hyde's face clearly enough, and could only have it described by Enfield or Utterson in some oblique, imaginative, suggestive way, which, however, would not be a likely manner of expression on the part of these stolid souls.

I suggest that given the situation and the characters, the only way to solve the problem is to have the aspect of Hyde cause in Enfield and Utterson not only a shudder of repulsion but also something else. I suggest that the shock of Hyde's presence brings out the hidden artist in Enfield and the hidden artist in Utterson. Otherwise the bright perceptions that illumine Enfield's story of his journey through the lighted, empty streets before he witnessed Mr. Hyde's assault on the child, and the colorful imaginings of Utterson's dreams after he has heard the story can only be explained by the abrupt intrusion of the author with his own set of artistic values and his own diction and intonation. A curious problem indeed.

There is a further problem. Stevenson gives us the specific, lifelike description of events by humdrum London gentlemen, but contrasting with this are the unspecified, vague, but ominous allusions to pleasures and dreadful vices somewhere behind the scenes. On the one side there is "reality"; on the other, "a nightmare world." If the author really means there to be a sharp contrast between the two, then the story could strike us as a little disappointing. If we are really being told "never mind what the evil was—just believe it was something very bad," then we might feel ourselves cheated and bullied. We could feel cheated by vagueness in the most interesting part of the story just because its setting is so matter of fact and realistic. The question that must be asked of the work is whether Utterson and the fog and the cabs and the pale butler are more "real" than the weird experiments and unmentionable adventures of Jekyll and Hyde.

————

Critics such as Stephen Gwynn have noticed a curious flaw in the story's so-called familiar and commonplace setting. "There is a certain characteristic avoidance: the tale, as it develops, might almost be one of a community of monks. Mr. Utterson is a bachelor, so is Jekyll himself, so by all indications is Enfield, the younger man who first brings to Utterson a tale of Hyde's brutalities. So, for that matter, is Jekyll's butler, Poole, whose part in the story is not negligible. Excluding two or three vague servant maids, a conventional hag and a faceless little girl running for a doctor, the gentle sex has no part in the action. It has been suggested that Stevenson, 'working as he did under Victorian restrictions,' and not wishing to bring colours into the story alien to its monkish pattern, consciously refrained from placing a painted feminine mask upon the secret pleasures in which Jekyll indulged."

If, for instance, Stevenson had gone as far as, say, Tolstoy, who was also a Victorian and also did not go very far—but if Stevenson had gone as far as Tolstoy had in depicting the light loves of Oblonski, the French girl, the singer, the little ballerina, etc., it would have been artistically very difficult to have Jekyll-Oblonski exude a Hyde. A certain amiable, jovial, and lighthearted strain running through the pleasures of a gay blade would then have been difficult to reconcile with the medieval rising as a black scarecrow against a livid sky in the guise of Hyde. It was safer for the artist not to be specific and to leave the pleasures of Jekyll undescribed. But does not this safety, this easy way, does it not denote a certain weakness in the artist? I think it does.

First of all, this Victorian reticence prompts the modern reader to grope for conclusions that perhaps Stevenson never intended to be groped for. For instance, Hyde is called Jekyll's protégé and his benefactor, but one may be puzzled by the implication of another epithet attached to Hyde, that of Henry Jekyll's favorite, which sounds almost like *minion*. The all-male pattern that Gwynn has mentioned may suggest by a twist of thought that Jekyll's secret adventures were homosexual practices so common in London behind the Victorian veil. Utterson's first supposition is that Hyde blackmails the good doctor—and it is hard to imagine what special grounds for blackmailing would there have been in a bachelor's consorting with ladies of light morals. Or do Utterson and Enfield suspect that Hyde is Jekyll's illegitimate son? "Paying for the capers of his youth" is what Enfield suggests. But the difference in age as implied by the difference in their appearance does not seem to be quite sufficient for Hyde to be Jekyll's son. Moreover, in his will Jekyll calls Hyde his "friend and benefactor," a curious choice of words perhaps bitterly ironic but hardly referring to a son.

In any case, the good reader cannot be quite satisfied with the mist surrounding Jekyll's adventures. And this is especially irritating since Hyde's adventures, likewise anonymous, are supposed to be monstrous

---

Nabokov's notes on the setting of "Dr. Jekyll and Mr. Hyde"

ɔ)

Stevenson, artistic purpose was to make a fantastic dream pass" in the
presence of plain sensible men", in an ~~familiar~~ at mosphere —
familiar to the readers of Dickens, ~~and the~~ in ⟨a⟩ settings

of London's bleak fog , of solemn elderly gentlemen drinking old port ,
of ugly faced houses, of ~~bad~~ family lawyers and devoted butlers , of anonymous
vices thriving somewhere behind the solemn square fog and of cold
mornings and of hansom cabs.
~~and hansom cabs~~.

grosse

A S K

As ~~what~~ such ~~folk~~ people as Mr. Utterson, Jekyll's lawyer, is " a decent,
reticent, likeable ,trustworthy ,courageous and crusty gentleman , and what such
people can accept as "real", the readers are supposed also to accept no real.
Critics [e.g. Stephen Gwynn , 1939, from whom the quotation come) have
noticed , however , a curious flaw in this (so-called familiar and story's)
commonplace ~~and~~ setting . " There is a ⟨certain⟩ characteristic avoidance :
the tale ,as it develops , might almost be one of a community
of monks . Mr. Utterson is a bachelor , so is Jekyll himself ;
so by all indications is Enfield, the younger man who first
brings to ~~a~~ Utterson a tale of Hyde's brutalities . So,
for that matter, is Jekyll's butler , Poole ~~the~~ whose part in the story
is important ... Excluding two or three vague servant maids,
not negligible
a conventional hag and ⟨a⟩ faceless little girl running for a doctor —

exaggerations of Jekyll's wayward whims. Now the only thing that we do guess about Hyde's pleasures is that they are sadistic—he enjoys the infliction of pain. "What Stevenson desired to convey in the person of Hyde was the presence of evil wholly divorced from good. Of all wrongs in the world Stevenson most hated cruelty; and the inhuman brute whom he imagines is shown not in his beastly lusts, whatever they specifically were, but in his savage indifference" to the human beings whom he hurts and kills.

———

In his essay "A Gossip on Romance" Stevenson has this to say about narrative structure: "The right kind of thing should fall out in the right kind of place; the right kind of thing should follow; and . . . all the circumstances in a tale answer one another like notes in music. The threads of a story come from time to time together and make a picture in the web; the characters fall from time to time into some attitude to each other or to nature, which stamps the story home like an illustration. Crusoe recoiling from the footprint [*Emma smiling under her iridescent sunshade; Anna reading the shop signs along the road to her death*], these are the culminating moments in the legend, and each has been printed on the mind's eye for ever. Other things we may forget; . . . we may forget the author's comment, although perhaps it was ingenious and true; but these epoch-making scenes which put the last mark of [artistic] truth upon a story and fill up, at one blow, our capacity for [artistic] pleasure, we so adopt into the very bosom of our mind that neither time nor tide can efface or weaken the impression. This, then, is [the highest,] the plastic part of literature: to embody character, thought, or emotion in some act or attitude that shall be remarkably striking to the mind's eye."

"Dr. Jekyll and Mr. Hyde," as a phrase, has entered the language for just the reason of its epoch-making scene, the impression of which cannot be effaced. The scene is, of course, the narrative of Jekyll's transformation into Mr. Hyde which, curiously, has the more impact in that it comes as the explanation contained in two letters after the chronological narrative has come to an end, when Utterson—alerted by Poole that it is someone other than the doctor who for days has immured himself in the laboratory—breaks down the door and finds Hyde in Jekyll's too-large clothes, dead on the floor and with the reek of the cyanide capsule he has just crushed in his teeth. The brief narrative passage between Hyde's murder of Sir Danvers and this discovery merely prepares for the explanation. Time passed but Hyde had disappeared. Jekyll seemed his old self and on the eighth of

January gave a small dinner party attended by Utterson and his now reconciled friend, Dr. Lanyon. But four days later Jekyll was not at home to Utterson although they have been seeing each other daily for over two months. On the sixth day when he was refused admission he called on Dr. Lanyon for advice only to find a man with death written on his face, who refused to hear the name of Jekyll. After taking to his bed Dr. Lanyon dies within a week, and Utterson receives a letter in the doctor's hand marked not to be opened before the death or disappearance of Henry Jekyll. A day or two later, Utterson is taking a walk with Enfield, who once again enters the story, and in passing the court on the bystreet they turn in and converse briefly with an ill-looking Jekyll sitting in the window of his laboratory, an interview that ends when "the smile was struck out of [Jekyll's] face and succeeded by an expression of such abject terror and despair, as froze the very blood of the two gentlemen below. They saw it but for a glimpse for the window was instantly thrust down; but that glimpse had been sufficient, and they turned and left the court without a word."

It is not long after that episode that Poole comes to see Mr. Utterson and the action is taken that leads to the forced entry. " 'Utterson,' said the voice, 'for God's sake, have mercy!'

" 'Ah, that's not Jekyll's voice—it's Hyde's!' cried Utterson. 'Down with the door, Poole!'

"Poole swung the axe over his shoulder; the blow shook the building, and the red baize door leaped against the lock and hinges. A dismal screech, as of mere animal terror, rang from the cabinet. Up went the axe again, and again the panels crashed and the frame bounded; four times the blow fell; but the wood was tough and the fittings were of excellent workmanship; and it was not until the fifth, that the lock burst and the wreck of the door fell inwards on the carpet."

At first Utterson thinks that Hyde has killed Jekyll and hidden the body, but a search is fruitless. However, he finds a note from Jekyll on the desk asking him to read Dr. Lanyon's letter and then, if he is still curious, to read the enclosed confession, which Utterson sees is contained in a bulky sealed packet. The narrative proper ends as Utterson, back in his office, breaks the seals and starts to read. The interlocking explanation contained in the narrative-within-a-narrative of the two letters concludes the story.

Briefly, Dr. Lanyon's letter describes how he received an urgent registered letter from Jekyll requesting him to go to the laboratory, to remove a certain drawer containing various chemicals, and to give it to a messenger who would arrive at midnight. He secures the drawer (Poole had also had a registered letter) and returning to his house examines the contents: "when I opened one of the wrappers I found what seemed to me a simple crystalline salt of a white colour. The phial, to which I next turned my attention, might have been about half full of a blood-red liquor, which was highly pungent to the sense of smell and seemed to me to contain phosphorus and some volatile ether. At the other ingredients I could make no guess." At midnight the messenger comes: "He was small, as I have said; I was struck besides with the shocking expression of his face, with his remarkable combination of great muscular activity and great apparent debility of constitution, and—last but not least—with the odd, subjective disturbance caused by his neighbourhood. This bore some resemblance to incipient rigor, and was accompanied by a marked sinking of the pulse." The man is clothed in garments enormously too large for him. As Dr. Lanyon shows him the drawer, "He sprang to it, and then paused, and laid his hand upon his heart: I could hear his teeth grate with the convulsive action of his jaws; and his face was so ghastly to see that I grew alarmed both for his life and reason.

" 'Compose yourself,' said I.

"He turned a dreadful smile to me, and as if with the decision of despair, plucked away the sheet. At sight of the contents, he uttered one loud sob of such immense relief that I sat petrified. And the next moment, in a voice that was already fairly well under control, 'Have you a graduated glass?' he asked.

"I rose from my place with something of an effort and gave him what he asked.

"He thanked me with a smiling nod, measured out a few minims of the red tincture and added one of the powders. The mixture, which was at first of a reddish hue, began, in proportion as the crystals melted, to brighten in colour, to effervesce audibly, and to throw off small fumes of vapour. Suddenly and at the same moment, the ebullition ceased and the compound changed to a dark purple, which faded again more slowly to a watery green. My visitor, who had watched these metamorphoses with a keen eye, smiled, set down the glass upon the table."

Lanyon is invited to withdraw, or to remain if he is curious so long as what transpires will be kept secret "under the seal of our profession." Lanyon stays. " 'It is well,' replied my visitor. 'Lanyon, you remember your vows: . . . And now, you who have so long been bound to the most narrow and material views, you who have denied the virtue of transcendental medicine, you who have derided your superiors—behold!'

"He put the glass to his lips and drank at one gulp. A cry followed; he reeled, staggered, clutched at the table and held on, staring with injected eyes, gasping with open mouth; and as I looked there came, I thought, a change—he seemed to swell—his face became suddenly black and the features seemed to melt and alter—and the next moment, I had sprung to my feet and leaped back against the wall, my arm raised to shield me from that prodigy, my mind submerged in terror.

" 'O God!' I screamed, and 'O God!' again and again; for there before my eyes—pale and shaken, and half fainting, and groping before him with his hands, like a man restored from death—there stood Henry Jekyll!

"What he told me in the next hour, I cannot bring my mind to set on paper. I saw what I saw, I heard what I heard, and my soul sickened at it; and yet now when that sight has faded from my eyes, I ask myself if I believe it, and I cannot answer. . . . As for the moral turpitude that man unveiled to me, even with tears of penitence, I cannot, even in memory, dwell on it without a start of horror. I will say but one thing, Utterson, and that (if you can bring your mind to credit it) will be more than enough. The creature who crept into my house that night was, on Jekyll's own confession, known by the name of Hyde and hunted for in every corner of the land as the murderer of Carew."

Dr. Lanyon's letter leaves quite enough suspense to be filled in by "Henry Jekyll's Full Statement of the Case" which Utterson then reads, bringing the story to a close. Jekyll recounts how his youthful pleasures, which he concealed, hardened into a profound duplicity of life. "It was thus rather the exacting nature of my aspirations than any particular degradation in my faults, that made me what I was, and, with even a deeper trench than in the majority of men, severed in me those provinces of good and ill which divide and compound man's dual nature." His scientific studies led wholly towards the mystic and the transcendental and drew him steadily toward the truth "that man is not truly one, but truly two." And even before the course of his scientific experiments had "begun to suggest the most naked possibility of such a miracle, I had learned to dwell with pleasure, as a beloved daydream, on the thought of the separation of these elements. If each, I told myself, could be housed in separate identities, life would be relieved of all that was unbearable; the unjust might go his way, delivered from the aspirations and remorse of his more upright twin; and the just could walk steadfastly and securely on his upward path, doing the good things in which he found his pleasure, and no longer exposed to disgrace and penitence by the hands of this extraneous evil. It was the curse of mankind that these incongruous faggots were thus bound together— that in the agonised womb of consciousness, these polar twins should be continually struggling. How, then, were they dissociated."

We then have the vivid description of his discovery of the potion and, in testing it, the emergence of Mr. Hyde who, "alone in the ranks of mankind, was pure evil." "I lingered but a moment at the mirror: the second and conclusive experiment had yet to be attempted; it yet remained to be seen if I had lost my identity beyond redemption and must flee before daylight from a house that was no longer mine; and hurrying back to my cabinet, I once more prepared and drank the cup, once more suffered the pangs of dissolution, and came to myself once more with the character, the stature and the face of Henry Jekyll."

For a time all is well. "I was the first that could plod in the public eye with a load of genial respectability, and in a moment, like a schoolboy, strip off these lendings and spring headlong into the sea of liberty. But for me, in my impenetrable mantle, the safety was complete. Think of it—I did not even exist! Let me but escape into my laboratory door, give me but a second or two to mix and swallow the draught that I had always standing ready; and whatever he had done, Edward Hyde would pass away like the stain of breath upon a mirror; and there in his stead, quietly at home, trimming the midnight lamp in his study, a man who could afford to laugh at suspicion, would be Henry Jekyll." The pleasures Jekyll experiences as Mr. Hyde, while his own conscience slumbered, are passed over without detail except that what in Jekyll had been "undignified; I would scarce use a harder term," in the person of Hyde "began to turn toward the monstrous. . . . This familiar that I called out of my own soul, and sent forth alone to do his good pleasure, was a being inherently malign and villainous; his every act and thought centered on self; drinking pleasure with bestial avidity from any degree of torture to another; relentless like a man of stone." Hyde's sadism is thus established.

Then things begin to go wrong. It becomes harder and harder to return to Jekyll from the person of Hyde. Sometimes a double dose of the elixir is required, and once at the risk of life, a triple dose. On one occasion there was total failure. Then one morning Jekyll woke up in his own bed in the house on the square and lazily began to examine the illusion that somehow he was in Hyde's house in Soho. "I was still so engaged when, in one of my more wakeful moments, my eyes fell upon my hand. Now the hand of Henry Jekyll (as you have often remarked) was professional in shape and size: it was large, firm, white and comely. But the hand which I now saw, clearly enough, in the yellow light of a mid-London morning, lying half shut on the bed clothes, was lean, corded, knuckly, of a dusky pallor and thickly shaded with a swart growth of hair. It was the hand of Edward

Hyde. . . . Yes, I had gone to bed Henry Jekyll, I had awakened Edward Hyde." He manages to make his way to the laboratory and to restore his Jekyll shape, but the shock of the unconscious transformation goes deep, and he determines to forsake his double existence. "Yes, I preferred the elderly and discontented doctor, surrounded by friends and cherishing honest hopes [*observe the alliteration in this passage*]; and bade a resolute farewell to the liberty, the comparative youth, the light step, leaping impulses and secret pleasures, that I had enjoyed in the disguise of Hyde."

For two months Jekyll persists in this resolution, although he does not give up his house in Soho or Hyde's smaller clothing that lies ready in his laboratory. Then he weakens. "My devil had been long caged, he came out roaring. I was conscious, even when I took the draught of a more unbridled, a more furious propensity to ill." In this furious mood he murders Sir Danvers Carew, stirred to rage by the old man's civilities. After his transports of glee as he mauls the body, a cold thrill of terror disperses the mists. "I saw my life to be forfeit; and fled from the scene of these excesses, at once glorifying and trembling, my lust of evil gratified and stimulated, my love of life screwed to the topmost peg. I ran to the house in Soho, and (to make assurance doubly sure) destroyed my papers; thence I set out through the lamplit streets, in the same divided ecstasy of mind, gloating on my crime, light-headedly devising others in the future, and yet still hastening and still hearkening in my wake for the steps of the avenger. Hyde had a song upon his lips as he compounded the draught, and as he drank it, pledged the dead man. The pangs of transformation had not done tearing him, before Henry Jekyll, with streaming tears of gratitude and remorse, had fallen upon his knees and lifted his clasped hands to God."

With a sense of joy Jekyll sees that his problem is solved and that he dare never again assume the form of the wanted murderer Hyde. For several months he lives a life of exemplary good works, but he was still cursed with duality of purpose and "the lower side of me, so long indulged, so recently chained down, began to growl for license." In his own person, for he can never again risk Hyde, he begins to pursue his secret vices. This brief excursion into evil finally destroyed the balance of his soul. One day, sitting in Regent's Park, "a qualm came over me, a horrid nausea and the most deadly shuddering. These passed away, and left me faint; and then as in its turn faintness subsided, I began to be aware of a change in the temper of my thoughts, a greater boldness, a contempt of danger, a solution of the bonds of obligation. I looked down; my clothes hung formlessly on my shrunken limbs; the hand that lay on my knees was corded and hairy. I was once more Edward Hyde. A moment before I had been safe of all men's respect, wealthy, beloved—the cloth laying for me in the dining-room at home; and now I was the common quarry of mankind, hunted, houseless, a known murderer, thrall to the gallows." As Hyde he cannot return to his house, and so he is forced into the expedient of calling on Dr. Lanyon's help, described in the doctor's letter.

The end now comes with rapidity. The very next morning, crossing the court of his own house, he is again seized by the vertigo of change and it took a double dose to restore him to himself. Six hours later the pangs returned and he had to drink the potion once more. From that time on he was never safe and it required the constant stimulation of the drug to enable him to keep the shape of Jekyll. (It was at one of these moments that Enfield and Utterson conversed with him at the window on the court, a meeting abruptly terminated by the onset of a transformation.) "At all hours of the day and night, I would be taken with the premonitory shudder; above all, if I slept, or even dozed for a moment in my chair, it was always as Hyde that I awakened. Under the strain of this continually impending doom and by the sleeplessness to which I now condemned myself, ay, even beyond what I had thought possible to man, I became, in my own person, a creature eaten up and emptied by fever, languidly weak both in body and mind, and solely occupied by one thought: the horror of my other self. But when I slept, or when the virtue of the medicine wore off, I would leap almost without transition (for the pangs of transformation grew daily less marked) into the possession of a fancy brimming with images of terror, a soul boiling with causeless hatreds, and a body that seemed not strong enough to contain the raging energies of life. The powers of Hyde seemed to have grown with the sickliness of Jekyll. And certainly the hate that now divided them was equal on each side. With Jekyll, it was a thing of vital instinct. He had now seen the full deformity of that creature that shared with him some of the phenomena of consciousness, and was co-heir with him to death: and beyond these links of community, which in themselves made the most poignant part of his distress, he thought of Hyde, for all his energy of life, as of something not only hellish but inorganic. This was the shocking thing; that the slime of the pit seemed to utter cries and voices; that the amorphous dust gesticulated and sinned; that what was dead, and had no shape, should usurp the offices of life. And this again, that that insurgent horror was knit to him closer than a wife, closer than an eye; lay caged in his flesh, where he heard it mutter and felt it struggle to be born; and at every hour of weakness, and in the confidence of slumber, prevailed against him, and deposed him out of life. The hatred of Hyde for Jekyll, was of a different order. His terror of the gallows drove him continually to commit temporary suicide, and return to his subordinate station of a part instead of a person; but he loathed the necessity, he loathed the despondency into which Jekyll was now fallen, and he resented the dislike with which he was himself regarded. Hence the apelike tricks that he would play me, scrawling in my own hand blasphemies on the pages of my books, burning the letters and destroying the portrait of my father; and indeed, had it not been for his fear of death, he would long ago have ruined himself in order to involve me in the ruin. But his love of life is wonderful; I go further: I, who sicken and freeze at the mere thought of him, when I recall the abjection and passion of this attachment, and when I know how he fears my power to cut him off by suicide, I find it in my heart to pity him."

The last calamity falls when the provision of the special salt for his potion begins to run low; when he sends for a fresh order the first change of color occurred but not the second, and no transformation took place. Poole had testified to Utterson of the desperate search for another supply. " 'All this last week (you must know) him, or it, whatever it is that lives in that cabinet, has been crying night and day for some sort of medicine and cannot get it to his mind. It was sometimes his way—the master's, that is— to write his orders on a sheet of paper and throw it on the stair. We've had nothing else this week back; nothing but papers, and a closed door, and the very meals left there to be smuggled in when nobody was looking. Well, sir, every day, ay, and twice and thrice in the same day, there have been orders and complaints, and I have been sent flying to all the wholesale chemists in town. Every time I brought the stuff back, there would be another paper telling me to return it, because it was not pure, and another order to a different firm. This drug is wanted bitter bad, sir, whatever for.'

" 'Have you any of these papers?' asked Mr. Utterson.

"Poole felt in his pocket and handed out a crumpled note, which the lawyer, bending nearer to the candle, carefully examined. Its contents ran thus: 'Dr. Jekyll presents his compliments to Messrs. Maw. He assures them that their last sample is impure and quite useless for his present purpose. In the year 18—, Dr. J. purchased a somewhat large quantity from Messrs. M. He now begs them to search with most sedulous care, and should any of the same quality be left, to forward it to him at once. Expense is no consideration. The importance of this to Dr. J. can hardly be exaggerated.' So far the letter had run composedly enough, but here with a sudden splutter of the pen, the writer's emotion had broken loose. 'For God's sake,' he added, 'find me some of the old.'

" 'This is a strange note,' said Mr. Utterson; and then sharply, 'How do you come to have it open?'

" 'The man at Maw's was main angry, sir, and he threw it back to me like so much dirt,' returned Poole."

Convinced at last that his first supply was impure, that it was the unknown impurity which gave efficacy to the draught, and that he can never renew his supply, Jekyll begins to write the confession and a week later is finishing it under the influence of the last of the old powders. "This, then, is the last time, short of a miracle, that Henry Jekyll can think his own thoughts or see his own face (now how sadly altered!) in the glass." He hastens to conclude lest Hyde suddenly take over and tear the papers to shreds. "Half an hour from now, when I shall again and forever reindue that hated personality, I know how I shall sit shuddering and weeping in my chair, or continue, with the most strained and fearstruck ecstasy of listening, to pace up and down this room (my last earthly refuge) and give ear to every sound of menace. Will Hyde die upon the scaffold? or will he find courage to release himself at the last moment? God knows; I am careless; this is my true hour of death, and what is to follow concerns another than myself. Here then, as I lay down the pen and proceed to seal up my confession, I bring the life of that unhappy Henry Jekyll to an end."

I would like to say a few words about Stevenson's last moments. As you know by now, I am not one to go heavily for the human interest stuff when speaking of books. Human interest is not in my line, as Vronski used to say. But books have their destiny, according to the Latin tag, and sometimes the destinies of authors follow those of their books. There is old Tolstoy in 1910 abandoning his family to wander away and die in a station master's room to the rumble of passing trains that had killed Anna Karenin. And there is something in Stevenson's death in 1894 on Samoa, imitating in a curious way the wine theme and the transformation theme of his fantasy. He went down to the cellar to fetch a bottle of his favorite burgundy, uncorked it in the kitchen, and suddenly cried out to his wife: what's the matter with me, what is this strangeness, has my face changed?—and fell on the floor. A blood vessel had burst in his brain and it was all over in a couple of hours.

What, has my face changed? There is a curious thematical link between this last episode in Stevenson's life and the fateful transformations in his most wonderful book.

Notes on lepidoptera omitted from Nabokov's lecture on "Dr. Jekyll and Mr. Hyde"

There was be a Chinese philosopher who all his life pondered the problem whether he was a chinese philosopher dreaming that he was a butterfly or a butterfly dreaming that he was a philosopher. All these things are concerned with transformation with metamorphosis. Who can explain the process ~~controls~~ in entomological terms?

Transformation Of transformation is a marvelous thing In my capacity of entomologist I am thinking especially of the transformation of ~~lepidoptera~~ butterflies ~~I am~~ Though wonderful to watch, transformation from larva to pupa or from pupa to butterfly is not ~~also~~ a particularly pleasant process for the subject involved. In the There comes a ~~moment in the course of~~ a difficult moment life ~~of~~ every for every caterpillar when he begins to feel pervaded by an odd sort of discomfort. It is a tight feeling here ~~about his neck~~ and here, and then an unbearable itch. Of course he has moulted a few times before but ~~that~~ ~~sensation~~ that was nothing in comparison to the ~~urge~~ particular that he feels now. He must shed that ~~tight~~ dry skin, or die As you have guessed under that skin the armor of a pupa ~~are so impossible to compare ones over ones~~ armor is already forming. I am especially concerned at the moment with those ~~cabbage~~ butterflies carried over that have golden pupa, called also chrysalis which hang from some surface in the open ~~you~~ air.

Well the caterpillar must do something about that horrible feeling. He walks about looking for a suitable place. He li finds it He crawls up a ~~wall or a~~ He makes for himself a little pad of silk on the underside of that perch. twig He B hangs himself by ~~means~~ by the ~~hooks~~ of his ~~cat~~ tail or last legs from ~~the~~ from the silk pad so as to dangle head downwards in the position of an inverted question mark.

I expect you by monday to have finished
Swann's way, ~~by day ach for youto~~
~~and~~ first reading. Then reread the 70 first ~~pages~~ pages twice
give section

Take a sheet of paper. Write a the top: Marcel Proust, 1871 - 1922
Now divide the ~~the~~ paper. On the left you will write the literal
translations of the titles. On the right the more or less fancy
translations that the Moncrieff inflicted upon Proust. ~~Th~~ For
some reason they are lifted from Shakespeare's sonnets.
The title of the whole work ~~with three or other parts~~ is:

parts	P vols	In search of lost time publ. dates: 1913 - 1927	M. ("Remembrance of things Past)
1	(I - II)	The walk by Swann's place oneself	"Swann's way"
2	(III - V)	In the shade of girls becoming young	"Within a budding grove"
3	(VI - VIII)	The Guermantes Walk	"The Guermantes Way"
4	(IX - X)	Sodom and Gomorrah	"Cities of the Plain"
5	(XI - XII)	The captive girl	The captive
6	(XIII)	Vanished Albertine Even	"The sweet cheat gone"
7	(XIV - XV)	Time found again	"The Past recaptured"

(Moncrieff died while translating the work, which
is no wonder and the last volume was
translated by a man called Blossom)
who did quite well.

These seven parts (published
in French in fifteen volumes) make
four thousand pages - about
a month's reading, if you read four
hours per day. It totals about
a million and a half words. Its
scope covers the ~~half century preceding~~ more than a half a century before the past World War One
the treaty of Versailles and it has a   1890   1915
cast of over 200 characters.

25 minutes

The Walk by Swann's Place (1913)

The seven parts of Proust's great novel *In Search of Lost Time* (translated by Moncrieff as *Remembrance of Things Past*) are as follows, the Moncrieff titles in parentheses:

The Walk by Swann's Place (*Swann's Way*)
In the Shade of Blooming Young Girls (*Within a Budding Grove*)
The Guermantes Walk (*The Guermantes Way*)
Sodom and Gomorrah (*Cities of the Plain*)
The Captive Girl (*The Captive*)
Vanished Albertine (*The Sweet Cheat Gone*)
Time Found Again (*The Past Recaptured*)

Moncrieff died while translating the work, which is no wonder, and the last volume was translated by a man called Blossom who did quite well. These seven parts, published in French in fifteen volumes between 1913 and 1927, make 4,000 pages in English or about a million and a half words. In scope the work covers more than half a century from 1840 to 1915, into the First World War, and it has a cast of over two hundred characters. Generally speaking, the society Proust invents belongs to the early 1890s.

Proust began the work in the autumn of 1906 in Paris and completed the first draft in 1912; then he rewrote most of it and kept rewriting and correcting until his very death in 1922. The whole is a treasure hunt where the treasure is time and the hiding place the past: this is the inner meaning of the title *In Search of Lost Time*. The transmutation of sensation into sentiment, the ebb and tide of memory, waves of emotions such as desire, jealousy, and artistic euphoria—this is the material of the enormous and yet singularly light and translucid work.

The opening page from Nabokov's lecture notes on *The Walk by Swann's Place*

In his youth Proust had studied the philosophy of Henri Bergson. Proust's fundamental ideas regarding the flow of time concern the constant evolution of personality in terms of duration, the unsuspected riches of our subliminal minds which we can retrieve only by an act of intuition, of memory, of involuntary associations; also the subordination of mere reason to the genius of inner inspiration and the consideration of art as the only reality in the world; these Proustian ideas are colored editions of the Bergsonian thought. Jean Cocteau has called the work "A giant miniature, full of mirages, of superimposed gardens, of games conducted between space and time."

One thing should be firmly impressed upon your minds: the work is not an autobiography; the narrator is not Proust the person, and the characters never existed except in the author's mind. Let us not, therefore, go into the author's life. It is of no importance in the present case and would only cloud the issue, especially as the narrator and the author do resemble each other in various ways and move in much the same environment.

Proust is a prism. His, or its, sole object is to refract, and by refracting to recreate a world in retrospect. The world itself, the inhabitants of that world, are of no social or historical importance whatever. They happen to be what the gazettes call society people, men and ladies of leisure, the wealthy unemployed. The only professions we are shown in action, or in result, are artistic and scholarly ones. Proust's prismatic people have no jobs: their job is to amuse the author. They are as free to indulge in conversation and pleasure as those legendary ancients that we see so clearly reclining around fruit-laden tables or walking in high discourse over painted floors, but whom we never see in the countinghouse or the shipyard.

In Search of Lost Time is an evocation, not a description of the past, as Arnaud Dandieu, a French critic, has remarked. This evocation of the past, he continues, is made possible by bringing to light a number of exquisitely chosen moments which are a sequence of illustrations, of images. Indeed, the whole enormous work, he concludes, is but an extended comparison revolving on the words *as if*——.* The key to the problem of reestablishing the past turns out to be the key of art. The treasure hunt

*Middleton Murry wrote that if you try to be precise you are bound to be metaphorical. VN

(French) *do not take down the French* In ~~search~~ of lost time

À la Recherche du Temps perdu (1913-1927)   *Remembrance of things past.* (different F.)

"by way of Swann's place"   Scott Moncrieff

296

281 / 218 $\overline{I - II}$ Du côté de chez Swann   ("Swann's Way")   1913

207 / 230 $\overline{III - V}$ À l'ombre des jeune filles en fleurs   1918

" In the shade of ~~groves~~ *fullbloom*   ("Within a Budding" grove)
blooming young girls

224 / 254 / 261 $\overline{VI - VIII}$ ● Le côté de Guermantes   ("The Guermantes Way")   1920-21

The Guermantes ~~side~~ Wall   ("The Guermantes Way")
(places, persons & complex)

337 / 338 $\overline{IX - X}$ Sodome + Gomorrhe   Sôdom and Gomorrah   ("Cities of the Plain")   1921-1922

354 / 263 $\overline{XI - XII}$ La Prisonnière   The captive girl   ("The captive")   1923-24

333 $\overline{XIII}$ Albertine disparue   ● Vanished albertine.   ("The sweet cheat gone")   1925

210 / 230 $\overline{XIV - XV}$ Le temps retrouvé   *time again* Time retrieved   ("The Past recaptured")   *Frederic Blossom*   (6)   1927

4000 pages
(one single the Scott in the English ed.)
8000 minutes
100 hours
one month
4 hours a day

~~The Book which [...] the 20th letters~~   Begun in the autumn of 1906 in Paris; first draft of the whole completed in 1912; then he ~~kept~~ rewrote most of it and kept recasting and correcting till his very death in 1922 [Another title might have been As if going Myself we will take it]

A treasure hunt   where the treasure is time   and the *hiding place* ~~archipelago~~ the past — this is the inner meaner of the title — "In search of lost Time"

The transmutation of sensation into sentiment, the ebb and tide of memory, waves of emotions such as desire, jealousy, *and* and artistic euphoria — ~~these are the ~~reminiscences~~~~ this is the material of their enormous and yet singularly lypt and translucid work.

● " A giant miniature, full of mirages, of superimposed gardens, of ~~interplay~~ *games conducted* between space and time" (Cocteau)

One thing should be firmly imprinted upon your minds: the work is not an autobiography. The ~~I~~ narrator is not Proust the person. ~~The~~ The ~~throughout~~ never existed except in the author's mind. To ~~never~~ come up with the information that Albertine, the young lady of the book was really a man

see 62-64
64-64 *garden*

He means chapps portraits

comes to a happy end in a cave full of music, in a temple rich with stained glass. The gods of standard religions are absent, or, perhaps more correctly, they are dissolved in art.

To a superficial reader of Proust's work—rather a contradiction in terms since a superficial reader will get so bored, so engulfed in his own yawns, that he will never finish the book—to an inexperienced reader, let us say, it might seem that one of the narrator's main concerns is to explore the ramifications and alliances which link together various houses of the nobility, and that he finds a strange delight when he discovers that a person whom he has been considering as a modest businessman revolves in the *grand monde*, or when he discovers some important marriage that has connected two families in a manner such as he had never dreamed possible. The matter-of-fact reader will probably conclude that the main action of the book consists of a series of parties; for example, a dinner occupies a hundred and fifty pages, a soirée half a volume. In the first part of the work, one encounters Mme. Verdurin's philistine salon in the days when it was frequented by Swann and the evening party at Mme. de Saint-Euverte's when Swann first realizes the hopelessness of his passion for Odette; then in the next books there are other drawing rooms, other receptions, a dinner party at Mme. de Guermantes', a concert at Mme. Verdurin's, and the final afternoon party at the same house of the same lady who has now become a Princesse de Guermantes by marriage—that final party in the last volume, *Time Found Again*, during which the narrator becomes aware of the changes that time has wrought upon all his friends and he receives a shock of inspiration—or rather a series of shocks—causing him to decide to set to work without delay upon his book, the reconstruction of the past.

At this late point, then, one might be tempted to say that Proust *is* the narrator, that he *is* the eyes and ears of the book. But the answer is still no. The book that the narrator in Proust's book is supposed to write is still a book-within-the-book and is not quite *In Search of Lost Time*—just as the narrator is not quite Proust. There is a focal shift here which produces a rainbow edge: this is the special Proustian crystal through which we read the book. It is not a mirror of manners, not an autobiography, not a historical account. It is pure fantasy on Proust's part, just as *Anna Karenin* is a fantasy, just as Kafka's "The Metamorphosis" is fantasy—just as Cornell University will be a fantasy if I ever happen to write about it some day in retrospect. The narrator in the work is one of its characters, who is called Marcel. In other words, there is Marcel the eavesdropper and there is Proust the author. Within the novel the narrator Marcel contemplates, in the last volume, the ideal novel he will write. Proust's work is only a copy of that ideal novel—but what a copy!

———————

The Walk by Swann's Place (*Swann's Way*) must be viewed from the correct angle; it must be seen in relation to the completed work as Proust meant it to be seen. In order to understand in full the initial volume we must first accompany the narrator to the party in the last volume. This will be taken up in greater detail later, but for the moment one must listen to what Marcel says there as he is beginning to understand the shocks that he has experienced. "What we call reality is a certain relationship between sensations and memories which surround us at the same time, the only true relationship, which the writer must recapture so that he may for ever link together in his phrase its two distinct elements. One may list in an interminable description the objects that figured in the place described, but truth will begin only when the writer takes two different objects, establishes their relationship, and encloses them in the necessary rings of his style (art), or even when, like life itself, comparing similar qualities in two sensations, he makes their essential nature stand out clearly by joining them in a metaphor in order to remove them from the contingencies (the accidents) of time, and links them together by means of timeless words. From this point of view regarding the true way of art [Marcel asks himself], was not nature herself a beginning of art, she who had often allowed me to know the beauty of something only a long time afterwards and only through something else—midday at Combray through the remembered sound of its bells and the tastes of its flowers."

This mention of Combray introduces the important theme of the two walks. The flow of the novel in all its seven parts (seven parts like the seven days of an initial creative week with no rest on Sunday)—through all those volumes the narrator keeps in his field of vision those two walks that he used to take as a child in the tiny town of Combray: the walk in the direction of Méséglise by way of Swann's place, Tansonville, and the walk in the direction of the Guermantes' country place. The whole story through all its fifteen volumes in the French edition is an investigation of the people related in one way or another to the two walks of his young life. Particularly, the narrator's distress about his mother's kiss is a foreglimpse of Swann's distress and love, just as the child's love for Gilberte and then the main love affair with a girl called Albertine are amplifications of the affair that Swann has with Odette. But the two walks have a further significance. As Derrick Leon writes in his *Introduction to Proust* (1940): "Marcel does not realize until he sees the two walks of his childhood united in Swann's granddaughter (Gilberte's child) that the segments into which we splice life are purely arbitrary, and correspond not to any aspect of life itself, but only to the deficient vision through which we perceive it. The separate worlds of Madame Verdurin, Madame Swann, and Madame de Guermantes are essentially the same world, and it is only snobbery or some accident of social custom that has ever separated them. They are the same world not because Madame Verdurin finally marries the Prince de Guermantes, not because Swann's daughter eventually marries Madame de Guermantes' nephew, and not because Odette herself crowns her career by becoming Monsieur de Guermantes' mistress, but because each of them revolves in an orbit which is formed by similar elements—and this is the automatic, superficial, mechanical quality of existence" that we already know from Tolstoy's works.*

———

Style, I remind you, is the manner of an author, the particular manner that sets him apart from any other author. If I select for you three passages from three different authors whose works you know—if I select them in such a way that nothing in their subject matter affords any clue, and if then you cry out with delightful assurance: "That's Gogol, that's Stevenson, and by golly that's Proust"—you are basing your choice on striking differences in style. The style of Proust contains three especially distinctive elements:

1. A wealth of metaphorical imagery, layer upon layer of comparisons. It is through this prism that we view the beauty of Proust's work. For Proust the term *metaphor* is often used in a loose sense, as a synonym for the hybrid form,** or for comparison in general, because for him the simile constantly grades into the metaphor, and vice versa, with the metaphorical moment predominating.

2. A tendency to fill in and stretch out a sentence to its utmost breadth and length, to cram into the stocking of the sentence a miraculous number

———

*Here and elsewhere VN has occasionally included his own phrasing or interpolated remarks in quotations. Ed.
**VN illustrates a simple simile as "the mist was like a veil"; a simple metaphor as "there was a veil of mist"; and a hybrid simile as "the veil of the mist was like the sleep of silence," combining both simile and metaphor. Ed.

———

Nabokov's notes on imagery from his lecture on *The Walk by Swann's Place*

I want to refresh your memories in regard to
the use of such terms as Imagery, metaphor, simile,
etcetera.

Imagery

Comparison · · world picture · · · · · · other

simile · metaphor · · · · · · · · · · · · combination of both.

Dummies

Simile :   the mist ~~was~~ like a veil

(integrated simile =)
~~metaphor~~   there is as a
metaphor :   ~~~~~ veil of the mist

hybrid :   the veil of the mist ~~was~~ like ~~~~ the sleep
                                                    ~~~~~ of silence

In the case of Proust the term metaphor
is often used in a loose sense — as
a synonym of hybrid form or, generally, comparison,
because in Proust the simile constantly
grades into the metaphor and vice versa, with
the metaphorical moment predominating

of clauses, parenthetic phrases, subordinate clauses, sub-subordinate clauses. Indeed, in verbal generosity he is a veritable Santa.

3. With older novelists there used to be a very definite distinction between the descriptive passage and the dialogue part: a passage of descriptive matter and then the conversation taking over, and so on. This of course is a method still used today in conventional literature, B-grade and C-grade literature that comes in bottles, and an ungraded literature that comes in pails. But Proust's conversations and his descriptions merge into one another, creating a new unity where flower and leaf and insect belong to one and the same blossoming tree.

"For a long time I used to go to bed early." This opening sentence of the work is the key to the theme, with its center in a sensitive boy's bedroom. The boy tries to sleep. "I could hear the whistling of trains, which, now nearer and now farther off, underscoring the distance like the note of a bird in a forest, unfolded for me in perspective the deserted countryside through which a traveller would be hurrying towards the nearest station: the path that he followed being fixed for ever in his memory by the general excitement due to being in a strange place, to doing unusual things, to the last words of conversation, to farewells exchanged beneath an unfamiliar lamp which echoed still in his ears amid the silence of the night; and to the delightful prospect of being once again home." The whistling of the train underscores the distance like the note of a bird in a wind, an additional simile, an inner comparison, which is a typical Proustian device to add all possible color and force to a picture. Then follows the logical development of the train idea, the description of a traveler and of his sensations. This unfolding of an image is a typical Proustian device. It differs from Gogol's rambling comparisons by its logic and by its poetry. Gogol's comparison is always grotesque, a parody of Homer, and his metaphors are nightmares, whereas Proust's are dreams.

A little later we have the metaphorical creation of a woman in the boy's sleep. "Sometimes, too, just as Eve was created from a rib of Adam, so a woman would come into existence while I was sleeping, conceived from some strain in the position of my thigh.... My body, conscious that its own warmth was permeating hers, would strive to become one with her, and I would awake. The rest of humanity seemed very remote in comparison with this woman whose company I had left but a moment ago: my cheek was still warm with her kiss, my body bent beneath the weight of hers. If, as would sometimes happen, she had the appearance of some woman whom I had known in waking hours, I would abandon myself altogether to the sole quest of her, like people who set out on a journey to see with their own eyes some city that they have always longed to visit, and imagine that they can taste in reality what has charmed their fancy. Gradually, the memory of her would dissolve and vanish, until I had forgotten the daughter of my dream." Again we have the unfolding device: the quest of the woman likened to people who journey to places, and so forth. Incidental quests and visitations and disappointments will form one of the main themes of the whole work.

The unfolding may cover years in a single passage. From the boy dreaming, waking, and falling asleep again, we pass imperceptibly to his habits of sleeping and waking as a man, in the present time of his narration. "When a man is asleep, he has in a circle round him the chain of the hours, the order of years and worlds. Instinctively, when he awakes, he looks to these, and in an instant reads off his own position on the earth's surface and the amount of time that has elapsed during his slumbers. . . . But for me [as a man] it was enough if, in my own bed, my sleep was so heavy as completely to relax my consciousness; for then I lost all sense of the place in which I had gone to sleep, and when I awoke at midnight, not knowing where I was, I could not be sure at first who I was; I had only the most rudimentary sense of existence, such as may lurk and flicker in the depths of an animal's consciousness; I was more destitute of things than the cave-dweller; but then the memory, not yet of the place in which I was, but of various other places where I had lived, and might now very possibly be, would come like a rope let down from heaven to draw me up out of the abyss of not-being, from which I could never have escaped myself. . . ."

The body's memory would then take over, and "would make an effort to deduce first from the form which its tiredness took the orientation of its various members, and then to deduce from that where the wall lay and the furniture stood, to piece together and to give a name to the house in which it must be living. The body's memory, the composite memory of its ribs, knees, and shoulder-blades, offered it a whole series of rooms in which it had at one time or another slept; while the unseen walls kept changing, adapting themselves to the shape of each successive room that it remembered, whirling through the darkness. And even before my brain, hesitating on the threshold of time and forms, had collected sufficient impressions to enable it to identify the room, it, my body, would recall from each room in succession what the bed was like, where the doors were, how daylight came in the windows, whether there was a passage outside, what I had had in my mind when I went to sleep, and had found there when I awoke." We go through a succession of rooms and their metaphors. For a moment he is a child again in a big bed with a canopy, "and at once I would say to myself, 'Why, I must have gone to sleep after all, and Mamma never came to say good night!' " At such a moment he was back in the country with his grandfather, who had died years ago. Then he is at Gilberte's house (she is now Mme. de Saint-Loup) in Swann's old house in Tansonville, and in a succession of rooms in winter and in summer. Finally he actually wakes up in present time (as a man) in his own house in Paris, but his memory having been set in motion: "usually I did not attempt to go to sleep again at once, but used to spend the greater part of the night recalling our life in the old days at Combray with my great-aunt, at Balbec, Paris, Doncières, Venice, and the rest; recalling all the places and people that I had known, what I had actually seen of them, and what others had told me."

Then with this mention of Combray, he is once more in his childhood and back in the time of the narrative: "At Combray, as every afternoon ended, long before the time when I should have to go up to bed, and to lie there, unsleeping, far from my mother and grandmother, my bedroom became the fixed point on which my melancholy and anxious thoughts were centered." When he was especially wretched, the time before dinner was occupied by a magic lantern telling a medieval tale of the evil Golo and the good Geneviève de Brabant (a forerunner of the Duchess de Guermantes). This magic lantern "movement," or "event," becomes connected by the dining-room lamp to the little parlor where the family would adjourn after dinner on wet evenings, and the rain then serves to introduce his grandmother—the most noble and pathetic character in the book—who would insist on walking in the wet garden. Swann is introduced: "we heard, from the far end of the garden, not the profuse and shrill bell which drenched and stunned with its icy, rusty, interminable sound any passing member of the household who set it going by pushing through 'without ringing,' but the double peal—timid, oval, golden—of the visitor's bell. . . . and then, soon after, my grandfather would say: 'I can hear Swann's voice.' . . . Although a far younger man, M. Swann was very much attached to my grandfather, who had been an intimate friend, in his time, of Swann's father, an excellent but an eccentric man in whom the least little thing would, it seemed, often check the flow of his spirits and divert the current of his thoughts." Swann is a man of fashion, an art expert, an exquisite Parisian greatly in vogue in the highest society; but his Combray friends, the narrator's family, have no idea of his position and think of him only as the son of their old friend, the stockbroker. One of the elements of the book is the various ways in which a person is seen by various eyes, as for instance Swann through the prism of Marcel's great aunt's notions: "One day when he had come to see us after dinner in Paris, and had apologized for being in evening clothes, Françoise [the cook], when he had gone, told us that she had got it from his coachman that he had been dining 'with a princess.' 'Some princess of the demi-monde, a courtesan,' drawled my aunt; and she shrugged her shoulders without raising her eyes from her knitting, serenely ironical."

One essential difference exists between the Proustian and the Joycean methods of approaching their characters. Joyce takes a complete and absolute character, God-known, Joyce-known, then breaks it up into fragments and scatters these fragments over the space-time of his book. The good rereader gathers these puzzle pieces and gradually puts them together. On the other hand, Proust contends that a character, a personality, is never known as an absolute but always as a comparative one. He does not chop it up but shows it as it exists through the notions about it of other characters. And he hopes, after having given a series of these prisms and shadows, to combine them into an artistic reality.

The introduction ends with Marcel's description of his despair when visitors forced him to say goodnight downstairs and his mother would not come up to his bedroom for a goodnight kiss; and the story proper begins with a particular arrival of Swann: "We were all in the garden when the double peal of the gate-bell sounded shyly. Everyone knew that it must be Swann, and yet they looked at one another inquiringly and sent my grandmother scouting." The metaphor of the kiss is complex and will run through the whole work. "I never took my eyes off my mother. I knew that when they were at table I should not be permitted to stay there for the whole of dinner-time, and that Mamma, for fear of annoying my father, would not allow me to give her in public the series of kisses that she would have had in my room. And so I promised myself that in the dining-room as they began to eat and drink and as I felt the hour approach, I would put beforehand into this kiss, which was bound to be so brief and stealthy in execution, everything that my own efforts could put into it: would look out very carefully first the exact spot on her cheek where I would imprint it, and would so prepare my thoughts that I might be able, thanks to these mental preliminaries, to consecrate the whole of the minute Mamma would allow me to the sensation of her cheek against my lips, as a painter who can have his subject for short sittings only prepares his palette beforehand, and from what he remembers and from rough notes does in advance everything which he can possibly do in the sitter's absence. But that night, before the dinner-bell had sounded, my grandfather said with unconscious ferocity: 'The little man looks tired; he'ld better go up to bed. Besides, we are dining late tonight.' . . .

"I was about to kiss Mamma, but at that moment the dinner-bell rang.

" 'No, no, leave your mother alone. You've said good night quite enough. These exhibitions are absurd. Go on upstairs.' "

The agony the young Marcel undergoes, the note he writes to his mother, his anticipation, and his tears when she does not appear foreshadow the theme of despairing jealousy he will endure, so that a direct connection is established between his emotions and Swann's emotions. He imagines that Swann would have laughed heartily could he have seen the contents of the letter to his mother, "whereas, on the contrary, as I was to learn in due course, a similar anguish had been the bane of his life for many years, and no one perhaps could have understood my feelings at that moment so well as himself; to him, that anguish which lies in knowing that the creature one adores is in some place of enjoyment where oneself is not and cannot follow—to him that anguish came through Love, to which it is in a sense predestined, by which it must be taken over and specialized. . . . And the joy with which I first bound myself apprentice when Françoise returned to tell me that my letter would be delivered, Swann, too, had known well that false joy which a friend can give us, or some relative of the woman we love, when on his arrival at the private house or theatre where she is to be found, for some ball or party or 'first night' at which he is to see her, he finds us wandering outside, desperately awaiting some opportunity of communicating with her. He recognises us, greets us familiarly, and asks what we are doing there. And when we invent a story of having some urgent message to give to her (his relative or friend), he assures us that nothing could be more simple, takes us in at the door, and promises to send her down to us in five minutes. . . . Alas! Swann had learned by experience that the good intentions of a third party are powerless to control a woman who is annoyed to find herself pursued even into a ball-room by a man whom she does not love. Too often, the kind friend comes down again alone.

"My mother did not appear, but with no attempt to safeguard my self-respect (which depended upon her keeping up the fiction that she had asked me to let her know the result of my search for something or other) made Françoise tell me, in so many words 'There is no answer'—words I have so often, since then, heard the janitors of public dancing-halls and the flunkeys in gambling-clubs and the like, repeat to some poor girl, who replies in bewilderment: 'What! he's said nothing? It's not possible. You did give him my letter, didn't you? Very well, I shall wait a little longer.' And just as she invariably protests that she does not need the extra gas which the janitor offers to light for her, and sits on there . . . so, having declined Françoise's offer to make me some tisane or to stay beside me, I let her go off again to the servants' hall, and lay down and shut my eyes, and tried not to hear the voices of my family who were drinking their after-dinner coffee in the garden."

This episode is followed by a description of the moonlight and silence which perfectly illustrates Proust's working of metaphors within metaphors.

The boy opens his window and sits on the foot of his bed, hardly daring to move lest he be heard by those below. (1) "Things outside seemed also fixed in mute expectation." (2) They seemed not to wish "to disturb the moonlight." (3) Now what was the moonlight doing? The moonlight duplicated every object and seemed to push it back owing to the forward extension of a shadow. What kind of a shadow? A shadow that seemed "denser and more concrete than the object" itself. (4) By doing all this the moonlight "made the whole landscape at once leaner and larger like [*additional simile*] a map which is unfolded and spread out" f'at. (5) There was some movement: "What had to move—the leafage of some chestnut-tree, for instance—moved. But its punctilious shiver [*what kind of shiver?*] complete, finished to the least shade, to the least delicate detail [*this fastidious shiver*] did not encroach upon the rest of the scene, did not grade into it, remaining clearly limited"—since it happened to be illumined by the moon and all the rest was in shadow. (6) The silence and the distant sounds. Distant sounds behaved in relation to the surface of silence in the same way as the patch of moonlit moving leafage in relation to the velvet of the shade. The most distant sound, coming from "gardens at the far end of the town, could be distinguished with such exact 'finish,' that the impression they gave of remoteness [*an additional simile follows*] seemed due only to their 'pianissimo' execution [*again a simile follows*] like those movements on muted strings" at the Conservatory. Now those muted strings are described: "although one does not lose one single note," they come from "outside, a long way from the concert hall so that [*and now we are in that concert hall*] all the old subscribers, and my grandmother's sisters too, when Swann gave them his seats, used to strain their ears as if [*final simile*] they had caught the distant approach of an army on the march, which had not yet rounded the corner" of the street.

The pictorial effects of moonlight change with era and author. There is a resemblance between Gogol, writing *Dead Souls* in 1840, and Proust composing this description about 1910. But Proust's description makes the metaphoric system still more complicated, and it is poetic, not grotesque. In describing a moonlit garden Gogol would also have used rich imagery, but his rambling comparisons would have turned the way of grotesque exaggeration and some beautiful bit of irrational nonsense. For instance, he might have compared the moonlit effect to linen fallen from a wash line, as he does somewhere in *Dead Souls*; but then he might ramble away and say the moonlight on the ground was like sheets and shirts that the wind had scattered while the washerwoman peacefully slept, dreaming of suds and starch and the pretty new frock her sister-in-law had bought. In Proust's case the peculiar point is that he drifts from the idea of pale light to that of remote music—the sense of vision grades into the sense of hearing.

But Proust had a precursor. In part six, chapter 2, of Tolstoy's *War and Peace* (1864-1869) Prince Andrey stays at the country manor of an acquaintance, Count Rostov. He cannot sleep. I have slightly revised Garnett: "Prince Andrey left his bed and went up to the window to open it. As soon as he had unfolded its shutters, the moonlight broke into the room as if it had been waiting a long time outside on the watch for such a chance. He opened the window. The night was cool and motionlessly luminous. The trimmed trees that stood in a row just in front of the window were black on one side and silvery bright on the other. . . . Beyond them was [some kind of] a roof all shining with dew. On the right stood a great thick-leaved tree, its bole and branches a brilliant white, and overhead an almost full moon was riding the starless spring sky.

"Presently at the window of the floor above him he hears two young feminine voices—one of them belongs to Natasha Rostov—singing and repeating a musical phrase. . . . A little later Natasha leans out of that window above and he hears the rustle of her dress and the sound of her breathing," and "The sounds became still like the moon and the shadows."

Three things are to be noted in Tolstoy as foreglimpses of Proust:

1. The expectancy of the moonlight lying in wait (a pathetic fallacy). Beauty ready to rush in, a fawning and dear creature at the moment it is perceived by the human mind.

2. The clearcut quality of the description, a landscape firmly etched in silver and black, with no conventional phrases and with no borrowed moons. It is all real, authentic, sensuously seen.

3. The close association of the visible and the heard, of shadow light and shadow sound, of ear and eye.

Compare these to the evolution of the image in Proust. Notice the elaboration of the moonlight in Proust, the shadows that come out of the light like the drawers of a chest, and the remoteness and the music.

The various layers and levels of sense in Proust's own metaphors are interestingly illustrated by the description of his grandmother's method of selecting gifts. *First layer:* "She would have liked me to have in my room photographs of ancient buildings or of the most beautiful landscapes. But at the moment of buying them, and for all that the subject of the picture had an aesthetic value of its own, she would find that vulgarity and utility had too prominent a part in them, through the mechanical nature of their reproduction by photography. [*Second layer:*] She attempted by a subterfuge, if not to eliminate altogether their commercial banality, at least to minimise it, to substitute for the bulk of it what was art still, to introduce, as it might be, several 'layers' of art; instead of photographs of Chartres Cathedral, of the Fountains of Saint-Cloud, or of Vesuvius she would inquire of Swann if some great painter had not made pictures of them, and preferred to give me photographs of 'Chartres Cathedral' after Corot, of the 'Fountains of Saint-Cloud' after Hubert Robert, and of 'Vesuvius' after Turner, and this brought her present up to an additional stage in the scale of art. [*Third layer:*] But although the photographer had been prevented from reproducing directly the masterpieces or the beauties of nature, and had there been replaced by a great artist, he was there again, in possession of his rights, when it came to reproducing the artist's interpretation. Accordingly, having to reckon again with vulgarity, my grandmother would endeavour to make it recede still farther. She would ask Swann if the picture had not been engraved, [*fourth layer:*] preferring, when possible, old engravings with some interest of association apart from themselves, such, for example, as shew us a masterpiece in a state in which we can no longer see it today, as Morghen's print of the 'Last Supper' of Leonardo before it was spoiled by restoration." The same method was followed when she made presents of antique furniture or when she gave Marcel the old-fashioned novels of George Sand (1804-1876) written fifty years before.

With his mother reading to him—from these George Sand novels—the first bedtime theme ends. These first sixty pages of the English translation are complete in themselves and contain most of the stylistic elements found throughout the novel. As Derrick Leon remarks: "Enriched by his remarkable and comprehensive culture, by his deep love and understanding of classical literature, of music and of painting, the whole work displays a wealth of similes derived with an equal aptness and facility from biology, from physics, from botany, from medicine, or from mathematics, that never ceases to astonish and delight."

The next six pages also form a complete episode, or theme, which in fact serves as a foreword to the Combray part of the novel's narrative. This episode, which can be titled "The Miracle of the Linden Blossom Tea," is the famous recollection of the madeleine. These pages start with a metaphorical summary of the first, or bedtime theme. "And so it was that, for a long time afterwards, when I lay awake at night and revived old memories of Combray, I saw no more of it than this sort of luminous wedge, sharply defined against a vague and shadowy background, like the triangles of light which a Bengal fire or some electric sign will bring out and dissect on the front of a building the other parts of which remain plunged in darkness: at the broadest base of this wedge there was the little parlour, the dining-room, the thrill of the dark path along which would come M. Swann, the unconscious author of my sufferings, the hall through which I would journey to the first step of that staircase; so hard to climb, which constituted, all by itself, the tapering part of that irregular pyramid; and, at the summit, my bedroom, with the little passage through whose glazed door Mamma would enter. . . ."

It is important to recognize that the significance of these memories is at this time, even as they accumulate, lost on the narrator. "It is a labour in vain to attempt to recapture [the past]: all the efforts of our intellect must prove futile. The past is hidden somewhere outside the realm, beyond the reach of intellect, in some material object (in the sensation which that material object will give us) which we do not suspect. And as for that object, it depends on chance whether we come upon it or not before we ourselves must die." It is only at the last party, in the final volume of the whole work, that the narrator, by then an old man of fifty, received in rapid succession three shocks, three revelations (what present-day critics would call an *epiphany*)—the combined sensations of the present and recollections of the past—the uneven cobbles, the tingle of a spoon, the stiffness of a napkin. And for the first time he realizes the *artistic importance* of this experience.

In the course of his life the narrator had experienced several such shocks,

---

Nabokov's annotations on Marcel's recollection of the madeleine

of it. I place in position before my mind's eye the still recent taste of that first mouthful, and I feel something starting within me, something that leaves its resting-place and attempts to rise, something that ~~has been~~ embedded like an anchor at a great depth; I do not know yet what it is, but I can feel it mounting slowly; I can measure the resistance, I can hear the echo of great spaces traversed.

Undoubtedly what is thus palpitating in the depths of my being must be the image, the visual memory which, being linked to that taste, has tried to follow it into my conscious mind. But its struggles are too far off, too much confused; scarcely can I perceive the ~~colourless~~ reflection in which are blended the ~~inextinguishable~~ whirling medley of ~~radiant~~ hues, and I cannot distinguish its form, cannot invite it, as the one possible interpreter, to translate to me the evidence of its contemporary, its inseparable paramour, the taste of cake soaked in tea; cannot ask it to inform me what special circumstance is in question, of what period in my past life.

Will it ultimately reach the clear surface of my consciousness, this old, dead moment which the magnetism of an identical moment has travelled so far to importune, to disturb, to raise up out of the very depths of my being? I cannot tell. Now ~~that~~ I feel nothing, it has stopped, has perhaps gone down again into its darkness; from which who can say whether it will ever rise? Ten times over I must essay the task, must lean down over the abyss. And each time ~~the natural~~ laziness which deters us from every difficult enterprise, every work of importance, has urged me to leave the thing alone, to drink my tea and to think merely of the worries of today and of my hopes for tomorrow, which let themselves be pondered over without effort or distress of mind.

And suddenly the memory returns. The taste was that of the little ~~crumb~~ of madeleine which on Sunday mornings at Combray (because on those mornings I did not go out before church-time), when I went to say good day to her in her bedroom, my aunt Léonie used to give me, dipping it first in her own cup of tea or of lime-flower tea. The sight of the little madeleine had recalled nothing to my mind before I tasted it; perhaps because I had so often seen such things in the interval, without tasting them, on the trays in pastry-cooks' windows, that their image had dissociated itself from those Combray days to take its place among others more recent; perhaps because of those memories, so long abandoned and put out of mind, nothing now survived, everything was scattered; the forms of things, including that of the little scallop-shell of pastry, so richly sensual under its severe, religious folds, were either obliterated or had been so long dormant as to have lost the power of expansion which would have allowed them to resume their place in my consciousness. But when from a long-distant past nothing subsists, after the people are dead, after the things are broken and scattered, still, alone, more fragile, but with more vitality, more unsubstantial, more persistent, more faithful, the smell and taste of things remain poised a long time, like souls, ready to remind us, waiting and hoping ~~for their moment,~~ amid the ruins of all the rest; and bear unfaltering, ~~in the tiny and~~ almost impalpable drop, ~~of their essence, the vast~~ structure of recollection.

And once I had recognised the taste of the ~~crumb~~ of madeleine soaked in her decoction of lime-flowers which my aunt used to give me (although I did not yet know and must long postpone the discovery of why this memory made me so happy) immediately the old grey house upon the

however, without then recognizing their importance. The first of these is the madeleine. One day when he was a man of, say, thirty, long after the days spent in Combray as a child, "one day in winter, as I came home, my mother, seeing that I was cold, offered me some tea, a thing I did not ordinarily take. I declined at first, and then, for no particular reason, changed my mind. She sent out for one of those stubby, plump little cakes called 'petites madeleines,' which look as though they had been moulded in the fluted scallop of a pilgrim's shell. And soon, mechanically, weary after a dull day with the prospect of a depressing morrow, I raised to my lips a spoonful of the tea in which I had soaked a morsel of the cake. No sooner had the warm liquid, and the crumbs with it, touched my palate than a shudder ran through me, and I stopped, intent upon the extraordinary changes that were taking place in me. An exquisite pleasure had invaded my senses, but individual, detached, with no suggestion of its origin. And at once the vicissitudes of life had become indifferent to me, its disasters innocuous, its brevity an illusion—this new sensation having had on me the effect which love has of filling me with a precious essence; or rather this essence was not in me, it was myself. I had ceased now to feel mediocre, accidental, mortal. Whence could it have come to me, this mighty joy? I was conscious that it was connected with the taste of tea and cake, but that it infinitely transcended those savours, could not, indeed, be of the same nature as theirs. Whence did it come? What did it signify? How could I seize upon and define it?"

Further mouthfuls begin to lose their magic. Marcel puts down the cup and compels his mind to examine the sensation until he is fatigued. After a rest he resumes the concentration of all his energies. "I place in position before my mind's eye the still recent taste of that first mouthful, and I feel something start within me, something that leaves its resting-place and attempts to rise, something that is loosened like an anchor that had been embedded at a great depth; I do not know yet what it is, but I can feel it mounting slowly; I can measure the resistance, I can hear the confused echo of great spaces traversed." There is a further struggle to clarify from the sensation of taste the visual memory of the occasion in the past that gave rise to the experience. "And suddenly the memory returns. The taste was that of the little bit of madeleine which on Sunday mornings at Combray (because on those mornings I did not go out before church-time), when I

Nabokov's map of the streets of Combray in his teaching copy of *Swann's Way*

street, where her room was, rose up like the scenery of a theatre to attach itself to the little pavilion, opening on to the garden, which had been built out behind it for my parents (the isolated panel which until that moment had been all that I could see); and with the house the town, from morning to night and in all weathers, the Square where I was sent before luncheon, the streets along which I used to run errands, the country roads we took when it was fine. And just as the Japanese amuse themselves by filling a porcelain bowl with water and steeping in it little crumbs of paper which until then are without character or form, but, the moment they become wet, stretch themselves and bend, take on colour and distinctive shape, become flowers or houses or people, permanent and recognisable, so in that moment all the flowers in our garden and in M. Swann's park, and the water-lilies on the Vivonne and the good folk of the village and their little dwellings and the parish church and the whole of Combray and of its surroundings, taking their proper shapes and growing solid, sprang into being, town and gardens alike, from my cup of tea.

COMBRAY at a distance, from a twenty-mile radius, as we used to see it from the railway when we arrived there every year in Holy Week, was no more than a church epitomising the town, representing it, speaking of it and for it to the horizon, and as one drew near, gathering close about its long, dark cloak, sheltering from the wind, on the open plain, as a shepherd gathers his sheep, the woolly grey backs of its flocking houses, which a fragment of its mediaeval ramparts enclosed, here and there, in an outline as scrupulously circular as that of a little town in a primitive painting. To live in, Combray was a trifle depressing, like its streets, whose houses, built of the blackened stone of the country, fronted with outside steps, capped with gables which projected long shadows downwards, were so dark that one had, as soon as the sun began to go down, to draw back the curtains in the sitting-room windows; streets with the solemn names of Saints, not a few of whom figured in the history of the early lords of Combray, such as the Rue Saint-Hilaire, the Rue Saint-Jacques, in which my aunt's house stood, the Rue Sainte-Hildegarde, which ran past her railings, and the Rue du Saint-Esprit, on to which the little garden gate opened; and these Combray streets exist in so remote a quarter of my memory, painted in colours so different from those in which the world is decked for me today, that in fact one and all of them, and the church which towered above them in the Square, seem to me now more unsubstantial than the projections of my magic-lantern; while at times I feel that to be able to cross the Rue Saint-Hilaire again, to engage a room in the Rue de l'Oiseau, in the old hostelry of the Oiseau Flesché, from whose windows in the pavement

went to say good day to her in her bedroom, my aunt Léonie used to give me, dipping it first in her own cup of tea or of lime-flower infusion. . . .

"And once I had recognised the taste of the bit of madeleine soaked in her decoction of lime-flowers which my aunt used to give me (although I did not yet know and must long postpone the discovery of why this memory made me so happy) immediately the old grey house upon the street, where her room was, rose up like the scenery of a theatre to attach itself to the little pavilion, opening on to the garden. . . . And just as the Japanese amuse themselves by filling a porcelain bowl with water and steeping in it little bits of paper which until then are without character or form, but, the moment they become wet, stretch themselves and bend, take on colour and distinctive shape, become flowers or houses or people, permanent and recognisable, so in that moment all the flowers in our garden and in M. Swann's park, and the water-lilies on the Vivonne and the good folk of the village and their little dwellings and the parish church and the whole of Combray and of its surroundings, taking their proper shapes and acquiring substance, sprang into being, town and gardens alike, from my cup of tea."

This is the end of the second theme and the magical introduction to the Combray section of the volume. For the larger purposes of the work as a whole, however, attention must be called to the confession, "although I did not yet know and must long postpone the discovery of why this memory made me so happy." Other recalls of the past will come from time to time in this work, also making him happy, but their significance is never apprehended until, extraordinarily, in the final volume the series of shocks to his senses and to his memories fuse into one great apprehension and, triumphantly—to repeat—he realizes the artistic importance of his experience and so can begin to write the great account of *In Search of Lost Time*.

———

The section titled "Combray" comes in a part of the book devoted to this Aunt Léonie—her room, her relationship with Françoise the cook, her interest in the life of the town in which she could not join physically, being an invalid. These are easy pages to read. Note Proust's system. For a hundred and fifty pages before her casual death, Aunt Léonie is the center in the web from which radiations go to the garden, to the street, to the church, to the walks around Combray, and every now and then back to Aunt Léonie's room.

Leaving his aunt to gossip with Françoise, Marcel accompanies his parents to church and the famous description of the church of Saint-Hilaire at Combray follows, with all its iridescent reflections, its fantasies of glass and of stone. When the name of Guermantes is mentioned for the first time, that romantically noble family emerges from the inner colors of the church. "Two tapestries of high warp represented the coronation of Esther (in which tradition would have it that the weaver had given to Ahasuerus the features of one of the kings of France and to Esther those of a lady of Guermantes whose lover he had been); their colours had melted into one another, so as to add expression, relief, light to the pictures." One need not repeat that since Proust had invented the whole Guermantes family he could not specify the king. We inspect the inside of the church and then we are outside again; and here begins the lovely theme of the steeple—the steeple that is seen from everywhere, "inscribing its unforgettable form upon a horizon beneath which Combray had not yet appeared," as when one approached by train. "And on one of the longest walks we ever took from Combray there was a spot where the narrow road emerged suddenly on to an immense plain, closed at the horizon by strips of forest over which rose and stood alone the fine point of Saint-Hilaire's steeple, but so sharpened and so pink that it seemed to be no more than sketched on the sky by the finger-nail of a painter anxious to give such a landscape, to so pure a piece of 'nature,' this little sign of art, this single indication of human existence." The whole of the description merits careful study. There is an intense vibration of poetry about the whole passage, about the purple spire rising above the jumbled roofs, a kind of pointer to a series of recollections, the exclamation mark of tender memory.

A simple transition leads us to a new character. We have been to church, we are on our way home, and we often meet M. Legrandin, a civil engineer who would visit his Combray home on weekends. He is not only a civil engineer, he is also a man of letters and, as it gradually will appear through the book, the most perfect specimen of vulgar snob. On coming home we find Aunt Léonie again, who has a visitor, a certain energetic albeit deaf spinster, Eulalie. We are ready for a meal. The cooking abilities of Françoise are beautifully brought into juxtaposition with the artistic carving of the quatrefoils on the porches of thirteenth-century cathedrals. In other words, the steeple is still with us, looming above the fancy food. The chocolate cream is to be marked. Taste buds play a very poetical part in Proust's system of reconstructing the past. This cream of chocolate was as "light and fleeting as an 'occasional piece' of music, into which [Françoise] had poured the whole of her talent. . . . To have left even the tiniest morsel in the dish would have shewn as much discourtesy as to rise and leave a concert hall while the 'piece' was still being played, and under the composer's very eyes."

An important theme is taken up in the next pages, leading to one of the main ladies in the book, the lady whom we shall later know as Odette Swann, Swann's wife, but who in these pages appears as an anonymous earlier recollection of Marcel—the lady in pink. This is how her appearance is brought about. At one time an uncle lived in the same house in Combray, Uncle Adolphe, but he is no longer there. In his boyhood the author visited him in Paris and liked to discuss theatrical matters with him. Names of great actresses pop up with one invented character named Berma among them. Uncle Adolphe was apparently a gay dog, and on one rather embarrassing occasion Marcel meets there a young woman in a pink silk dress, a *cocotte*, a lady of light morals, whose love may be bought for a diamond or a pearl. It is this charming lady who is going to become Swann's wife; but her identity is a secret well kept from the reader.

Back we go again to Combray and Aunt Léonie, who as a kind of household goddess dominates this whole part of the book. She is an invalid lady, somewhat grotesque, but also very pathetic, who is cut off from the world by sickness but is intensely curious about every piece of gossip in Combray. In a way she is a kind of parody, a grotesque shadow, of Marcel himself in his capacity of sick author spinning his web and catching up into that web the life buzzing around him. A pregnant servant maid is momentarily featured and compared to an allegorical figure in a Giotto picture, just as Mme. de Guermantes appeared in a church tapestry. It is noteworthy that throughout the whole work either the narrator or Swann often sees the physical appearance of this or that character in terms of paintings by famous old masters, many of them of the Florentine School. There is one main reason behind this method, and a secondary reason. The main reason is of course that for Proust art was the essential reality of life. The other reason is of a more private kind: in describing young men he disguised his keen appreciation of male beauty under the masks of recognizable paintings; and in describing young females he disguised under the same masks of paintings his sexual indifference to women and his inability to describe their charm. But by this time, the fact that reality is a mask should not disturb us in Proust.

A hot summer afternoon follows, a very concentration of summer color

---

Nabokov's comments on the translation in his teaching copy of *Swann's Way*

⊛ now to translate
literally from the
French

instance, literally saintly examples of practical charity, they
have generally had the brisk, decided, undisturbed, and
slightly brutal air of a busy surgeon, the face in which one
can discern no commiseration, no tenderness at the sight
of suffering humanity, and no fear of hurting it, the face
devoid of gentleness or sympathy, the sublime face of true
goodness.

Then while the kitchen-maid—who, all unawares, made
the superior qualities of Françoise shine with added
lustre, just as Error, by force of contrast, enhances the
triumph of Truth—took in coffee which (according to
Mamma) was nothing more than hot water, and then
carried up to our rooms hot water which was barely tepid,
I would be lying stretched out on my bed, a book in my
hand, in my room which trembled with the effort to
defend its frail, transparent coolness against the afternoon
sun, behind its almost closed shutters through which, however, a reflection of the sunlight had contrived to ~~slip in
on its golden wings,~~ remaining motionless, between glass
and woodwork, in a corner, like a butterfly ~~poised upon a
flower.~~ It was hardly light enough for me to read, and my
feeling of the day's brightness and splendour was derived
solely from the blows struck down below, in the Rue de la
Cure, by Camus (whom Françoise had assured that my
aunt was not 'resting' and that he might therefore make a
noise), upon some old packing-cases from which nothing
would really be sent flying but the dust, though the din of
them, in the resonant atmosphere that accompanies hot
weather, seemed to scatter broadcast a rain of blood-red
stars; and from the flies who performed for my benefit, in
their small concert, as it might be the chamber music of
summer; evoking heat and light quite differently from an

made its yellow wing slip in
and
folded

'idiot'

you will note that Monsieur
is a conventional golden butterfly poised delicately
a conventional flower, muddles things

and heat, with a garden and a book in the middle; one should note how the book merges with the surroundings of Marcel, the reader. Remember that after some thirty-five years have elapsed Marcel is all the time searching for new methods of reconstructing this little town of his early adolescence. In a kind of pageant, soldiers pass beyond the garden, and presently the theme of reading brings about the author of a book whom Proust calls Bergotte. This character has some affinities with Anatole France, a real writer mentioned separately, but on the whole Bergotte is a complete creation by Proust. (Bergotte's death is beautifully described in the pages of a later volume.) Once more we meet Swann, and there is a first allusion to Swann's daughter Gilberte with whom Marcel is later to fall in love. Gilberte is linked with Bergotte, her father's friend, who explains to her the beauties of a cathedral. Marcel is impressed by the fact that this favorite author of his is a guide to the little girl in her studies and her interests: here is one of those romantic projections and relationships in which so many characters of Proust appear.

A friend of Marcel's, a young man called Bloch, a somewhat pompous and extravagant young fellow in whom culture, snobbism, and a high-strung temperament are combined, is introduced; and with him comes the theme of racial intolerance. Swann is Jewish, as is Bloch, and so was Proust on his mother's side. It follows that Proust was greatly concerned with the anti-Semitic trends in the bourgeois and noble circles of his day, trends that culminated historically in the Dreyfus affair, the main political event discussed in the later volumes.

Back to Aunt Léonie who is visited by a learned priest. The theme of the church steeple looms again, and like the chimes of a clock, the theme of Eulalie, Françoise, and the pregnant maid reverberates as the various attitudes and relations between these women are established. We find Marcel actually eavesdropping on his aunt's dream—a very singular event in the annals of literature. Eavesdropping is, of course, one of the oldest literary devices, but here the author goes to the limits of the device. Luncheon is earlier on Saturday. Proust makes much of little family traditions, of those capricious patterns of domestic customs that cheerfully isolate one family from another. Then in the next few pages starts the beautiful theme of the hawthorn flowers which will be more fully developed later. We are again in the church where the flowers adorn the altar: "they were made more lovely still by the scalloped outline of the dark leaves, over which were scattered in profusion, as over a bridal train, little clusters of buds of a dazzling whiteness. Though I dared not look at them save through my fingers, I could feel that the formal scheme was composed of living things, and it was Nature herself who, by trimming the shape of the foliage, and by adding the crowning ornament of those snowy buds, had made the decorations worthy of what was at once a public rejoicing and a solemn mystery. Higher up on the altar, a flower had opened here and there with a careless grace, holding so unconcernedly, like a final, almost vapourous bedizening, its bunch of stamens, slender as gossamer, which clouded the flower itself in a white mist, that in following these with my eyes, in trying to imitate, somewhere inside myself, the action of their blossoming, I imagined it as a swift and thoughtless movement of the head with an enticing glance from her contracted pupils, by a young girl in white, careless and alive."

At the church we meet a certain M. Vinteuil. Vinteuil is accepted by everybody in this provincial town of Combray as a vague crank dabbling in music, and neither Swann nor the boy Marcel realizes that in reality his music is tremendously famous in Paris. This is the beginning of the important music theme. As already remarked, Proust is intensely interested in the various masks under which the same person appears to various other persons. Thus Swann is merely a stockbroker's son to Marcel's family, but to the Guermantes he is a charming and romantic figure in Paris society. Throughout this shimmering book there are many other examples of these changing values in human relationship. Vinteuil not only brings in the theme of a recurrent musical note, the "little theme," as we shall see later, but also the theme of homosexual relationship which is developed throughout the novel, shedding new light on this or that character. In the present case it is Vinteuil's homosexual daughter who is involved in the theme.

Marcel is a very fantastic Sherlock Holmes and is extremely lucky in the glimpses of gestures and snatches of tales that he sees and hears. (Incidentally, the first homosexuals in modern literature are described in *Anna Karenin*, namely in chapter 19, part two, where Vronski is breakfasting in the mess room of his regiment. Two officers are briefly but vividly described—and the description leaves no doubt about the relationship between those two.) Vinteuil's house stood in a hollow surrounded by the steep slopes of a hill, and on that escarpment, hidden among its shrubs, the narrator stood a few feet from the drawing-room window and saw old Vinteuil lay out a sheet of music—his own music—so as to catch the eye of his approaching visitors, Marcel's parents, but at the last moment he snatched it away so as not to have his guests suspect that he was glad to see them only because it would give him a chance to play to them his compositions. Some eighty pages later the narrator is again hidden among the shrubs and again watches the same window. Old Vinteuil by then has died. His daughter is in deep mourning. The narrator sees her place her father's photograph on a little table, with the same gesture as when her father had prepared that sheet of music. Her purpose, as it proves, is a rather sinister, sadistic one: her lesbian friend insults the picture in preparation for their making love. The whole scene, incidentally, is a little lame from the point of view of actions to come, with the eavesdropping business enhancing its awkwardness. Its purpose, however, is to start the long series of homosexual revelations and revaluations of characters that occupy so many pages in the later volumes and produce such changes in the aspects of various characters. Also, later, the possible relations of Albertine with Vinteuil's daughter will become a form of jealous fixation for Marcel.

But let us return to the walk home from the church and the return to Aunt Léonie, the spider in the web, and to Françoise's dinner preparations, where her vulgar cruelty both to chickens and to people is revealed. Legrandin reappears a little later. He is a philistine and a snob, toadying to a duchess and not wishing her to see his humble friends, the narrator's family. It is interesting to see how false and pompous Legrandin's speeches sound about the beauties of a landscape.

———

The theme of the two walks the family would take in the neighborhood of Combray now enters its main stage of development. One walk led towards Méséglise, called the Swann way because it passed along the boundary of Swann's estate of Tansonville; the other was the Guermantes way leading towards the estate of the Duke and Duchess of Guermantes. It is on the Swann way walk that the theme of the hawthorns and the theme of love, of Swann's little daughter Gilberte, come together in a splendid flash of pictorial art. "I found the whole path throbbing with the fragrance of hawthorn-blossom. The hedge resembled a series of chapels, whose walls were no longer visible under the mountains of flowers that were heaped upon their altars [*a reminiscence of the first introduction of the hawthorn theme in the church*]; while underneath the sun cast a square of light upon the ground, as though it had shone in upon them through a stained window; the scent that swept out over me from them was as rich, and as circumscribed in its range, as though I had been standing before the Lady-altar. . . .

"But it was in vain that I lingered before the hawthorns, to breathe in, to marshal before my mind (which knew not what to make of it), to lose in order to rediscover their invisible and unchanging odour, to absorb myself in the rhythm which disposed their flowers here and there with the lightheartedness of youth, and at intervals as unexpected as certain intervals of music; they offered me an indefinite continuation of the same charm, in an inexhaustible profusion, but without letting me delve into it any more deeply, like those melodies which one can play over a hundred times in succession without coming any nearer their secret. I turned away from them for a moment so as to be able to return to them with renewed strength."

But on his return to viewing them the hawthorns still offer no enlightenment (for Marcel is not to know the full significance of these experiences until the illumination that comes to him in the last volume) but his rapture is increased when his grandfather points out to him one particular blossom. "And it was indeed a hawthorn, but one whose flowers were pink, and lovelier even than the white. It, too, was in holiday attire ... but it was attired even more richly than the rest, for the flowers which clung to its branches, one above another, so thickly as to leave no part of the tree undecorated, [*first comparison*:] like the tassels on the crook of a rococo shepherdess, were every one of them 'in colour,' and consequently of a superior quality, by the aesthetic standards of Combray, to the 'plain,' [*second comparison*:] if one was to judge by the scale of prices at the main 'store' in the Square, or at Camus's, where the most expensive biscuits were those whose sugar was pink. And for my own part [*third comparison*:] I set a higher value on cream cheese when it was pink, when I had been allowed to tinge it with crushed strawberries. And these flowers [*now the combination of all the senses*:] had chosen precisely the colour of some edible and delicious thing, or of some exquisite addition to one's costume for a great festival, which colours, inasmuch as they make plain the reason for their superiority, are those whose beauty is most evident to the eyes of children. .... High up on the branches, like so many of those tiny rose-trees, their pots concealed in jackets of paper lace, whose slender stems rise in a forest from the altar on the greater festivals, a thousand buds were swelling and opening, paler in colour, but each disclosing as it burst, as at the bottom of a cup of pink marble, its blood-red stain, and suggesting even more strongly than the full-blown flowers the special, irresistible quality of the hawthorn-tree, which, wherever it budded, wherever it was about to blossom, could bud and blossom in pink flowers alone."

We then come to Gilberte, who in Marcel's mind is forever after associated with this glory of hawthorn blossoms. "A little girl, with fair, reddish hair, who appeared to be returning from a walk, and held a trowel in her hand, was looking at us, raising towards us a face sprinkled with pinkish freckles. . . .

"I gazed at her, at first with that gaze which is not merely a messenger from the eyes, but in whose window all the senses assemble and lean out, petrified and anxious, that gaze which would fain reach, touch, capture, bear off in triumph the body at which it is aimed, and the soul with the body . . . an unconsciously appealing look, whose object was to force her to pay attention to me, to see, to know me. She cast a glance forwards and sideways, so as to take stock of my grandfather and father, and doubtless the impression she formed of them was that we were all absurd people, for she turned away with an indifferent and contemptuous air, withdrew herself so as to spare her face the indignity of remaining within their field of vision; and while they, continuing to walk on without noticing her, had overtaken and passed me, she allowed her eyes to wander, over the space that lay between us, in my direction, without any particular expression, without appearing to have seen me, but with an intensity, a half-hidden smile which I was unable to interpret, according to the instruction I had received in the ways of good breeding, save as a mark of infinite disgust; and her hand, at the same time, sketched in the air an indelicate gesture, for which, when it was addressed in public to a person whom one did not know, the little dictionary of manners which I carried in my mind supplied only one meaning, namely, a deliberate insult.

" 'Gilberte, come along; what are you doing?' called out in a piercing tone of authority a lady in white, whom I had not seen until that moment, while, a little way beyond her, a gentleman in a suit of linen 'ducks,' whom I did not know either, stared at me with eyes which seemed to be starting from his head; the little girl's smile abruptly faded, and, seizing her trowel, she made off without turning to look again in my direction, with an air of obedience, inscrutable and sly.

"And so was wafted to my ears the name of Gilberte, bestowed on me like a talisman . . . with the mystery of the life of her whom its syllables designated to the happy creatures that lived and walked and travelled in her company; unfolding through the arch of the pink hawthorn, which opened at the height of my shoulder, the quintessence of their familiarity—so exquisitely painful to myself—with her, and with all that unknown world of her existence, into which I should never penetrate." Of course, Marcel does penetrate this world, not only the world of Odette but also that of the gentleman Charlus, who will develop later into the greatest portrait in literature of a homosexual. In their innocence, however, Marcel's family believe that he is Madame Swann's lover and are disgusted that the child is living in such an atmosphere. It is much later that Gilberte confesses to Marcel that she had been offended at his immobility as he looked at her without a gesture towards a friendship to which she would have responded.

The walk along the Guermantes way follows in part a lovely river, the Vivonne, flowing through its clusters of water lilies. The Guermantes theme gains body when Marcel sees the duchess attending a ceremony in the very church where her prototypical image had appeared in the tapestry. He finds that the name is more than its bearer. "Suddenly, during the nuptial mass, the beadle, by moving to one side, enabled me to see, sitting in a chapel, a lady with fair hair and a large nose, piercing blue eyes, a billowy neckerchief of mauve silk, glossy and new and brilliant, and a little pimple at the corner of her nose. . . . My disappointment was immense. It arose from my not having borne in mind, when I thought of Mme. de Guermantes, that I was picturing her to myself in the colours of a tapestry or a painted window, as living in another century, as being of another substance than the rest of the human race. . . . I was gazing upon this image, which, naturally enough, bore no resemblance to those that had so often, under the same title of 'Mme. de Guermantes,' appeared to me in dreams, since this one had not been, like the others, formed by myself, but had sprung into sight for the first time, only a moment ago, here in church; an image which was not of the same nature, was not colourable at will, like those others that allowed themselves to be suffused by the orange tint of a sonorous syllable [*Marcel saw sounds in color*], but which was so real that everything, even to the fiery little pimple at the corner of her nose, gave an assurance of her subjection to the laws of life, as in a transformation scene on the stage a crease in the dress of a fairy, a quivering of her tiny finger, indicate the material presence of a living actress before our eyes, whereas we were uncertain, till then, whether we were not looking merely at a projection of limelight from a lantern. . . . But this Mme. de Guermantes of whom I had so often dreamed, now that I could see that she had a real existence independent of myself, acquired a fresh increase of power over my imagination, which, paralysed for a moment by contact with a reality so different from anything that it had expected, began to react and to say within me: 'Great and glorious before the days of Charlemagne, the Guermantes had the right of life and death over their vassals; the Duchesse de Guermantes descends from Geneviève de Brabant.' . . . And my gaze resting upon her fair hair, her blue eyes, the lines of her neck, and overlooking the features which might have reminded me of the faces of other women, I cried out within myself, as I admired this deliberately unfinished sketch: 'How lovely she is! What true nobility! it is indeed a proud Guermantes, the descendant of Geneviève de Brabant, that I have before me!' "

After the ceremony when the duchess was standing outside the church, her glance passed over Marcel: "And at once I fell in love with her. . . . Her eyes waxed blue as a periwinkle flower, wholly beyond my reach, yet dedicated by her to me; and the sun, bursting out again from behind a threatening cloud and darting the full force of its rays on to the Square and into the sacristy, shed a geranium glow over the red carpet laid down for the wedding, along which Mme. de Guermantes smilingly advanced, and covered its woollen texture with a nap of rosy velvet, a bloom of light, giving it that sort of tenderness, of solemn sweetness in the pomp of a joyful celebration, which characterise certain pages of *Lohengrin*, certain paintings by Carpaccio, and make us understand how Baudelaire was able to apply to the sound of the trumpet the epithet 'delicious.' "

It is in the course of his walks in the Guermantes direction that Marcel reflects on his future as a writer and is discouraged at his lack of qualification, at the "sense of my own impotence which I had felt whenever I had sought a philosophic theme for some great literary work." The most vivid sensations come to him but he does not understand that they have a literary significance. "Then, quite apart from all those literary preoccupations, and without definite attachment to anything, suddenly a roof, a gleam of sunlight reflected from a stone, the smell of a road would make me stop still, to enjoy the special pleasure that each of them gave me, and also because they appeared to be concealing, beneath what my eyes could see, something which they invited me to approach and seize from them, but which, despite all my efforts, I never managed to get at, to possess. As I felt that the mysterious object was to be found in them, I would stand there in front of them, motionless, gazing, breathing, endeavouring to penetrate with my mind beyond the thing seen or heard or smelt. And if I had then to hasten after my grandfather, to proceed on my way, I would still seek to recover my sense of them by closing my eyes; I would concentrate upon recalling exactly the line of the roof, the colour of the stone, which, without my being able to understand why, had seemed to me to be teeming, ready to open, to yield up to me the secret treasure of which they were themselves no more than the outer coverings. It was certainly not any impression of this kind that could or would restore the hope I had lost of succeeding one day in becoming a writer, for each of them was associated with some material object devoid of any intellectual value, and suggesting no abstract truth." Contrasted here are the literature of the senses, true art, and the literature of ideas, which does not produce true art unless it stems from the senses. To this profound connection Marcel is blind. He wrongly thinks he had to write about things of intellectual value when in reality it was that system of sensations he was experiencing that without his knowledge was slowly making an authentic writer of him.

Some intimations come to him, as when the steeples theme turns up again in triple form during a drive: "At a bend in the road I experienced, suddenly, that special pleasure, which bore no resemblance to any other, when I caught sight of the twin steeples of Martinville, on which the setting sun was playing, while the movement of the carriage and the windings of the road seemed to keep them continually changing their position; and then of a third steeple, that of Vieuxvicq, which although separated from them by a hill and a valley, and rising from rather higher ground in the distance, appeared none the less to be standing by their side.

"In ascertaining and noting the shape of their spires, the changes of aspect, the sunny warmth of their surfaces, I felt that I was not penetrating to the full depth of my impression, that something more lay behind that mobility, that luminosity, something which they seemed at once to contain and to conceal."

Proust now does a most interesting thing: he confronts the style of his present with the style of his past. Marcel borrows a piece of paper and composes a description of these three steeples which the narrator then proceeds to reproduce. It is Marcel's first attempt at writing and it is charming although some of the comparisons, such as those of the flowers and of the maidens, are made deliberately juvenile. The comparison comes, however, between the steeples which the narrator has just described from his later vantage point and Marcel's literary attempt, which is surface description without the significance for which he was groping when he first experienced the sensation of these steeples. It is doubly significant that writing this piece "relieved my mind of the obsession of the steeples."

The Combray part of the volume, which is about his childhood impressions, ends with a theme that started in the beginning—the reconstruction of his room in Combray, in which he would lie awake at night. In later life, when lying awake he would feel himself back in this room: "All these memories, following one after another, were condensed into a single substance, but it had not coalesced completed, and I could discern between the three layers (my oldest, my instinctive memories, those others, inspired more recently by a taste or 'perfume,' and those which were actually the memories of another, from whom I had acquired them at second hand) not fissures, not geological faults, but at least those veins, those streaks of colour which in certain rocks, in certain marbles, point to differences of origin, age, and formation." Proust is here describing three layers of impressions: (1) simple memory as a deliberate act; (2) an old memory stirred by a sensation in the present repeating a sensation in the past; and (3) memorized knowledge of another man's life, though acquired at second hand. The point is again that simple memory cannot be relied upon to reconstruct the past.

The Combray section has been devoted to Proust's first two categories; it is the third that is the subject of the second main section of the volume, entitled "Swann in Love," in which Swann's passion for Odette leads to an understanding of Marcel's for Albertine.

———

Several important themes occupy this latter section of the volume. One of these is "the little musical phrase." The year before, Swann had heard a piece of music for violin and piano played at an evening party. "And it had been a source of keen pleasure when, below the narrow line of the violin-part, delicate, unyielding, substantial and governing the whole, he had suddenly perceived, where it was trying to surge upwards in a plashing tide of sound, the mass of the piano-part, multiform, coherent, level, and interclashing like the mauve tumult of the sea, charmed into a minor key by the moonlight." And "hardly had the delicious sensation, which Swann had experienced, died away, before his memory had furnished him with an immediate transcript, summary, it is true, and provisional, but one on which he had kept his eyes fixed while the playing continued, so effectively that, when the same impression suddenly returned, it was no longer uncapturable. . . . This time he had distinguished, quite clearly, a phrase which emerged for a few moments from the waves of sound. It had at once held out to him an invitation to partake of intimate pleasures, of whose existence, before hearing it, he had never dreamed, into which he felt that nothing but this phrase could initiate him; and he had been filled with love for it, as with a new and strange desire.

"With a slow and rhythmical movement it led him here, there, everywhere, towards a state of happiness noble, unintelligible, yet clearly indicated. And then, suddenly having reached a certain point from which he was prepared to follow it, after pausing for a moment, abruptly it changed its direction, and in a fresh movement, more rapid, multiform, melancholy, incessant, gentle, it bore him off with it towards a vista of joys unknown."

This passion for a phrase of music brought on in Swann's life the possibility of a sort of rejuvenation, renovation, for he had grown dull, but not being able to discover the composer and secure the music, at last he ceased to think of it. But now, at Mme. Verdurin's party, where he had gone only to be with Odette, a pianist plays a work that he recognizes, and he learns that it is the andante movement of a sonata for piano and violin by Vinteuil. With this knowledge, Swann has the feeling of holding the phrase secure in his power, of possessing it, as the narrator dreamed of possessing the landscapes that he saw. The same musical phrase not only speaks to Swann again later in the work but also delights the narrator at a certain point in his life. It should be borne in mind that Swann is a kind of fancy mirror of the narrator himself. Swann sets the pattern, and the narrator follows it.

Another important episode, and an example of the way in which Proust unfolds an incident, is that of Swann at Odette's window. He has come to see her after eleven at night, but she is tired and irresponsive and asks him to leave in half an hour. "She begged him to put out the light before he went; he drew the curtains close round her bed and left her." But in a fit of jealousy about an hour later it occurs to him that perhaps she rid herself of him because she was expecting someone else. He took a cab and came out almost opposite her house. Proust's metaphor is that of golden fruit. "Amid the blackness of all the row of windows, the lights in which had long since been put out, he saw one, and only one, from which overflowed, between the slats of its shutters, closed like a wine-press over its mysterious golden pulp, the light that filled the room within, a light which on so many evenings, as soon as he saw it, far off, as he turned into the street, had rejoiced his heart with its message: 'She is there—expecting you,' and now tortured him with: 'She is there with the man she was expecting.' He must know who; he tiptoed along by the wall until he reached the window, but between the slanting bars of the shutters he could see nothing; he could hear, only, in the silence of the night, the murmur of conversation."

Despite the pain, he derives an intellectual pleasure, the pleasure of the truth: the same inner truth above emotion that Tolstoy was after. He feels "the same thirst for knowledge with which he had once studied history. And all manner of actions, from which, until now, he would have recoiled in shame, such as spying, tonight, outside a window, tomorrow, for all he knew, putting adroitly provocative questions to casual witnesses, bribing servants, listening at doors, seemed to him, now, to be precisely on a level with the deciphering of manuscripts, the weighing of evidence, the interpretation of old texts, that was to say, so many different methods of scientific investigation, each one having a definite intellectual value and being legitimately employable in the search for truth." The next metaphor combines the idea of the golden light and the pure, scholarly search for knowledge: the secret of a lighted window and the interpretation of some old text. "But his desire to know the truth was stronger, and seemed to him nobler, than his desire for her. He knew that the true story of certain events, which he would have given his life to be able to reconstruct accurately and in full, was to be read within that window, streaked with bars of light, as within the illuminated, golden boards of one of those precious manuscripts, by whose wealth of artistic treasures the scholar who consults them cannot remain unmoved. He yearned for the satisfaction of knowing the truth which so impassioned him in that brief, fleeting, precious transcript, on that translucent page, so warm, so beautiful. And besides, the advantage which he felt—which he so desperately wanted to feel—that he had over them, lay perhaps not so much in knowing as in being able to shew them that he knew."

He knocks and finds two old gentlemen facing him from the window. It was the wrong one. "Having fallen into the habit, when he came late to Odette, of identifying her window by the fact that it was the only one still lighted in a row of windows otherwise all alike, he had been misled, this time, by the light, and had knocked at the window beyond hers, in the adjoining house." This mistake of Swann's may be compared to the narrator's mistake when relying solely upon memory, he tried to reconstruct his room from gleams in the dark, at the end of the Combray section, and found that he had misplaced everything when daylight came.

———

In Paris, in the park of the Champs-Elysées, "a little girl with reddish hair was playing with a racquet and a shuttlecock; when, from the path, another little girl, who was putting on her cloak and covering up her battledore, called out sharply: 'Good-bye, Gilberte, I'm going home now; don't forget, we're coming to you this evening, after dinner.' The name Gilberte passed close by me, evoking all the more forcibly her whom it labelled in that it did not merely refer to her, as one speaks of a person in his absence, but was directly addressed to her"; and thus carried in the little girl's memory all of the unknown shared existence possessed by her, an existence from which Marcel was excluded. The metaphor of the name's trajectory, which begins the description, is followed by one of the name's perfume, Gilberte's friend "flung it on the air with a light-hearted cry: letting float in the atmosphere the delicious perfume which that message had distilled, by touching the two girls with precision, from certain invisible points in Mlle. Swann's life." In its passage the celestial quality of the name is compared to "Poussin's little cloud, exquisitely coloured, like the cloud that, curling over one of Poussin's gardens, reflects minutely, like a cloud in the opera, teeming with chariots and horses, some apparition of the life of the gods." To these images is now added that of space-time in parentheses, the content of which should be noted for its bit of lawn and bit of time in the girl's afternoon, with the shuttlecock beating time: the cloud casts a light "on that ragged grass, at the spot on which she stood (at once a scrap of withered lawn and a moment in the afternoon of the fair player, who continued to beat up and catch her shuttlecock until a governess, with a blue feather in her hat, had called her away)." The light that the name, like a cloud passing over, sheds for Marcel was "a marvellous little band of light, of the colour of heliotrope," and then with an inner simile it turns the lawn to a magic carpet.

This band of light was of a mauve color, the violet tint that runs through the whole book, the very color of time. This rose-purple mauve, a pinkish lilac, a violet flush, is linked in European literature with certain sophistications of the artistic temperament. It is the color of an orchid, *Cattleya labiata* (the genus called thus after William Cattley, a solemn British botanist), an orchid, which today, in this country, regularly adorns the bosoms of matrons at club festivities. This orchid in the nineties of the last century in Paris was a very rare and expensive flower. It adorns Swann's lovemaking in a famous but not very convincing scene. From this mauve to the delicate pink of hawthorns in the Combray chapters there are all kinds of shadings within Proust's flushed prism. One should recall the pink dress worn many years before by the pretty lady (Odette de Crécy) in Uncle Adolphe's apartment, and now the association with Gilberte, her daughter. Notice, moreover, as a kind of exclamation mark punctuating the passage, the blue feather in the hat of the girl's governess—which the boy's old nurse lacked.

More metaphors within metaphors may be observed in the passage after Marcel has become acquainted with Gilberte and plays with her in the park. If the weather threatens rain he worries that Gilberte will not be allowed to go to the Champs-Elysées. "And so, if the heavens were doubtful, from early morning I would not cease to interrogate them, observing all the omens." If he sees the lady in the apartment across the way putting on her hat, he hopes that Gilberte can do the same. But the day grew dark and remained so. Outside the window the balcony was gray. Then we have a series of inner comparisons: (1) "Suddenly, on [the balcony's] sullen stone, I did not indeed see a less negative colour, but I felt as it were an effort towards a less negative colour, [2] the pulsation of a hesitating ray that struggled to discharge its light. [3] A moment later the balcony was as pale and luminous as a standing water at dawn, and a thousand shadows from the iron-work of its balustrade had come to rest on it." Then the inner comparisons again: a breath of wind disperses the shadows and the stone turns dark again, (1) "but, like tamed creatures, [the shadows] returned; they began, imperceptibly, to grow lighter, [2] and by one of those continuous crescendos, such as, in music, at the end of an overture, carry a single note to the extreme fortissimo, making it pass rapidly through all the intermediate stages, I saw it attain to that fixed, inalterable gold of fine days, [3] on which the sharply cut shadows of the wrought iron of the balustrade were outlined in black like a capricious vegetation. . . ." The comparisons end with the pledge of happiness: "with a fineness in the delineation of [the shadows'] smallest details which seemed to indicate a deliberate application, an artist's satisfaction, and with so much relief, so velvety a bloom in the restfulness of their sombre and happy mass that in truth those large and leafy shadows which lay reflected on that lake of sunshine seemed aware that they were pledges of happiness and peace of mind." Finally, the shadows of the filigree ironwork, resembling ivy, become "like the very shadow of the presence of Gilberte, who was perhaps already in the Champs-Elysées, and as soon as I arrived there would greet me with: 'Let's begin at once. You are on my side.' "

The romantic view of Gilberte is transferred to her parents. "Everything that concerned them was on my part the object of so constant a preoccupation that the days on which, as on this day, M. Swann (whom I had seen so often, long ago, without his having aroused my curiosity, when he was still on good terms with my parents) came for Gilberte to the Champs-Elysées, once the pulsations to which my heart had been excited by the appearance of his grey hat and hooded cape had subsided, the sight

---

Nabokov's drawing of "a gorgeous, mauve-colored orchid"

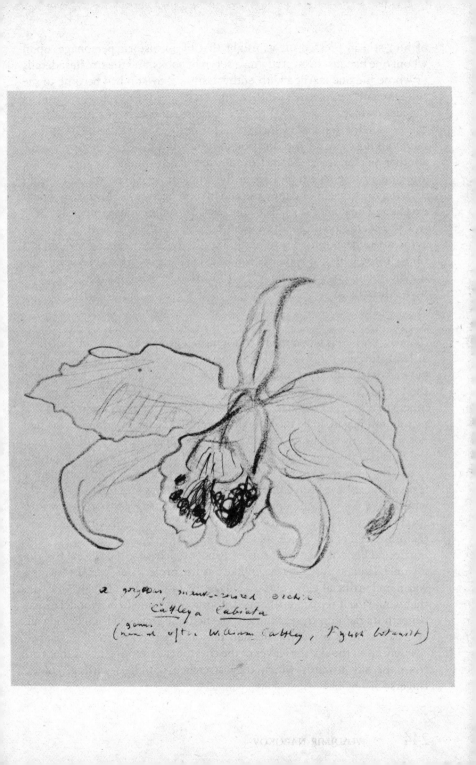

a golden, mentioned orchis
Cattleya Labiata
(genus named after William Cattley, English botanist)

of him still impressed me as might that of an historic personage, upon whom one had just been studying a series of books, and the smallest details of whose life one learned with enthusiasm. . . . Swann had become to me pre-eminently [Gilberte's] father, and no longer the Combray Swann; as the ideas which, nowadays, I made his name connote were different from the ideas in the system of which it was formerly comprised, which I utilised not at all now when I had occasion to think of him, he had become a new, another person. . . ." Marcel even attempts to imitate Swann: "in my attempts to resemble him, I spent the whole time, when I was at table, in drawing my finger along my nose and in rubbing my eyes. My father would exclaim: 'The child's a perfect idiot, he's becoming quite impossible.' "

The dissertation on Swann's love that occupies the middle of the volume evinces the narrator's desire to find a resemblance between Swann and himself: the pangs of jealousy Swann experiences will be repeated in the middle volume of the whole work in relation to the narrator's love affair with Albertine.

———————

Swann's Way ends when the narrator, now a grown-up man of thirty-five, at least, revisits the Bois de Boulogne early on a November day, and we have an extraordinary record of his impressions and his memories. Against the background of dark and distant woods, some trees still in foliage but others now bare, a double row of orange red chestnut trees "seemed, as in a picture just begun, to be the only thing painted, so far, by an artist who had not yet laid any colour on the rest. . . ." The appearance is artificial: "And the Bois had the temporary, unfinished, artificial look of a nursery garden or a park in which, either for some botanic purpose or in preparation for a festival, there have been embedded among the trees of commoner growth, which have not yet been uprooted and transplanted elsewhere, a few rare specimens, with fantastic foliage, which seem to be clearing all round themselves an empty space, making room, giving air, diffusing light." The horizontal light of the sun at this early hour touches the tops of the trees as it would, later, at dusk, "flame up like a lamp, project afar over the leaves a warm and artificial glow, and set ablaze the few topmost boughs of a tree that would itself remain unchanged, a sombre incombustible candelabrum beneath its flaming crest. At one spot the light grew solid as a brick wall, and like a piece of yellow Persian masonry, patterned in blue, daubed coarsely upon the sky the leaves of the chestnuts; at another, it cut them off from the sky towards which they stretched out their curling, golden fingers."

As on a colored map the different places in the Bois could be traced. For years the trees had shared the life of the beautiful ladies who in the past walked under them: "forced for so many years now, by a sort of grafting process, to share the life of feminine humanity, they called to my mind the figure of the dryad, the fair worldling, swiftly walking, brightly coloured, whom they sheltered with their branches as she passed beneath them, and obliged to acknowledge, as they themselves acknowledged, the power of the season; they recalled to me the happy days when I was young and had faith, when I would hasten eagerly to the spots where masterpieces of female elegance would be incarnate for a few moments beneath the unconscious, accomodating boughs." The inelegant people he now passes in the Bois recall what he had earlier known. "Could I ever have made them understand the emotion that I used to feel on winter mornings, when I met Mme. Swann on foot, in a seal-skin coat, with a woollen cap from which stuck out two blade-like partridge-feathers, but enveloped also in the deliberate, artificial warmth of her own house, which was suggested by nothing more than the bunch of violets crushed into her bosom, whose flowering, vivid and blue against the grey sky, the freezing air, the naked boughs, had the same charming effect of using the season and the weather merely as a setting, and of living actually in a human atmosphere, in the atmosphere of this woman, as had in the vases and beau-pots of her drawing-room, beside the blazing fire, in front of the silk-covered sofa, the flowers that looked out through closed windows at the falling snow?"

The volume ends with the narrator's view of the past in time and space. "The sun's face was hidden. Nature began again to reign over the Bois, from which had vanished all trace of the idea that it was the Elysian Garden of Woman. . . ." The return of a semblance of reality over this artificial wood "helped me to understand how paradoxical it is to seek in reality for the pictures that are stored in one's memory, which must inevitably lose the charm that comes to them from memory itself and from their not being apprehended by the senses. The reality that I had known no longer existed. It sufficed that Mme. Swann did not appear, in the same attire and at the same moment, for the whole avenue to be altered. The places that we have known belong not only to the little world of space on which we map them for our own convenience. None of them was ever more than a thin layer between the contiguous impressions that composed our life at that time; remembrance of a particular form is but regret for a particular moment; and houses, roads, avenues are as fugitive, alas, as the years."

The point he makes is that simple memory, the act of visualizing something in retrospect, is not the correct method: it does not recreate the past. The ending of *Swann's Way* is only one of the different aspects of viewing the past that in the gradual building up of Marcel's understanding prepare for the final experience that reveals to him the reality for which, throughout the work, he has been searching. This event takes place in the great third chapter, "The Princesse de Guermantes Receives," in the final volume, *The Past Recaptured*, when he discovers why simple memory is insufficient and what, instead, is required. The process begins when Marcel, entering the court of the Prince de Guermantes's residence, on his way to the final party, hastily avoids an oncoming automobile "and, in stepping back, struck my foot against some unevenly cut flagstones leading to a carriage house. In recovering my balance, I put my foot on a stone that was a little lower than the one next to it; immediately all my discouragement vanished before a feeling of happiness which I had experienced at different moments of my life, at the sight of trees I thought I recognised when driving around Balbec, or the church spires of Martinville, or the savour of a *madeleine*, dipped in herb tea, or from many other sensations I have mentioned which had seemed to me to be synthesised in the last works of Vinteuil. Just as when I had tasted the *madeleine*, all anxiety as to the future, all intellectual doubt was dispelled. The misgivings that had been harassing me a moment before concerning the reality of my literary gifts, and even of literature itself, were suddenly banished as if by magic. But this time I made a firm resolve that I would not be satisfied to leave the question unanswered (as I did the day I tasted of a *madeleine* dipped in herb tea) as to why, without my having worked out any new line of reasoning or found any decisive argument, the difficulties that had seemed insoluble a short time before had now lost all their importance. The feeling of happiness which had just come over me was, indeed, exactly the same as I had experienced while eating the *madeleine*, but at that time I put off seeking the deep-lying causes of it."

The narrator is able to identify the sensation rising from the past as what he had once felt when he stood on two uneven stones in the baptistry of Saint Mark's in Venice, "and with that sensation came all the others connected with it that day, which had been waiting in their proper place in the series of forgotten days, until a sudden happening had imperiously commanded them to come forth. It was in the same way that the taste of the little *madeleine* had recalled Combray to my mind." This time he determines to get to the root of the matter, and while waiting to make his entrance to the drawing room, his sensations being actively aroused, the tinkle of a spoon against a plate, the feeling of a starched napkin, even the noise of a hot-water pipe bring back to him floods of memories of similar sensations in the past. "Even at this moment, in the mansion of the Prince de Guermantes, I heard the sound of my parents' footsteps as they accompanied M. Swann and the reverberating ferruginous, interminable, sharp, jangling tinkle of the little bell which announced to me that at last M. Swann had gone and Mamma was going to come upstairs—I heard these sounds again, the very identical sounds themselves, although situated so far back in the past."

But the narrator knows that this is not enough. "It was not in the Piazza San Marco any more than it had been on my second visit to Balbec or on my return to Tansonville to see Gilberte, that I would recapture past Time, and the journey which was merely suggested to me once more by the illusion that these old impressions existed outside myself, at the corner of a certain square, could not be the means I was seeking. . . . Impressions such as those which I was endeavouring to analyse and define could not fail to vanish away at the contact of a material enjoyment that was unable to bring them into existence. The only way to get more joy out of them was to try to know them more completely at the spot where they were to be found, namely, within myself, and to clarify them to their lowest depths." The problem to be solved is how to keep these impressions from vanishing under the pressure of the present. One answer is found in his new recognition of the continuity of present with past. "I had to descend again into my own consciousness. It must be, then, that this tinkling [of the bell at Swann's departure] was still there and also, between it and the present moment, all the infinitely unrolling past which I had been unconsciously carrying within me. When the bell tinkled, I was already in existence and, since that night, for me to have been able to hear the sound again, there must have been no break of continuity, not a moment of rest for me, no cessation of existence, of thought, of consciousness of myself, since this distant moment still clung to me and I could recapture it, go back to it, merely by descending more deeply within myself. It was this conception of time as incarnate, of past years as still close held within us, which I was now determined to bring out in such bold relief in my book."

Still, something more than memory, no matter how vivid and continuous, is involved. The inner meaning must be sought. "For the truths that the intelligence grasps directly and openly in the full-lighted world are somehow less profound, less indispensable than those which life has communicated to us without our knowledge through the form of impressions, material because they have come to us through the senses, but the inner meaning of which we can discern. In short, in this case as in the other, whether objective impressions such as I had received from the sight of the spires of Martinville, or subjective memories like the unevenness of the two steps or the taste of the *madeleine*, I must try to interpret the sensations as the indication of corresponding laws and ideas; I must try to think, that is to say, bring out of the obscurity what I had felt, and convert it into a spiritual equivalent." What he has learned is that intellectual scrutiny of past memories or sensations alone has not revealed to him their significance. For many years he has tried: "even when I was at Combray, I used to hold attentively before my mind some object that had forced itself upon my attention—a cloud, a triangle, a steeple, a flower, a pebble—because I felt there might be underneath these signs something quite different which I ought to try to discover, a thought which they transcribed after the manner of those hieroglyphics which one might think represented only material objects."

The truth he now sees is that he is not free, as by an intellectual effort at recovery, to choose memories from the past for scrutiny, "but they came to my mind pell-mell. And I felt that that must surely be the hall mark of their genuineness. I had not set out to seek the two paving stones in the court which I struck my foot against. But it was precisely the fortuitous, unavoidable way in which I had come upon the sensation that guaranteed the truth of a past which that sensation revived and of the mental images it released, since we feel its effort to come up into the light and also the thrill of recapturing reality. That sensation is the guarantee of the truth of the entire picture composed of contemporary impressions which the sensation brings in its train, with that unerring proportion of light and shadow, emphasis and omission, remembrance and oblivion, which conscious memory and observation will never know." Conscious memory merely reproduces "the chain of all the inaccurate impressions in which there is nothing left of what we really experienced, which constitutes for us our thoughts, our life, reality; and a so-called 'art taken from life' would simply reproduce that lie, an art as thin and poor as life itself, without any beauty, a repetition of what our eyes see and our intelligence notes," whereas "The grandeur of real art, on the contrary, ... is to rediscover, grasp again and lay before us that reality from which we live so far removed and from which we become more and more separated as the formal knowledge which we substitute for it grows in thickness and imperviousness—that reality which there is grave danger we might die without ever having known and yet which is simply our life, life as it really is, life disclosed at last and made clear. . . ."

The bridge between past and present that Marcel then discovers is that "What we call reality is a certain relationship between sensations and memories which surround us at the same time." In short, to recreate the past something other than the operation of memory must happen: there must be a combination of a present sensation (especially taste, smell, touch, sound) with a recollection, a remembrance, of the sensuous past. To quote Leon: "Now, if at the moment of this resurrection [as of Venice from the uneven stones in the Guermantes courtyard], instead of obliterating the present we can continue to be aware of it: if we can retain the sense of our own identity, and at the same time live fully in that moment which we had for long believed to be no more, then, and only then, we are at last in full possession of lost time." In other words, a nosegay of the senses in the present *and* the vision of an event or sensation in the past, this is when sense and memory come together and lost time is found again.

The illumination is then completed when the narrator realizes that a work of art is our only means of thus recapturing the past, and to this end he dedicates himself: for "recreating through the memory impressions which must then be plumbed to their depths, brought into the light and transformed into intellectual equivalents, was this not one of the prerequisites, almost the very essence of a work of art such as I had conceived . . . ?" And he finds, at last, that "all these materials for literary work were nothing else than my past life and that they had come to me in the midst of frivolous pleasures, in idleness, through tender affection and through sorrow, and that I had stored them up without foreseeing their final purpose or even their survival, any more than does the seed when it lays by all the sustenance that is going to nourish the seedling."

"It did not seem," he writes in conclusion, "as if I should have the strength to carry much longer attached to me that past which already extended so far down and which I was bearing so painfully within me! If, at least, there were granted me time enough to complete my work, I would not fail to stamp it with the seal of that Time the understanding of which was this day so forcibly impressing itself upon me, and I would therein describe men—even should that give them the semblance of monstrous creatures—as occupying in Time a place far more considerable than the so restricted one allotted them in space, a place, on the contrary, extending boundlessly since, giant-like, reaching far back into the years, they touch simultaneously epochs of their lives—with countless intervening days between—so widely separated from one another in Time."

The Metamorphosis

just over 3 feet long

wings

very smooth

correct ...

I

AS GREGOR SAMSA awoke one morning from ~~uneasy~~ *a troubled* dreams he found himself transformed in his bed into a *monstrous* ~~gigantic~~ insect. He was lying on his hard, as it were armor-plated, back and when he lifted his head a little he could see his dome-like brown belly divided into ~~stiff arched~~ *corrugated* segments on top of which the bed quilt could hardly keep in position and was about to slide off completely. His numerous legs, which were pitifully thin compared to the rest of his bulk, ~~waved~~ *flimmered* helplessly before *go on to p 20* his eyes.

the verb waved is inaccurate

flimmerten flitters & shimmers

What has happened to me? he thought. It was no dream. His room, a regular human bedroom, ~~only~~ *though* rather ~~too~~ small, lay quiet ~~between the~~ *within its* four familiar walls. Above the table on which a collection of cloth samples was unpacked and spread out—Samsa was a commercial traveler—hung the picture which he had recently cut out of an illustrated magazine and put into a pretty gilt frame. It showed a lady, with a fur cap on and a fur ~~stole~~, sitting ~~upright~~ *very straight* and holding out to the spectator a huge fur muff into which the whole of her forearm had vanished!

he had ... the made the frame himself, of wood, coated with gold paint

FRANZ KAFKA (1883-1924)

"The Metamorphosis" (1915)

Of course, no matter how keenly, how admirably, a story, a piece of music, a picture is discussed and analyzed, there will be minds that remain blank and spines that remain unkindled. "To take upon us the mystery of things"—what King Lear so wistfully says for himself and for Cordelia—this is also my suggestion for everyone who takes art seriously. A poor man is robbed of his overcoat (Gogol's "The Greatcoat," or more correctly "The Carrick"); another poor fellow is turned into a beetle (Kafka's "The Metamorphosis")—so what? There is no rational answer to "so what." We can take the story apart, we can find out how the bits fit, how one part of the pattern responds to the other; but you have to have in you some cell, some gene, some germ that will vibrate in answer to sensations that you can neither define, nor dismiss. *Beauty plus pity*—that is the closest we can get to a definition of art. Where there is beauty there is pity for the simple reason that beauty must die: beauty always dies, the manner dies with the matter, the world dies with the individual. If Kafka's "The Metamorphosis" strikes anyone as something more than an entomological fantasy, then I congratulate him on having joined the ranks of good and great readers.

I want to discuss fantasy and reality, and their mutual relationship. If we consider the "Dr. Jekyll and Mr. Hyde" story as an allegory—the struggle between Good and Evil within every man—then this allegory is tasteless and childish. To the type of mind that would see an allegory here, its shadow play would also postulate physical happenings which common sense knows to be impossible; but actually in the setting of the story, as viewed by a commonsensical mind, nothing at first sight seems to run

The opening page of "The Metamorphosis" from Nabokov's teaching copy

counter to general human experience. I want to suggest, however, that a second look shows that the setting of the story does run counter to general human experience, and that Utterson and the other men around Jekyll are, in a sense, as fantastic as Mr. Hyde. Unless we see them in a fantastic light, there is no enchantment. And if the enchanter leaves and the storyteller and the teacher remain alone together, they make poor company.

The story of Jekyll and Hyde is beautifully constructed, but it is an old one. Its moral is preposterous since neither good nor evil is actually depicted: on the whole, they are taken for granted, and the struggle goes on between two empty outlines. The enchantment lies in the art of Stevenson's fancywork; but I want to suggest that since art and thought, manner and matter, are inseparable, there must be something of the same kind about the structure of the story, too. Let us be cautious, however. I still think that there is a flaw in the artistic realization of the story—if we consider form and content separately—a flaw which is missing in Gogol's "The Carrick" and in Kafka's "The Metamorphosis." The fantastic side of the setting—Utterson, Enfield, Poole, Lanyon, and their London—is not of the same quality as the fantastic side of Jekyll's hydization. There is a crack in the picture, a lack of unity.

"The Carrick," "Dr. Jekyll and Mr. Hyde," and "The Metamorphosis": all three are commonly called fantasies. From my point of view, any outstanding work of art is a fantasy insofar as it reflects the unique world of a unique individual. But when people call these three stories fantasies, they merely imply that the stories depart in their subject matter from what is commonly called reality. Let us therefore examine what *reality* is, in order to discover in what manner and to what extent so-called fantasies depart from so-called reality.

Let us take three types of men walking through the same landscape. Number One is a city man on a well-deserved vacation. Number Two is a professional botanist. Number Three is a local farmer. Number One, the city man, is what is called a realistic, commonsensical, matter-of-fact type: he sees trees as *trees* and knows from his map that the road he is following is a nice new road leading to Newton, where there is a nice eating place recommended to him by a friend in his office. The botanist looks around and sees his environment in the very exact terms of plant life, precise biological and classified units such as specific trees and grasses, flowers and ferns, and for him *this* is reality; to him the world of the stolid tourist (who cannot distinguish an oak from an elm) seems a fantastic, vague, dreamy, never-never world. Finally, the world of the local farmer differs from the two others in that his world is intensely emotional and personal since he has been born and bred there, and knows every trail and individual tree, and every shadow from every tree across every trail, all in warm connection with his everyday work, and his childhood, and a thousand small things and patterns which the other two—the humdrum tourist and the botanical taxonomist—simply cannot know in the given place at the given time. Our farmer will not know the relation of the surrounding vegetation to a botanical conception of the world, and the botanist will know nothing of any importance to him about that barn or that old field or that old house under its cottonwoods, which are afloat, as it were, in a medium of personal memories for one who was born there.

So here we have three different worlds—three men, ordinary men who have different *realities*—and, of course, we could bring in a number of other beings: a blind man with a dog, a hunter with a dog, a dog with his man, a painter cruising in quest of a sunset, a girl out of gas—— In every case it would be a world completely different from the rest since the most objective words *tree, road, flower, sky, barn, thumb, rain* have, in each, totally different subjective connotations. Indeed, this subjective life is so strong that it makes an empty and broken shell of the so-called objective existence. The only way back to objective reality is the following one: we can take these several individual worlds, mix them thoroughly together, scoop up a drop of that mixture, and call it *objective reality*. We may taste in it a particle of madness if a lunatic passed through that locality, or a particle of complete and beautiful nonsense if a man has been looking at a lovely field and imagining upon it a lovely factory producing buttons or bombs; but on the whole these mad particles would be diluted in the drop of objective reality that we hold up to the light in our test tube. Moreover, this *objective reality* will contain something that transcends optical illusions and laboratory tests. It will have elements of poetry, of lofty emotion, of energy and endeavor (and even here the button king may find his rightful place), of pity, pride, passion—and the craving for a thick steak at the recommended roadside eating place.

So when we say *reality*, we are really thinking of all this—in one drop— an average sample of a mixture of a million individual realities. And it is in this sense (of human reality) that I use the term *reality* when placing it against a backdrop, such as the worlds of "The Carrick," "Dr. Jekyll and Mr. Hyde," and "The Metamorphosis," which are specific fantasies.

In "The Carrick" and in "The Metamorphosis" there is a central figure endowed with a certain amount of human pathos among grotesque, heartless characters, figures of fun or figures of horror, asses parading as zebras, or hybrids between rabbits and rats. In "The Carrick" the human quality of the central figure is of a different type from Gregor in Kafka's story, but this human pathetic quality is present in both. In "Dr. Jekyll and Mr. Hyde" there is no such human pathos, no throb in the throat of the story, none of that intonation of " 'I cannot get out, I cannot get out,' said the starling" (so heartrending in Sterne's fantasy *A Sentimental Journey*). True, Stevenson devotes many pages to the horror of Jekyll's plight, but the thing, after all, is only a superb Punch-and-Judy show. The beauty of Kafka's and Gogol's private nightmares is that their central human characters belong to the same private fantastic world as the inhuman characters around them, but the central one tries to get out of that world, to cast off the mask, to transcend the cloak or the carapace. But in Stevenson's story there is none of that unity and none of that contrast. The Uttersons, and Pooles, and Enfields are meant to be commonplace everyday characters; actually they are characters derived from Dickens, and thus they constitute phantasms that do not quite belong to Stevenson's own artistic reality, just as Stevenson's fog comes from a Dickensian studio to envelop a conventional London. I suggest, in fact, that Jekyll's magic drug is more real than Utterson's life. The fantastic Jekyll-and-Hyde theme, on the other hand, is supposed to be in contrast to this conventional London, but it is really the difference between a Gothic medieval theme and a Dickensian one. It is not the same kind of difference as that between an absurd world and pathetically absurd Bashmachkin, or between an absurd world and tragically absurd Gregor.

The Jekyll-and-Hyde theme does not quite form a unity with its setting because its fantasy is of a different type from the fantasy of the setting. There is really nothing especially pathetic or tragic about Jekyll. We enjoy every detail of the marvellous juggling, of the beautiful trick, but there is no artistic emotional throb involved, and whether it is Jekyll or Hyde who gets the upper hand remains of supreme indifference to the good reader. I am speaking of rather nice distinctions, and it is difficult to put them in simple form. When a certain clear-thinking but somewhat superficial French philosopher asked the profound but obscure German philosopher Hegel to state his views in a concise form, Hegel answered him harshly, "These things can be discussed neither concisely nor in French." We shall ignore the question whether Hegel was right or not, and still try to put into a nutshell the difference between the Gogol-Kafka kind of story and Stevenson's kind.

In Gogol and Kafka the absurd central character belongs to the absurd world around him but, pathetically and tragically, attempts to struggle out of it into the world of humans—and dies in despair. In Stevenson the unreal central character belongs to a brand of unreality different from that of the world around him. He is a Gothic character in a Dickensian setting, and when he struggles and then dies, his fate possesses only conventional pathos. I do not at all mean that Stevenson's story is a failure. No, it is a minor masterpiece in its own conventional terms, but it has only two dimensions, whereas the Gogol-Kafka stories have five or six.

Born in 1883, Franz Kafka came from a German-speaking Jewish family in Prague, Czechoslovakia. He is the greatest German writer of our time. Such poets as Rilke or such novelists as Thomas Mann are dwarfs or plaster saints in comparison to him. He read for law at the German university in Prague and from 1908 on he worked as a petty clerk, a small employee, in a very Gogolian office for an insurance company. Hardly any of his now famous works, such as his novels *The Trial* (1925) and *The Castle* (1926), were published in his lifetime. His greatest short story "The Metamorphosis," in German "Die Verwandlung," was written in the fall of 1912 and published in Leipzig in October 1915. In 1917 he coughed blood, and the rest of his life, a period of seven years, was punctuated by sojourns in Central European sanatoriums. In those last years of his short life (he died at the age of forty-one), he had a happy love affair and lived with his mistress in Berlin, in 1923, not far from me. In the spring of 1924 he went to a sanatorium near Vienna where he died on 3 June, of tuberculosis of the larynx. He was buried in the Jewish cemetery in Prague. He asked his friend Max Brod to burn everything he had written, even published material. Fortunately Brod did not comply with his friend's wish.

Before starting to talk of "The Metamorphosis," I want to dismiss two points of view. I want to dismiss completely Max Brod's opinion that the category of sainthood, not that of literature, is the only one that can be applied to the understanding of Kafka's writings. Kafka was first of all an artist, and although it may be maintained that every artist is a manner of saint (I feel that very clearly myself), I do not think that any religious implications can be read into Kafka's genius. The other matter that I want to dismiss is the Freudian point of view. His Freudian biographers, like Neider in *The Frozen Sea* (1948), contend, for example, that "The Metamorphosis" has a basis in Kafka's complex relationship with his father and his lifelong sense of guilt; they contend further that in mythical symbolism children are represented by vermin—which I doubt—and then go on to say that Kafka uses the symbol of the bug to represent the son according to these Freudian postulates. The bug, they say, aptly characterizes his sense of worthlessness before his father. I am interested here in bugs, not in humbugs, and I reject this nonsense. Kafka himself was extremely critical of Freudian ideas. He considered psychoanalysis (I quote) "a helpless error," and he regarded Freud's theories as very approximate, very rough pictures, which did not do justice to details or, what is more, to the essence of the matter. This is another reason why I should like to dismiss the Freudian approach and concentrate, instead, upon the artistic moment.

The greatest literary influence upon Kafka was Flaubert's. Flaubert who loathed pretty-pretty prose would have applauded Kafka's attitude towards his tool. Kafka liked to draw his terms from the language of law and science, giving them a kind of ironic precision, with no intrusion of the author's private sentiments; this was exactly Flaubert's method through which he achieved a singular poetic effect.

The hero of "The Metamorphosis" is Gregor Samsa (pronounced *Zamza*), who is the son of middle-class parents in Prague, Flaubertian philistines, people interested only in the material side of life and vulgarians in their tastes. Some five years before, old Samsa lost most of his money, whereupon his son Gregor took a job with one of his father's creditors and became a traveling salesman in cloth. His father then stopped working altogether, his sister Grete was too young to work, his mother was ill with asthma; thus young Gregor not only supported the whole family but also found for them the apartment they are now living in. This apartment, a flat in an apartment house, in Charlotte Street to be exact, is divided into segments as he will be divided himself. We are in Prague, central Europe, in the year 1912; servants are cheap so that the Samsas can afford a servant maid, Anna, aged sixteen (one year younger than Grete), and a cook. Gregor is mostly away traveling, but when the story starts he is spending a night at home between two business trips, and it is then that the dreadful thing happened. "As Gregor Samsa awoke one morning from a troubled dream he found himself transformed in his bed into a monstrous insect. He was lying on his hard, as it were armor-plated, back and when he lifted his head a little he could see his dome-like brown belly divided into corrugated segments on top of which the bed quilt could

VLADIMIR NABOKOV

The Samsa flat

Hotel +
Home Ec. students will help us

Street

Charlotte Street

| Parents' R. (later Lodgers') | Living-Dining R. (later Sister & Gregor's Room) | Hospital | Gregor's R. | Sister's R. (later Parents') |

F (closet, H)

table

Sister appears p. 23

Mother

Corridor

Corridor

Taps p. 22

Scene

Hallway

Front door

maid

cook

Kitchen

open book
on p. 22

Third with floor

Scene 14

hardly keep in position and was about to slide off completely. His numerous legs, which were pitifully thin compared to the rest of his bulk, flimmered [*flicker* + *shimmer*] helplessly before his eyes.

"What has happened to me? he thought. It was no dream. . . .

"Gregor's eyes turned next to the window—one could hear rain drops beating on the tin of the windowsill's outer edge and the dull weather made him quite melancholy. What about sleeping a little longer and forgetting all this nonsense, he thought, but it could not be done, for he was accustomed to sleep on his right side and in his present condition he could not turn himself over. However violently he tried to hurl himself on his right side he always swung back to the supine position. He tried it at least a hundred times, shutting his eyes* to keep from seeing his wriggly legs, and only desisted when he began to feel in his side a faint dull ache he had never experienced before.

"Ach Gott, he thought, what an exhausting job I've picked on! Traveling about day in, day out. Many more anxieties on the road than in the office, the plague of worrying about train connections, the bad and irregular meals, casual acquaintances never to be seen again, never to become intimate friends. The hell with it all! He felt a slight itching on the skin of his belly; slowly pushed himself on his back nearer the top of the bed so that he could lift his head more easily; identified the itching place which was covered with small white dots the nature of which he could not understand and tried to touch it with a leg, but drew the leg back immediately, for the contact made a cold shiver run through him."

Now what exactly is the "vermin" into which poor Gregor, the seedy commercial traveler, is so suddenly transformed? It obviously belongs to the branch of "jointed leggers" (*Arthropoda*), to which insects, and spiders, and centipedes, and crustaceans belong. If the "numerous little legs" mentioned in the beginning mean more than six legs, then Gregor would not be an insect from a zoological point of view. But I suggest that a man awakening on his back and finding he has as many as six legs vibrating in the air might feel that six was sufficient to be called numerous. We shall therefore assume that Gregor has six legs, that he is an insect.

Next question: what insect? Commentators say *cockroach*, which of course does not make sense. A cockroach is an insect that is flat in shape

---

*VN's note in his annotated copy: "A regular beetle has no eyelids and cannot close its eyes—a beetle with human eyes." About the passage in general he has the note: "In the original German there is a wonderful flowing rhythm here in this dreamy sequence of sentences. He is half-awake—he realizes his plight without surprise, with a childish acceptance of it, and at the same time he still clings to human memories, human experience. The metamorphosis is not quite complete as yet." Ed.

258   VLADIMIR NABOKOV

with large legs, and Gregor is anything but flat: he is convex on both sides, belly and back, and his legs are small. He approaches a cockroach in only one respect: his coloration is brown. That is all. Apart from this he has a tremendous convex belly divided into segments and a hard rounded back suggestive of wing cases. In beetles these cases conceal flimsy little wings that can be expanded and then may carry the beetle for miles and miles in a blundering flight. Curiously enough, Gregor the beetle never found out that he had wings under the hard covering of his back. (This is a very nice observation on my part to be treasured all your lives. Some Gregors, some Joes and Janes, do not know that they have wings.) Further, he has strong mandibles. He uses these organs to turn the key in a lock while standing erect on his hind legs, on his third pair of legs (a strong little pair), and this gives us the length of his body, which is about three feet long. In the course of the story he gets gradually accustomed to using his new appendages— his feet, his feelers. This brown, convex, dog-sized beetle is very broad. I should imagine him to look like this:

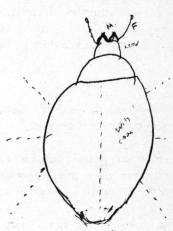

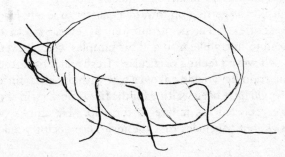

In the original German text the old charwoman calls him *Mistkafer*, a "dung beetle." It is obvious that the good woman is adding the epithet only to be friendly. He is not, technically, a dung beetle. He is merely a big beetle. (I must add that neither Gregor nor Kafka saw that beetle any too clearly.)

Let us look closer at the transformation. The change, though shocking and striking, is not quite so odd as might be assumed at first glance. A commonsensical commentator (Paul L. Landsberg in *The Kafka Problem* [1946], ed. Angel Flores) notes that "When we go to bed in unfamiliar surroundings, we are apt to have a moment of bewilderment upon awakening, a sudden sense of unreality, and this experience must occur over and over again in the life of a commercial traveller, a manner of living that renders impossible any sense of continuity." The sense of reality depends upon continuity, upon duration. After all, awakening as an insect is not much different from awakening as Napoleon or George Washington. (I knew a man who awoke as the Emperor of Brazil.) On the other hand, the isolation, and the strangeness, of so-called reality—this is, after all, something which constantly characterizes the artist, the genius, the discoverer. The Samsa family around the fantastic insect is nothing else than mediocrity surrounding genius.

PART ONE

I am now going to speak of structure. Part one of the story can be divided into seven scenes or segments:

Scene I: Gregor wakes up. He is alone. He has already been changed into a beetle, but his human impressions still mingle with his new insect instincts. The scene ends with the introduction of the still human time element.

"He looked at the alarm clock ticking on the chest. Good Lord! he thought. It was half-past six and the hands were quietly moving on, it was even past the half-hour, it was getting on toward a quarter to seven. Had the alarm clock not gone off? . . . The next train went at seven o'clock; to catch that he would need to hurry like mad and his samples weren't even packed up, and he himself wasn't feeling particularly fresh and active. And even if he did catch the train he wouldn't avoid a row with the boss, since the firm's messenger would have been waiting for the five o'clock train and would have long since reported his failure to turn up." He thinks of reporting that he is sick, but concludes that the insurance doctor would certify him as perfectly healthy. "And would he be so far wrong on this occasion? Gregor really felt quite well, apart from a drowsiness that was utterly superfluous after such a long sleep, and he was even unusually hungry."

Scene II: The three members of the family knock on his doors and talk to him from, respectively, the hallway, the living room, and his sister's room. Gregor's family are his parasites, exploiting him, eating him out from the inside. This is his beetle itch in human terms. The pathetic urge to find some protection from betrayal, cruelty, and filth is the factor that went to form his carapace, his beetle shell, which at first seems hard and secure but eventually is seen to be as vulnerable as his sick human flesh and spirit had been. Who of the three parasites—father, mother, sister—is the most cruel? At first it would seem to be the father. But he is not the worst: it is the sister, whom Gregor loves most but who betrays him beginning with the furniture scene in the middle of the story. In the second scene the door theme begins: "there came a cautious tap at the door behind the head of his bed. 'Gregor,' said a voice—it was his mother's—'it's a quarter to seven. Hadn't you a train to catch?' That gentle voice! Gregor had a shock as he heard his own voice answering hers, unmistakably his own voice, it was true, but with a persistent pitiful squeaky undertone. . . . 'Yes, yes, thank you, Mother, I'm getting up now.' The wooden door between them must have kept the change in his voice from being noticeable outside. . . . Yet this brief exchange of words had made the other members of the family aware that Gregor was still in the house, as they had not expected, and at one of the side doors his father was already knocking gently, yet with his fist. 'Gregor, Gregor,' he called, 'what's the matter with you?' And after a while he called again in a deeper voice: 'Gregor! Gregor!' At the other side door his sister was saying in a low, plaintive tone: 'Gregor? Aren't you well? Do you need anything?' He answered them both at once: 'I'm just ready,' and did his best to make his voice sound as normal as possible by enunciating the words very clearly and leaving long pauses between them. So his father went back to his breakfast, but his sister whispered: 'Gregor, open the door, do.' However, he was not thinking of opening the door, and felt thankful for the prudent habit he had acquired in traveling of locking all doors during the night, even at home."

Scene III: The getting out of bed ordeal in which man plans but beetle acts. Gregor still thinks of his body in human terms, but now a human's lower part is a beetle's hind part, a human's upper part is a beetle's fore part. A man on all fours seems to him to correspond to a beetle on all sixes. He does not quite yet understand this and will persistently try to stand up on his third pair of legs. "He thought that he might get out of bed with the lower part of his body first, but this lower part, which he had not yet seen and of which he could form no clear conception, proved too difficult to move; it was all so slow; and when at last almost savagely he gathered his forces together and thrust out recklessly, he had miscalculated the direction and bumped heavily against the lower end of the bed, and the burning pain he felt taught him that it was the lower part of his body that probably for the time being was the most sensitive. . . . But then he said to himself: 'Before it strikes a quarter past seven I must be quite out of this bed, without fail. Anyhow, by that time someone will have come from the office to ask what is the matter with me, since it opens before seven.' And he set himself to rocking his whole body at once in a regular series of jolts, with the idea of swinging it out of the bed. If he tipped himself out in that way he could keep his head from injury by lifting it at an acute angle when he fell. His back seemed to be hard and was not likely to suffer from a fall on the carpet. His biggest worry was the loud crash he would not be able to help making, which would probably cause anxiety, if not terror, behind all the doors. Still, he must take the risk. . . . Well, ignoring the fact that the doors were all locked, ought he really to call for help? In spite of his misery he could not suppress a smile at the very idea of it."

Scene IV: He is still struggling when the family theme, or the theme of the many doors, takes over again, and in the course of this scene he falls out of bed at last, with a dull thud. The conversation is a little on the lines of a Greek chorus. From Gregor's office the head clerk has been sent to see why he has not yet turned up at the station. This grim speed in checking a remiss employee has all the qualities of a bad dream. The speaking through doors, as in the second scene, is now repeated. Note the sequence: the chief clerk talks to Gregor from the living room on the left; Gregor's sister, Grete, talks to her brother from the room on the right; the mother and father join the chief clerk in the living room. Gregor can still speak, but his voice becomes more and more indistinct, and soon his speech cannot be understood. (In *Finnegans Wake*, written twenty years later by James Joyce, two washerwomen talking across a river are gradually changed into a

---

Nabokov's notes on the triad theme in "The Metamorphosis"

(3 theme) Triptych theme

Triad theme

Add. one

It begins in the scene second (of the First Part) when p. 15-16 — the scene that floods in one reitered long paragraph, after we see when Father, for long room on the left out where with him before on the right talk to Gregor

The three main rooms correspond to the divisions of his body.

His family consists of three people Father. Mother. sister Daughter.

They are his parasites, exploiting him, eating him out from the inside. This is his beetle itch in human terms. The pathetic urge to find some protection from betrayal, cruelty and filth — this is the factor that went to form his carapace, his beetle shell which at first seems secure and hard; — but eventually is seen to be as vulnerable as his sick human flesh and spirit had been.

Who of the three parasites — Father Mother Sister is the worst most cruel? At first it would seem — the Father. But we know it is not he; the worst, — it is the Sister, whom he loves most and who betrays him, beginning with the furniture scene in the middle of the story

stout elm and a stone.) Gregor does not understand why his sister in the right-hand room did not join the others. "She was probably newly out of bed and hadn't even begun to put on her clothes yet. Well, why was she crying? Because he wouldn't get up and let the chief clerk in, because he was in danger of losing his job, and because the boss would begin dunning his parents again for the old debts?" Poor Gregor is so accustomed to be just an instrument to be used by his family that the question of pity does not arise: he does not even hope that Grete might be sorry for him. Mother and sister call to each other from the doors across Gregor's room. The sister and servant are dispatched for a doctor and a locksmith. "But Gregor was now much calmer. The words he uttered were no longer understandable, apparently, although they seemed clear enough to him, even clearer than before, perhaps because his ear had grown accustomed to the sound of them. Yet at any rate people now believed that something was wrong with him, and were ready to help him. The positive certainty with which these first measures had been taken comforted him. He felt himself drawn once more into the human circle and hoped for great and remarkable results from both the doctor and the locksmith, without really distinguishing precisely between them."

Scene V: Gregor opens the door. "Slowly Gregor pushed the chair towards the door, then let go of it, caught hold of the door for support—the soles at the end of his little legs were somewhat sticky—and rested against it for a moment after his efforts. Then he set himself to turning the key in the lock with his mouth. It seemed, unhappily, that he hadn't really any teeth—what could he grip the key with?—but on the other hand his jaws were certainly very strong; with their help he did manage to set the key in motion, heedless of the fact that he was undoubtedly damaging them somewhere, since a brown fluid issued from his mouth, flowed over the key and dripped on the floor. . . . Since he had to pull the door towards him, he was still invisible when it was really wide open. He had to edge himself slowly round the near half of the double door, and to do it very carefully if he was not to fall plump upon his back just on the threshold. He was still carrying out this difficult manoeuvre, with no time to observe anything else, when he heard the chief clerk utter a loud 'Oh!'—it sounded like a gust of wind—and now he could see the man, standing as he was nearest to the door, clapping one hand before his open mouth and slowly backing away as if driven by some invisible steady pressure. His mother—in spite of the chief clerk's being there her hair was still undone and sticking up in all directions—first clasped her hands and looked at his father, then took two steps towards Gregor and fell on the floor among her outspread skirts, her face quite hidden on her breast. His father knotted his fist with a fierce expression on his face as if he meant to knock Gregor back into his room, then looked uncertainly round the living room, covered his eyes with his hands and wept till his great chest heaved."

Scene VI: Gregor tries to calm the chief clerk so that he will not be discharged. " 'Well,' said Gregor, knowing perfectly that he was the only one who had retained any composure, 'I'll put my clothes on at once, pack up my samples and start off. Will you only let me go? You see, sir, I'm not obstinate, and I'm willing to work; traveling is a hard life, but I couldn't live without it. Where are you going, sir? To the office? Yes? Will you give a true account of all this? One can be temporarily incapacitated, but that's just the moment for remembering former services and bearing in mind that later on, when the incapacity has been got over, one will certainly work with all the more industry and concentration.' " But the chief clerk in horror and as if in a trance is stumbling towards the staircase to escape. Gregor starts to walk towards him—a wonderful bit here—on the hind pair of his three pairs of legs, "but immediately, as he was feeling for a support, he fell down with a little cry upon his many little legs. Hardly was he down when he experienced for the first time this morning a sense of physical comfort; his legs had firm ground under them; they were completely obedient, as he noted with joy; they even strove to carry him forward in whatever direction he chose; and he was inclined to believe that a final relief from all his sufferings was at hand." His mother springs up, and in backing away from him she upsets the coffeepot on the breakfast table so that it pours over the rug. " 'Mother, Mother,' said Gregor in a low voice, and looked up at her. The chief clerk, for the moment, had quite slipped from his mind; instead, he could not resist snapping his jaws together at the sight of the streaming coffee. That made his mother scream again." Gregor, looking now for the chief clerk, "made a spring, to be as sure as possible of overtaking him; the chief clerk must have divined his intention, for he leaped down several steps and vanished; he was still yelling 'Ugh!' and it echoed through the whole staircase."

Scene VII: The father brutally drives Gregor back into his room, stamping his feet and flourishing a stick in one hand and a newspaper in the other. Gregor has difficulty getting through the partly opened door, but forced by his father he tries until he gets stuck. "One side of his body rose up, he was tilted at an angle in the doorway, his flank was quite bruised, horrid blotches stained the white door, soon he was stuck fast and, left to himself, could not have moved at all, his legs on one side fluttered trembling in the air, those on the other were crushed painfully to the floor—when from behind his father gave him a strong push which was literally a deliverance and he flew far into the room, bleeding freely. The father caught at the handle of the door with the stick and slammed it behind him, and then at last there was silence."

PART TWO

Scene I: The first attempt is made to feed coleopteron Gregor. Under the impression that his condition is some kind of foul but not hopeless illness that may pass with time, he is placed at first on the diet of a sick human being and he finds that a human meal of milk has been offered to him. We are always aware of those doors, doors opening and closing stealthily in the dusk. From the kitchen, across the hallway, to the hallway door of Gregor's room light footsteps had come, his sister's, awakening him from sleep, and he discovers that a basin with milk has been placed within his room. One of his little legs has been damaged in the collision with his father; it will grow better, but in this scene he limps and trails it uselessly behind him. He is a big beetle as beetles go, but he is smaller and more brittle than a human being. Gregor makes for the milk. Alas, while his still human mind eagerly accepts the notion of that sweetish sop, with soft white bread in the milk, his beetle stomach and beetle taste buds refuse a mammal's meal. Although he is very hungry the milk is repulsive to him and he crawls back to the middle of the room.

Scene II: The door theme continues and the duration theme settles in. We shall begin to witness Gregor's usual day and dusk during this fantastic winter of 1912, and his discovery of the security of the couch. But let us look and listen with Gregor through the crack of the parlor door on the left. His father used to read aloud the newspapers to his wife and daughter. True, this has now been interrupted and the flat is silent though not empty of occupants, but on the whole the family is getting used to the situation. Here is the son and brother plunged into a monstrous change that should have sent them scuttling out into the streets for help with shrieks and tears, in wild compassion—but here they are, the three philistines, cosily taking it in their stride.

I don't know if you read a couple of years ago in the papers about that teenage girl and boy who murdered the girl's mother. It starts with a very

Kafkaesque scene: the girl's mother has come home and found her daughter and the boy in the bedroom, and the boy has hit the mother with a hammer—several times—and dragged her away. But the woman is still thrashing and groaning in the kitchen, and the boy says to his sweetheart, "Gimme that hammer. I think I'll have to knock her again." But the girl gives her mate a knife instead and he stabs the girl's mother many, many times, to death—under the impression, probably, that this all is a comic strip: you hit a person, the person sees lots of stars and exclamation marks but revives by and by, in the next installment. Physical life however has no next installment, and soon boy and girl have to do something with dead mother. "Oh, plaster of paris, it will dissolve her completely!" Of course, it will—marvelous idea—place body in bathtub, cover with plaster, and that's all. Meanwhile, with mother under the plaster (which does not work—wrong plaster, perhaps) boy and girl throw several beer parties. What fun! Lovely canned music, and lovely canned beer. "But you can't go, fellas, to the bathroom. The bathroom is a mess."

I'm trying to show you that in so-called real life we find sometimes a great resemblance to the situation in Kafka's fantastic story. Mark the curious mentality of the morons in Kafka who enjoy their evening paper despite the fantastic horror in the middle of their apartment. " 'What a quiet life our family has been leading,' said Gregor to himself, and as he sat there motionless staring into the darkness he felt great pride in the fact that he had been able to provide such a life for his parents and sister in such a fine flat." The room is lofty and empty and the beetle begins to dominate the man. The high room "in which he had to lie flat on the floor filled him with an apprehension he could not account for, since it had been his very own room for the past five years—and with a half-unconscious action, not without a slight feeling of shame, he scuttled under the couch, where he felt comfortable at once, although his back was a little cramped and he could not lift his head up, and his only regret was that his body was too broad to get the whole of it under the couch."

Scene III: Gregor's sister brings a selection of foods. She removes the basin of milk, not by means of her bare hands but with a cloth, for it has been touched by the disgusting monster. However, she is a clever little creature, that sister, and brings a whole selection—rotten vegetables, old cheese, bones glazed with dead white sauce—and Gregor whizzed towards this feast. "One after another and with tears of satisfaction in his eyes he quickly devoured the cheese, the vegetables and the sauce; the fresh food, on the other hand, had no charms for him, he could not even stand the smell of it and actually dragged away to some little distance the things he could eat." The sister turns the key in the lock slowly as a warning that he should retreat, and she comes and cleans up while Gregor, full of food, tries to hide under the couch.

Scene IV: Grete, the sister, takes on a new importance. It is she who feeds the beetle; she alone enters the beetle's lair, sighing and with an occasional appeal to the saints—it is such a Christian family. In a wonderful passage the cook goes down on her knees to Mrs. Samsa and begs to leave. With tears in her eyes she thanks the Samsas for allowing her to go—as if she were a liberated slave—and without any prompting she swears a solemn oath that she will never say a single word to anyone about what is happening in the Samsa household. "Gregor was fed, once in the early morning while his parents and the servant girl were still asleep, and a second time after they had all had their midday dinner, for then his parents took a short nap and the servant girl could be sent out on some errand or other by his sister. Not that they would have wanted him to starve, of course, but perhaps they could not have borne to know more about his feeding than from hearsay, perhaps too his sister wanted to spare them such little anxieties wherever possible, since they had quite enough to bear as it was."

Scene V: This is a very distressing scene. It transpires that in his human past Gregor has been deceived by his family. Gregor had taken that dreadful job with that nightmare firm because he wished to help his father who five years ago had gone bankrupt. "They had simply got used to it, both the family and Gregor; the money was gratefully accepted and gladly given, but there was no special uprush of warm feeling. With his sister alone had he remained intimate, and it was a secret plan of his that she, who loved music, unlike himself, and could play movingly on the violin, should be sent next year to study at the School of Music, despite the great expense that would entail, which must be made up in some other way. During his brief visits home the School of Music was often mentioned in the talks he had with his sister, but always merely as a beautiful dream which could never come true, and his parents discouraged even these innocent references to it; yet Gregor had made up his mind firmly about it and meant to announce the fact with due solemnity on Christmas Day." Gregor now overhears his father explaining "that a certain amount of investments, a very small amount it was true, had survived the wreck of their fortunes and had even increased a little because the dividends had not been touched meanwhile. And besides that, the money Gregor brought home every month—he had kept only a few dollars for himself—had never been quite used up and now amounted to a small capital sum. Behind the door Gregor nodded his head eagerly, rejoiced at his evidence of unexpected thrift and foresight. True, he could really have paid off some more of his father's debts to the boss with this extra money, and so brought much nearer the day on which he could quit his job, but doubtless it was better the way his father had arranged it." The family believes this sum should be kept untouched for a rainy day, but in the meantime how are the living expenses to be met? The father has not worked for five years and could not be expected to do much. And Gregor's mother's asthma would keep her from working. "And was his sister to earn her bread, she who was still a child of seventeen and whose life hitherto had been so pleasant, consisting as it did in dressing herself nicely, sleeping long, helping in the housekeeping, going out to a few modest entertainments and above all playing the violin? At first whenever the need for earning money was mentioned Gregor let go his hold on the door and threw himself down on the cool leather sofa beside it, he felt so hot with shame and grief."

Scene VI: A new relationship begins between brother and sister, this time having to do with a window instead of a door. Gregor "nerved himself to the great effort of pushing an armchair to the window, then crawled up over the window sill and, braced against the chair, leaned against the windowpanes, obviously in some recollection of the sense of freedom that looking out of a window always used to give him." Gregor, or Kafka, seems to think that Gregor's urge to approach the window was a recollection of human experience. Actually, it is a typical insect reaction to light: one finds all sorts of dusty bugs near windowpanes, a moth on its back, a lame daddy longlegs, poor insects cobwebbed in a corner, a buzzing fly still trying to conquer the glass pane. Gregor's human sight is growing dimmer so that he cannot see clearly even across the street. The human detail is dominated by the insect general idea. (But let us not ourselves be insects. Let us first of all study every detail in this story; the general idea will come of itself later when we have all the data we need.) His sister does not understand that Gregor has retained a human heart, human sensitivity, a human sense of decorum, of shame, of humility and pathetic pride. She disturbs him horribly by the noise and haste with which she opens the window to breathe some fresh air, and she does not bother to conceal her disgust at the awful smell in his den. Neither does she conceal her feelings when she actually sees him. One day, about a month after Gregor's metamorphosis, "when there was surely no reason for her to be still startled at his appearance, she came a little earlier than usual and found him gazing out of the window, quite motionless, and thus well placed to look like a bogey.... She jumped back as if in alarm and banged the door shut; a stranger might well have thought that he had been lying in wait for her there meaning to bite her. Of course he hid himself under the couch at once, but he had to wait until midday before she came again, and she seemed more ill at ease than usual." These things hurt, and nobody understood how they hurt. In an exquisite display of feeling, in order to spare her the repulsive sight of him, Gregor one day "carried a sheet on his back to the couch—it cost him four hours' labor—and arranged it there in such a way as to hide him completely, so that even if she were to bend down she could not see him.... Gregor even fancied that he caught a thankful glance from her eye when he lifted the sheet carefully a very little with his head to see how she was taking the new arrangement."

It should be noted how kind, how good our poor little monster is. His beetlehood, while distorting and degrading his body, seems to bring out in him all his human sweetness. His utter unselfishness, his constant preoccupation with the needs of others—this, against the backdrop of his hideous plight comes out in strong relief. Kafka's art consists in accumulating on the one hand, Gregor's insect features, all the sad detail of his insect disguise, and on the other hand, in keeping vivid and limpid before the reader's eyes Gregor's sweet and subtle human nature.

Scene VII: Here occurs the furniture-moving scene. Two months have passed. Up to now only his sister has been visiting him; but, Gregor says to himself, my sister is only a child; she has taken on herself the job of caring for me merely out of childish thoughtlessness. My mother should understand the situation better. So here in the seventh scene the mother, asthmatic, feeble, and muddleheaded, will enter his room for the first time. Kafka prepares the scene carefully. For recreation Gregor had formed the habit of walking on the walls and ceiling. He is at the height of the meagre bliss his beetlehood can produce. "His sister at once remarked the new distraction Gregor had found for himself—he left traces behind him of the sticky stuff on his soles wherever he crawled—and she got the idea in her head of giving him as wide a field as possible to crawl in and of removing the pieces of furniture that hindered him, above all the chest of drawers and the writing desk." Thus the mother is brought in to help move the furniture. She comes to his door with exclamations of joyful eagerness to see her son, an incongruous and automatic reaction that is replaced by a certain hush when she enters the mysterious chamber. "Gregor's sister, of course, went in first, to see that everything was in order before letting his mother enter. In great haste Gregor pulled the sheet lower and rucked it more in folds so that it really looked as if it had been thrown accidentally over the couch. And this time he did not peer out from under it; he renounced the pleasure of seeing his mother on this occasion and was only glad that she had come at all. 'Come in, he's out of sight,' said his sister, obviously leading her mother in by the hand."

The women struggle to move the heavy furniture until his mother voices a certain human thought, naive but kind, feeble but not devoid of feeling, when she says: "doesn't it look as if we were showing him, by taking away his furniture, that we have given up hope of his ever getting better and are just leaving him coldly to himself? I think it would be best to keep his room exactly as it has always been, so that when he comes back to us he will find everything unchanged and be able all the more easily to forget what has happened in between." Gregor is torn between two emotions. His beetlehood suggests that an empty room with bare walls would be more convenient for crawling about—all he needed would be some chink to hide in, his indispensable couch—but otherwise he would not need all those human conveniences and adornments. But his mother's voice reminds him of his human background. Unfortunately, his sister has developed a queer self-assurance and has grown accustomed to consider herself an expert in Gregor's affairs as against her parents. "Another factor might have been also the enthusiastic temperament of an adolescent girl, which seeks to indulge itself on every opportunity and which now tempted Grete to exaggerate the horror of her brother's circumstances in order that she might do all the more for him." This is a curious note: the domineering sister, the strong sister of the fairy tales, the handsome busybody lording it over the fool of the family, the proud sisters of Cinderella, the cruel emblem of health, youth, and blossoming beauty in the house of disaster and dust. So they decide to move the things out after all but have a real struggle with the chest of drawers. Gregor is in an awful state of panic. He kept his fretsaw in that chest, with which he used to make things when he was free at home, his sole hobby.

Scene VIII: Gregor tries to save at least the picture in the frame he had made with his cherished fretsaw. Kafka varies his effects in that every time the beetle is seen by his family he is shown in a new position, some new spot. Here Gregor rushes from his hiding place, unseen by the two women now struggling with his writing desk, and climbs the wall to press himself over the picture, his hot, dry belly against the soothing cool glass. The mother is not much help in this furniture-moving business and has to be supported by Grete. Grete always remains strong and hale whereas not only her brother but both parents are going to be soon (after the apple-pitching scene) on the brink of sinking into some dull dream, into a state of torpid and decrepit oblivion; but Grete with the hard health of her ruddy adolescence keeps propping them up.

Scene IX: Despite Grete's efforts, the mother catches sight of Gregor, a "huge brown mass on the flowered wallpaper, and before she was really conscious that what she saw was Gregor screamed in a loud, hoarse voice: 'Oh God, oh God!' fell with outspread arms over the couch as if giving up and did not move. 'Gregor!' cried his sister, shaking her fist and glaring at him. This was the first time she had directly addressed him since his metamorphosis." She runs into the living room for something to rouse her mother from the fainting fit. "Gregor wanted to help too—there was still time to rescue the picture—but he was stuck fast to the glass and had to tear himself loose; he then ran after his sister into the next room as if he could advise her, as he used to do; but then had to stand helplessly behind her; she meanwhile searched among various small bottles and when she turned round started in alarm at the sight of him; one bottle fell on the floor and broke; a splinter of glass cut Gregor's face and some kind of corrosive medicine splashed him; without pausing a moment longer Grete gathered up all the bottles she could carry and ran to her mother with them; she banged the door shut with her foot. Gregor was now cut off from his mother, who was perhaps nearly dying because of him; he dared not open the door for fear of frightening away his sister, who had to stay with her mother; there was nothing he could do but wait; and harassed by self-reproach and worry he began now to crawl to and fro, over everything, walls, furniture and ceiling, and finally in his despair, when the whole room seemed to be reeling around him, fell down on to the middle of the big table." There is a change in the respective position of the various members of the family. Mother (on the couch) and sister are in the middle room; Gregor is in the corner in the left room. And presently his father comes home and enters the living room. "And so [Gregor] fled to the door of his own room and crouched against it, to let his father see as soon as he came in from the hall that his son had the good intention of getting back into his own room immediately and that it was not necessary to drive him there, but that if only the door were opened he would disappear at once."

Scene X: The apple-pelting scene comes now. Gregor's father has changed and is now at the summit of his power. Instead of the man who used to lie wearily sunk in bed and could scarcely wave an arm in greeting, and when he went out shuffled along laboriously with a crook-handled stick, "Now he was standing there in fine shape; dressed in a smart blue uniform with gold buttons, such as bank messengers wear; his strong double chin bulged over the stiff high collar of his jacket; from under his bushy eyebrows his black eyes darted fresh and penetrating glances; his onetime tangled white hair had been combed flat on either side of a shining and carefully exact parting. He pitched his cap, which bore a gold monogram, probably the badge of some bank, in a wide sweep across the whole room on to a sofa and with the tail-ends of his jacket thrown back, his hands in his trouser pockets, advanced with a grim visage towards Gregor. Likely enough he did not himself know what he meant to do; at any rate he lifted his feet uncommonly high and Gregor was dumbfounded at the enormous size of his shoe soles."

As usual, Gregor is tremendously interested in the movement of human legs, big thick human feet, so different from his own flimmering appendages. We have a repetition of the slow motion theme. (The chief clerk, backing and shuffling, had retreated in slow motion.) Now father and son slowly circle the room: indeed, the whole operation hardly looked like pursuit it was carried out so slowly. And then his father starts to bombard Gregor with the only missiles that the living-dining room could provide—apples, small red apples—and Gregor is driven back into the middle room, back to the heart of his beetlehood. "An apple thrown without much force grazed Gregor's back and glanced off harmlessly. But another following immediately landed right on his back and sank in; Gregor wanted to drag himself forward, as if this startling, incredible pain could be left behind him; but he felt as if nailed to the spot and flattened himself out in a complete derangement of all his senses. With his last conscious look he saw the door of his room being torn open and his mother rushing out ahead of his screaming sister, in her underbodice, for her daughter had loosened her clothing to let her breathe more freely and recover from her swoon; he saw his mother rushing towards his father, leaving one after another behind her on the floor her loosened petticoats, stumbling over her petticoats straight to his father and embracing him, in complete union with him—but here Gregor's sight began to fail—with her hands clasped round his father's neck as she begged for her son's life."

This is the end of part two. Let us sum up the situation. The sister has become frankly antagonistic to her brother. She may have loved him once, but now she regards him with disgust and anger. In Mrs. Samsa asthma and emotion struggle. She is a rather mechanical mother, with some mechanical mother love for her son, but we shall soon see that she, too, is ready to give him up. The father, as already remarked, has reached a certain summit of impressive strength and brutality. From the very first he had been eager to hurt physically his helpless son, and now the apple he has thrown has become embedded in poor Gregor's beetle flesh.

PART THREE

Scene I: "The serious injury done to Gregor, which disabled him for more than a month—the apple went on sticking in his body as a visible reminder, since no one ventured to remove it—seemed to have made even his father recollect that Gregor was a member of the family, despite his present unfortunate and repulsive shape, and ought not to be treated as an enemy, that, on the contrary, family duty required the suppression of disgust and the exercise of patience, nothing but patience." The door theme is taken up again since now, in the evening, the door leading from Gregor's darkened room to the lighted living room is left open. This is a subtle situation. In the previous scene father and mother had reached their highest point of energy, he in his resplendent uniform pitching those little red bombs, emblems of fruitfulness and manliness; and she, the mother, actually moving furniture despite her frail breathing tubes. But after that peak there is a fall, a weakening. It would almost seem that the father himself is on the point of disintegrating and becoming a feeble beetle. Through the opened door a curious current seems to pass. Gregor's beetle illness is catching, his father seems to have caught it, the weakness, the drabness, the dirt. "Soon after supper his father would fall asleep in his armchair; his mother and sister would admonish each other to be silent; his mother, bending low over the lamp, stitched at fine sewing for an underwear firm; his sister, who had taken a job as a salesgirl, was learning shorthand and French in the evenings on the chance of bettering herself. Sometimes his father woke up, and as if quite unaware that he had been sleeping said to the mother: 'What a lot of sewing you're doing today!' and at once fell asleep again, while the two women exchanged a tired smile.

"With a kind of mulishness his father persisted in keeping his uniform on even in the house; his dressing gown hung uselessly on its peg and he slept fully dressed where he sat, as if he were ready for service at any moment and even here only at the beck and call of his superior. As a result, his uniform, which was not brand new to start with, began to look dirty, despite all the loving care of the mother and sister to keep it clean, and Gregor often spent whole evenings gazing at the many greasy spots on the garment, gleaming with gold buttons always in a high state of polish, in which the old man sat sleeping in extreme discomfort and yet quite peacefully." The father always refused to go to bed when the time had arrived, despite every inducement offered by the mother and sister, until finally the two women would hoist him up by his armpits from the chair, "And leaning on the two of them he would heave himself up, with difficulty, as if he were a great burden to himself, suffer them to lead him as far as the door and then wave them off and go on alone, while the mother abandoned her needlework and the sister her pen in order to run after him and help him farther." The father's uniform comes close to resembling that of a big but somewhat tarnished scarab. His tired overworked family must get him from one room to another and to bed.

Scene II: The disintegration of the Samsa family continues. They dismiss the servant girl and engage a still cheaper charwoman, a gigantic bony creature who comes in to do the rough work. You must remember that in Prague, 1912, it was much more difficult to clean and cook than in Ithaca, 1954. They have to sell various family ornaments. "But what they lamented most was the fact that they could not leave the flat which was much too big for their present circumstances, because they could not think of any way to shift Gregor. Yet Gregor saw well enough that consideration for him was not the main difficulty preventing the removal, for they could have easily shifted him in some suitable box with a few air holes in it; what really kept them from moving into another flat was rather their own complete hopelessness and the belief that they had been singled out for a misfortune such as had never happened to any of their relations or acquaintances." The family is completely egotistic and has no more strength left after fulfilling its daily obligations.

Scene III: A last flash of human recollections comes to Gregor's mind, prompted by the still living urge in him to help his family. He even remembers vague sweethearts, "but instead of helping him and his family they were one and all unapproachable and he was glad when they vanished." This scene is mainly devoted to Grete, who is now clearly the villain of the piece. "His sister no longer took thought to bring him what might especially please him, but in the morning and at noon before she went to business hurriedly pushed into his room with her foot any food that was available, and in the evening cleared it out again with one sweep of the broom, heedless of whether it had been merely tasted, or—as most frequently happened—left untouched. The cleaning of his room, which she now did always in the evenings, could not have been more hastily done. Streaks of dirt stretched along the walls, here and there lay balls of dust and filth. At first Gregor used to station himself in some particularly filthy corner when his sister arrived, in order to reproach her with it, so to speak. But he could have sat there for weeks without getting her to make any improvement; she could see the dirt as well as he did, but she had simply made up her mind to leave it alone. And yet, with a touchiness that was new to her, which seemed anyhow to have infected the whole family, she jealously guarded her claim to be the sole caretaker of Gregor's room." Once when his mother had given the room a thorough cleaning with several buckets of water—the dampness upset Gregor—a grotesque family row ensues. The sister bursts into a storm of weeping while her parents look on in helpless amazement; "then they too began to go into action; the father reproached the mother on his right for not having left the cleaning of Gregor's room to his sister; shrieked at the sister on his left that never again was she to be allowed to clean Gregor's room; while the mother tried to pull the father into his bedroom, since he was beyond himself with agitation; the sister, shaken with sobs, then beat upon the table with her small fists; and Gregor hissed loudly with rage because not one of them thought of shutting the door to spare him such a spectacle and so much noise."

Scene IV: A curious relationship is established between Gregor and the bony charwoman who is rather amused by him, not frightened at all, and in fact she rather likes him. "Come along, then, you old dung beetle," she says. And it is raining outside, the first sign of spring perhaps.

Scene V: The lodgers arrive, the three bearded boarders, with a passion for order. These are mechanical beings; their beards are masks of respectability but actually they are shoddy scoundrels, these serious-looking gentlemen. In this scene a great change comes over the apartment. The boarders take the parents' bedroom on the far left of the flat, beyond the living room. The parents move across to the sister's room on the right of Gregor's room, and Grete has to sleep in the living room but has now no room of her own since the lodgers take their meals in the living room and spend their evenings there. Moreover, the three bearded boarders have brought into this furnished flat some furniture of their own. They have a fiendish love for superficial tidiness, and all the odds and ends which they do not need go into Gregor's room. This is exactly the opposite to what had been happening in the furniture scene of part two, scene 7, where there had been an attempt to move everything out of Gregor's room. Then we had the ebb of the furniture, now the return flow, the jetsam washed back, all kinds of junk pouring in; and curiously enough Gregor, though a very sick beetle—the apple wound is festering, and he is starving—finds some beetle pleasure in crawling among all that dusty rubbish. In this fifth scene of part three where all the changes come, the alteration in the family meals is depicted. The mechanical movement of the bearded automatons is matched by the automatic reaction of the Samsas. The lodgers "set themselves at the top end of the table where formerly Gregor and his father and mother had eaten their meals, unfolded their napkins and took knife and fork in hand. At once his mother appeared in the other doorway with a dish of meat and close behind her his sister with a dish of potatoes piled high. The food steamed with a thick vapor. The lodgers bent over the food set before them as if to scrutinize it before eating, in fact the man in the middle, who seemed to pass for an authority with the other two, cut a piece of meat as it lay on the dish, obviously to discover if it were tender or should be sent back to the kitchen. He showed satisfaction, and Gregor's mother and sister, who had been watching anxiously, breathed freely and began to smile." Gregor's keen envious interest in large feet will be recalled; now toothless Gregor is also interested in teeth. "It seemed remarkable to Gregor that among the various noises coming from the table he could always distinguish the sound of their masticating teeth, as if this were a sign to Gregor that one needed teeth in order to eat, and that with toothless jaws even of the finest make one could do nothing. 'I'm hungry enough,' said Gregor sadly to himself, 'but not for that kind of food. How these lodgers are stuffing themselves, and here am I dying of starvation!'"

Scene VI: In this great music scene the lodgers have heard Grete playing the violin in the kitchen, and in automatic reaction to the entertainment value of music they suggest that she play for them. The three roomers and the three Samsas gather in the living room.

Without wishing to antagonize lovers of music, I do wish to point out that taken in a general sense music, as perceived by its consumers, belongs to a more primitive, more animal form in the scale of arts than literature or painting. I am taking music as a whole, not in terms of individual creation, imagination, and composition, all of which of course rival the art of literature and painting, but in terms of the impact music has on the average listener. A great composer, a great writer, a great painter are brothers. But I think that the impact music in a generalized and primitive form has on the listener is of a more lowly quality than the impact of an average book or an average picture. What I especially have in mind is the soothing, lulling, dulling influence of music on some people, such as of the radio or records.

In Kafka's tale it is merely a girl pitifully scraping on a fiddle, and this corresponds in the piece to the canned music or plugged-in music of today. What Kafka felt about music in general is what I have just described: its stupefying, numbing, animallike quality. This attitude must be kept in mind in interpreting an important sentence that has been misunderstood by some translators. Literally, it reads "Was Gregor an animal to be so affected by music?" That is, in his human form he had cared little for it, but in this scene, in his beetlehood, he succumbs: "He felt as if the way were opening before him to the unknown nourishment he craved." The scene goes as follows. Gregor's sister begins to play for the lodgers. Gregor is attracted by the playing and actually puts his head into the living room. "He felt hardly any surprise at his growing lack of consideration for the others; there had been a time when he prided himself on being considerate. And yet just on this occasion he had more reason than ever to hide himself, since owing to the amount of dust which lay thick in his room and rose into the air at the slightest movement, he too was covered with dust; fluff and hair and remnants of food trailed with him, caught on his back and along his sides; his indifference to everything was much too great for him to turn on his back and scrape himself clean on the carpet, as once he had done several times a day. And in spite of his condition, no shame deterred him from advancing a little over the spotless floor of the living room."

At first no one was aware of him. The lodgers, disappointed in their expectation of hearing good violin playing, were clustered near the window, whispering among themselves and waiting only for the music to stop. And yet, to Gregor, his sister was playing beautifully. He "crawled a little farther forward and lowered his head to the ground so that it might be possible for his eyes to meet hers. Was he an animal, that music had such an effect upon him? He felt as if the way were opening before him to the unknown nourishment he craved. He was determined to push forward till he reached his sister, to pull at her skirt and so let her know that she was to come into his room with her violin, for no one here appreciated her playing as he would appreciate it. He would never let her out of his room, at least, not so long as he lived; his frightful appearance would become, for the first time, useful to him; he would watch all the doors of his room at once and spit at intruders; but his sister should need no constraint, she should stay with him of her own free will; she should sit beside him on the couch, bend down her ear to him and hear him confide that he had had the firm intention of sending her to the School of Music, and that, but for his mishap, last Christmas—surely Christmas was long past?—he would have announced it to everybody without allowing a single objection. After this confession his sister would be so touched that she would burst into tears, and Gregor would then raise himself to her shoulder and kiss her on the neck, which, now that she went to business, she kept free of any ribbon or collar."

Suddenly the middle lodger sees Gregor, but instead of driving Gregor out the father tries to soothe the lodgers and (in a reversal of his actions) "spreading out his arms, tried to urge them back into their own room and at the same time to block their view of Gregor. They now began to be really a little angry, one could not tell whether because of the old man's behavior or because it had just dawned on them that all unwittingly they had such a neighbor as Gregor next door. They demanded explanations of his father, they waved their arms like him, tugged uneasily at their beards, and only with reluctance backed towards their room." The sister rushes into the lodgers' room and quickly makes up their beds, but "The old man seemed once more to be so possessed by his mulish self-assertiveness that he was forgetting all the respect he should show to his lodgers. He kept driving them on and driving them on until in the very door of the bedroom the middle lodger stamped his foot loudly on the floor and so brought him to a halt. 'I beg to announce,' said the lodger, lifting one hand and looking also at Gregor's mother and sister, 'that because of the disgusting conditions prevailing in this household and family'—here he spat on the floor with emphatic brevity—'I give you notice on the spot. Naturally I won't pay you a penny for the days I have lived here; on the contrary I shall consider bringing an action for damages against you, based on claims—believe me—that will be easily susceptible of proof.' He ceased and stared straight in front of him, as if he expected something. In fact his two friends at once rushed into the breach with these words: 'And we too give notice on the spot.' On that he seized the door-handle and shut the door with a slam."

Scene VII: The sister is completely unmasked; her betrayal is absolute and fatal to Gregor. " 'I won't utter my brother's name in the presence of this creature, and so all I say is: we must try to get rid of it. . . .

" 'We must try to get rid of it,' his sister now said explicitly to her father, since her mother was coughing too much to hear a word. 'It will be the death of both of you, I can see that coming. When one has to work as hard as we do, all of us, one can't stand this continual torment at home on top of it. At least I can't stand it any longer.' And she burst into such a passion of sobbing that her tears dropped on her mother's face, where she wiped them off mechanically." Both the father and sister agree that Gregor cannot understand them and hence no agreement with him is possible.

" 'He must go,' cried Gregor's sister, 'that's the only solution, Father. You must just try to get rid of the idea that this is Gregor. The fact that we've believed it for so long is the root of all our trouble. But how can it be Gregor? If this were Gregor, he would have realized long ago that human beings can't live with such a creature, and he'd have gone away on his own accord. Then we wouldn't have any brother, but we'd be able to go on living and keep his memory in honor. As it is, this creature persecutes us, drives away our lodgers, obviously wants the whole apartment to himself and would have us all sleep in the gutter.' "

That he has disappeared as a human brother and should now disappear as a beetle deals Gregor the last blow. Painfully, because he is so weak and maimed, he crawls back to his own room. At the doorway he turns and his last glance falls on his mother, who was, in fact, almost asleep. "Hardly was he well inside his room when the door was hastily pushed shut, bolted and locked. The sudden noise in his rear startled him so much that his little legs gave beneath him. It was his sister who had shown such haste. She had been standing ready waiting and had made a light spring forward. Gregor had not even heard her coming, and she cried 'At last!' to her parents as she turned the key in the lock." In his darkened room Gregor discovers that he cannot move and though he is in pain it seems to be passing away. "The rotting apple in his back and the inflamed area around it, all covered with soft dust, already hardly troubled him. He thought of his family with tenderness and love. The decision that he must disappear was one that he held to even more strongly than his sister, if that were possible. In this state of vacant and peaceful meditation he remained until the tower clock struck three in the morning. The first broadening of light in the world outside the window entered his consciousness once more. Then his head sank to the floor of its own accord and from his nostrils came the last faint flicker of his breath."

Scene VIII: Gregor's dead, dry body is discovered the next morning by the charwoman and a great warm sense of relief permeates the insect world of his despicable family. Here is a point to be observed with care and love. Gregor is a human being in an insect's disguise; his family are insects disguised as people. With Gregor's death their insect souls are suddenly aware that they are free to enjoy themselves. " 'Come in beside us, Grete, for a little while,' said Mrs. Samsa* with a tremulous smile, and Grete, not without looking back at the corpse, followed her parents into their bedroom." The charwoman opens the window wide and the air has a certain warmth: it is the end of March when insects come out of hibernation.

Scene IX: We get a wonderful glimpse of the lodgers as they sullenly ask for their breakfast but instead are shown Gregor's corpse. "So they entered and stood around it, with their hands in the pockets of their shabby coats, in the middle of the room already bright with sunlight." What is the key word here? *Shabby* in the sun. As in a fairy tale, in the happy end of a fairy tale, the evil charm is dissipated with the magician's death. The lodgers are seen to be seedy, they are no longer dangerous, whereas on the other hand the Samsa family ascends again, gains in power and lush vitality. The scene ends with a repetition of the staircase theme, just as the chief clerk had retreated in slow motion, clasping the banisters. At the orders of Mr. Samsa that they must leave the lodgers are quelled. "In the hall they all three took their hats from the rack, their sticks from the umbrella stand, bowed in silence and quitted the apartment." Down they go now, three bearded borders, automatons, clockwork puppets, while the Samsa family leans over the banisters to watch them descend. The staircase as it winds down through the apartment house imitates, as it were, an insect's jointed legs; and the lodgers now disappear, now come to view again, as they descend lower and lower, from landing to landing, from articulation to articulation. At one point they are met by an ascending butcher boy with his basket who is first seen rising towards them, then above them, in proud deportment with his basket full of red steaks and luscious innards—red raw meat, the breeding place of fat shiny flies.

Scene X: The last scene is superb in its ironic simplicity. The spring sunshine is with the Samsa family as they write their three letters— articulation, jointed legs, happy legs, three insects writing three letters—of excuse to their employers. "They decided to spend this day in resting and going for a stroll; they had not only deserved such a respite from work, but absolutely needed it." As the charwoman leaves after her morning's work, she giggles amiably as she informs the family: " 'you don't need to bother

*In a note in his annotated copy VN observes that after Gregor's death it is never "father" and "mother" but only Mr. and Mrs. Samsa. Ed.

about how to get rid of the thing next door. It's been seen to already.' Mrs. Samsa and Grete bent over their letters again, as if preoccupied; Mr. Samsa, who perceived that she was eager to begin describing it all in detail, stopped her with a decisive hand. . . .

" 'She'll be given notice tonight,' said Mr. Samsa, but neither from his wife nor his daughter did he get any answer, for the charwoman seemed to have shattered again the composure they had barely achieved. They rose, went to the window and stayed there, clasping each other tight. Mr. Samsa turned in his chair to look at them and quietly observed them for a little. Then he called out: 'Come along, now, do. Let bygones be bygones. And you might have some consideration for me.' The two of them complied at once, hastened to him, caressed him and quickly finished their letters.

"Then they all three left the apartment together, which was more than they had done for months, and went by trolley into the open country outside the town. The trolley, in which they were the only passengers, was filled with warm sunshine. Leaning comfortably back in their seats they canvassed their prospects for the future, and it appeared on closer inspection that these were not at all bad, for the jobs they had got, which so far they had never really discussed with each other, were all three admirable and likely to lead to better things later on. The greatest immediate improvement in their condition would of course arise from moving to another house; they wanted to take a smaller and cheaper but also better situated and more easily run apartment than the one they had, which Gregor had selected. While they were thus conversing, it struck both Mr. and Mrs. Samsa, almost at the same moment, as they became aware of their daughter's increasing vivacity, that in spite of all the sorrow of recent times, which had made her cheeks pale, she had bloomed into a buxom girl. They grew quieter and half unconsciously exchanged glances of complete agreement, having come to the conclusion that it would soon be time to find a good husband for her. And it was like a confirmation of their new dreams and excellent intentions that at the end of their journey their daughter sprang to her feet first and stretched her young body."*

Let me sum up various of the main themes of the story.

1. The number *three* plays a considerable role in the story. The story is divided into three parts. There are three doors to Gregor's room. His

---

· *"The soul has died with Gregor; the healthy young animal takes over. The parasites have fattened themselves on Gregor." VN note in his annotated copy. Ed.

family consists of three people. Three servants appear in the course of the story. Three lodgers have three beards. Three Samsas write three letters. I am very careful not to overwork the significance of symbols, for once you detach a symbol from the artistic core of the book, you lose all sense of enjoyment. The reason is that there are artistic symbols and there are trite, artificial, or even imbecile symbols. You will find a number of such inept symbols in the psychoanalytic and mythological approach to Kafka's work, in the fashionable mixture of sex and myth that is so appealing to mediocre minds. In other words, symbols may be original, and symbols may be stupid and trite. And the abstract symbolic value of an artistic achievement should never prevail over its beautiful burning life.

So, the only emblematic or heraldic rather than symbolic meaning is the stress which is laid upon *three* in "The Metamorphosis." It has really a technical meaning. The trinity, the triplet, the triad, the triptych are obvious art forms such as, say, three pictures of youth, ripe years, and old age, or any other threefold triplex subject. Triptych means a picture or carving in three compartments side by side, and this is exactly the effect that Kafka achieves, for instance, with his three rooms in the beginning of the story—living room, Gregor's bedroom, and sister's room, with Gregor in the central one. Moreover, a threefold pattern suggests the three acts of a play. And finally it must be observed that Kafka's fantasy is emphatically logical; what can be more characteristic of logic than the triad of thesis, antithesis, and synthesis. We shall, thus, limit the Kafka symbol of three to its aesthetic and logical significance and completely disregard whatever myths the sexual mythologists read into it under the direction of the Viennese witch doctor.

2. Another thematic line is the theme of the doors, of the opening and closing of doors that runs through the whole story.

3. A third thematic line concerns the ups and downs in the well-being of the Samsa family, the subtle state of balance between their flourishing condition and Gregor's desperate and pathetic condition.

There are a few other subthemes but the above are the only ones essential for an understanding of the story.

You will mark Kafka's style. Its clarity, its precise and formal intonation in such striking contrast to the nightmare matter of his tale. No poetical metaphors ornament his stark black-and-white story. The limpidity of his style stresses the dark richness of his fantasy. Contrast and unity, style and matter, manner and plot are most perfectly integrated.

Joyce

For Next time read to the end of the funeral chapter p. 114

In order to discuss Ulysses intelligently we should plan very carefully our ~~thirteen or thirteen~~ sessions and the reading in between. I do not usually urge my students to attend my ~~own~~ lectures with unswerving devotion, But in the last spurt of the year, at the culmination of a very special course, at ~~xxxxxxxxxxxxx~~ a final stage marked by the masterpiece of a difficult writer, I do hope that vernal indolence will not interfere with academic diligence.

So here is my plan: I shall start by dividing the book into chapters and telling you what to ~~xxxxxxx~~ read with special attention ~~then what to skim over~~ ~~and what~~ with a less attentive eye; ~~then I shall make some remarks about that xxxx xxxx the book and again~~ Then, I shall review the whole book ~~xxxxx~~ chapter by chapter ~~from the p.~~ in answer to the question what is it all about ~~After that~~ I shall analyze not explain several obligatory chapters and passages ~~from less~~ obligatory ones. Finally I shall discuss ~~their~~ characters, ~~and~~ the style ~~xxxxxxxxxxxx~~

Ulysses
(1922)

James Joyce was born in 1882 in Ireland, left Ireland in the first decade of the twentieth century, lived most of his life as an expatriate in continental Europe, and died in 1941 in Switzerland. *Ulysses* was composed between 1914 and 1921 in Trieste, Zurich, and Paris. In 1918 parts began to appear in the so-called *Little Review*. *Ulysses* is a fat book of more than two hundred sixty thousand words; it is a rich book with a vocabulary of about thirty thousand words. The Dublin setting is built partly on data supplied by an exile's memory, but mainly on data from *Thom's Dublin Directory*, whither professors of literature, before discussing *Ulysses*, secretly wing their way in order to astound their students with the knowledge Joyce himself stored up with the aid of that very directory. He also used, throughout the book, a copy of the Dublin newspaper the *Evening Telegraph* of Thursday, 16 June 1904, price one halfpenny, which among other things featured that day the Ascot Gold Cup race (with Throwaway, an outsider, winning), an appalling American disaster (the excursion steamer *General Slocum* on fire), and a motorcar race for the Gordon Bennett Cup in Homburg, Germany.

Ulysses is the description of a single day, the sixteenth of June 1904, a Thursday, a day in the mingled and separate lives of a number of characters walking, riding, sitting, talking, dreaming, drinking, and going through a number of minor and major physiological and philosophical actions during this one day in Dublin and the early morning hours of the next day. Why did Joyce choose that particular day, 16 June 1904? In an otherwise rather poor though well-meaning work, *Fabulous Voyager: James Joyce's Ulysses* (1947), Mr. Richard Kain informs me that this was the day on which Joyce

Opening page from Nabokov's lecture notes on *Ulysses*

met his future wife Nora Barnacle. So much for human interest.

Ulysses consists of a number of scenes built around three major characters; of these major characters the dominant one is Leopold Bloom, a small businessman in the advertisement business, an advertisement canvasser to be exact. At one time he was with the firm of Wisdom Hely, stationer, in the capacity of a traveler for blotting paper, but now he is on his own, soliciting ads and not doing too well. For reasons that I shall mention presently Joyce endowed him with a Hungarian-Jewish origin. The two other major characters are Stephen Dedalus, whom Joyce had already depicted in *Portrait of the Artist as a Young Man* (1916), and Marion Bloom, Molly Bloom, Bloom's wife. If Bloom is the central figure, Stephen and Marion are the lateral ones in this triptych: the book begins with Stephen and ends with Marion. Stephen Dedalus, whose surname is that of the mythical maker of the labyrinth at Knossos, the royal city of ancient Crete; other fabulous gadgets; wings for himself and Icarus, his son—Stephen Dedalus, aged twenty-two, is a young Dublin schoolteacher, scholar, and poet, who in his days of schooling had been subjected to the discipline of a Jesuit education and now violently reacts against it but remains of an essentially metaphysical nature. He is a rather abstract young man, a dogmatist even when drunk, a freethinker imprisoned in his own self, a brilliant pronouncer of abrupt aphoristic sayings, physically fragile, and as unwashed as a saint (his last bath took place in October, and this is June), a bitter and brittle young fellow—never quite clearly visualized by the reader, a projection of the author's mind rather than a warm new being created by an artist's imagination. Critics tend to identify Stephen with young Joyce himself, but that is neither here nor there. As Harry Levin has put it, "Joyce lost his religion, but kept his categories," which is also true of Stephen.

Marion (Molly) Bloom, Bloom's wife, is Irish on her father's side and Spanish-Jewish on her mother's side. She is a concert singer. If Stephen is a highbrow and Bloom a middlebrow, Molly Bloom is definitely a lowbrow and a very vulgar one at that. But all three characters have their artistic sides. In Stephen's case the artistic is almost too good to be true—one never meets anybody in "real life" who has anything approaching such a perfect artistic control over his casual everyday speech as Stephen is supposed to have. Bloom the middlebrow is less of an artist than Stephen but is much more of an artist than critics have discerned: in fact, his mental stream flows now and then very close to Stephen's mental stream, as I will explain later. Finally, Molly Bloom, despite her triteness, despite the conventional quality of her ideas, despite her vulgarity, is capable of rich emotional response to the superficially lovely things of life, as we shall see in the last part of her extraordinary soliloquy on which the book ends.

Before discussing the matter and manner of the book, I have still a few words to say about the main character Leopold Bloom. When Proust portrayed Swann, he made Swann an individual, with individual, unique characteristics. Swann is neither a literary type nor a racial type, though he happens to be the son of a Jewish stockbroker. In composing the figure of Bloom, Joyce's intention was to place among endemic Irishmen in his native Dublin someone who was as Irish as he, Joyce, was, but who also was an exile, a black sheep in the fold, as he, Joyce, was. Joyce evolved the rational plan, therefore, of selecting for the type of an outsider, the type of the Wandering Jew, the type of the exile. However, I shall explain later that Joyce is sometimes crude in the way he accumulates and stresses so-called racial traits. Another consideration in relation to Bloom: those so many who have written so much about *Ulysses* are either very pure men or very depraved men. They are inclined to regard Bloom as a very ordinary nature, and apparently Joyce himself intended to portray an ordinary person. It is obvious, however, that in the sexual department Bloom is, if not on the verge of insanity, at least a good clinical example of extreme sexual preoccupation and perversity with all kinds of curious complications. His case is strictly heterosexual, of course—not homosexual as most of the ladies and gentlemen are in Proust (*homo* is Greek for same, not Latin for man as some students think)—but within the wide limits of Bloom's love for the opposite sex he indulges in acts and dreams that are definitely subnormal in the zoological, evolutional sense. I shall not bore you with a list of his curious desires, but this I will say: in Bloom's mind and in Joyce's book the theme of sex is continually mixed and intertwined with the theme of the latrine. God knows I have no objection whatsoever to so-called frankness in novels. On the contrary, we have too little of it, and what there is has become in its turn conventional and trite, as used by so-called tough writers, the darlings of the book clubs, the pets of clubwomen. But I do object to the following: Bloom is supposed to be a rather ordinary citizen. Now it is not true that the mind of an ordinary citizen continuously dwells on physiological things. I object to the continuously, not to the disgusting. All this very special pathological stuff seems artificial and unnecessary in this particular context. I suggest that the squeamish among you regard the special preoccupation of Joyce with perfect detachment.

Ulysses is a splendid and permanent structure, but it has been slightly overrated by the kind of critic who is more interested in ideas and generalities and human aspects than in the work of art itself. I must especially warn against seeing in Leopold Bloom's humdrum wanderings and minor adventures on a summer day in Dublin a close parody of the *Odyssey*, with the adman Bloom acting the part of Odysseus, otherwise Ulysses, man of many devices, and Bloom's adulterous wife representing chaste Penelope while Stephen Dedalus is given the part of Telemachus. That there is a very vague and very general Homeric echo of the theme of wanderings in Bloom's case is obvious, as the title of the novel suggests, and there are a number of classical allusions among the many other allusions in the course of the book; but it would be a complete waste of time to look for close parallels in every character and every scene of the book. There is nothing more tedious than a protracted and sustained allegory based on a well-worn myth; and after the work had appeared in parts, Joyce promptly deleted the pseudo-Homeric titles of his chapters when he saw what scholarly and pseudoscholarly bores were up to. Another thing. One bore, a man called Stuart Gilbert, misled by a tongue-in-cheek list compiled by Joyce himself, found in every chapter the domination of one particular organ—the ear, the eye, the stomach, etc.—but we shall ignore that dull nonsense too. All art is in a sense symbolic; but we say "stop, thief" to the critic who deliberately transforms an artist's subtle symbol into a pedant's stale allegory—a thousand and one nights into a convention of Shriners.

What then is the main theme of the book? It is very simple.

1. The hopeless past. Bloom's infant son has died long ago, but the vision remains in his blood and brain.

2. The ridiculous and tragic present. Bloom still loves his wife Molly, but he lets Fate have its way. He knows that in the afternoon at 4:30 of this mid-June day Boylan, her dashing impresario, concert agent, will visit Molly—and Bloom does nothing to prevent it. He tries fastidiously to keep out of Fate's way, but actually throughout the day is continuously on the point of running into Boylan.

3. The pathetic future. Bloom also keeps running into another young man—Stephen Dedalus. Bloom gradually realizes that this may be another little attention on the part of Fate. If his wife *must* have lovers then sensitive, artistic Stephen would be a better one than vulgar Boylan. In fact, Stephen could give Molly lessons, could help her with her Italian pronunciations in her profession as a singer, could be in short a refining influence, as Bloom pathetically thinks.

This is the main theme: Bloom and Fate.

Each chapter is written in a different style, or rather with a different style predominating. There is no special reason why this should be—why one chapter should be told straight, another through a stream-of-consciousness gurgle, a third through the prism of a parody. There is no special reason, but it may be argued that this constant shift of the viewpoint conveys a more varied knowledge, fresh vivid glimpses from this or that side. If you have ever tried to stand and bend your head so as to look back between your knees, with your face turned upside down, you will see the world in a totally different light. Try it on the beach: it is very funny to see people walking when you look at them upside down. They seem to be, with each step, disengaging their feet from the glue of gravitation, without losing their dignity. Well, this trick of changing the vista, of changing the prism and the viewpoint, can be compared to Joyce's new literary technique, to the kind of new twist through which you see a greener grass, a fresher world.

The characters are constantly brought together during their peregrinations through a Dublin day. Joyce never loses control over them. Indeed, they come and go and meet and separate, and meet again as the live parts of a careful composition in a kind of slow dance of fate. The recurrence of a number of themes is one of the most striking features of the book. These themes are much more clear-cut, much more deliberately followed, than the themes we pick up in Tolstoy or in Kafka. The whole of *Ulysses*, as we shall gradually realize, is a deliberate pattern of recurrent themes and synchronization of trivial events.

Joyce writes in three main styles:

1. The original Joyce: straightforward, lucid and logical and leisurely. This is the backbone of chapter 1 of the first part and of chapters 1 and 3 of the second part; and lucid, logical, and leisurely parts occur in other chapters.

2. Incomplete, rapid, broken wording rendering the so-called stream of consciousness, or better say the stepping stones of consciousness. Samples may be found in most chapters, though ordinarily associated only with major characters. A discussion of this device will be found in connection with its most famous example, Molly's final soliloquy, part three, chapter 3; but one can comment here that it exaggerates the verbal side of thought. Man thinks not always in words but also in images, whereas the stream of consciousness presupposes a flow of words that can be notated: it is difficult, however, to believe that Bloom was continuously talking to himself.

3. Parodies of various nonnovelistic forms: newspaper headlines (part two, chapter 4), music (part two, chapter 8), mystical and slapstick drama (part two, chapter 12), examination questions and answers in a catechistic pattern (part three, chapter 2). Also, parodies of literary styles and

authors: the burlesque narrator of part two, chapter 9, the lady's magazine type of author in part two, chapter 10, a series of specific authors and literary periods in part two, chapter 11, and elegant journalese in part three, chapter 1.

At any moment, in switching his styles, or within a given category, Joyce may intensify a mood by introducing a musical lyrical strain, with alliterations and lilting devices, generally to render wistful emotions. A poetic style is often associated with Stephen, but an example from Bloom occurs, for instance, when he disposes of the envelope of the letter from Martha Clifford: "Going under the railway arch he took out the envelope, tore it swiftly to shreds and scattered them towards the road. The shreds fluttered away, sank in the dank air: a white flutter then all sank." Or, a few sentences later, the end of the vision of a huge flood of spilled beer "winding through mudflats all over the level land, a lazy pooling swirl of liquor bearing along wideleaved flowers of its froth." At any other moment, however, Joyce can turn to all sorts of verbal tricks, to puns, transposition of words, verbal echoes, monstrous twinning of verbs, or the imitation of sounds. In these, as in the overweight of local allusions and foreign expressions, a needless obscurity can be produced by details not brought out with sufficient clarity but only suggested for the knowledgeable.

PART ONE, CHAPTER 1

Time: Around eight in the morning, 16 June 1904, a Thursday.

Place: In Dublin Bay, Sandycove, Martello Tower—an actually existing structure not unlike a squat chess rook—one of a number of towers built against French invasion in the first decade of the nineteenth century. William Pitt, the statesman, the younger Pitt, had these towers built, says Buck Mulligan, "when the French were on the sea." (A snatch from the song goes, "Oh the French are on the sea says [it continues in Irish] the poor old woman," that is, Ireland), but Martello Tower, Mulligan continues, is the *omphalos* among towers, the navel, the center of the body, the starting point and center of the book; and also the seat of the Delphic oracle in ancient Greece. Stephen Dedalus, Buck Mulligan, and the Englishman Haines lodge in this *omphalos*.

Characters: Stephen Dedalus, a young Dubliner, aged twenty-two, a student, philosopher, and poet. He has recently in the beginning of the year 1904 returned to Dublin from Paris where he had spent about a year. He has now been teaching school (Dingy's School) for three months, getting paid on the day following mid-month, a monthly salary of £3.12, at contemporaneous rates less than twenty dollars. He had been recalled from Paris by a telegram from his father, "—Mother dying come home father," to find that she was dying of cancer. When she asked him to kneel down at the recitation of the prayer for the dying, he refused, a refusal that is the clue to Stephen's dark brooding grief throughout the book. He had placed his newfound spiritual freedom above his mother's last request, last comfort. Stephen has renounced the Roman Catholic church, in the bosom of which he had been brought up, and has turned to art and philosophy in a desperate quest for something that would fill the empty chambers vacated by faith in the God of Christians.

The two other male characters who appear in this first chapter are Buck Mulligan ("Malachi Mulligan, two dactyls . . . with a Hellenic ring"), a medical student, and Haines, an Englishman, an Oxford student visiting Dublin and collecting folklore. Renting the tower costs twelve pounds per year (sixty dollars in those days), as we learn, and it is Stephen who has paid it so far, Buck Mulligan being the gay parasite and usurper. He is, in a sense, Stephen's parody and grotesque shadow, for if Stephen is the type of the serious young man with a tortured soul, one for whom loss or change of faith is a tragedy, Mulligan on the other hand is the happy, robust, blasphemous vulgarian, a phony Greek pagan, with a wonderful memory, a lover of purple patches. At the opening of the chapter he comes from the stairhead bearing his shaving bowl with mirror and razor crossed, and chanting in a mockery of the Mass, the ceremony commemorating in the Catholic church the sacrifice of the body and blood of Jesus Christ under the appearance of bread and wine. "He held the bowl aloft and intoned:

—*Introibo ad altare Dei.*

Halted, he peered down the dark winding stairs and called up coarsely:

—Come up, Kinch. Come up, you fearful jesuit."

Mulligan's nickname for Stephen is Kinch, dialect for "knife blade." His presence, everything about him, is oppressive and repulsive to Stephen, who in the course of the chapter tells him what he has against him. "Stephen, depressed by his own voice, said:

—Do you remember the first day I went to your house after my mother's death?

Buck Mulligan frowned quickly and said:

Overleaf: The opening pages of Nabokov's teaching copy of *Ulysses*

Stephen and four other young men
leave in a tower - Martello Tower
that [Recanthology] stood in Dublin bay.
This is [Dublin]:

Blasphemously the happy Bulgarian,
a medical student, [pro fluong Greek pagans]
Mulligan uses his shaving bowl as
a mockery of Mass — the ceremony
commemorating, in the Latin Church,
the sacrifice of the body and blood of Jesus Christ
under the appearances of bread and wine.

Stephen Dedalus has renounced the Catholic church
in the bosom of which he has been brought up, and has
turned to art and philosophy in a desperate quest
for faith. He has lost his religious faith but the
shadow of its vessel, like a casement crossed
by its frame, lies across his path.

TATELY, PLUMP

who is a vulgarian,

Buck Mulligan came from the stairhead, bearing a bowl of lather on which a mirror and a razor lay crossed. A yellow dressinggown, ungirdled, was sustained gently behind him by the mild morning air. He held the bowl aloft and intoned:

— *Introibo ad altare Dei.*

Halted, he peered down the dark winding stairs and called up coarsely:

— Come up, Kinch. Come up, you fearful jesuit.

Solemnly he came forward and mounted the round gunrest. He faced about and blessed gravely thrice the tower, the surrounding country and the awaking mountains. Then, catching sight of Stephen Dedalus, he bent towards him and made rapid crosses in the air, gurgling in his throat and shaking his head. Stephen Dedalus, displeased and sleepy, leaned his arms on the top of the staircase and looked coldly at the shaking gurgling face that blessed him, equine in its length, and at the light untonsored hair, grained and hued like pale oak.

Buck Mulligan peeped an instant under the mirror and then covered the bowl smartly.

— Back to barracks, he said sternly.

He added in a preacher's tone:

— For this, O dearly beloved, is the genuine Christine: body and soul and blood and ouns. Slow music, please. Shut your eyes, gents. One moment. A little trouble about those white corpuscles. Silence, all.

He peered sideways up and gave a long low whistle of call, then paused awhile in rapt attention, his even white teeth glistening here and there with gold points. Chrysostomos. Two strong shrill whistles answered through the calm.

— Thanks, old chap, he cried briskly. That will do nicely. Switch off the current, will you?

He skipped off the gunrest and looked gravely at his watcher, gathering about his legs the loose folds of his gown. The plump shadowed face and sullen oval jowl recalled a prelate, patron of arts in the middle ages. A pleasant smile broke quietly over his lips.

— The mockery of it, he said gaily. Your absurd name, an ancient Greek.

He pointed his finger in friendly jest and went over the parapet, laughing to himself. Stephen Dedalus stepped up, followed him wearily halfway and sat down on the edge of the gunrest, watching him still as he propped his mirror on the parapet,

[5]

—What? Where? I can't remember anything. I remember only ideas and sensations. Why? What happened in the name of God?

—You were making tea, Stephen said, and I went across the landing to get more hot water. Your mother and some visitor came out of the drawingroom. She asked you who was in your room.

—Yes? Buck Mulligan said. What did I say? I forget.

—You said, Stephen answered, *O, it's only Dedalus whose mother is beastly dead.*

A flush which made him seem younger and more engaging rose to Buck Mulligan's cheek.

—Did I say that? he asked. Well? What harm is that?

He shook his constraint from him nervously.

—And what is death, he asked, your mother's or yours or my own? You saw only your mother die. I see them pop off every day in the Mater and Richmond and cut into tripes in the dissecting room. It's a beastly thing and nothing else. It simply doesn't matter. You wouldn't kneel down to pray for your mother on her deathbed when she asked you. Why? Because you have the cursed jesuit strain in you, only it's injected the wrong way. To me it's all a mockery and beastly. Her cerebral lobes are not functioning. She calls the doctor Sir Peter Teazle and picks buttercups off the quilt. Humour her till it's over. You crossed her last wish in death and yet you sulk with me because I don't whinge like some hired mute from Lalouette's. Absurd! I suppose I did say it. I didn't mean to offend the memory of your mother.

He had spoken himself into boldness. Stephen, shielding the gaping wounds which the words had left in his heart, said very coldly:

—I am not thinking of the offence to my mother.

—Of what, then? Buck Mulligan asked.

—Of the offence to me, Stephen answered.

Buck Mulligan swung round on his heel.

—O, an impossible person! he exclaimed."

Buck Mulligan not only [paralyzes] Stephen's *omphalos*, he also has a friend of his own lodging there, Haines, the English literary tourist. There is nothing especially wrong with Haines, but for Stephen he is both a representative of the hated usurper England and a friend of the private usurper Buck whose brogues Stephen is wearing and whose breeches fit him second-leg and who will annex that tower.

The action: The action of the chapter starts with Buck Mulligan shaving—and borrowing Stephen's snotgreen dirty handkerchief to wipe his razor. As Mulligan shaves, Stephen protests against Haines staying in the tower. Haines has raved in his dream about shooting a black panther, and Stephen is afraid of him. "If he stays on here I am off." There are allusions to the sea, to Ireland, to Stephen's mother again, to the £3.12 Stephen will be paid by the school. Then Haines, Mulligan, and Stephen have breakfast in a most appetizing scene. An old milkwoman brings the milk and there is a delightful exchange of remarks. All three set out for the beach. Mulligan goes at once for a swim. Haines will plunge presently after his breakfast has settled, but Stephen, who hates water as much as Bloom loves it, does not bathe. Presently Stephen leaves his two companions and makes his way to the school, not far off, where he teaches.

The style: Chapters 1 and 2 of part one are composed in what I shall call normal style; that is, in the style of normal narration, lucid and logical Joyce. True, here and there the flow of narrative prose is interrupted briefly by the inner monologue technique which in other chapters of the book blurs and breaks so much the author's diction; but here the logical flow predominates. A brief example of the stream of consciousness comes on the first page when Mulligan is about to shave. "He peered sideways up and gave a long low whistle of call, then paused awhile in rapt attention, his even white teeth glistening here and there with gold points. Chrysostomos. Two strong shrill whistles answered through the calm." Here is a typical Joycean device which will be repeated and greatly developed throughout the book. Chrysostomos, "gold mouth," is of course John, patriarch of Constantinople, fourth century. But why does the name crop up? Quite simple: it is Stephen's stream of thought interrupting the description. Stephen sees and hears Buck whistling down to Haines to wake him—then pausing in rapt attention—Stephen sees Buck's gold-stopped teeth gleaming in the sun—gold, gold mouth, Mulligan the oracle, the eloquent speaker—and a brief image of the church father flits across Stephen's mind, after which the narrative is immediately resumed with Haines whistling in answer. This is pronounced a miracle by Buck who now tells God to switch off the current.

This is simple, and there are other simple examples in the chapter, but soon we find a more enigmatic interruption of the tale by Stephen's stream of thought. Stephen has just flashed one of his marvelous aphorisms which so fascinate Mulligan. Pointing at Buck's broken little shaving mirror which he has lifted from a maid's room, Stephen bitterly says: "—It is a symbol of Irish art. The cracked lookingglass of a servant." Mulligan suggests that Stephen sell this aphorism to "the oxy chap" Haines for a guinea, and adds that he, Mulligan, together with Stephen, whose arm he clasps confidentially, should hellenize Ireland with bright crisp thought.

Now comes the stream of Stephen's thought: "Cranly's arm. His arm." A first reading of *Ulysses* will hardly help here, but at a second reading we will know who Cranly is, since he is alluded to later, a false friend of Stephen's boyhood who used to take Stephen to the races—"led me to get rich quick, hunting his winners . . . amid the bawls of bookies on their pitches" as Mulligan is now suggesting they get rich quick by selling bright sayings: "Even money Fair Rebel: ten to one the field. Dicers and thimble riggers we hurried by after the hoofs, the vying caps and jackets and past the meatfaced woman, a butcher's dame, nuzzling thirstily her clove of orange." This dame is a first cousin of Marion Bloom, a fore-glimpse of that carnal lady.

Another good example of Stephen's stream in this easy first chapter occurs when Stephen, Mulligan, and Haines are finishing their breakfast. Mulligan turned to Stephen and said: "—Seriously, Dedalus. I'm stony. Hurry out to your school kip and bring us back some money. Today the bards must drink and junket. Ireland expects that every man this day will do his duty.

—That reminds me, Haines said, rising, that I have to visit your national library today.

—Our swim first, Buck Mulligan said.

He turned to Stephen and asked blandly:

—Is this the day for your monthly wash, Kinch?

Then he said to Haines:

—The unclean bard makes a point of washing once a month.

—All Ireland is washed by the gulf stream, Stephen said as he let honey trickle over a slice of the loaf.

Haines from the corner where he was knotting easily a scarf about the loose collar of his tennis shirt spoke:

I intend to make a collection of your sayings if you will let me.

Speaking to me. They wash and tub and scrub. Agenbite of inwit. Conscience. Yet here's a spot.

—That one about the cracked lookingglass of a servant being the symbol of Irish art is deuced good."

Stephen's thought runs as follows: he is speaking to me—the Englishman. Englishmen tub and scrub because of their bad conscience in regard to the countries they oppress, and he remembers Lady Macbeth and her bad conscience—yet here's a spot of blood which she cannot wash off. *Agenbite of inwit* is Middle English for the French *remords de conscience*, the bite of conscience, remorse. (It is the title of a religious tract of the fourteenth century.)

The technique of this stream of thought has, of course, the advantage of brevity. It is a series of brief messages jotted down by the brain. But it does demand from the reader more attention and sympathy than an ordinary description such as: Stephen realized Haines was speaking to him. Yes, he thought, the English wash a good deal, trying perhaps to scrub away the spot on their conscience which old Northgate called agenbite of inwit, etc.

Inner thoughts rising to the surface and prompted to do so by an outside impression lead to significant word connections, verbal links, in the mind of the thinker. For instance, look at the way the notion of the sea leads to the most hidden thoughts within Stephen's tortured soul. As he is shaving Mulligan gazes out over Dublin Bay and remarks quietly: "God.... Isn't the sea what Algy [*that is, Algernon Swinburne, an English postromantic minor poet*] calls it: a grey sweet mother?" (Mark the word *sweet*.) Our great sweet mother, he adds, improving as it were on the *grey* by adding the *t*. —Our mighty mother, he goes on, polishing up a nice alliteration. Then he refers to Stephen's mother, to Stephen's sinister sin. My aunt thinks you killed your mother, he says. —But what a lovely mummer (that is, mime) you are, he murmurs (look at the coils of the alliterating dragging up sense after sense: mighty mother, mummer, murmur). And Stephen listens to the well-fed voice; and mother and murmuring mighty sweet bitter sea merge, as it were, and there are other mergings. "The ring of bay and skyline held a dull green mass of liquid." This is inwardly transposed by Stephen's thought into the "bowl of white china [that] had stood beside her deathbed holding the green sluggish bile which she had torn up from her rotting liver by fits of loud groaning vomiting." The sweet mother becomes the bitter mother, bitter bile, bitter remorse. Then Buck Mulligan wipes his razor blade on Stephen's handkerchief: "—Ah, poor dogsbody, he said in a kind voice. I must give you a shirt and a few noserags." This links up the snotgreen sea with Stephen's filthy handkerchief and the green bile in the bowl; and the bowl of bile and the shaving bowl and the bowl of the sea, bitter tears and salty mucous, all fuse for a second into one image. This is Joyce at his best.

Notice, by the way, the term *poor dogsbody*. The symbol of a forlorn dog will be attached to Stephen through the book, just as the symbol of a soft-bodied cat, a padded-footed pard will be attached to Bloom. And this leads me to my next point: Haines's nightmare of the black panther somehow foreshadows for Stephen the image of Bloom, whom he has not yet met, but who will pad silently after him, a black catlike soft shadow. You will also note that Stephen had a troubled dream that night—saw an Oriental offer him a woman while Bloom too had an Oriental dream of Molly in

Turkish garb among the trappings of the slave market.

Time: Between nine and ten of the same day. It being Thursday, a half holiday, school stops at ten, with hockey to follow immediately.

Action: Stephen is teaching a high school class in ancient history. "—You, Cochrane, what city sent for him?

—Tarentum, sir.

—Very good. Well?

—There was a battle, sir.

—Very good. Where?

The boy's blank face asked the blank window."

Stephen's stream of thought takes over. "Fabled by the daughters of memoty. And yet it was in some way if not as memory fabled it. A phrase, then, of impatience, thud of Blake's wings of excess. I hear the ruin of all space, shattered glass and toppling masonry, and time one livid final flame. What's left us then?"

In the space of one moment, while a schoolboy pauses in blankness of mind, Stephen's vivid thought evokes the torrent of history, shattered glass, falling walls, the livid flame of time. What's left us then? Apparently the comfort of oblivion: "—I forget the place, sir. 279 B.C.

—Asculum, Stephen said, glancing at the name and date in the gorescarred book" (red-inked, bloody history book).

The fig rolls that one of the boys is eating are what we call fig newtons. The young idiot makes a poor pun: Pyrrhus—a pier. Stephen launches one of his typical epigrams. What is a pier? A disappointed bridge. Not all the students understand this.

All through the chapter the events at school are interrupted, or better say annotated, by Stephen's stream of inner thought. He thinks of Haines and England, of the library in Paris where he had read Aristotle "sheltered from the sin of Paris, night by night." "The soul is in a manner all that is: the soul is the form of forms." The soul is the form of forms will be the leading theme in the next chapter. Stephen asks a riddle:

> *The cock crew*
> *The sky was blue:*
> *The bells in heaven*
> *Were striking eleven.*
> *'Tis time for this poor soul*
> *To go to heaven.*

At eleven that morning Patrick Dignam, a friend of his father's, is to be buried, but Stephen is also obsessed with the memory of his mother's recent death. She has been buried in that cemetery; his father at Dignam's funeral will be shown sobbing as he passes his wife's grave, but Stephen will not go to Paddy Dignam's funeral. He answers his riddle, "—The fox burying his grandmother under a hollybush."

He goes on brooding on his mother and his guilt: "A poor soul gone to heaven: and on a heath beneath winking stars a fox, red reek of rapine in his fur, with merciless bright eyes scraped in the earth, listened, scraped up the earth, listened, scraped and scraped." The sophist Stephen can prove anything, for instance that Hamlet's grandfather is Shakespeare's ghost. Why grandfather and not father? Because of grandmother, meaning to him mother, in the line about the fox. In the next chapter Stephen, walking on the beach, sees a dog, and the dog idea and fox idea merge as the dog foxily scrapes up the sand, and listens, for he has buried something, his grandmother.

While the boys play hockey, Stephen talks to the schoolmaster Mr. Deasy and is paid his salary. Study the beautifully detailed way in which Joyce describes this transaction. "He brought out of his coat a pocketbook bound by a leather thong. It slapped open and he took from it two notes, one of joined halves, and laid them carefully on the table.

—Two, he said, strapping and stowing his pocketbook away.

And now his strongroom for the gold. Stephen's embarrassed hand moved over the shells heaped in the cold stone mortar: whelks and money cowries and leopard shells: and this, whorled as an emir's turban, and this, the scallop of Saint James. An old pilgrim's hoard, dead treasure, hollow shells.

A sovereign fell, bright and new, on the soft pile of the tablecloth.

—Three, Mr Deasy said, turning his little savingsbox about in his hand. These are handy things to have. See. This is for sovereigns. This is for shillings, sixpence, halfcrowns. And here crowns. See.

He shot from it two crowns and two shillings.

—Three twelve, he said. I think you'll find that's right.

—Thank you, sir, Stephen said, gathering the money together with shy haste and putting it all in a pocket of his trousers.

—No thanks at all, Mr Deasy said. You have earned it.

Stephen's hand, free again, went back to the hollow shells. Symbols too of beauty and of power. A lump in my pocket. Symbols soiled by greed and misery."

You will notice with a little pang of pleasure the shell of Saint James, prototype of a cake in Proust, the madeleine, la coquille de Saint Jacques. These shells were used as money by the Africans.

Deasy asks him to take a letter he has typed and have it printed in the *Evening Telegraph*. Mr. Deasy, a philistine and a busybody, not unlike M. Homais in Flaubert's *Madame Bovary*, Mr. Deasy pompously discusses in his letter a local cattle plague. Deasy is full of vicious political clichés taking a philistine's usual crack at minorities. England he says "is in the hands of the jews. . . . As sure as we are standing here the jew merchants are already at their work of destruction." To which Stephen very sensibly replies that a merchant is one who buys cheap and sells dear, Jew or Gentile: a wonderful squelching answer to bourgeois anti-Semitism.

PART ONE, CHAPTER 3

Time: Between ten and eleven in the morning.

Action: Stephen walks to the city by way of the beach, Sandymount strand. We shall glimpse him later, still walking steadily, on our way to Dignam's funeral when Bloom, Cunningham, Power, and Simon Dedalus, Stephen's father, drive in a carriage to the cemetery; and then we shall meet him again at his first destination, the (*Telegraph*) newspaper office. As Stephen walks on the beach he meditates on many things: the "ineluctable modality of the visible," *ineluctable* meaning "not to be overcome" and *modality* "form as opposed to substance"; the two old women, midwives, whom he sees; the resemblance of the cocklepicker's bag to a midwife's bag; his mother; his uncle Richie; various passages from Deasy's letter; Egan the Irish revolutionary in exile; Paris; the sea; his mother's death. He sees two other cocklepickers, two gypsies (*Egyptians* means "gypsies"), a man and a woman, and his mind immediately supplies him with samples of rogues' lingo, rogue words, gypsy talk.*

White thy fambles, red thy gan
And thy quarrons dainty is.
Couch a hogshead with me then.
In the darkmans clip and kiss.

A man has been recently drowned. He has already been mentioned by the boatmen when Mulligan and Haines were bathing and Stephen watching; he is a character who will reappear. "Five fathoms out there. Full

---

*"I have looked this up in the same special dictionary where Stephen and Joyce found the words: *mort* means 'woman ; *bing awast, to Romeville*—'going to London'; *wap*—'love'; *dimber wapping dell*—'a pretty loving woman ; *fambles*—'hands'; *gan*—'mouth'; *quarrons*—'body'; *couch a hogshead*—'lie down'; *darkmans*—'night.' " VN

fathom five thy father lies. At once he said. Found drowned. High water at Dublin bar. Driving before it a loose drift of rubble, fanshoals of fishes, silly shells. A corpse rising saltwhite from the undertow, bobbing landward, a pace a pace a porpoise. There he is. Hook it quick. Sunk though he be beneath the watery floor. We have him. Easy now.

Bag of corpsegas sopping in foul brine. A quiver of minnows, fat of a spongy titbit, flash through the slits of his buttoned trouserfly. God becomes man becomes fish becomes barnacle goose becomes featherbed mountain. Dead breaths I living breathe, tread dead dust, devour a urinous offal from all dead. Hauled stark over the gunwhale he breathes upward the stench of his green grave, his leprous nosehole snoring to the sun. . . .

My handkerchief. He threw it. I remember. Did I not take it up?

His hand groped vainly in his pockets. No, I didn't. Better buy one.

He laid the dry snot picked from his nostril on a ledge of rock, carefully. For the rest let look who will.

Behind. Perhaps there is someone.

He turned his face over a shoulder, rere regardant. Moving through the air high spars of a threemaster, her sails brailed up on the crosstrees, homing, upstream, silently moving, a silent ship."

In chapter 7 of part two we learn that this is the schooner *Rosevean* from Bridgwater, loaded with bricks. It is bringing Murphy, who will meet Bloom in the cabman's shelter, like two ships meeting at sea.

PART TWO, CHAPTER 1

Style: Joyce logical and lucid.

Time: Eight in the morning, synchronized with Stephen's morning.

Place: 7 Eccles Street, where the Blooms live in the northwest part of the town; Upper Dorset Street is in the immediate vicinity.

Main characters: Bloom; his wife; incidental characters: the pork-butcher Dlugacz, from Hungary like Bloom, and the maid servant of the Woods family next door, 8 Eccles Street. Who is Bloom? Bloom is the son of a Hungarian Jew Rudolph Virag (which means "flower" in Hungarian), who changed his name to Bloom, and of Ellen Higgins, of mixed Irish and Hungarian descent. Thirty-eight years old, born in 1866 in Dublin. Attended a school conducted by a Mrs. Ellis, then high school with Vance as a teacher, finished schooling in 1880. Because of neuralgia and loneliness after his wife's death, Bloom's father committed suicide in 1886. Bloom met Molly, the daughter of Brian Tweedy, when they were paired off in a game of musical chairs in Mat Dillon's house. He married her on 8 October

1888, he being twenty-two and she eighteen. Their daughter Milly was born on 15 June 1889, son Rudy in 1894, died when only eleven days old. At first Bloom was an agent for the stationery firm of Wisdom Hely's, at one time he had also been with a firm of cattle dealers working at the cattle market. Lived in Lombard Street from 1888 to 1893, in Raymond Terrace from 1893 to 1895, at Ontario Terrace in 1895 and for a period before that at the City Arms Hotel, and then in Holles Street in 1897. In 1904 they live in 7 Eccles Street.

Their house is narrow, with two front windows in each of its three front stories. The house no longer exists, but was actually empty in 1904, the year which Joyce some fifteen years later after correspondence with a relative, Aunt Josephine, selected for his invented Blooms. When a Mr. Finneran took over in 1905, he little imagined (says my informer Patricia Hutchins who wrote a charming book on *James Joyce's Dublin* [1950]) Mr. Finneran little imagined the literary ghosts which were yet to have lived there. The Blooms occupy two rooms on the hall floor (if seen from the front, Eccles Street; in the second story if seen from the rear), of their three-story rented house (if seen from the front), with the kitchen in the basement (or first story, if seen from the rear). The parlor is the front room; the bedroom is on the other side, and there is a little back garden. It is a cold-water flat with no bathroom, but a water closet on the landing and a rather mouldy privy in the back garden. The two stories above the Blooms are empty and for rent—in fact the Blooms have put a card on the front room window sash of the hall floor, saying "unfurnished apartments."

Action: Bloom in the basement kitchen prepares breakfast for his wife, talks charmingly to the cat; then while the kettle sits sideways on the fire "dull and squat, its spout stuck out," he walks up to the hallway and, having decided to buy for himself a pork kidney, tells Molly through the bedroom door that he is going round the corner. A sleepy soft grunt answered: "Mn." A certain slip of paper is safe in the leather headband of his hat, "the sweated legend in the crown of his hat told him mutely: Plasto's high grade ha" (sweat has obliterated the *t*). The slip of paper is the card with a phony name Henry Flower which he will produce in the next chapter at the postal substation on Westland Row to obtain a letter from a Martha Clifford, pseudonym, with whom he is carrying on a clandestine correspondence that originated in the lovelorn column in the *Irish Times*. He has forgotten

---

Nabokov's map of Bloom's and Stephen's travels in *Ulysses*, part two

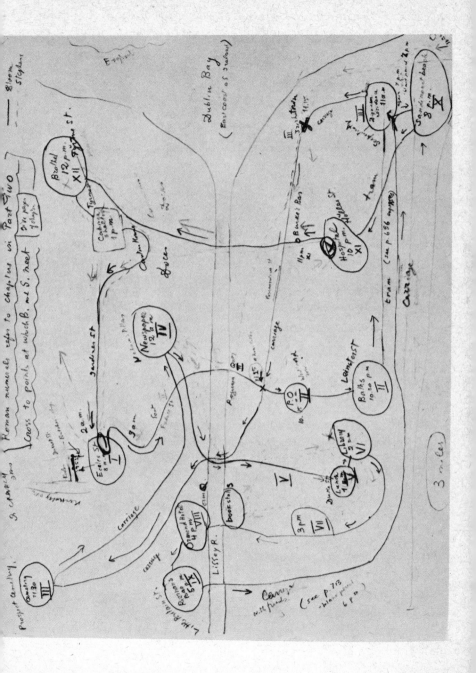

his key left in his everyday trousers, for he is wearing today a black suit in view of Dignam's funeral, which is scheduled for 11 A.M. He has, however, not forgotten to transfer into his hip pocket a potato which he carries, a mascot, a talisman, poor mother's panacea. (It saves him much later in the day from a sand-strewing trolley.) His stream of consciousness trickles over various pebbles of thought. "Creaky wardrobe. No use disturbing her. She turned over sleepily that time. He pulled the halldoor to after him very quietly, more, till the footleaf dropped gently over the threshold, a limp lid. Looked shut. All right till I come back anyhow." He turns the corner of Dorset Street, greets the grocer, "lovely weather," in passing, enters the butcher's shop and notices the next-door servant girl buying sausages at the counter. Shall he and Dlugacz, both from Hungary, shall they hail each other as compatriots? Bloom puts it off again. No, another time. He reads the advertisement of a planter's company in Palestine and his thought wanders east to the Orient. The synchronizing cloud. "A cloud began to cover the sun wholly slowly wholly. Grey. Far." This is a synchronization. Stephen saw the same cloud before breakfast: "A cloud began to cover the sun slowly, shadowing the bay in deeper green. It lay behind him, a bowl of bitter waters." The green is a bitter memory in Stephen's mind, the gray of the cloud suggests to Bloom a gray desolation, a barren land in the Orient unlike the voluptuous orchards of the advertisement.

He returns with the kidney; meantime the mail has come, two letters and a postcard. "He stooped and gathered them. Mrs Marion Bloom. His quick heart slowed at once. Bold hand. Mrs Marion." (The letter is in a bold hand, and Mrs. Marion is a bold hand.) Why did his heart miss a beat? Well, as we shortly discover the letter is from Blazes Boylan, Marion's impresario. He is coming around four o'clock with the program for her next tour, and Bloom has a hunch that if he, the husband, does not interfere and keeps away that afternoon, four o'clock will prove to be a critical time mark: that afternoon Boylan will become Molly's lover. Mark Bloom's fatalistic attitude: "A soft qualm regret, flowed down his backbone, increasing. Will happen, yes. Prevent. Useless: can't move. Girl's sweet light lips. Will happen too. He felt the flowing qualm spread over him. Useless to move now. Lips kissed, kissing kissed. Full gluey woman's lips."

The other letter and postcard are from Milly, Bloom's daughter, now in Mullingar, Westmeath County, central Ireland. The letter is for him, the

---

Nabokov's notes on the Blooms' house at 7 Eccles Street

a narrow house with two front windows in each
of its three front stories, a house

The Blooms live at 7 Eccles Street , (which does not exist,
but was actually empty in 1904   the year when   some 15 years later sold
when Joyce, after some
correspondence from Paris with a creative aunt Josephine,
selected it for the Blooms. [When a Mr Finnegan took over
in 1905, he still had and Eccles 7 informer Patricia Hutchins
who wrote a charming book in "James Joyce's Dublin" (1950) — Mr Finnegan
little imagined the literary ghosts which were yet to have lived there]
The Blooms occupy
[a two rooms apartment on the second floor of a three (if seen
from the front, Eccles street), [on the second story if seen from
the rear] of a three story house (if seen from the front), with
the kitchen in the basement [or first story (if seen from the rear)]
The parlor is the front room, hall floor (690) ; and the bedroom
is on the other side ; and there is a little
back garden.   It is a cold water flat, with no bathroom,
with a water closet on the landing, and a privy in the
back garden   The two stories above the Blooms are empty and
are for rent — in fact there is a card on the front room window sash
of the hall floor saying "unfurnished apartments [see 222, 230]

According to a photograph I have studied,
that house 7 Eccles Street looks unequivocally
like the corner house with the drugstore opposite the big garage
in College avenue, Ithaca, same dreary idea.

Front   Back   they rent the whole house
but it is too big for them

empty floor   empty floor

unoccupied room   milly's former room (see 765)
("Cunningham", 1765)

Front room (parlor)   bedroom

Kitchen

card for her mother to thank her for a 15 June birthday present, a lovely box of chocolate creams. Milly writes "I am getting on swimming in the photo business now." When Mulligan was swimming after breakfast a young friend told him he had received a card from Bannon in Westmeath: "Says he found a sweet young thing down there. Photo girl he calls her." Milly's letter continues: "There is to be a concert in the Greville Arms on Saturday. There is a young student comes here some evenings named Bannon his cousins or something are big swells he sings Boylan's . . . song about those seaside girls." In a sense, to Bloom, Blazes Boylan, Molly's four o'clock lover, is what, to Stephen, Buck Mulligan is, the gay usurper. All of Joyce's pieces fit: Molly, Bannon, Mulligan, Boylan. You will enjoy the wonderfully artistic pages, one of the greatest passages in all literature, when Bloom brings Molly her breakfast. How beautifully the man writes! "—Who was the letter from? he asked.

Bold hand. Marion.

—O, Boylan, she said. He's bringing the programme.

—What are you singing?

—*Là ci darem* with J. C. Doyle, she said, and *Love's Old Sweet Song*.

Her full lips, drinking, smiled. Rather stale smell that incense leaves next day. Like foul flowerwater.

Would you like the window open a little?

She doubled a slice of bread in her mouth, asking:

—What time is the funeral?

—Eleven, I think, he answered. I didn't see the paper.

Following the pointing of her finger he took up a leg of her soiled drawers from the bed. No? Then, a twisted grey garter looped round a stocking: rumpled, shiny sole.

—No: that book.

Other stocking. Her petticoat.

—It must have fell down, she said.

He felt here and there. *Voglio e non vorrei*. Wonder if she pronounces that right: *voglio*. Not in the bed. Must have slid down. He stooped and lifted the valance. The book, fallen, sprawled against the bulge of the orangekeyed chamberpot.

—Show here, she said. I put a mark in it. There's a word I wanted to ask you.

She swallowed a draught of tea from her cup held by nothandle and, having wiped her finger tips smartly on the blanket, began to search the text with the hairpin till she reached the word.

—Met him what? he asked.

—Here, she said. What does that mean?

He leaned downward and read near her polished thumbnail.

—Metempsychosis?

—Yes. Who's he when he's at home?

—Metempsychosis, he said, frowning. It's Greek: from the Greek. That means the transmigration of souls.

—O, rocks! she said. Tell us in plain words.

He smiled, glancing askance at her mocking eye. The same young eyes. The first night after the charades. Dolphin's Barn. He turned over the smudged pages. *Ruby: the Pride of the Ring*. Hello. Illustration. Fierce Italian with carriagewhip. Must be Ruby pride of the on the floor naked. Sheet kindly lent. *The monster Maffei desisted and flung his victim from him with an oath*. Cruelty behind it all. Doped animals. Trapeze at Hengler's. Had to look the other way. Mob gaping. Break your neck and we'll break our sides. Families of them. Bone them young so they metempsychosis. That we live after death. Our souls. That a man's soul after he dies. Dignam's soul . . .

—Did you finish it? he asked.

—Yes, she said. There's nothing smutty in it. Is she in love with the first fellow all the time?

—Never read it. Do you want another?

—Yes. Get another of Paul de Kock's. Nice name he has.

She poured more tea into her cup, watching its flow sideways.

Must get that Capel street library book renewed or they'll write to Kearney, my guarantor. Reincarnation: that's the word.

—Some people believe, he said, that we go on living in another body after death, that we lived before. They call it reincarnation. That we all lived before on the earth thousands of years ago or some other planet. They say we have forgotten it. Some say they remember their past lives.

The sluggish cream wound curdling spirals through her tea. Better remind her of the word: metempsychosis. An example would be better. An example?

The *Bath of the Nymph* over the bed. Given away with the Easter number of *Photo Bits*: Splendid masterpiece in art colours. Tea before you put milk in. Not unlike her with her hair down: slimmer. Three and six I gave for the frame. She said it would look nice over the bed. Naked nymphs: Greece: and for instance all the people that lived then.

He turned the pages.

—Metempsychosis, he said, is what the ancient Greeks called it. They used to believe you could be changed into an animal or a tree, for instance. What they called nymphs, for example.

Her spoon ceased to stir up the sugar. She gazed straight before her, inhaling through her arched nostrils.

—There's a smell of burn, she said. Did you leave anything on the fire?

—The kidney! he cried suddenly."

Equally artistic is the end of the chapter where through the back door into the garden, to the earth closet, goes Bloom. The hat is the link for some musings. He mentally hears the bell of Drago, the barbershop (Drago, however, is on Dawson Street far to the south)—and mentally sees Boylan, with brown glossy hair, coming out after having had a wash and a brush up, which suggests to Bloom a bath at the Taro Street baths, but he will go to Leinster Street instead.

In the beautifully described scene in the privy Bloom reads a magazine story, "Matcham's Masterstroke," and echoes of this will vibrate here and there throughout *Ulysses*. There is something of an artist about old Bloom, as in the dance of the hours that he on his warm seat imagines. "Evening hours, girls in grey gauze. Night hours then black with daggers and eyemasks. Poetical idea pink, then golden, then grey, then black. Still true to life also. Day, then the night.

He tore away half the prize story sharply and wiped himself with it. Then he girded up his trousers, braced and buttoned himself. He pulled back the jerky shaky door of the jakes and came forth from the gloom into the air.

In the bright light, lightened and cooled in limb, he eyed carefully his black trousers, the ends, the knees, the houghs of the knees. What time is the funeral? Better find out in the paper."

The clock tolls a quarter to nine. Dignam will be buried at eleven.

PART TWO, CHAPTER 2

Time: Between ten and eleven in the morning of 16 June.

Place: Various streets to the south of the Liffey, the river that crosses Dublin from west to east.

Characters: Bloom; an acquaintance M'Coy who stops him in the street and asks him to put his name down at Dignam's funeral which he cannot attend since "There's a drowning case at Sandycove may turn up and then the coroner and myself would have to go down if the body is found."

M'Coy's wife is a singer but not as good as Marion Bloom is. Another character who talks to Bloom in the street at the end of the chapter is Bantam Lyons, of whom I shall speak presently in connection with the Ascot race theme.

Action and style: Bloom is at first seen on Sir John Rogerson's Quay, which runs south of the Liffey and which he has reached on foot from Eccles Street, his home, a mile away northwest of the Liffey. On the way he has bought a morning paper, the *Freeman*. The stream of consciousness is the main device in this chapter. From the quay Bloom walks south to the post office, transferring the address card from behind the headband of his hat to his waistcoat pocket. His thoughts float from the window of the Oriental Tea Company into a world of fragrancy and flowers. At the post office there is a letter for him from the unknown Martha Clifford whom we shall never meet. While Bloom talks to M'Coy in the street his roving eye watches a woman about to get into a carriage. "Watch! Watch! Silk flash rich stockings white. Watch!" Ankles in 1904 were more seldom seen than today. But a heavy tramcar honks and lumbers between Bloom's watchful eye and the lady. "Lost it. Curse your noisy pugnose. Feels locked out of it. Paradise and the peri. Always happening like that. The very moment. Girl in Eustace street hallway Monday was it settling her garter. Her friend covering the display of. *Esprit de corps*. Well, what are you gaping at?"

Now walking down Cumberland Street Bloom reads Martha's letter. Its sentimental vulgarity affects his senses, and his thoughts run to soft satisfactions. He passes under a railway bridge. The image of the barrels of beer, Dublin's chief item of export, is suggested by the rumble of the train above, just as the sea suggests barreled porter to Stephen walking on the beach. "In cups of rocks it slops: flop, slop, slap: bounded in barrels. And, spent, its speech ceases. It flows purling, widely flowing, floating foampool, flower unfurling." This is quite close to Bloom's vision of flowing beer: "An incoming train clanked heavily above his head, coach after coach. Barrels bumped in his head: dull porter slopped and churned inside. The bungholes sprang open and a huge dull flood leaked, flowing together, winding through mudflats all over the level land, a lazy pooling swirl of liquor bearing along wideleaved flowers of its froth." This is still another synchronization. One should note that this chapter will end with the word *flower* in a paragraph of Bloom in his bath that has some relation to Stephen's imaginings of the drowned man. Bloom foresees: "his trunk and limbs riprippled over and sustained, buoyed lightly upward, lemonyellow: his navel, bud of flesh: and saw the dark tangled curls of his bush floating, floating hair of the stream around the limp father of thousands, a languid floating flower." And the chapter ends on the word *flower.*

Continuing on Cumberland Street after reading Martha's letter Bloom, in passing, enters for a moment a Catholic church. His thoughts flow on. A few minutes later, around a quarter past ten, he walks along Westland Row to a drugstore to order a certain hand lotion for his wife. Sweet almond oil and tincture of benzoin, and orange-flower water. He buys a cake of soap and says he will call later for the lotion, but he will forget to do so. The soap, however, is going to be quite a character in the story.

Let me at this point follow up two themes in this chapter—the soap and the Ascot Gold Cup. The soap is a cake of Barrington's lemon-flavored, soap which costs fourpence and smells of sweet lemony wax. After Bloom's bath, on the way to the funeral in the horse-drawn carriage, the soap is lodged in his hip pocket. "I am sitting on something hard. Ah, that soap in my hip pocket. Better shift it out of that. Wait for an opportunity." This comes when they reach Prospect Cemetery. He gets out. Only then does he make the transfer of the paper-stuck soap from hip to inner handkerchief pocket. In the newspaper office, after the funeral, he takes out his handkerchief, and here the theme of lemon perfume is mingled with Martha's letter and his wife's unfaithfulness. Still later, in the early afternoon, near the library and near the museum in Kildare Street Bloom catches a glimpse of Blazes Boylan. Why the museum? Well, Bloom had decided to investigate out of sheer curiosity certain details of anatomy in marble goddesses. "Straw hat in sunlight. Tan shoes. Turnedup trousers. It is. It is.

His heart quopped softly. To the right. Museum. Goddesses. He swerved to the right.

Is it? Almost certain. Won't look. Wine in my face. Why did I? Too heady. Yes, it is. The walk. Not see. Not see. Get on.

Making for the museum gate with long windy strides he lifted his eyes. Handsome building. Sir Thomas Deane designed. Not following me?

Didn't see me perhaps. Light in his eyes.

The flutter of his breath came forth in short sighs. Quick. Cold statues: quiet there. Safe in a minute.

No, didn't see me. After two. Just at the gate.

My heart!

His eyes beating looked steadfastly at cream curves of stone. Sir Thomas Deane was the Greek architecture.

Look for something I.

His hasty hand went quick into a pocket, took out, read unfolded Agendath Netaim. Where did I?

Busy looking for.

He thrust back quickly Agendath.

Afternoon she said.

I am looking for that. Yes, that. Try all pockets. Handker. *Freeman.* Where did I? Ah, yes. Trousers. Purse. Potato. Where did I?

Hurry. Walk quietly. Moment more. My heart.

His hand looking for the where did I put found in his hip pocket soap lotion have to call tepid paper stuck. Ah, soap there! Yes. Gate.

Safe!"

The soap is mentioned as being sticky in his hip pocket at four o'clock, and then in the tremendous comedy nightmare at midnight in the house of ill fame, a cake of new clean lemon soap arises diffusing light and perfume, a perfumed moon in an advertisement come to celestial life, and the soap actually sings as it soars in its adman's paradise:

We're a capital couple are Bloom and I;
He brightens the earth, I polish the sky—

The apotheosis of the soap theme is here identified as the *wandering soap*; the cake finally is used by Bloom at home to wash his soiled hands. "Having set the halffilled kettle on the now burning coals, why did he return to the stillflowing tap?

To wash his soiled hands with a partially consumed tablet of Barrington's lemonflavoured soap, to which paper still adhered (bought thirteen hours previously for fourpence and still unpaid for), in fresh cold neverchanging everchanging water and dry them, face and hands, in a long redbordered holland cloth passed over a wooden revolving roller."

At the end of part two, chapter 2, the rereader will discover the starting point of a theme that runs through the whole day of the book—the Ascot Gold Cup race which is to take place that afternoon, 16 June 1904, at three o'clock at Ascot Heath in Berkshire, England. The results of the Gold Cup event reach Dublin an hour later, at four o'clock. This race with these horses took place in so-called reality. A number of Dubliners are betting on the four runners: the horses are Maximum the second, a French horse and last year's winner; Zinfandel, a favorite after his display in the Coronation Cup at Epsom; Sceptre, which is the choice of the sports editor Lenehan; and finally Throwaway, an outsider.

Let us now look at the evolution of the theme throughout the book. It starts, as I said, at the end of Bloom's second chapter: "At his armpit Bantam Lyons' voice and hand said:

—Hello, Bloom, what's the best news? Is that today's? Show us a minute.

Shaved off his moustache again, by Jove! Long cold upper lip. To look younger. He does look balmy. Younger than I am.

Bantam Lyons' yellow blacknailed fingers unrolled the baton. Wants a wash too. Take off the rough dirt. Good morning, have you used Pears' soap? Dandruff on his shoulders. Scalp wants oiling.

—I want to see about the French horse that's running today, Bantam Lyons said. Where the bugger is it?

He rustled the pleated pages, jerking his chin on his high collar. Barber's itch. Tight collar he'll lose his hair. Better leave him the paper and get shut of him.

—You can keep it, Mr Bloom said.

—Ascot. Gold cup. Wait, Bantam Lyons muttered. Half a mo. Maximum the second.

—I was just going to throw it away, Mr Bloom said.

Bantam Lyons raised his eyes suddenly and leered weakly.

—What's that? his sharp voice said.

—I say you can keep it, Mr Bloom answered. I was going to throw it away that moment.

Bantam Lyons doubted an instant, leering: then thrust the outspread sheets back on Mr Bloom's arms.

—I'll risk it, he said. Here, thanks.

He sped off towards Conway's corner. God speed scut."

Apart from the beautiful display of the stream-of-thought technique in this passage, what should we mark? Two facts: (1) that Bloom has no interest in (and perhaps no knowledge of) this race whatsoever, and (2) that Bantam Lyons, a casual acquaintance, mistakes Bloom's remark for a tip concerning the horse Throwaway. Bloom is not only indifferent to the Ascot Gold Cup race, he remains serenely unaware that his remark has been misinterpreted as a tip.

Now look at the evolution of the theme. The racing edition of the *Freeman* appears at noon, and Lenehan, the sports editor, picks Sceptre, a tip that Bloom then overhears in the newspaper office. At two o'clock Bloom is standing at a food counter having a snack beside a very stupid fellow, Nosey Flynn, who is discussing the form sheet. "Mr Bloom, champing standing, looked upon his sigh. Nosey numskull. Will I tell him that horse Lenehan? He knows already. Better let him forget. Go and lose more. Fool and his money. Dewdrop coming down again. Cold nose he'd have kissing a woman. Still they might like. Prickly beards they like. Dog's cold noses. Old Mrs Riordan with the rumbling stomach's Skye terrier in the City Arms hotel. Molly fondling him in her lap. O the big doggybowwowsywowsy!

Wine soaked and softened rolled pith of bread mustard a moment mawkish cheese. Nice wine it is. Taste it better because I'm not thirsty. Bath of course does that. Just a bite or two. Then about six o'clock I can. Six, six. Time will be gone then. She . . ."

Coming in later into the eating place after Bloom has left, Bantam Lyons hints to Flynn that he has a good bet and will plunge five bob on his own, but he does not mention Throwaway, only says that Bloom gave him that tip. When the sports editor Lenehan pops into a bookie's to find out about Sceptre's starting price, he meets Lyons there and dissuades him from betting on Throwaway. In the great chapter in the Ormond bar, around four in the afternoon, Lenehan tells Blazes Boylan that he is sure Sceptre will win in a canter, and Boylan, who is on his way to his date with Molly Bloom, admits that he has plunged a bit for the benefit of a lady-friend (Molly). The wire with the result will be in any time now. In the Kiernan bar chapter, sports editor Lenehan enters the bar and gloomily announces that Throwaway has won "at twenty to one. A rank outsider. . . . Frailty, thy name is *Sceptre*." Now look at the way all this fatefully reacts on Bloom, who has no interest in the Gold Cup whatsoever. Bloom leaves Kiernan's bar to walk over to the courthouse on a mission of mercy (concerning the life insurance of his dead friend Pat Dignam), and Lenehan at the bar remarks: "—I know where he's gone, says Lenehan, cracking his fingers.

—Who? says I.

—Bloom, says he, the courthouse is a blind. He had a few bob on *Throwaway* and he's gone to gather in the shekels.

—Is it that whiteeyed kaffir? says the citizen, that never backed a horse in anger in his life.

That's where he's gone, says Lenehan. I met Bantam Lyons going to back that horse, only I put him off it and he told me Bloom gave him the tip. Bet you what you like he has a hundred shillings to five on. He's the only man in Dublin has it. A dark horse.

—He's a bloody dark horse himself, says Joe."

The *I* of the chapter in Kiernan's bar is an anonymous narrator, a drunken muddleheaded fellow with a lynching streak in him. Aroused by Bloom's gentle ways and humane wisdom, he is now—this anonymous narrator—inflamed by the suspicion that a Jew has won a hundred to five on the dark horse Throwaway. The anonymous narrator views with pleasure the brawl that follows when a hoodlum (the so-called citizen of the chapter) throws a biscuit tin at Bloom.

The race results appear later in the *Evening Telegraph* that Bloom reads in the cabman's shelter at the end of his long day, where there is also an account of Dignam's funeral and Deasy's letter appears—a newspaper summing up the events of the day. And finally, in the last but one chapter of the book when Bloom comes home at last, we note two things: (1) he finds on the apron of the dresser in the kitchen four fragments of two torn red betting slips that Blazes Boylan on his visit to Molly in a blazing rage tore up on learning that Sceptre had not won; and (2) kindly Bloom reflects with satisfaction that he had not risked, had not been disappointed, and also had not at lunch urged Flynn to put money on Lenehan's choice, Sceptre.

———

Let me say at this point between chapters 2 and 3 of part two a few words about Bloom's character. One of his main characteristics is kindness to animals, kindness to the weak. Although he has eaten with relish the inner organ of a beast, the pork kidney, for his breakfast that day, and can actually experience a sense of acute hunger when thinking of smoking, hot, thick sugary blood, despite these somewhat coarse tastes he feels a keen compassion for man-degraded, man-injured animals. One may note his kindly attitude at breakfast towards his little black cat: "Mr Bloom watched curiously, kindly, the lithe black form. Clean to see: the gloss of her sleek hide, the white button under the butt of her tail, the green flashing eyes. He bent down to her, his hands on his knees.

—Milk for the pussens, he said.

—Mrkgnao! the cat cried."

Also his understanding of dogs, as when, for example, he recalls on the way to the cemetery his dead father's dog Athos. "Poor old Athos! Be good to Athos, Leopold, is my last wish." And the picture of Athos in Bloom's mind is that of a "Quiet brute. Old men's dogs usually are." Bloom's mind reveals a sympathetic participation in animal emblems of life that in artistic and human values vies with Stephen's understanding of dogs, as in the Sandymount beach scene. Likewise Bloom experiences a pang of pity and tenderness as after his meeting with M'Coy he passes, near the cabman's stop, the drooping nags at nosebag time. "He came nearer and heard a crunching of gilded oats, the gently champing teeth. Their full buck eyes regarded him as he went by, amid the sweet oaten reek of horsepiss.

Their Eldorado. Poor jugginses! Damn all they know or care about anything with their long noses stuck in nosebags. Too full for words. Still they get their feed all right and their doss. Gelded too: a stump of black guttapercha wagging limp between their haunches. Might be happy all the same that way. Good poor brutes they look. Still their neigh can be very irritating." (Joyce's curious interest in the bladder is shared by Bloom.) In his compassionate attitude to animals Bloom even feeds sea gulls, which I personally consider to be nasty birds with drunkard's eyes—and there are other of his kindnesses to animals throughout the book. It is interesting that on his walk before luncheon his passing thought regarding a flock of pigeons before the Irish House of Parliament, the tone of his definition "Their little frolic after meals" corresponds exactly in intonation and meter to Stephen's musing on the beach, "The simple pleasures of the poor" (an ironic distortion of Thomas Gray's *Elegy Written in a Country Churchyard*, 1751), as a dog, being called, lifted his hindleg and "pissed quick short at an unsmelt rock."

PART TWO, CHAPTER 3

Style: Lucid and logical Joyce, with Bloom's thoughts easily followed by the reader.

Time: Just after eleven o'clock.

Place: Bloom has taken a tram from the baths on Leinster Street eastward to Dignam's residence, 9 Serpentine Avenue, southeast of the Liffey, from which the funeral starts. Instead of going immediately in a western direction towards the center of Dublin and then northwest to Prospect Cemetery, the procession goes by way of Irishtown, curving northeast and then west. It is a fine old custom to take Dignam's body first through Irishtown, up Tritonville Road, north of Serpentine Avenue, and only after passing through Irishtown to turn west by way of Ringsend Road and New Brunswick Street, then across the Liffey River and northwest to Prospect Cemetery.

Characters: A dozen or so mourners, among them in the backseat of a horse-drawn four-seat carriage Martin Cunningham, a good kind man, beside Power, who unthinkingly talks of suicide in Bloom's presence; and facing them, Bloom and Simon Dedalus, Stephen's father, an extremely witty, ferocious, cranky, talented fellow.

Action: The action of this chapter is very simple and easily read. I prefer to discuss it from the point of view of certain themes.

Bloom's Jewish-Hungarian father (whose suicide is mentioned in this chapter) married an Irish girl, Ellen Higgins, of Christian Hungarian ancestry on her father's side and a Protestant so that Bloom was baptised as a Protestant and only later became a Catholic in order to marry Marion Tweedy, also of mixed Hungarian-Irish parentage. In Bloom's ancestry there is also, in the past, a blonde Austrian soldier. Despite these complications, Bloom considers himself a Jew, and anti-Semitism is the constant shadow hanging over him throughout the book. He is always in danger of being insulted and hurt, even by otherwise respectable people, and he is regarded as an outsider. Looking up the question, I find that in 1904, the date of our day in Dublin, the number of Jews living in Ireland was around four thousand in a population of four million and a half. Vicious or conventional prejudice animates most of the people whom Bloom meets in the course of his dangerous day. In the carriage going to the cemetery Simon Dedalus lustily ridicules Reuben J. Dodd, a Jewish moneylender, whose son was almost drowned. Bloom eagerly tries to tell the story first in order to have some control over it and to avoid insulting innuendos. Throughout the book the theme of racial persecution pursues Bloom: even Stephen Dedalus rudely offends him with a song, in the next to last chapter, which is a parody of the sixteenth-century ballad about young Saint Hugh of Lincoln, believed in early times to have been crucified by Jews in the twelfth century.

Synchronization is a device rather than a theme. Throughout the book people keep running into each other—paths meet, diverge, and meet again. Turning from Tritonville Road to Ringsend Road, the four men in the carriage overtake Stephen Dedalus, Simon's son, who is walking from Sandycove to the newspaper office along much the same route as the funeral procession is following. Then further on, in Brunswick Street, not far from the Liffey, just as Bloom is reflecting that Boylan is coming that afternoon, Cunningham sees Boylan in the street and Boylan receives the salutations of Bloom's companions in the carriage.

The Man in the Brown Macintosh is, however, a theme. Among the incidental characters of the book there is one of very special interest to the Joycean reader, for I need not repeat that every new type of writer evolves a new type of reader; every genius produces a legion of young insomniacs. The very special incidental character I have in mind is the so-called Man in the Brown Macintosh, who is alluded to in one way or another eleven times in the course of the book but is never named. Commentators have, as far as I know, not understood his identity. Let us see if we can identify him.

He is first seen at the funeral of Paddy Dignam; nobody knows who he is, his appearance is sudden and unexpected, and throughout the long day

Mr. Bloom will keep reverting in thought to this small but irritating mystery—who was the man in the brown raincoat? This is how he appears at the funeral. Bloom is thinking of dead Dignam while the grave diggers set the nose of the coffin on the brink of the grave and loop the bands around it to sink it into the hole. "Burying him. . . . He doesn't know who is here nor care." At this point Bloom's eye roving for a minute over those "who are here," is arrested by the sight of a person he does not know. The stream of thought takes a new turn. "Now who is that lankylooking galoot over there in the macintosh? Now who is he I'd like to know? Now, I'd give a trifle to know who he is. Always someone turns up you never dreamt of." This thought bumbles on, and presently he is counting the small number of people at the funeral. "Mr Bloom stood far back, his hat in his hand, counting the bared heads. Twelve. I'm thirteen. No. The chap in the macintosh is thirteen. Death's number. Where the deuce did he pop out of? He wasn't in the chapel, that I'll swear. Silly superstition that about thirteen." Bloom's thought wanders to other things.

So who is that lanky fellow who seems to have been engendered out of nothing at the very moment when Patrick Dignam's coffin is lowered into the grave? Let us pursue our inquiry. At the end of the ceremony Joe Hynes, a reporter who is taking down names at the funeral, asks Bloom, "—And tell us, Hynes said, do you know that fellow in the . . ." but at this point he notices that the fellow has disappeared, and the sentence remains unfinished. The dropped word is, of course, *macintosh*. Then Hynes goes on, "—fellow was over there in the. . . ." Again he does not finish and looks round. Bloom supplements the end of the sentence: "—Macintosh. Yes, I saw him. . . . Where is he now?" Hynes misunderstands: he thinks the name of the man is Macintosh (compare this with the Throwaway horse theme), and this he scribbles down. "—Macintosh, Hynes said, scribbling. I don't know who he is. Is that his name?" Hynes moves away, looking around him to see if he had jotted down everybody. "—No, Mr Bloom began, turning and stopping. I say, Hynes!

Didn't hear. What? Where has he disappeared to? Not a sign. Well of all the. Has anybody here seen? Kay ee double ell. Become invisible. Good Lord, what became of him?" At this point Bloom's thoughts are interrupted when a seventh grave digger comes beside him to pick up an idle spade.

In the last section of the seventh chapter of part two, the chapter devoted to the synchronization of the various people in the streets of Dublin around three o'clock of the afternoon, we find another allusion to the mystery man. The viceroy, the governor of Ireland, on his way to inaugurate the Mirus bazaar in aid of funds for Mercer's Hospital (it is at this bazaar that later, at nightfall, a certain significant display of fireworks is produced in chapter 10)—the viceroy as he drives with his following past a blind youth, then "In Lower Mount street a pedestrian in a brown macintosh, eating dry bread, passed swiftly and unscathed across the viceroy's path." What new clues are added here? Well, the man exists; after all, he is a live individual, he is poor, he walks with light steps, he somehow resembles Stephen Dedalus in contemptuous and aloof motion. But of course he is not Stephen. England, the viceroy, leaves him unscathed— England cannot molest him. A live man and at the same time as light as a ghost—who on earth is he?

The next reference comes in chapter 9 of part two, the chapter where kind, gentle Bloom in Kiernan's bar is pestered by a hoodlum, the anonymous citizen, and the dreadful dog belonging to Gerty's grandfather. Bloom with a very tender and grave intonation (which raises him above his own too physical individual level in other parts of the book), Bloom the Jew is speaking: "—And I belong to a race too, says Bloom, that is hated and persecuted. Also now. This very moment. This very instant." The citizen sneers at him, "Are you talking about the new Jerusalem? says the citizen.

—I'm talking about injustice, says Bloom. . . .

—But it's no use, says he. Force, hatred, history, all that. That's not life for men and women, insult and hatred. And everybody knows that it's the very opposite of that that is really life."

What is that, asks Alf, the barkeeper. "—Love, says Bloom." Incidentally this is a main support of Tolstoy's philosophy—human life is divine love. Love is understood by the simpler minds in the bar as sexual love. But among the various statements: "Constable 14 A loves Mary Kelly. Gerty MacDowell loves the boy that has the bicycle. . . . His Majesty the King loves Her Majesty the Queen," etc.—our mystery man reappears for a moment. "The man in the brown macintosh loves a lady who is dead." We note that he stands out here in marked contrast to the constable and even to "Old Mr Verschoyle with the ear trumpet [who] loves old Mrs Verschoyle with the turnedin eye." A poetical something has been added to the mystery man. But who is he—he who appears at crucial points of the book—is he death, oppression, persecution, life, love?

In chapter 10 at the end of the masturbation scene on the beach, during the bazaar fireworks Bloom briefly recalls the Man in the Brown Macintosh he had seen at the grave side; and, in chapter 11, in a bar just before closing time at eleven o'clock, a bar between a maternity hospital and a house of ill-fame, the mystery man through the fog of liquor is briefly seen: "Golly, whatten tunket's yon guy in the macintosh? Dusty Rhodes. Peep at his wearables. By mighty! What's he got? Jubilee mutton. Bovril, by James. Wants it real bad. D'ye ken bare socks? Seedy cuss in the Richmond? Rawthere! Thought he had a deposit of lead in his penis. Trumpery insanity. Bartle the Bread we calls him. That, sir, was once a prosperous cit. Man all tattered and torn that married a maiden all forlorn. Slung her hook, she did. Here see lost love. Walking Macintosh of lonely canyon. Tuck and turn in. Schedule time. Nix for the hornies. Pardon? See him today at a runefal? Chum o yourn passed in his checks?" The passage, like the whole last scene of the chapter, is unnecessarily obscure, but there are clearly references to the man avidly eating Bovril soup and to his dusty shoes, torn socks, and lost love.

A brown-macintoshed man pops up in the bordello scene, chapter 12, which is a grotesque exaggeration of broken thoughts passing through the mind of Bloom: broken thoughts acting on a dim stage in a nightmare comedy. This chapter should not be taken seriously, nor should we take seriously Bloom's brief vision of the Man in the Brown Macintosh who denounces him as the son of a Christian mother: "Don't you believe a word he says. That man is Leopold M'Intosh, the notorious fireraiser. His real name is Higgins." Bloom's mother, who married Rudolph Virag of Szombathely, Vienna, Budapest, Milan, London, and Dublin, was born Ellen Higgins, second daughter of Julius Higgins (born Karoly—a Hungarian) and Fanny Higgins, born Hegarty. In the same nightmare Bloom's grandfather Lipoti (Leopold) Virag is sausaged into several overcoats over which he wears a brown macintosh obviously borrowed from the mystery man. When after midnight Bloom orders coffee for Stephen in a cabman's shelter (part three, chapter 1), he picks up a copy of the *Evening Telegraph* and reads therein the account of Patrick Dignam's funeral as reported by Joe Hynes: The mourners included—here follows a list of names ending with M'Intosh. And finally, in chapter 2 of this last part, a chapter which is composed in question and answer form, there occurs the following: "What selfinvolved enigma did Bloom [as he undressed and gathered his garments] voluntarily apprehending, not comprehend?

Who was M'Intosh?"

This is the last we hear of the Man in the Brown Macintosh.

Do we know who he is? I think we do. The clue comes in chapter 4 of part two, the scene at the library. Stephen is discussing Shakespeare and affirms that Shakespeare himself is present in his, Shakespeare's, works. Shakespeare, he says, tensely: "He has hidden his own name, a fair name,

William, in the plays, a super here, a clown there, as a painter of old Italy set his face in a dark corner of his canvas. . . ." and this is exactly what Joyce has done—setting his face in a dark corner of this canvas. The Man in the Brown Macintosh who passes through the dream of the book is no other than the author himself. Bloom glimpses his maker!

PART TWO, CHAPTER 4

Time: Noon.

Place: Newspaper offices, the *Freeman's Journal* and *Evening Telegraph*, at Nelson's Pillar, the center of the city just north of the Liffey.

Characters: Among the characters there is Bloom, who has come in order to arrange for the publication of an advertisement of Alexander Keyes: high class licensed premises, a liquor store or pub. (Later, in chapter 5, he will go to the National Library to procure the design of the two crossed keys with the legend, house of keys, the name of the Manx parliament—an innuendo bearing on home rule for Ireland. To the same newspaper office comes Stephen with Deasy's letter on hoof-and-mouth disease, but Joyce does not bring Bloom and Stephen together. Bloom is aware of Stephen, however; and other citizens, including Stephen's father, back from the cemetery with Bloom, are glimpsed at the newspaper office. Among the journalists there is Lenehan, who riddles a pun, "What opera resembles a railway line?" Answer: The Rose of Castille (rows of cast steel).

Style: The sections of the chapter bear humorous titles in parody of newspaper headlines. The chapter seems to me to be poorly balanced, and Stephen's contribution to it is not especially witty. You may peruse it with a skimming eye.

PART TWO, CHAPTER 5

Time: After one o'clock, early afternoon.

Place: Streets south of Nelson's Pillar.

Characters: Bloom and several people he happens to meet.

Action: From Nelson's Pillar Bloom walks south, riverward. A somber YMCA man places a leaflet, "Elijah is Coming," "in a hand of Mr Bloom." Why this odd construction, "in a hand of Mr Bloom"? Because for the distributor of leaflets a hand is merely a hand into which to place something: that it belongs to Mr. Bloom is incidental. "Heart to heart talks.

Bloo . . . Me? No.

Blood of the Lamb.

His slow feet walked him riverward, reading. Are you saved? All are washed in the blood of the lamb. God wants blood victim. Birth, hymen, martyr, war, foundation of a building, sacrifice, kidney burntoffering, druid's altars. Elijah is coming. Dr. John Alexander Dowie, restorer of the church in Zion, is coming.

Is coming! Is coming!! Is coming!!!
All heartily welcome."

Presently we shall follow the fate of that pamphlet, called a *throwaway*. On his way to lunch in town Bloom passes a few people. Stephen's sister is outside Dillon's auction rooms, selling off some old things. They are very poor, Stephen's motherless family of four girls and Stephen, and the father, an old egoist, does not seem to care. Bloom sets foot on O'Connell bridge and sees gulls flapping and wheeling. He is still holding in his hand the leaflet he has been given by the YMCA man, announcing the evangelist Dr. Dowie on the subject Elijah is coming. Now Bloom crumples it into a ball and throws it from the bridge to see if the gulls will snatch at it. "Elijah thirty-two feet per sec is com." (Scientific Bloom.) The gulls ignore it.

Let us briefly follow through three chapters the Elijah theme, the fate of that scrap of paper. It has fallen into the flowing Liffey and will be instrumental to mark the passage of time. It started on its river voyage eastward, seaward, at about half past one. An hour later, riding lightly down the Liffey, it has sailed under Loopline bridge, two blocks east from its starting point: "A skiff, a crumpled throwaway, Elijah is coming, rode lightly down the Liffey, under Loopline bridge, shooting the rapids where water chafed around the bridgepiers, sailing eastward past hulls and anchorchains, between the Customhouse old dock and George's quay." A few minutes later, "North wall and sir John Rogerson's quay, with hulls and anchorchains, sailing westward, sailed by a skiff, a crumpled throwaway, rocked on the ferry-wash, Elijah is coming." Finally, a little after three o'clock it reaches Dublin Bay: "Elijah, skiff, light crumpled throwaway, sailed eastward by flanks of ships and trawlers, amid an archipelago of corks, beyond new Wapping street past Benson's ferry, and by the threemasted schooner *Rosevean* from Bridgwater with bricks." At about the same time, Mr. Farrell, just before he brushes by the blind stripling, frowns "at Elijah's name announced on the Metropolitan Hall" where the evangelist is to speak.

In another synchronizing theme, a procession of white-smocked sandwich-board men march slowly towards Bloom in the vicinity of

Westmoreland Street. Bloom is brooding over Molly's coming betrayal and thinks of ads at the same time. He has seen a sign on a urinal—post no bills—and some chap has changed bills to pills. This leads Bloom to reflect in terror—what if Boylan has gonorrhea? These sandwich men advertising Wisdom Hely's stationery shop are also going to walk through the book. In Bloom's mind they are associated with his happy past when he worked at Hely's in the first years of his marriage.

In this same chapter 5, Bloom on his way south to lunch meets an old flame of his, then Josephine Powell, now Mrs. Denis Breen. She tells him that some anonymous joker has sent her husband an insulting postcard with the message U. P.: you pee, up (a reference to the tag "U.P. spells goslings," meaning it's all up with a person). Bloom changes the subject and asks of Mrs. Breen if she has seen anything of Mrs. Beaufoy. She corrects him, you mean Purefoy, Mina Purefoy. Bloom's slip of the tongue is due to his mixing up the name Purefoy with that of Philip Beaufoy, the pseudoelegant name of the chap who wrote the prize titbit "Matcham's Masterstroke" in the *Titbits* pages which Bloom took with him to the toilet after his breakfast. As he talks to Mrs. Breen, Bloom even remembers part of the passage. The mention of Mina Purefoy being in the maternity hospital and going through the throes of a very stiff birth suggests to compassionate Bloom visiting the hospital, which he does eight hours later, in chapter 11, to find out how she is. One thing leads to another in this marvelous book. And meeting Josephine Powell, now Mrs. Breen, sets going a train of retrospective thought in Bloom's mind, the happy past when he first met Molly and now the bitter and ugly present. He remembers a recent night when he, Molly, and Boylan were walking along the River Tolka, near Dublin. She was humming. Perhaps it was then that her fingers and Boylan's touched, and a question was asked and the reply was yes. The change in Molly, the change in their love, occurred some ten years before, in 1894, after their little boy's birth and his death a few days later. He thinks about giving Molly a present of a pin cushion, perhaps for her birthday on 8 September. "Women won't pick up pins. Say it cuts lo." The *ve* in *love* has been cut off to show what happens. But he cannot prevent her affair with Boylan. "Useless to go back. Had to be. Tell me all."

Bloom enters the Burton restaurant, but it is noisy, crowded, dirty, and he decides not to eat there. But being very careful not to offend anybody, even stinking Burton, kindly Bloom goes through a little rigmarole of private courtesy. He "raised two fingers doubtfully to his lips. His eyes said.

—Not here. Don't see him."

An invented person, a pretext for leaving the place, the mannerism of a very good-hearted and very vulnerable Bloom. This is a preview of his motions at the end of the chapter when he runs into Boylan and feigns to be searching in his pocket so as not to give the appearance of seeing him. He finally has a snack at Byrne's pub in Duke Street—a gorgonzola cheese sandwich and a glass of burgundy—where he talks to Nosey Flynn, and the Gold Cup is on everybody's mind. Crushing the glowing wine in his mouth, Bloom thinks of the first kiss Molly gave him and the wild fern on Howth hill, just north of Dublin on the bay, and the rhododendron and her lips and breasts.

He walks on, now heading for the Art Museum and National Library where he wants to look up an advertisement in an old issue of the *Kilkenny People* paper. "At Duke lane a ravenous terrier choked up a sick knuckly cud on the cobble stones and lapped it with new zest. Surfeit. Returned with thanks having fully digested the contents. . . . Mr Bloom coasted warily. Ruminants. His second course." Much in the same way will Stephen, poor dogsbody, disgorge brilliant literary theories in the library scene. Walking along the street Bloom thinks of the past and the present, and whether *teco* in the *Don Giovanni* aria means "tonight" (it does not: it means "with thee"). "Could buy one of those silk petticoats for Molly, colour of her new garters."* But the shadow of Boylan, of four o'clock, only two hours to go, intervenes. "Today. Today. Not think." He pretends not to see Boylan passing.

Towards the end of the chapter you will notice the first appearance of a minor character who will walk through several chapters as one of the many synchronizing agents in the book; that is, characters or things whose changing place marks the flow of time throughout that particular day. "A blind stripling stood tapping the curbstone with his slender cane. No tram in sight. Wants to cross.

—Do you want to cross? Mr Bloom asked.

The blind stripling did not answer. His wall face frowned weakly. He moved his head uncertainly.

—You're in Dawson street, Mr Bloom said. Molesworth street is opposite. Do you want to cross? There's nothing in the way.

The cane moved out trembling to the left. Mr Bloom's eye followed its line and saw again the dyeworks' van drawn up before Drago's [the barber]. Where I saw [Boylan's] brilliantined hair just when I was. Horse drooping. Driver in John Long's. Slaking his drouth.

*Molly's new garters are violet colored, as we have learned during the Oriental fantasy Bloom enjoyed while on his way earlier that morning to purchase his breakfast kidney. Ed.

—There's a van there, Mr Bloom said, but it's not moving. I'll see you across. Do you want to go to Molesworth street?

—Yes, the stripling answered. South Frederick street. [*Actually he heads for Clare Street.*]

—Come, Mr Bloom said.

He touched the thin elbow gently: then took the limp seeing hand to guide it forward. . . .

—Thanks, sir.

Knows I'm a man. Voice.

—Right now? First turn to the left.

The blind stripling tapped the curbstone and went on his way, drawing his cane back, feeling again."

Bloom having crossed the Liffey again by another bridge at about half past one, walks south and runs into Mrs. Breen and presently they both see the insane Mr. Farrell striding by. After lunching at Byrne's pub, Bloom walks on, heading for the National Library. It is here in Dawson Street that he helps the blind stripling to cross, and the youth continues east towards Clare Street. In the meantime, Farrell, who has gone by way of Kildare Street and reached Merrion Square, has turned back and brushes by the blind youth. "As he strode past Mr Bloom's dental windows [*another Bloom*] the sway of his dustcoat brushed rudely from its angle a slender tapping cane and swept onwards, having buffeted a thewless body. The blind stripling turned his sickly face after the striding form.

—God's curse on you, he said sourly, whoever you are! You're blinder nor I am, you bitch's bastard!"

Thus madness and blindness meet. Shortly, the viceroy driving to open the bazaar, "passed a blind stripling opposite Broadbent's." Still later, the blind youth will be tapping his way back, westward back to Ormond's where he had been tuning the piano and has forgotten his tuning fork. We shall hear the approaching tip-tap throughout the Ormond chapter around four o'clock.

PART TWO, CHAPTER 6

Time: Around two o'clock.
Place: The National Library.

Nabokov's map of the blind stripling's route in *Ulysses*, part two

The Blind Stripling

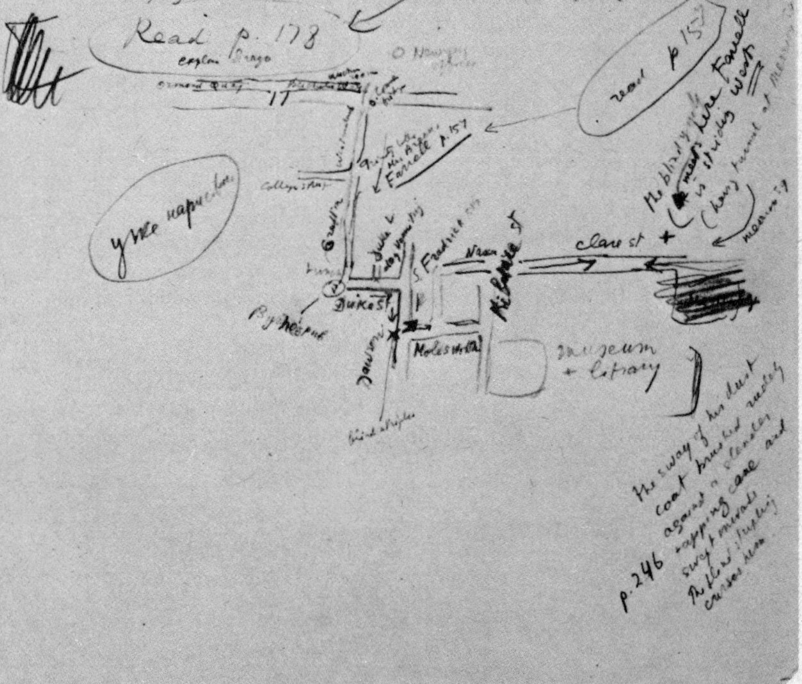

Characters: Stephen has sent Buck Mulligan a telegram implying that he should relinquish the tower to him, and in the meantime, at the library, is discussing Shakespeare with certain members of the Irish Revival group of writers and scholars. There is Thomas Lyster (real name), here dubbed the quaker librarian because he wears a broad-brimmed hat to cover a big bald head; there is in the shadow George Russell, pen name A.E., a tall figure and well-known Irish writer in bearded homespun whom Bloom saw passing in the precedent chapter; there is John Eglinton, a merry puritan; there is Mr. Richard Best, who gets mixed up with the second-best bed that Shakespeare left to his widow Anne Hathaway (this Best is depicted as a somewhat shallow and conventional man of letters); and presently comes, primrose-vested, the mocking Malachi Mulligan with Stephen's cryptic telegram just received.

Action: Stephen discoursing on Shakespeare argues (1) that the Ghost in *Hamlet* is really Shakespeare himself, (2) that Hamlet is to be identified with Hamnet, Shakespeare's little son; and (3) that Richard Shakespeare, William's brother, had an intrigue with Anne, Shakespeare's wife, thus accounting for the bitterness of the play. When he is asked if he believes his own thesis, Stephen promptly answers: no. Everything is fouled up in this book.* The discussion in this chapter is one of those things that is more amusing for a writer to write than for a reader to read, and so its details need not be examined. However, it is in this chapter at the library that Stephen first becomes aware of Bloom.

Joyce has intertwined the Stephen and Bloom patterns much more closely than is generally thought. The connection begins in the book long before Bloom passes Stephen on the library steps. It begins in a dream. Nobody has noticed yet—it is true not much has been written about the real Joyce, Joyce the artist—no commentator has noticed yet that as in Tolstoy's *Anna Karenin* there is in *Ulysses* a significant double dream; that is, the same dream seen by two people at the same time.

On an early page, Stephen complains to Mulligan, who is shaving, that Haines awoke him during the night by raving about shooting a black

---

*In a deleted passage, following, VN wrote: "Those who will read out of artistic curiosity the house-of-ill-fame chapter 12 will find, at one point, Bloom seeing himself in the mirror under the reflection of a deer-horned hat hanger—and the cuckold's face is fleetingly identified with Shakespeare's face—the two themes Bloom's betrayal and Shakespeare's betrayal come together in a whore's looking glass." Ed.

Nabokov's notes on the routes followed by Bloom, Farrell, and the blind stripling

Who has unlocked the Meatland used in 1881 to explain by cable that the Journalist galloped from Dublin to America

the route followed by the newscables in the Phoenix Park murder case.

Chapter V

The route followed by
Bloom, Farrell and the Blind Boy

☐ Nelson Pillar
○ Newspaper office

Liffey R.

Ormond Bar and restaurant
Ormond Quay   Bachelor Walk   anchor

1.30 a.m.   10 a.m.

Westmoreland St
College St   Trinity College
Grafton St   Dawson St   Nassau   Clare St   ← Farrell starting out   merrion sq
Byron's Pub   Duke St
Molesworth St   Kildare St
Mus. Library
Nat L

Bloom having crossed the Liffey again by another bridge (and at about half past one) walking south runs into MacKernan, and presently they both see the insane Mr Farrell striding by. After lunching at the Byron's Pub Bloom walks on heading for the Library. In Dawson St he helps a blind stripling to cross. The blind youth continues ... east towards Clare street. In the meantime Farrell who has gone by way of Kildare St and reached Merrion sq has turned back and brushes past the blind youth. Still later the blind youth will be tap-tapping his way back ... Westland back to Ormond's where he has been tuning the piano and has forgotten his tuning fork. We shall hear the approach tap-tap through the Ormond chapter about four o'clock

panther. The black panther leads to Bloom, in black, the kindly black cat. This is how it goes. Walking along the beach after being paid by Deasy, Stephen observes the cocklepickers and their dog, who has just enjoyed the simple pleasures of the poor by cocking his leg against a rock. In a reminiscence of his riddle to his pupils about the fox, Stephen's stream of thought is at first colored by his guilt: "His hindpaws then scattered sand: then his forepaws dabbled and delved. Something he buried there, his grandmother. He rooted in the sand, dabbling, delving and stopped to listen to the air, scraped up the sand again with a fury of his claws, soon ceasing, a pard, a panther, got in spousebreach, vulturing the dead.

After [Haines] woke me up last night same dream or was it? Wait. Open hallway. Street of harlots. Remember. Haroun al Raschid. I am almosting it. That man led me, spoke. I was not afraid. The melon he had he held against my face. Smiled: creamfruit smell. That was the rule, said. In. Come. Red carpet spread. You will see who."

Now this is a prophetic dream. But let us mark that near the end of part two, chapter 10—a chapter where Bloom is also on a beach, Bloom briefly and dimly recalls the dream he saw the same night as Stephen saw his. At first his stream of thought, caught by an advertisement, hovers over his old flame, now the aging and unattractive Mrs. Breen, with her husband who was tricked and went off to see a lawyer about the insulting anonymous message he had received. "Ladies' grey flannelette bloomers, three shillings a pair, astonishing bargain. Plain and loved, loved for ever, they say. Ugly: no woman thinks she is. Love, lie and be handsome for tomorrow we die. See him sometimes walking about trying to find out who played the trick. U.p.: up. Fate that is. He, not me. Also a shop often noticed. Curse seems to dog it. Dreamt last night? Wait. Something confused. She had red slippers on. Turkish. Wore the breeches." And then his thought wanders on in another direction. In chapter 11, the maternity hospital chapter, another reference is slipped in although without further detail: "Bloom there for a languor he had but was now better, he having dreamed tonight a strange fancy of his dame Mrs Moll with red slippers on in pair of Turkey trunks which is thought by those in ken to be for a change. . . ."

So on the night of 15 June to 16 June, Stephen Dedalus in his tower at Sandycove, and Mr. Bloom in the connubial bed in his house on Eccles Street dream the same dream. Now, what is Joyce's intention here, in these twin dreams? He wishes to show that in his Oriental dream Stephen foresaw a stranger offering him the opulent charms of his, the dark stranger's, wife. This dark stranger is Bloom. Let us look at another passage. During his walk before breakfast to purchase a kidney, Bloom conjures up a very similar Oriental vision: "Somewhere in the east: early morning: set off at dawn, travel round in front of the sun, steal a day's march on him. Keep it up for ever never grow a day older technically. Walk along a strand, strange land, come to a city gate, sentry there, old ranker too, old Tweedy's [Molly's father's] big moustaches leaning on a long kind of a spear. Wander through awned streets. Turbaned faces going by. Dark caves of carpet shops, big man, Turko the terrible, seated crosslegged smoking a coiled pipe. Cries of sellers in the streets. Drink water scented with fennel, sherbet. Wander along all day. Might meet a robber or two. Well, meet him. Getting on to sundown. The shadows of the mosques along the pillars: priests with a scroll rolled up. A shiver of the trees, signal, the evening wind. I pass on. Fading gold sky. A mother watches from her doorway. She calls her children home in their dark language. High wall: beyond strings twanged. Night sky moon, violet, colour of Molly's new garters. Strings. Listen. A girl playing one of these instruments what do you call them: dulcimers. I pass."

Around two o'clock Bloom visits the National Library, and Stephen, walking out with Mulligan, sees Bloom, whom he knows slightly, for the first time that day. Here is Stephen seeing the dream stranger Bloom: "A man passed out between them, bowing, greeting.

—Good day again, Buck Mulligan said.

The portico.

Here I watched the birds for augury. Aengus of the birds. They go, they come. Last night I flew. Easily flew. Men wondered. Street of harlots after. A creamfruit melon he held to me. In. You will see.*

—The wandering jew, Buck Mulligan whispered with clown's awe. Did you see his eye?" and he cracks an obscene joke. A few lines down: "A dark back went before them. Step of a pard, down, out by the gateway, under portcullis barbs.

They followed."

Bloom's dark back, his step of a pard. The link is complete.

Further on, in the nightmare chapter in the house of ill-fame, we find an echo of the Bloom-Stephen twin dream. The stage direction reads: "([Bloom] looks up. Beside her mirage of datepalms a handsome woman in Turkish costume stands before him. Opulent curves fill out her scarlet trousers and jacket slashed with gold. A wide yellow cummerbund girdles

*In his annotated copy VN wrote in the margin of this paragraph: "NB Stephen recalls his dream at the moment he notices Bloom bowing, greeting." Ed.

her. *A white yashmak violet in the night, covers her face, leaving free only her large dark eyes and raven hair.*)" Bloom calls out, "Molly!" Then much later in the same scene Stephen says to one of the girls: "Mark me. I dreamt of a watermelon," to which the girl replies, "Go abroad and love a foreign lady." The melons Stephen dreamed of, originally the creamfruit offered him, are finally identified as Molly Bloom's opulent curves in the question-and-answer chapter 2 of part three: Bloom "kissed the plump mellow yellow smellow melons of her rump, on each plump melonous hemisphere, in their mellow yellow furrow, with obscure prolonged provocative melonsmellonous osculation."

The twin dreams of Stephen and Bloom prove prophetic, because in the next to last chapter of the book it is Bloom's intention to do exactly what the stranger in Stephen's dream wished to do—namely, Bloom wishes to bring Stephen and Marion, Bloom's wife, together as a means of displacing Boylan, a theme which is especially stressed in the chapter of the cabman's shelter at the beginning of part three.

PART TWO, CHAPTER 7

This consists of nineteen sections.

Time: Five minutes to three.

Place: Dublin.

Characters: Fifty characters, including all our friends and their various activities within the same time limits, around three in the afternoon of 16 June.

Action: These characters cross and recross each other's trails in a most intricate counterpoint—a monstrous development of Flaubert's counterpoint themes, as in the agricultural show scene in *Madame Bovary*. So the device here is synchronization. It starts with the Jesuit Father Conmee of Saint Xavier's Church, Upper Gardiner Street, an optimistic and elegant priest, nicely combining this world and the other, and concludes with the viceroy, the governor of Ireland, driving through the town. Father Conmee is followed on his rounds, blessing a one-legged sailor, speaking to parishioner after parishioner as he walks, passing the O'Neill funeral establishment, until at Newcomen Bridge he boards a tramcar that takes him to the Howth Road stop, to Malahide, northeast of Dublin. It was a charming day, elegant and optimistic. In a field a flushed young man came from a gap in the hedge, and after him came a young woman with wild nodding daisies in her hand. The young man, a medical student, named Vincent Lynch we learn later, raised his cap abruptly; the young woman abruptly bent and with slow care detached from her light skirt a clinging twig (*marvelous* writer). Father Conmee blessed both gravely.

In the second section the synchronization begins. Near Newcomen Bridge, at the undertaker O'Neill's, the undertaker's assistant Kelleher, who has taken care of the Dignam funeral, closes his daybook and chats with the constable, the same policeman who had saluted Father Conmee in passing a few moments earlier. By this time Father John Conmee has gone towards the bridge and now (synchronization!) steps into the tram on Newcomen Bridge in between the sentences referring to Kelleher. See the technique? It is now three. Kelleher sends a silent jet of hayjuice (produced by the blade of hay that he was chewing while checking figures in his daybook when Father Conmee passed a moment ago), Kelleher sends the silent jet from his mouth and at the same time in another part of the town (section 3) a generous white arm (Molly Bloom's) from a window in Eccles Street, three miles away to the northwest, flings forth a coin to the one-legged sailor who has by now reached Eccles Street. Molly is grooming herself for her date with Blazes Boylan. And also at the same time J. J. O'Molloy is told that Ned Lambert has come to the warehouse with a visitor, a visit taken care of later in section 8.

There is not time or space to go through all the detailed synchronizing mechanisms in all nineteen sections of this chapter. We must hit only the high spots. In section 4 Katy, Boody, and Maggy Dedalus, Stephen's young sisters (he has four in all) return empty-handed from the pawnshop while Father Conmee, walking through the Clongowes fields, has his thin socked ankles tickled by the stubble. Where is the crumpled skiff Elijah? Find her. What lackey rings what bell—barang! The man at the auction rooms—at Dillon's.

About 3:15, we start to follow Blazes Boylan, who has begun his little journey Mollyward, to Molly Bloom whom he will reach in a jaunting car around a quarter to four. But this is still around three o'clock (he will stop at the Ormond Hotel on the way); and at Thornton's, a fruit shop, he is sending fruit to Molly by tram. It will take ten minutes to reach her. Hely's sandwich men by this time are plodding by the fruit shop. Bloom is now under Merchant's Arch, near Metal Bridge, and bends, dark-backed, over a book hawker's cart. The end of the section gives us the origin in the fruit shop of the red carnation that Boylan is to carry with its stem between his teeth throughout the chapter. At the time he cadges the carnation he begs the use of the phone, and as we later learn calls his secretary.

Now Stephen walks. In the vicinity of Trinity College he meets his former teacher of Italian, Almidano Artifoni, and they talk briskly in

Italian. Artifoni accuses Stephen of sacrificing his youth to his ideals. A bloodless sacrifice, says Stephen smiling. The seventh section is synchronized with the fifth. Boylan's secretary, Miss Dunn, has been reading a novel and now answers the telephone call Boylan makes in the fruit shop. She tells Boylan that the sports editor Lenehan has been looking for him and will be in the Ormond Hotel at four. (We shall meet them there in a later chapter.) In this section two other synchronizations occur. A disk that shoots down a groove and ogles the onlookers with the number *six* refers to a betting machine which Tom Rochford, bookie, demonstrates farther on in the ninth section. And we follow the five tall white-hatted sandwich men who having reached their limit, beyond Monypeny's Corner, eel themselves around and begin their return.

Ned Lambert, in section 8, with Jack O'Molloy shows a visitor, a Protestant clergyman, the Reverend Love, his warehouse which was formerly the council chamber of Saint Mary's Abbey. At this moment the girl with the medical student in that country lane where Father Conmee has walked is picking the twig from her skirt. This is synchronization: while this happens here, that happens there. Soon after three o'clock (section 9) Rochford the bookie shows Lenehan his gadget and the disk slides down the groove and reveals a six. At the same time there goes Richie Goulding, a law clerk, Stephen's uncle, with whom Bloom will eat at the Ormond Hotel in the next chapter. Lenehan leaves Rochford with M'Coy (who had asked Bloom to put down his name at Dignam's funeral when he could not attend) and they visit another bookie. On their way to the Ormond Hotel, after stopping at Lynam's to see Sceptre's starting odds, they observe Mr. Bloom "—*Leopold or the Bloom is on the Rye*," Lenehan quips. Bloom is scanning those books on the hawker's cart. Lenehan's walking towards the Ormond Hotel is synchronized with Molly Bloom replacing the card advertising an unfurnished apartment that has slipped from the sash when she opened it to fling the one-legged sailor a penny. And since at the same time Kelleher was talking to the constable, and Father Conmee had boarded a trolley, we conclude with a tinge of artistic pleasure that sections 2, 3, and 9 occurred simultaneously in different places.

After three o'clock Mr. Bloom is still idling over the books for rent. He finally rents for Molly *Sweets of Sin*, an American novel, slightly risqué in an old-fashioned manner. "He read where his finger opened.

—All the dollarbills her husband gave her were spent in the stores on wondrous gowns and costliest frillies. For him! For Raoul!

Yes. This. Here. Try.

—Her mouth glued on his in a luscious voluptuous kiss while his hands felt for the opulent curves inside her deshabilé.

Yes. Take this. The end.

—You are late, he spoke hoarsely, eyeing her with a suspicious glare. The beautiful woman threw off her sabletrimmed wrap, displaying her queenly shoulders and heaving embonpoint. An imperceptible smile played round her perfect lips as she turned to him calmly."

Dilly Dedalus, Stephen's fourth sister, who has been hanging around Dillon's auction rooms since Bloom saw her there about one o'clock, listens to the auction hand bell ringing at the sales. Her father, hard, selfish, clever, artistic old Simon Dedalus comes by and Dilly gets a shilling and tuppence out of him. This is synchronized with the viceroy's cavalcade starting out at Parkgate, Phoenix Park, the western suburb of Dublin, and heading for the center of the city, thence eastward to Sandymount, to inaugurate a bazaar. They pass through the whole city from west to east.

Just after three o'clock Tom Kernan, tea merchant, walks, pleased with the order he has just got. He is a pompous and plump Protestant, Mr. Kernan, beside whom Bloom stood at the funeral of Dignam. Kernan is one of the few minor characters in the book whose stream of consciousness is given in detail, here in the twelfth section. In the same section Simon Dedalus meets on the street a priest, Father Cowley, with whom he is on intimate first-name terms. Elijah sails down the Liffey past Sir John Rogerson's Quay, and the viceregal cavalcade passes along Pembroke Quay. Kernan just misses it.

In the next, a few moments after Bloom, Stephen in his turn stops at the bookstalls in Bedford Row. Father Conmee is now walking through the hamlet of Donnycarney, reading his vespers. Stephen's sister Dilly, with her high shoulders and shabby dress, halts next to him. She has bought a French primer with one of the pennies she got from her father. Abstract Stephen, although acutely aware of the misery of his four young sisters, seems to forget that he still has gold in his pocket, what is left of his schoolteacher's salary. He will be ready to give that money away for no reason at all, when drunk, in a later chapter. The section ends with his sorrow for Dilly, and the repetition of *agenbite*, remorse, which we heard from him in the first chapter of part one.

In section 14 we repeat the greeting of Simon Dedalus and Father Cowley and the conversation is recorded. The priest is having money troubles with the moneylender Reuben J. Dodd and with his landlord. Then Ben Dollard comes up, an amateur singer, who is trying to be helpful to Father Cowley in staving off the bailiffs. Mr. Cashel Boyle O'Connor

Fitzmaurice Tisdall Farrell, the demented gentleman, murmuring and glassy eyed, strides down Kildare Street; this is the man who passed Bloom talking to Mrs. Breen. The Reverend Mr. Love, who toured the warehouse-abbey with Lambert and O'Molloy, is mentioned as Father Cowley's landlord who had put out a writ for his rent.

Next Cunningham and Power (also of the funeral party) discuss the fund for Dignam's widow, to which Bloom has contributed five shillings. Father Conmee is mentioned, and we meet for the first time two barmaids, the Misses Kennedy and Douce, who will come in later in chapter 8. The viceroy now passes Parliament Street. In section 16 the brother of the Irish patriot Parnell plays chess in a café where Buck Mulligan points him out to Haines, the Oxford student of folklore. The two discuss Stephen. Synchronized in this section is the one-legged sailor, growling his song and swinging along on his crutches on Nelson Street. And the crumpled pamphlet Elijah meets in the bay a home-come ship, the *Rosevean*.

Then in section 17 Stephen's Italian teacher walks and so does the mad gentleman Farrell, with the long name. We shall soon realize that the most important synchronizing agent in the whole chapter is the blind youth, the blind piano tuner, whom Bloom helped to cross the street in an eastward direction, about two o'clock. Demented Farrell now walks westward on Clare Street, while the blind youth is walking eastward on the same street, still unaware that he has left his tuning fork in the Ormond Hotel. Opposite number 8, the office of a dentist Mr. Bloom, already referred to in the description of the funeral procession, no relation to Leopold, mad Farrell brushes against the frail soft body of the blind youth, who curses him.

The eighteenth section is devoted to the late Mr. Dignam's son, Patrick, Jr., a boy of twelve or so, who heads west on Wicklow Street, carrying some pork steaks for which he had been sent. He dawdles and looks into a shop window at the picture of two boxers who have fought recently, on 21 May. In chapter 9 one finds a delightful parody of a journalistic description of a boxing match: the sports stylist keeps varying his epithets—it is one of the funniest passages in this amusing book—Dublin's pet lamb, the sergeant major, the artilleryman, the soldier, the Irish gladiator, the redcoat, the Dubliner, the Portobello bruiser. In Grafton Street, the brightest street in

3

Buck Mulligan and Haines discuss Stephen — p. 245

Synchronised in this section you will find the one-legged sailor growling his song, now in Nelson street and at the end of the section the crumpled pamphlet Elijah meets in the bay a homecome ship. Then too as sailor sings is ---

Section 17 p.246 is important Stephen's Italian teacher walk, and so does the demented gentleman with the long name, and Cashel ... Farrell the street umbrella'd dou. We shall soon realise that the most important synchronising agent in the whole chapter is the blind youth, the blind piano tuner whom Bloom helped to cross a street, in an eastward afterward around two o'clock an hour ago direction in sextern chapter Five. p.173

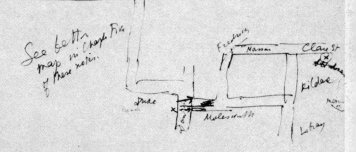

See better map in chapter Five of these notes.

ormond Key

Liffey R.

Freds ... Hanan Clare st

Kildare

Duke

Molesworth

Lahay

[We see now in Clare st Demented Farrell walks now in Clare street grinding his fierce word about "wishing to compel"] The blind youth is walking eastward in Clare st still unaware he has left his tuning fork in the ormond Hotel In Clare street opposite number eight the office of a dentist Mr Bloom - no relation to our Bloom, mad Farrell brushes against the frail body of the blind youth, who curses him.

Dublin, Master Dignam notices a red flower in a smartly dressed fellow's mouth—Blazes Boylan, of course. One may compare the boy's thought about his dead father with the thoughts of Stephen in the first chapter about his mother.

In the last section the viceregal procession comes into vivid existence. It is instrumental in bringing into focus all the people we have been following through the preceding sections, plus a few others, who either salute the viceroy or ignore him. Making an appearance are Kernan, Richie Goulding, the Ormond bar girls, Simon Dedalus who salutes the viceroy with a low servile hat, Gerty MacDowell whom we shall meet in chapter 10 on the rocks, the Reverend Hugh Love, Lenehan and M'Coy, Nolan, Rochford, Flynn, gay Mulligan and grave Haines, John Parnell who does not glance up from the chessboard, Dilly Dedalus with her French primer, Mr. Menton with his oyster eyes, Mrs. Breen and her husband, and the sandwich men. Blazes Boylan, straw hatted in his indigo suit and sky blue tie, red carnation between his lips, on his way to the Ormond Hotel and thence to Eccles Street ogles the ladies in the carriage, and the mad Cashel Boyle O'Connor Fitzmaurice Tisdall Farrell stares through a fierce eyeglass across the carriages at somebody in the window of the Austro-Hungarian consulate. Also Hornblower, the Trinity College porter whom Bloom had met on his way to the baths, Paddy Dignam, Jr., two cockle gatherers, and Almidano Artifoni. The procession going towards Lower Mount Street passes the blind piano tuner still heading east, but he will recall in a minute the tuning fork he forgot at his last job and will be coming back west in a moment towards the Ormond Hotel. There is also on the list the Man in the Brown Macintosh, James Joyce, master of synchronization.

Bloom runs into Boylan three times during the day (at 11 A.M., at 2 P.M., and at 4 P.M.) in three separate spots, and none of the times does Boylan see Bloom. The first time is in part two, chapter 3, in the carriage driving with Cunningham, Power, and Simon Dedalus to the funeral, a little after eleven, just as Bloom sees the wet bright bills of the opera on the hoardings near the Queen's Theatre. He sees Boylan emerging from the door of a restaurant, the Red Bank, a seafood place, and while the others salute him, Bloom inspects his fingernails. Boylan notices the funeral but does not notice the carriage.

The second time is in part two, chapter 5, as Bloom enters Kildare Street on his way to the National Library just after 2 P.M. soon after seeing the blind stripling heading for Frederick Street "perhaps to Levinston's dancing academy piano"—where, if so, he did not miss his tuning fork since we see him still proceeding eastward in chapter 7. Bloom sees Boylan

"Straw hat in sunlight. Tan shoes" and swerves to the right, to the museum connected with the library.

The third time is in part two, chapter 8, as Bloom crosses Ormond Quay (after crossing Essex Bridge from Wellington Quay, north bank to south bank of the Liffey) to buy some notepaper at Daly's stationers; he turns his head and sees Boylan in a jaunty hackney cab coming the same way Bloom just came. Boylan, to meet Lenehan for a moment, enters the bar of the Ormond Hotel. Bloom decides to enter the dining room with Richie Goulding whom he happens to meet at the door. Bloom watches Boylan from there. It is a few minutes to four now, and Boylan presently leaves the Ormond bar for Eccles Street.

PART TWO, CHAPTER 8

The characters in chapter 8 are

1. In the saloon of the hotel and at the bar:
two barmaids—bronze-haired Lydia Douce and gold-haired Mina Kennedy;
the boots, a saucy young fellow who brings them their tea;
Simon Dedalus, Stephen's father;
the racing editor Lenehan, who comes in shortly afterwards to wait for Boylan;
Boylan himself on his way to Molly;
fat Ben Dollard and thin Father Cowley who join Simon Dedalus at the piano;
Mr. Lidwell, a lawyer who courts Miss Douce;
Tom Kernan, the pompous tea merchant;
there are also two anonymous gentlemen drinking beer from tankards;
and finally at the end of the chapter the blind piano tuner returns for his tuning fork.

2. In the adjacent dining room there are the waiter Pat (bald, deaf Pat), Bloom, and Richie Goulding. They hear the songs in the bar, and Bloom glimpses the barmaids.

In the course of chapter 8 three people are sensed approaching, before they actually enter, the Ormond Hotel: Bloom, Boylan, and the blind youth coming back for his tuning fork. The tap of his approaching stick on the sidewalk—his leitmotiv—is heard midway through the chapter, and these taps can be traced here and there, increasing on the next pages—tap, tap, tap—, then four taps repeated. His tuning fork lying on the piano is noticed by Simon Dedalus. He is sensed coming by Daly's shop window, and finally "Tap. A youth entered a lonely Ormond hall."

Bloom and Boylan are not only sensed coming—they are sensed going. Boylan, after talking horses with Lenehan, drinking a slow, syrupy sloe gin, and watching coy Miss Douce imitate a ringing clock by smacking her garter against her thigh, impatiently leaves, heading for Molly, but with Lenehan starting to go with him to tell him about Tom Rochford. As the drinkers continue in the bar, and the eaters in the restaurant, his jingle jaunty jingle is sensed receding both by Bloom and the author, and his progress in the jaunting car (also known as a jaunty car) to Eccles Street is marked by such notices as "Jingle a tinkle jaunted" and "Jingle jaunted down the quays. Blazes sprawled on bounding tyres" and "By Bachelors walk jogjaunty jingled Blazes Boylan, bachelor, in sun, in heat, mare's glossy rump atrot, with flick of whip, on bounding tyres: sprawled, warmseated, Boylan impatience, ardentbold" and "By Graham Lemon's pineapple rock, by Elvery's elephant jingle jogged." Moving at a slower rate than in Bloom's mind, "Jingle by monuments of sir John Gray, Horatio onehanded Nelson, reverend father Theobald Matthew, jaunted as said before just now. Atrot, in heat, heatseated. *Cloche. Sonnez la. Cloche. Sonnez la.* Slower the mare went up the hill by the Rotunda, Rutland square. Too slow for Boylan, blazes Boylan, impatience Boylan, joggled the mare." Then "Jingle into Dorset street" and, coming closer, "A hackney car, number three hundred and twenty-four, driver Barton, James of number one Harmony avenue, Donnybrook, on which sat a fare, a young gentleman, stylishly dressed in an indigoblue serge suit made by George Robert Mesias, tailor and cutter, of number five Eden quay, and wearing a straw hat very dressy, bought of John Plasto of number one Great Brunswick street, hatter. Eh? This is the jingle that joggled and jingled. By Dlugacz' porkshop bright tubes of Agendath trotted a gallantbuttocked mare." The jingle even imposes itself on Bloom's stream of thought in the hotel as he is composing a letter in return to Martha: "Jingle, have you the?" The missing word is, of course, *horn*, for Bloom is mentally following Boylan's progress. In fact, in Bloom's feverish imagination he has Boylan arrive and make love to Molly sooner than he actually does. While Bloom listens to the music in the bar and to Richie Goulding talking, his thought ranges, and one part is, "Her wavyavyeavyheavyeavyevyevy hair un comb:'d"— meaning that in Bloom's hasty mind her hair has been uncombed already by her lover. Actually, at this point Boylan has only reached Dorset Street. Finally, Boylan arrives: "Jog jig jogged stopped. Dandy tan shoe of dandy Boylan socks skyblue clocks came light to earth. . . .

One rapped on a door, one rapped with a knock, did he knock Paul de

Kock, with a loud proud knocker, with a cock carracarracarra cock. Cockcock."

Two songs are sung in the bar. First Simon Dedalus, a wonderful singer, sings Lionel's aria "All is lost now" from *Martha*, a French opera with an Italian libretto by a German composer von Flotow, 1847. The "All is lost now" nicely echoes Bloom's feelings about his wife. In the adjacent restaurant Bloom writes a letter to his mysterious correspondent Martha Clifford in as coy terms as she had used to him, enclosing a small money order. Then Ben Dollard sings a ballad "The Croppy Boy," which begins, if we look up the song:

> It was early, early in the spring,
> The birds did whistle and sweetly sing,
> Changing their notes from tree to tree,
> And the song they sang was Old Ireland free.

(Croppies were the Irish rebels of 1798 who cropped their hair in a token of sympathy with the French Revolution.)

Bloom leaves the Ormond Hotel before the singing has ended, heading for the nearest post office and then to a pub where he has agreed to meet Martin Cunningham and Jack Power. His stomach starts to rumble. "Gassy thing that cider: binding too." He notices on the quay a prostitute he knows, with a black straw sailor hat, and he avoids her. (That night she will briefly look in at the cabman's shelter.) Once again his stomach rumbles. "Must be the cider or perhaps the burgund" which he had had at lunch. These rumbles are synchronized with the conversation in the bar that he has left until the patriotic conversation gets all mixed up with Bloom's stomach. As Bloom views a picture of the Irish patriot Robert Emmet in Lionel Marks's window, the men in the bar begin to talk of him and to give a toast to Emmet just as the blind youth arrives. They quote "True men like you men," from a poem "The Memory of the Dead" (1843) by John Kells Ingram. The italicized phrases that accompany Bloom's internal difficulties represent Emmet's last words, which Bloom sees under the picture: "Seabloom, Greaseabloom viewed last words. Softly. *When my country takes her place among.*

Prrprr.

Must be the bur.

Overleaf: Nabokov's annotations in his teaching copy of *Ulysses*, part two, chapter 8

musical fugue
A ... of themes - broken phrases that will be repeated in a fuller form in the context that follows

the governor of Ireland passing
a bronze-haired barmaid and Kennedy *Douce*

1. BRONZE BY GOLD HEARD THE HOOFIRONS, STEELYRINGING *a golden haired one heard the iron and steel sound of the hoofs.*

the boots is rude to them — mimicing the violinist's...

2. Imperthnthn thnththnthn.

3. Chips, picking chips off rocky thumbnail, chips. *Steven's father, old Dedalus enters*

4. Horrid! And gold flushed more. *gold-hair refusing bronze for being vulgar*

5. A husky fifenote blew. *Dedalus blows across pipe*

5a. Blew. Blue bloom is on the *transition to Bloom. These are blue wildflowers* *rye* *in the restaurant*)

6. Gold pinnacled hair.

Kennedy
Douce
Douce

7. A jumping rose on satiny breasts of satin, rose of Castille.

8. Trilling, trilling: Idolores.

9. Peep! Who's in the . . . peepofgold? *Lenehan kidding Miss Kennedy*

10. Tink cried to bronze in pity. *A diner's bell asking for Lignor echoed Miss Douce with ... for a Blind Tuner*

11. And a call, pure, long and throbbing. Longindying call.

Blas
numbers refer to the different styles

12. Decoy. Soft word. But look! The bright stars fade. O rose! *Douce also...* Notes chirruping answer. Castille. The morn is breaking. *Miss Douce will... whispers dreams*

13. Jingle jingle jaunted jingling. *Boylan arrives*

14. Coin rang. Clock clacked. *pays for Lignor*

5

15. Avowal. *Sonnez.* I could. Rebound of garter. Not leave thee.
Smack. *La cloche!* Thigh smack. Avowal. Warm. Sweetheart, goodbye! *The garter scene*

16. Jingle. Bloo. *Bloom, over incomplete meal, hears Boylan depart*

17. Boomed crashing chords. When love absorbs. War! War! The *Dollard sings* tympanum. *Dedalus greets his friend Cowley and Dollard.*

18. A sail! A veil awave upon the waves. *Cowley sang "A Last Farewell"* *through*

19. Lost. Throstle fluted. All is lost now. *another sing*

allusion to Boylan's journey

20. Horn. Hawhorn. *that horn seducing*

21. When first he saw. Alas!

22. Full tup. Full throb. — *Boylan & Bloom's wife*

23. Warbling. Ah, lure! Alluring. *Dedalus sings "Martha"*

24. Martha! Come! *from the opera "Martha"*

25. Clapclop. Clipclap. Clappyclap.

26. Goodgod he never heard inall *Richie Goulding, Bloom's friend, Cousins...* *said he had never heard*

the waiter
27. Deaf bald Pat brought pad knife took up. *such a voice and...*

28. A moonlit nightcall: far: far.

29. I feel so sad. P. S. So lonely blooming. *Bloom writes letter*

30. Listen! *To Cowley's song*

Bloom also
listens to the sea-call
31. The spiked and winding cold seahorn. Have you the? *far* Each and for other plash and silent roar. *snake*

32. Pearls: when she. Liszt's rhapsodies. Hissss.
You don't? *plays* *music*

33. Did not: no, no: believe: Lidlyd. With a cock with a carra.

Bloom's
34. Black. *refers to Lidwell and Lydia* *Boylan's theme* *Kelvey*

35. Deepsounding. Do, Ben, do.

[252]

Ben is asked to sing "The Croppy Boy"

35 Wait while you wait. Hee hee. Wait while you hee. *the waiter Pat*

36 But wait! *echo of a song*

37 Low in dark middle earth. Embedded ore. *recollection of funeral*

38 Naminedamine. All gone. All fallen. *croppy boys* × *281, Miss Douce*

39 Tiny, her tremulous fernfoils of maidenhair. ×

40 Amen! He gnashed in fury. *croppy boy. Douce fingering things on the listens*

41 Fro. To, fro. A baton cool protruding.

42 Bronzelydia by Minagold. *Lidia Douce and Meena Kennedy*

43 By bronze, by gold, in oceangreen of shadow. Bloom. Old
Bloom. *exit Bloom*

44 One rapped, one tapped with a carra, with a cock.

45 Pray for him! Pray, good people! *The Croppy Boy*

46 His gouty fingers nakkering. *castagnetts*

⸙ Big Benaben. Big Benben.

47 Last rose Castille of summer left bloom I feel so sad alone.

48 Pwee! Little wind piped wee. *Gas on Bloom's stomach*

49 True men. Lid Ker Cow De and Doll. Ay, ay. Like you men. *Lidwel, Kernan, Cowley, Dedalus, Dollard*
Will lift your tschink with tschunk. *clinking glasses*

50 Fff! Oo! *Gas*

51 Where bronze from anear? Where gold from afar? Where
hoofs? *Yes, here, this is the place*

52 Rrrpr. Kraa. Kraandl. *The rearmon and the fart*
Then, not till then. My eppripffitaph. Be pfrwritt. *mingle with a patriot's epitaph.*

53 Done.

Begin! *the recital; Lydia oo* 〔First first here〕

Bronze by gold, Miss Douce's head by Miss Kennedy's head, *see 248, 249*
over the crossblind of the Ormond bar heard the viceregal hoofs *251*
go by, ringing steel. *Mina*
— Is that her? asked Miss Kennedy. *colleen*
Miss Douce said yes, sitting with his ex, pearl grey and *eau de* *wife of the governor of Ireland*
Nil.
— Exquisite contrast, Miss Kennedy said. *Among ladies are exquisite vulgar*
When all agog Miss Douce said eagerly: *Kennedys a little more genteel than Lydia Douce*
— Look at the fellow in the tall silk. *hat*
— Who? Where? gold asked more eagerly.
— In the second carriage, Miss Douce's wet lips said, laughing ‖ × *there is*
in the sun. He's looking. Mind till I see. *a glow of middle*
She darted, bronze, to the backmost corner, flattening her *sunshine*
face against the pane in a halo of hurried breath. *breaking into the bar.*
Her wet lips tittered:
— He's killed looking back. *good, ironic.*

[253]

Fff. Oo. Rrpr.

Nations of the earth. No-one behind. She's passed. *Then and not till then*. Tram. Kran, kran, kran. Good oppor. Coming Krandlkrankran [the trolley noise]. I'm sure it's the burgund. Yes. One, two. *Let my epitaph be*. Karaaaaaaa. *Written. I have.*

Pprrpffrrppfff

Done."

Joyce with all his genius has a perverse leaning towards the disgusting, and it is diabolically like him to end a chapter full of music, patriotic pathos, and broken heart song with a released *borborygmos* combining Emmet's last word with Bloom's murmur of satisfaction, "*Done*."*

PART TWO, CHAPTER 9

The anonymous narrator, a collector of debts, after loafing with old Troy of the Dublin Metropolitan Police Force, meets another friend, Joe Hynes, the reporter who took down the names of the mourners at Dignam's funeral, and they both turn into Barney Kiernan's pub. There we find the villain of the chapter, a "citizen" as he is termed. The citizen is there with a fierce mangy dog Garryowen, belonging to his father-in-law old Giltrap. Giltrap is the maternal grandfather of Gerty MacDowell, the leading young lady of the next chapter, where she thinks about her grandpapa's lovely dog. It would thus seem that the citizen is Gerty MacDowell's father. In the preceding chapter Gerty had had her view of the viceregal procession obstructed by a passing tram as she was carrying the mail from his office. (He was in the cork and linoleum business.) In the next chapter we discover that her father, a drunkard, could not attend Dignam's funeral because of his gout.

This chapter is timed at about five o'clock and we must suppose that citizen MacDowell's gout does not prevent him from limping into his favorite pub where the collector of debts and the reporter join him at the bar and are served three pints of ale by Terry O'Ryan, the bartender. Then comes another customer, Alf Bergan, who discovers Bob Doran snoring in

---

*In VN's annotated copy he remarks, "Moreover, the 'let my epitaph be' is linked up with the famous limerick about wind going free, and the 'done' ends the chapter in more ways than one." Ed.

Nabokov's transcription of the lyrics for "The Croppy Boy" in his teaching copy of *Ulysses*

see 180

see
p. 39 2 Browne

the author
see also p.108
and 207
and 285

cap with fingers greased by porksteak paper. His collar too
sprang up. The viceroy, on his way to inaugurate the Mirus
bazaar in aid of funds for Mercer's hospital, drove with his following towards Lower Mount street. He passed a blind stripling
opposite Broadbent's. In Lower Mount street a pedestrian in a
brown macintosh, eating dry bread, passed swiftly and unscathed across the viceroy's path. At the Royal Canal bridge,
from his hoarding, Mr. Eugene Stratton, his blub lips agrin,
bade all comers welcome to Pembroke township. At Hadding-
ton road corner two sanded women halted themselves, an umbrella and a bag in which eleven cockles rolled to view with
wonder the lord mayor and lady mayoress without his golden
chain. On Northumberland and Landsdowne roads His Excel-
lency acknowledged punctually salutes from rare male walkers,
the salute of two small schoolboys at the garden gate of the house
said to have been admired by the late queen when visiting the
Irish capital with her husband, the prince consort, in 1849 and
the salute of Almidano Artifoni's sturdy trousers swallowed by a
closing door.

---

p. 278   The Croppy Boy, anon.   "rebel, late 18th early"

(here is another passage; the priest who confessed the boy was
a yeoman in disguise. See p, 281)

It was early, early in the spring,
the birds did whistle and sweetly sing,
changing their notes from tree to tree,
and the song they sang was Old Ireland free.

It was early, early in the night,
(evening)
the yeoman cavalry gave me a fright; (*)
the yeoman cavalry was my downfall
and taken was I by Lord Cornwall.

'Twas in the guard-house where I was laid (air)
and   in a parlour where I was tried;
my sentence passed and my courage low
when to Dungannon I was forced to go.

As I was passing my father's own door,
my brother William stood at the door;
my aged father stood at the door,
and my tender mother her hair she tore.

As I was walking up Wexford Street
my own first cousin I chanced to meet;

(*) British cavalry acting as a defence force.

my own first cousin did me betray,
and for one bare guinea swore my life
etc

my sister Mary heard the express,
she ran upstairs in her morning-dress,
(saying) "Five hundred guineas I will lay
to see my brother safe in Wexford Town.

As I was walking up Wexford hill,
who could blame me to cry my fill?
I looked behind and I looked before
but my tender mother I shall see no more.

As I was mounted on the platform high,   scaffold
my aged father was standing by;
my aged father did me deny
and the name he gave me was Croppy Boy.

It was in Dungannon this young man died
[251]
and in Dungannon his body laid;
and you good Christians that do pass by,
just drop a tear for the croppy boy.

(**) declaration of his guilt

a corner. They talk about dead Dignam, and Bergan shows a curio, a hangman's letter of application to Dublin's high sheriff. It is here that Bloom comes into the bar looking for Martin Cunningham. Then two other characters enter, Jack O'Molloy, whom we met in the newspaper office and in Lambert's warehouse, and Ned Lambert himself. They are joined by John Wyse Nolan and Lenehan the racing editor, with a long face, having lost on Sceptre. Bloom goes to the courthouse just around the corner to see if Cunningham is perhaps there, and before Bloom returns Martin Cunningham turns up at the pub with Jack Power. Bloom comes back to the pub, and the three of them set out from there, in the northwest of Dublin, in a carriage for the Dignam's residence at the far southeast side, on the bay. Their visit to Dignam's widow, with talks about Dignam's insurance money, is somehow omitted from Bloom's consciousness.

The themes of this chapter develop in the bar before Bloom leaves. They consist of the Ascot Gold Cup race and the theme of anti-Semitism. A prejudiced discussion of patriotism which Bloom vainly tries to conduct in a rational and humane way is turned by the citizen into a brawl. A strain of parody, a grotesque travesty of legendary doings, runs through the chapter and ends with the citizen hurling an empty biscuit tin at the retreating carriage.

PART TWO, CHAPTER 10

Time: Between "the altercation with a truculent troglodyte" at Kiernan's bar around five o'clock and the present chapter 10 there is a blank period of time that includes a carriage drive and then a visit to a house of mourning, to Dignam's widow, in east Dublin, not far from Sandymount, but this visit is not described. When the action resumes with chapter 10 it is sunset time, around 8 P.M.

Place: Sandymount shore, Dublin Bay, southeast of Dublin, where Stephen had walked in the morning, in the direct vicinity of the Star of the Sea Church.

Characters: Seated on the rocks are three girls: two of them are named at once. Cissy Caffrey, "A truerhearted lass never drew the breath of life, always with a laugh in her gypsylike eyes and a frolicsome word on her cherryripe red lips, a girl lovable in the extreme." The style is a deliberate parody of feminine magazines and of commercial English prose. Edy Boardman is petite and shortsighted. The third girl, the heroine of the chapter, is named on its third page—"But who was Gerty?" And here we are told that Gerty MacDowell, who was seated near her companions, lost in thought, "was in very truth as fair a specimen of winsome Irish girlhood as one could wish to see," a beautiful parody of corny descriptions. Cissy Caffrey has with her her two little brothers, Tommy and Jacky, twins, "scarce four years old," and of course curly headed; and Edy Boardman is with her infant brother, a baby in a pushcar. There is yet another person present, sitting on some rocks opposite. He is mentioned on the third and eighth pages, but it is only later that he is identified as Leopold Bloom.

Action: The action of this chapter is difficult to separate from its very special style. In answer to a simple question what happens in this chapter, we can reply simply: the two little boys play and quarrel and play again, the baby gurgles and squalls, Cissy and Edy tend their respective brothers, Gerty daydreams, voices sing in the nearby translucent church, twilight comes, the fireworks at the bazaar (to which the viceroy had been heading) start, and Cissy and Edy with their charges run down the strand to see the display over the houses in the distance. But Gerty does not follow them immediately: if they could run like horses she could sit and see from where she sat. Bloom has been sitting on a rock opposite and staring at Gerty, who for all her coy girlishness realizes quite clearly what is going on behind his stares, and finally she leans back in a shameless show of garters while "a rocket sprang and bang shot blind and O! then the Roman candle burst and it was like a sigh of O! and everyone cried O! O! in raptures and it gushed out of it a stream of rain gold hair threads and they shed and ah! they were all greeny dewy stars falling with golden, O so lovely! O so soft, sweet, soft!" Shortly, Gerty rises and slowly walks away down the strand. "She walked with a certain quiet dignity characteristic of her but with care and very slowly because, because Gerty MacDowell was . . .

Tight boots? No. She's lame! O!

Mr Bloom watched her as she limped away. Poor girl!"

Style: The chapter consists of two parts totally different in technique. First, while the three girls are on the beach, sitting on the rocks, there is in describing them and their charges a sustained parody of feminine magazine or novelette prose with all the clichés and false elegancies of that kind.* Then comes the second part when Mr. Bloom's stream of consciousness takes over; in its familiar abrupt fashion there comes a medley of impressions and recollections until the end of the chapter.

The parody is full of wonderfully amusing clichés, the platitudes of gracious living and pseudopoetry. "The summer evening had begun to fold

---

*VN has interlined a later comment, in pencil: "This is fifty years ago. They would correspond in our time and place to stories about blonde office girls and boyish-looking executives in the *Saturday Evening Post* trash." Ed.

the world in its mysterious embrace. . . . the last glow of all too fleeting day lingered lovingly on sea and strand . . . and, last but not least, on. . . .

The three girl friends were seated on the rocks, enjoying the evening scene and the air which was fresh but not too chilly. . . . Many a time and oft were they wont to come there to that favourite nook to have a cosy chat beside the sparkling waves and discuss matters feminine." (The adjective placed for the sake of elegance after the noun is of course characteristic of the *House Beautiful* style.)

The very construction is corny: "For Tommy and Jacky Caffrey were twins, scarce four years old and very noisy and spoiled twins sometimes but for all that darling little fellows with bright merry faces and endearing ways about them. They were dabbling in the sand with their spades and buckets, building castles as children do, or playing with their big coloured ball, happy as the day was long." The baby is of course chubby and "that young gentleman fairly chuckled with delight." Not simply chuckled, but fairly chuckled—how arch and coy all this is. A number of these deliberately collected elegant clichés are found on each of the twenty pages of this part of the chapter.

When we say cliché, stereotype, trite pseudoelegant phrase, and so on, we imply, among other things, that when used for the first time in literature the phrase was original and had a vivid meaning. In fact, it became hackneyed because its meaning was at first vivid and neat, and attractive, and so the phrase was used over and over again until it became a stereotype, a cliché. We can thus define clichés as bits of dead prose and of rotting poetry. However, the parody has its interruptions. Now what Joyce does here is to cause some of that dead and rotten stuff to reveal here and there its live source, its primary freshness. Here and there the poetry is still alive. The description of the church service as it passes transparently through Gerty's consciousness has real beauty and a luminous pathetic charm. So has the tenderness of the twilight, and of course the description of the fireworks—the climactic passage quoted above—is really tender and beautiful: it is the freshness of poetry still with us before it becomes a cliché.

But Joyce manages to do something even more subtle than that. You will mark when Gerty's flowing stream of consciousness starts on its course, her thought lays great stress on her dignity of being and tasteful clothes, for she is a votary of the fashions suggested to her by the magazines the *Woman Beautiful* and the *Lady's Pictorial*: "A neat blouse of electric blue, selftinted by dolly dyes (because it was expected in the *Lady's Pictorial* that electric blue would be worn), with a smart vee opening down to the division and kerchief pocket (in which she always kept a piece of cottonwool scented with her favorite perfume because the handkerchief spoiled the sit) and a navy threequarter skirt cut to the stride showed off her slim graceful figure to perfection," etc. But when we realize with Bloom that the poor girl is hopelessly lame, the very clichés of her thought acquire a pathetic shade. In other words, Joyce manages to build up something real—pathos, pity, compassion—out of the dead formulas which he parodies.

Joyce goes even further. As the parody glides on its sweet course, the author with a demon's flash of gaiety leads Gerty's thought to a number of subjects dealing with physiological matters that would of course never be alluded to in the kind of novelette with which Gerty's consciousness is permeated: "Her figure was slight and graceful, inclining even to fragility but those iron jelloids she had been taking of late had done her a world of good much better than the Widow Welch's female pills and she was much better of those discharges she used to get and that tired feeling." Moreover, when she becomes aware of the gentleman in deep mourning with "the story of a haunting sorrow ... written on his face," a romantic vision comes into her mind: "Here was that of which she had so often dreamed. It was he who mattered and there was joy on her face because she wanted him because she felt instinctively that he was like no-one else. The very heart of the girlwoman went out to him, her dreamhusband, because she knew on the instant it was him. If he had suffered, more sinned against than sinning, or even, even, if he had been himself a sinner, a wicked man, she cared not. Even if he was a protestant or methodist she could convert him easily if he truly loved her. . . . Then mayhap he would embrace her gently, like a real man, crushing her soft body to him, and love her, his ownest girlie, for herself alone." Nevertheless, this romantic vision (of which there is much more) is quite simply continued in her mind with very realistic ideas about naughty gentlemen. "His hands and face were working and a tremor went over her. She leaned back far to look up where the fireworks were and she caught her knee in her hands so as not to fall back looking up and there was no-one to see only him and her when, she revealed all her graceful beautifully shaped legs like that, supply soft and delicately rounded, and she seemed to hear the panting of his heart, his hoarse breathing, because she knew about the passion of men like that, hotblooded, because Bertha Supple told her once in dead secret and made her swear she'd never about the gentleman lodger that was staying with them out of the Congested Districts Board that had pictures cut out of papers of those skirtdancers and highkickers and she said he used to do something not very nice that you could imagine sometimes in the bed. But this was altogether different from a thing like that because there was all the difference because she could almost feel him draw her face to his and the first quick hot touch of his handsome lips. Besides there was absolution so long as you didn't do the other thing before being married."

Of the stream of Bloom's thought little need be said. You understand the physiological situation—love at a distance (*Bloomism*). You recognize the stylistic contrast between the rendering of Bloom's thought, impressions, recollections, sensations, and the vicious parody of a literary girlishness in the first part of the chapter. His batlike thoughts vibrate and zigzag in the twilight. There is always, of course, his thought about Boylan and Molly; and there is also the earliest mention of Molly's first admirer in Gibraltar, Lieutenant Mulvey, who kissed her under the Moorish wall beside the gardens, when she was fifteen. We also realize with a pang of compassion that Bloom did notice, after all, the newsboys in the street near Nelson's Pillar in the newspaper-office chapter, who imitated him as he walked. Bloom's highly artistic definition of a bat ("Like a little man in a cloak he is with tiny hands") is absolutely enchanting, and an equally charming and artistic thought comes to him about the sun: "Stare the sun for example like the eagle then look at a shoe see a blotch blob yellowish. Wants to stamp his trademark on everything." This is as good as Stephen. There is the touch of the artist about old Bloom.

The chapter ends with Bloom dozing away for a few winks, and the clock on the mantelpiece of the priest's house nearby (the service in the church now over) proclaims with its cuckoo cuckoo cuckoo the plight of Bloom, the cuckold. It was very odd, he finds, that his watch had stopped at half past four.

PART TWO, CHAPTER 11

Time: Around ten o'clock at night.

Place: The first line means in Irish, "Let us go south [of the Liffey] to Holles Street," and it is thither that Bloom wanders. In the second paragraph the pun in Horhorn refers to the head of the maternity hospital in Holles Street, Sir Andrew Horne, a real person. And in the next paragraph in "hoopsa boyaboy" we hear a generalized midwife elevating a generalized newborn baby. Bloom comes to the hospital to visit Mrs. Purefoy in the throes of childbirth (her baby is born in the course of the chapter). Bloom is not able to see her but instead has beer and sardines in the medical mess.

Characters: Nurse Callan whom Bloom talks to; the resident doctor, Dixon, who once treated Bloom for a bee sting. Now, in keeping with the grotesquely epic tone of the chapter the bee is promoted to a dreadful dragon. There are also various medical students: Vincent Lynch, whom we and Father Conmee saw around three with a girl in a suburban field, Madden, Crotthers, Punch Costello, and a very drunken Stephen, all sitting at a table where Bloom joins them. A little later Buck Mulligan appears with his friend Alec Bannon, the Bannon from whom came the postcard in the first chapter that he was attracted by Milly, Bloom's daughter, in Mullingar.

Action: Dixon leaves the company to attend to Mrs. Purefoy. The rest sit and drink. "A gallant scene in truth it made. Crotthers was there at the foot of the table in his striking Highland garb, his face glowing from the briny airs of the Mull of Galloway. There too, opposite to him was Lynch, whose countenance bore already the stigmata of earbly depravity and premature wisdom. Next the Scotchman was the place assigned to Costello, the eccentric, while at his side was seated in stolid repose the squat form of Madden. The chair of the resident indeed stood vacant before the hearth but on either flank of it the figure of Bannon in explorer's kit of tweed shorts and salted cowhide brogues contrasted sharply with the primrose elegance and townbred manners of Malachi Roland St John Mulligan. Lastly at the head of the board was the young poet who found a refuge from his labours of pedagogy and metaphysical inquisition in the convivial atmosphere of Socratic discussion, while to right and left of him were accommodated the flippant prognosticator, fresh from the hippodrome [Lenehan], and that vigilant wanderer [Bloom], soiled by the dust of travel and combat and stained by the mire of an indelible dishonour, but from whose steadfast and constant heart no lure or peril or threat or degradation could ever efface the image of that voluptuous loveliness which the inspired pencil of Lafayette [the photographer who took a picture of Molly] has limned for ages yet to come."

Mrs. Purefoy's child is born. Stephen suggests that they all go to Burke's, a bar. The hullabaloo at the bar is rendered in a manner where I find reflected the grotesque, inflated, broken, mimicking, and punning style of the author's next and last novel, *Finnegans Wake* (1939), one of the greatest failures in literature.

Style: To quote from Richard M. Kain's *Fabulous Voyager* (1947): "The style of this chapter is a series of parodies of English prose from Anglo-Saxon down to modern slang. . . .*

*VN adds, "and is not a success." Ed.

For what they are worth, here are the most important parodies which have been identified: Anglo-Saxon, Mandeville, Malory, Elizabethan prose, Browne, Bunyan, Pepys, Sterne, the Gothic novel, Charles Lamb, Coleridge, Macaulay, Dickens (one of the most successful), Newman, Ruskin, Carlyle, modern slang, evangelistic oratory.

As the young medical students go off for drinks at Stephen's expense, the prose tumbles into broken sounds, echoes, and half-words, . . . a rendition of the stupor of intoxication."

PART TWO, CHAPTER 12

I do not know of any commentator who has correctly understood this chapter. The psychoanalytical interpretation I, of course, dismiss completely and absolutely, since I do not belong to the Freudian denomination with its borrowed myths, shabby umbrellas, and dark backstairs. To regard this chapter as the reactions of intoxication or lust on Bloom's subconscious is impossible for the following reasons:

1. Bloom is perfectly sober and for the moment impotent.

2. Bloom cannot possibly know of a number of events, characters, and facts that appear as visions in this chapter.

I propose to regard this chapter 12 as an hallucination on the author's part, an amusing distortion of his various themes. The book is itself dreaming* and having visions; this chapter is merely an exaggeration, a nightmare evolution of its characters, objects, and themes.

Time: Between eleven and midnight.

Place: Nighttown starts at the Mabbot Street entrance, in east Dublin, north of the Liffey, near the docks, exactly one mile west of Eccles Street.

Style: A nightmare comedy, with implied acknowledgement to the visions in a piece by Flaubert, *The Temptation of Saint Anthony*, written some fifty years earlier.

Action: The action can be split into five scenes.

Scene I: Main characters: Two English soldiers, Carr and Compton, who will attack Stephen later in scene 5. There is a streetwalker impersonating the innocent Cissy Caffrey of chapter 10, and there are Stephen and his friend the medical student Lynch. The two privates already in this first scene heckle Stephen: "Way for the parson." "What ho, parson!" Stephen

---

*Elsewhere in VN's notes is this passage: "Bernard Shaw writing of *Ulysses* in a letter to its publisher Sylvia Beach defined it as a revery—but truthful record of a disgusting phase of civilization." Ed.

looks like a priest, being in mourning for his mother. (Both Stephen and Bloom are in black.) Another prostitute resembles Edy Boardman. The Caffrey twins also appear: street urchins, phantasms resembling the twins, climbing up street lamps. It is worth notice that these thought associations do not occur in the mind of Bloom, who had noticed Cissy and Edy on the beach but who is absent from this first scene, whereas Stephen who is present cannot know of Cissy and Edy. The only real event in this first scene is the fact that Stephen and Lynch are heading for a house of ill-fame in Nighttown after the others, among them Buck Mulligan, have dispersed.

Scene II: Bloom appears on a stage, representing an oblique street with leaning lamps; he is anxious about Stephen and is following him. The beginning of the scene is a description of a real entrance: puffing from having run after Stephen, Bloom does buy a pig's foot and a sheep's trotter at the butcher Othousen and does narrowly miss being hit by a trolley. Then his dead parents appear—this is the author's hallucination, and Bloom's. Several other women known to Bloom, including Molly and Mrs. Breen, and Gerty, also make an appearance in this scene as well as the lemon soap, sea gulls, and other incidental characters, including even Beaufoy, the author of the story in *Titbits*. There are also religious allusions. One will remember that Bloom's father was a Hungarian Jew who turned Protestant, whereas Bloom's mother was Irish. Bloom, who was born a Protestant, was baptized a Catholic. He is, incidentally, a Freemason.

Scene III: Bloom reaches the house of ill-fame. Zoe, a young harlot in a sapphire slip, meets him at the door on Lower Tyrone Street, a landmark that no longer exists. Presently in the author's hallucination Bloom, the world's greatest reformer (an allusion to Bloom's interests in various civic improvements) is crowned emperor by the citizens of Dublin to whom he explains his schemes for social regeneration but then is denounced as a fiendish libertine and finally proclaimed a woman. Dr. Dixon (the resident at the maternity hospital) reads his bill of health: "Professor Bloom is a finished example of the new womanly man. His moral nature is simple and lovable. Many have found him a dear man, a dear person. He is a rather quaint fellow on the whole, coy though not feebleminded in the medical sense. He has written a really beautiful letter, a poem in itself, to the court missionary of the Reformed Priests' Protection Society which clears up everything. He is practically a total abstainer and I can affirm that he sleeps on a straw litter and eats the most Spartan food, cold dried grocer's peas. He wears a hairshirt winter and summer and scourges himself every Saturday. He was, I understand, at one time a firstclass misdemeanant in Glencree reformatory. Another report states that he was a very posthumous child. I appeal for clemency in the name of the most sacred word our vocal organs have ever been called upon to speak. He is about to have a baby.

(*General commotion and compassion. Women faint. A wealthy American makes a street collection for Bloom.*)"

Etc. At the end of the scene Bloom in the book's reality follows Zoe into the brothel in search of Stephen. We have now found how the machinery of the chapter works. This or that detail of reality bursts into elaborate life; an allusion starts to live on its own. Thus the "real" conversation at the door of the brothel between Zoe and Bloom is interrupted in order to interpolate the Rise and Fall of Bloom before his entrance into the house.

Scene IV: In the house of ill-fame Bloom meets Stephen and Lynch. Various visions appear. The author conjures up Bloom's grandfather Leopold Virag. Bella Cohen, a massive whoremistress with a sprouting moustache in yet another authorial hallucination evokes Bloom's past sins and in an amusing exchange of sexes is horribly cruel to impotent Bloom. Also water nymphs and waterfalls appear with the liquid musical theme so dear to Joyce. A glimpse of reality starts. Bloom gets back his talisman, the potato, from Zoe. Stephen attempts to squander his money. (Note that neither Stephen nor Bloom has any interest in the women around them.) Bloom manages to retrieve the money and to save it for Stephen. One pound seven "Doesn't matter a rambling damn," says Stephen. More authorial hallucinations follow—even Boylan and Marion appear in a vision. In the real life of the scene Stephen very comically imitates the Parisian brand of English. Then the author's hallucinations begin to harass Stephen. Stephen's mother horribly appears.

"THE MOTHER: (*With the subtle smile of death's madness.*) I was once the beautiful May Goulding. I am dead.

STEPHEN: (*Horrorstruck.*) Lemur, who are you? What bogeyman's trick is this?

BUCK MULLIGAN: (*Shakes his curling capbell.*) The mockery of it! Kinch killed her dogsbody bitchbody. She kicked the bucket. (*Tears of molten butter fall from his eyes into the scene.)* Our great sweet mother! *Epi oinopa ponton.*

THE MOTHER: *(Comes nearer, breathing upon him softly her breath of wetted ashes.)* All must go through it, Stephen. More women than men in the world. You too. Time will come.

STEPHEN: *(Choking with fright, remorse and horror.)* They said I killed you, mother. He offended your memory. Cancer did it, not I. Destiny.

THE MOTHER: *(A green rill of bile trickling from a side of her mouth.)* You sang that song to me. *Love's bitter mystery.*

STEPHEN: *(Eagerly.)* Tell me the word, mother, if you know now. The word known to all men.

THE MOTHER: Who saved you the night you jumped into the train at Dalkey with Paddy Lee? Who had pity for you when you were sad among the strangers? Prayer is all powerful. Prayer for the suffering souls in the Ursuline manual, and forty days' indulgence. Repent, Stephen.

STEPHEN: The ghoul! Hyena!

THE MOTHER: I pray for you in my other world. Get Dilly to make you that boiled rice every night after your brain work. Years and years I loved you, O my son, my firstborn, when you lay in my womb."

After more of this, Stephen with his cane smashes the lamp.

Scene V: Stephen and Bloom leave the house and are now in Beaver Street, not far from it. Stephen still drunk raves, and the two English soldiers Carr and Compton decide he has insulted their king, King Edward VII (who also appears in the author's hallucination). One of the soldiers, Carr, attacks Stephen and knocks him down. Watchmen loom. This is reality. Also in reality Kelleher, the undertaker's assistant, happens to be around and helps them to convince the watchmen that Stephen has merely been out on a spree—boys will be boys. At the end of the scene Bloom bends over fallen Stephen, who murmurs "Who? Black panther vampire" and quotes fragments of Yeats's "Who Goes with Fergus." The chapter ends with the hallucination appearing tò Bloom of his dead son Rudy as an eleven-year-old fairy boy, a changeling, who gazes unseeing into Bloom's eyes and kisses the page of the book he is reading from right to left.

Time: After midnight.

Place: Still near Nighttown, in the vicinity of Amiens Street, northeast Dublin, near the docks and the customhouse; then the cabman's shelter near Butt Bridge, its keeper said to be Skin-the-Goat Fitzharris who took part in the Phoenix Park political assassination. Fitzharris was one of the so-called Invincibles who in 1882 murdered Lord Frederick Cavendish, chief secretary, and Thomas H. Burke, under secretary, in Phoenix Park. Fitzharris was only the driver of the carriage and we are not even sure it is he.

Characters: Bloom and Stephen, who have now finally been brought together alone in the solitary night. Among the incidental night characters they meet, the most vivid one is the red-bearded sailor Murphy, back from his voyages in the three-master *Rosevean* which Elijah had met when it was at last swept into the bay.

Style: Most of the chapter is again a parody, an imitation of a jaunty journalistic style with masculine clichés replacing the woman's magazine clichés of the Gerty MacDowell chapter, which it otherwise resembles.

Action: Throughout the chapter kindly Bloom does his best to be friendly towards Stephen but is regarded by Stephen with a slightly contemptuous indifference. In this chapter and in the next, Joyce carefully outlines and illustrates the various differences in character, education, tastes, etc., between Bloom and Stephen. The differences between them far outweigh the main similarity that each has rejected the religion of his fathers.* However, Stephen's metaphysical aphorisms are not unrelated, generally, to Bloom's pseudoscientific tags. Both men have keen eyes and ears, both love music, both notice details such as gestures, colors, sounds. In the events of that particular day, a door key plays a curiously similar part in the lives of both men—and if Bloom has his Boylan, Stephen has his Mulligan. Both harbor phantoms in their respective pasts, retrovistas of

---

*In his annotated copy VN marked in the following chapter the end of Bloom's examination of the contents of the second drawer containing an addressed envelope *"To my Dear Son Leopold"* and evoking memories of his father's dying words. Joyce questions, "Why did Bloom experience a sentiment of remorse?" and answers "Because in immature impatience he had treated with disrespect certain beliefs and practices." In the margin, VN noted, "Cp. Stephen." The passage continues:

"As?

The prohibition of the use of fleshmeat and milk at one meal, the hebdomadary, symposium of incoordinately abstract, perfervidly concrete mercantile coexreligionist excompatriots: the circumcision of male infants: the supernatural character of Judaic scripture: the ineffability of the tetragrammaron: the sanctity of the sabbath.

How did these beliefs and practices now appear to him?

Not more rational than they had then appeared, not less rational than other beliefs and practices now appeared." Ed.

loss and betrayal. Both Bloom and Stephen suffer from loneliness; however, Stephen is lonely not because he has quarreled with his family's beliefs, revolted against the commonplace, etc., and certainly not in consequence (like Bloom) of any social condition, but because he has been created by the author as a budding genius, and genius, by necessity, is lonely. Both see their enemy in history—injustice for Bloom, a metaphysical prison for Stephen. Both are wanderers and exiles, and finally in both runs the singing blood of James Joyce, their maker.

In their dissimilarities, to put it very roughly, Bloom is the middlebrow; Stephen the highbrow. Bloom admires applied science and applied art; Stephen pure art and pure science. Bloom is the delighted reader of the Believe It or Not column; Stephen the maker of profound philosophic aphorisms. Bloom is the man of running water; Stephen of opalescent stone. There are also emotional contrasts. Bloom is the kindly, diffident, humane materialist; Stephen the ascetic, hard, brilliant, bitter egotist who in rejecting his God has also rejected mankind. Stephen's figure is built on contrasts. He is physically repulsive but intellectually exquisite. Joyce emphasizes his physical cowardice, dirt, bad teeth, untidy or disgusting manners (the whole play on his dirty handkerchief and later, on the beach, his lack of one), his physical lust and humiliating poverty with all its degrading implications. Yet set against all this is his lofty soaring mind, his enchanting creative imagination, fantastically rich and subtle frame of reference, freedom of spirit, unbending proud integrity and truthfulness, which calls for moral courage, his independence carried to the point of obstinacy. If there is a streak of the philistine in Bloom, there is something of the ruthless fanatic in Stephen. To Bloom's questions full of solicitude and fatherly tenderness Stephen retaliates with his hard aphorisms. Bloom says in the elegant journalese of the chapter, "I don't mean to presume to dictate to you in the slightest degree but why did you leave your father's house?

—To seek misfortune, was Stephen's answer." (Incidentally, look at one characteristic of elegant journalese—the variety of synonyms for *he said*: observed, responded, ejaculated, returned, repeated, ventured to throw out, etc.)

Then in a rambling talk, Bloom who is very diffident about his own shallow culture and is trying to be as nice as possible to Stephen, suggests that your country is the place where you can live well if you work, a simple practical approach. Count me out, Stephen answers. Work in the widest sense, Bloom hastens to explain, literary labor . . . poets have every bit as much right to live by their brain as the peasant by his brawn: both belong to

Ireland. You suspect, Stephen retorts with a sort of half-laugh, that I may be important because I belong to Ireland, but I suspect that Ireland must be important because it belongs to me. Bloom is taken aback and thinks he has been misunderstood. And Stephen rather rudely says: "—We can't change the country. Let us change the subject."

But the main subject of this chapter is Molly, whom we shall soon meet in the last chapter of the book. With a gesture analogical to that of the wave-worn sailor producing a picture postcard of Peruvians or showing the tattoo on his chest, with much the same gesture Bloom shows Stephen her photograph: "Carefully avoiding a book in his pocket *Sweets of*, which reminded him by the by of that Capel street library book out of date, he took out his pocketbook and, turning over the various contents rapidly, finally he . . .

—Do you consider, by the by, he said, thoughtfully selecting a faded photo which he laid on the table, that a Spanish type?

Stephen, obviously addressed, looked down on the photo showing a large sized lady, with her fleshy charms on evidence in an open fashion, as she was in the full bloom of womanhood, in evening dress cut ostentatiously low for the occasion to give a liberal display of bosom, with more than vision of breasts, her full lips parted, and some perfect teeth, standing near, ostensibly with gravity, a piano, on the rest of which was *In old Madrid*, a ballad, pretty in its way, which was then all the vogue. Her (the lady's) eyes, dark, large, looked at Stephen, about to smile about something to be admired. Lafayette of Westmoreland street, Dublin's premier photographic artist, being responsible for the esthetic execution.

—Mrs Bloom, my wife the *prima donna*, Madam Marion Tweedy, Bloom indicated. Taken a few years since. In or about '96. Very like her then."

Bloom discovers that Stephen had last dined on Wednesday. One night Bloom brought home a dog (breed unknown) with a lame paw, and now he decides to bring Stephen to Eccles Street. Although Stephen is sort of standoffish—not effusive at all—Bloom invites him to his house for a cup of cocoa. "My wife, he intimated, plunging *in medias res*, would have the greatest of pleasure in making your acquaintance as she is passionately attached to music of any kind." They walk to Bloom's house together—and this takes us to the next chapter.

PART THREE, CHAPTER 2

"The studied dulness of the preceding chapter is now reduced to the completely impersonal tone of questions phrased in scientific fashion and answered in an equally chilly manner" (Kain). The questions are set in a catechistic pattern, and the phrasing is more pseudoscientific than scientific. We are given a good deal of material in the way of information and recapitulation, and perhaps it would be wisest to discuss this chapter from the point of view of the facts it contains. It is a very simple chapter.

As for the facts, some elaborate or recapitulate information already contained in the book, but some are new. For example, two questions and answers about Bloom and Stephen:

"Of what did the duumvirate deliberate during their itinerary?

Music, literature, Ireland, Dublin, Paris, friendship, woman, prostitution, diet, the influence of gaslight or the light of arc and glowlamps on the growth of adjoining paraheliotropic trees, exposed corporation emergency dustbuckets, the Roman catholic church, ecclesiastical celibacy, the Irish nation, jesuit education, careers, the study of medicine, the past day, the maleficent influence of the presabbath, Stephen's collapse.

Did Bloom discover common factors of similarity between their respective like and unlike reactions to experience?

Both were sensitive to artistic impressions musical in preference to plastic or pictorial. . . . Both indurated by early domestic training and an inherited tenacity of heterodox resistance professed their disbelief in many orthodox religious, national, social and ethical doctrines. Both admitted the alternately stimulating and obtunding influence of heterosexual magnetism."

Bloom's sudden (to the reader) interest in civic duties exhibited in his conversation with Stephen at the cabman's shelter is shown by a question and answer that goes back to discussions with various people he had as early as 1884 and on various other occasions up to 1893.

"What reflection concerning the irregular sequence of dates 1884, 1885, 1886, 1888, 1892, 1893, 1904 did Bloom make before their arrival at their destination?

He reflected that the progressive extension of the field of individual development and experience was regressively accompanied by a restriction of the converse domain of interindividual relations."

Arriving at 7 Eccles Street, Bloom realizes he has forgotten his key, left in his other trousers. He climbs over the area railings and gains access to the basement kitchen through the scullery, and then:

"What discrete succession of images did Stephen meanwhile perceive?

Reclined against the area railings he perceived through the transparent kitchen panes a man regulating a gasflame of 14 C P, a man lighting a candle, a man removing in turn each of his two boots, a man leaving the kitchen holding a candle of 1 C P.

Did the man reappear elsewhere?

After a lapse of four minutes the glimmer of his candle was discernible through the semitransparent semicircular glass fanlight over the halldoor. The halldoor turned gradually on its hinges. In the open space of the doorway the man reappeared without his hat, with his candle.

Did Stephen obey his sign?

Yes, entering softly, he helped to close and chain the door and followed softly along the hallway the man's back and listed feet and lighted candle past a lighted crevice of doorway on the left [Molly had left the light on in the bedroom] and carefully down a turning staircase of more than five steps into the kitchen of Bloom's house."

Bloom prepares the cocoa for Stephen and himself, and there are various references to his fondness for gadgets, riddles, clever devices, word games, as in the anagrams to which he had subjected his name, the acrostic poem he had sent to Molly in 1888, or the topical song he had started to compose, but not completed, for one of the scenes of the Gaiety Theatre's Christmas pantomime, *Sinbad the Sailor*. The relation between the ages of the two is given: in 1904 Bloom is thirty-eight and Stephen twenty-two. Conversations and recollections are referred to in the next pages. We learn their respective parentages and even the rather pathetic facts about their baptisms.

Throughout the chapter both men are acutely aware of racial and religious differences, and Joyce overstresses a little this awareness. Fragments of verse from ancient Hebrew and ancient Irish languages are cited by guest to host and by host to guest.

"Was the knowledge possessed by both of each of these languages, the extinct and the revived, theoretical or practical?

Theoretical, being confined to certain grammatical rules of accidence and syntax and practically excluding vocabulary."

The next question is "What points of contact existed between these languages and between the peoples who spoke them?" The answer reveals the existence of a natural bond between Jew and Irish in that each is a subjugated race. After a pseudolearned discourse on the kinds of the two literatures, Joyce ends the answer, "the proscription of their national costumes in penal laws and jewish dress acts: the restoration in Chanan

David of Zion and the possibility of Irish political autonomy or devolution." In other words, the movement for a Jewish homeland is the same as that of Ireland for independence.

But then religion, the great divider, enters. In answer to two lines of lament that Bloom quotes in Hebrew, and his paraphrase of the rest, Stephen with his usual detached cruelty recites a little medieval ballad about the Jew's daughter dressed in green, who lures the Christian little boy Saint Hugh to his crucifixion, and then proceeds to discuss it from a rather absurd metaphysical angle. Bloom feels offended and sad, but at the same time he still pursues his curious vision of Stephen ("He saw in a quick young male familiar form the predestination of a future") as teaching Molly correct Italian pronunciation and perhaps marrying Bloom's daughter, blonde Milly. Bloom suggests that Stephen spend the night in the living room:

"What proposal did Bloom, diambulist [walker by day], father of Milly, somnambulist [walker in sleep], make to Stephen, noctambulist [walker by night]?

To pass in repose the hours intervening between Thursday (proper) and Friday (normal) on an extemporised cubicle in the apartment immediately above the kitchen and immediately adjacent to the sleeping apartment of his host and hostess.

What various advantages would or might have resulted from a prolongation of such extemporisation?

For the guest: security of domicile and seclusion of study. For the host: rejuvenation of intelligence, vicarious satisfaction. For the hostess: disintegration of obsession, acquisition of correct Italian pronunciation.

Why might these several provisional contingencies between a guest and a hostess not necessarily preclude or be precluded by a permanent eventuality of reconciliatory union between a schoolfellow and a jew's daughter?

Because the way to daughter led through mother, the way to mother through daughter."

Here we have an intimation of Bloom's obscure thought that Stephen would be a better lover for Molly than Boylan. The "disintegration of obsession" is presumably Molly's cooling to Boylan, and the next answer, though it can be read innocently enough, can also carry a hidden meaning.

The offer is declined, but apparently Stephen does agree to coach Bloom's wife in Italian, although the proposal and its acceptance are given in a curiously problematic way. And presently Stephen prepares to leave.

"For what creature was the door of egress a door of ingress?

For a cat.

What spectacle confronted them when they, first the host, then the guest, emerged silently, doubly dark, from obscurity by a passage from the rere of the house into the penumbra of the garden?

The heaventree of stars hung with humid nightblue fruit." Both men for an instant see the sky in the same way.

After the two men part we shall never discover how and where Stephen the wanderer spent the rest of the night. It is almost 2 A.M. by now, but he will not go to his father's house nor will he go back to the brick tower, the key of which he has relinquished to Mulligan. Bloom is half inclined to remain outside and wait for the diffusion of daybreak, but he thinks better of it and returns to the house, where we have a description of the contents of the living room and, later, a wonderful catalogue of his books, clearly reflecting both his haphazard culture and his eager mind. He makes out his budget, item by item, of expenditures and receipts for 16 June 1904, balancing at £2.19.3. Each entry has been described in the course of his wanderings that day. After the famous description of the contents of two drawers that he examines, we have some recapitulations concerning the fatigues of the day:

"What past consecutive causes, before rising preapprehended, of accumulated fatigue did Bloom, before rising, silently recapitulate?

The preparation of breakfast (burnt offering): intestinal congestion and premeditative defecation (holy of holies): the bath (rite of John): the funeral (rite of Samuel): the advertisement of Alexander Keyes (Urim and Thummin): unsubstantial lunch (rite of Melchisedek): the visit to museum and national library (holy place): the bookhunt along Bedford row, Merchants Arch, Wellington Quay (Simchath Torah): the music in the Ormond Hotel (Shira Shirim): the altercation with a truculent troglodyte in Bernard Kiernan's premises (holocaust): a blank period of time including a cardrive, a visit to a house of mourning, a leavetaking (wilderness): the eroticism produced by feminine exhibitionism (rite of Onan): the prolonged delivery of Mrs Mina Purefoy (heave offering): the visit to the disorderly house of Mrs Bella Cohen, 82 Tyrone street, lower, and subsequent brawl and chance medley in Beaver street (Armageddon): nocturnal perambulation to and from the cabman's shelter, Butt Bridge (atonement)."

Bloom walks from the living room into the bedroom, which is nicely described both as to Molly's attire scattered about, and the furniture. The room is lighted; Molly is dozing. Bloom enters the bed.

"What did his limbs, when gradually extended, encounter?

New clean bedlinen, additional odours, the presence of a human form, female, hers, the imprint of a human form, male, not his, some crumbs, some flakes of potted meat, recooked, which he removed."

His entering the double bed wakes up Molly:

"What followed this silent action?

Somnolent invocation, less somnolent recognition, incipient excitation, catechetical interrogation."

To the question, implied, what have you been doing all day? Bloom's answer occupies a singularly brief space, compared to the length of Molly's meditation in the next chapter. He deliberately omits mention of three things: (1) the clandestine correspondence between Martha Clifford and Henry Flower; (2) the altercation at Kiernan's bar; and (3) his onanistic response to Gerty's display. He tells three lies: (1) that he had been to the Gaiety Theatre; (2) that he had supper at Wynn's Hotel; and (3) that the reason for his bringing Stephen home for a moment was that Stephen had suffered a temporary concussion caused by a falsely calculated movement in the course of an after-dinner gymnastic performance. As appears later from Molly's mental monologue, Bloom also tells her three authentic things: (1) about the funeral; (2) about meeting Mrs. Breen (Molly's former friend Josie Powell); and (3) about his desire to have Stephen give her lessons in Italian.

The chapter ends with Bloom gradually falling asleep.

"In what posture?

Listener [Molly]: reclined semilaterally, left, left hand under head, right leg extended in a straight line and resting on left leg, flexed, in the attitude of Gea-Tellus, fulfilled, recumbent, big with seed. Narrator: reclined laterally, left, with right and left legs flexed, the indexfinger and thumb of the right hand resting on the bridge of the nose, in the attitude depicted on a snapshot photograph made by Percy Apjohn, the childman weary, the manchild in the womb.

Womb? Weary?
He rests. He has travelled.

With?
Sindbad the Sailor and Tinbad the Tailor and Jinbad the Jailer and Whinbad the Whaler and Ninbad the Nailer and Finbad the Failer and Binbad the Bailer and Pinbad the Pailer and Mindbad the Mailer and

Henbad the Hailer and Rinbad the Railer and Dinbad the Kailer and Vinbad the Quailer and Linbad the Yailer and Xinbad the Phthailer.

When?

Going to dark bed there was a square round Sinbad the Sailor roc's auk's egg in the night of the bed of all the auks of the rocs of Darkinbad the Brightdayler.

Where?"

No answer is forthcoming. But it would be—Nowhere: he is asleep.

PART THREE, CHAPTER 3

It is around two in the morning, or a little later. Bloom in the position of a foetus has fallen asleep, but Molly remains awake for forty pages. The style is a sustained stream of consciousness running through Molly's lurid, vulgar, and hectic mind, the mind of a rather hysterical woman, with commonplace ideas, more or less morbidly sensual, with a rich strain of music in her and with the quite abnormal capacity of reviewing her whole life in an uninterrupted inner verbal flow. A person whose thought tumbles on with such impetus and consistency is not a normal person. Readers who want to break down the flow of this chapter need to take a sharp pencil and separate the sentences, as illustrated in this quotation that begins the chapter: "Yes / because he never did a thing like that before / as ask to get his breakfast in bed with a couple of eggs / since the *City Arms* hotel when he used to be pretending to be laid up with a sick voice / doing his highness to make himself interesting to that old faggot Mrs Riordan that he thought he had a great leg of and she never left us a farthing / all for masses for herself and her soul / greatest miser ever was / actually afraid to lay out 4d for her methylated spirit / telling me all her ailments / she had too much old chat in her about politics and earthquakes and the end of the world / let us have a bit of fun first / God help the world if all the women were her sort / down on bathingsuits and lownecks / of course nobody wanted her to wear / I suppose she was pious because no man would look at her twice / I hope I'll never be like her / a wonder she didnt want us to cover our faces / but she was a welleducated woman certainly / and her gabby talk about Mr Riordan here and Mr Riordan there / I suppose he was glad to get shut of her / and her dog smelling my fur and always edging to get up under my petticoats especially then / still I like that in him [Bloom] / polite to old women like that and waiters and beggars too / hes not proud out of nothing but not always" etc.

Readers are unduly impressed by the stream-of-thought device. I want to submit the following considerations. First, the device is not more "realistic" or more "scientific" than any other. In fact if some of Molly's thoughts were described instead of all of them being recorded, their expression would strike one as more "realistic," more natural. The point is that the stream of consciousness is a stylistic convention because obviously we do not think continuously in words—we think also in images; but the switch from words to images can be recorded in direct words only if description is eliminated as it is here. Another thing: some of our reflections come and go, others stay; they stop as it were, amorphous and sluggish, and it takes some time for the flowing thoughts and thoughtlets to run around those rocks of thought. The drawback of simulating a recording of thought is the blurring of the time element and too great a reliance on typography.

These Joycean pages have had a tremendous influence. In this typographical broth many a minor poet has been generated: the typesetter of the great James Joyce is the godfather of tiny Mr. Cummings. We must not see in the stream of consciousness as rendered by Joyce a natural event. It is a reality only insofar as it reflects Joyce's cerebration, the mind of the book. This book is a new world invented by Joyce. In that world people think by means of words, sentences. Their mental associations are mainly dictated by the structural needs of the book, by the author's artistic purposes and plans. I should also add that if punctuation marks be inserted by an editor into the text, Molly's musings would not really become less amusing or less musical.

There is one thing that Bloom told Molly just before going to sleep, one thing which is not mentioned by the bedside report in the precedent chapter, one thing which has much struck Molly. Before going to sleep Bloom coolly asked her to bring him his breakfast in bed tomorrow—with a couple of eggs. Now that the crisis of Molly's betrayal is past, Bloom, I suggest, decides that by the mere fact of knowing about, and tacitly condoning the situation, and allowing his wife to go on next Monday with that sordid intrigue with Boylan, he, Bloom, has acquired, in a way, the upper hand, has a certain power over Molly—and thus need not bother about *her* breakfast anymore. Let her bring him his, in bed.

Molly's soliloquy starts with her irritated surprise at his request. She returns to that thought several times through the monologue. For instance, "then he starts giving us his orders for eggs and tea Findon haddy and hot buttered toast I suppose well have him sitting up like the king of the country pumping the wrong end of the spoon up and down in his egg wherever he learned that from. . . ." (You will have noticed that Bloom has a leaning towards all kinds of special little devices, methodical tricks. From Molly's soliloquy we learn that when she was pregnant he attempted to milk her into his tea, and of course his posture in sleeping and other little habits such as kneeling to the chamber pot are all his own.) Molly cannot get over that breakfast request and the eggs become new-laid eggs—"then tea and toast for him buttered on both sides and newlaid eggs I suppose Im nothing any more"—and it again bubbles up in her mind later, "and Im to be slooching around down in the kitchen to get his lordship his breakfast while hes rolled up like a mummy will I indeed did you ever see me running Id just like to see myself at it show them attention and they treat you like dirt. . . ." But somehow the idea sinks in, and Molly reflects "Id love a big juicy pear now to melt in your mouth like when I used to be in the longing way then Ill throw him up his eggs and tea in the moustachecup she gave him to make his mouth bigger I suppose hed like my nice cream too. . . ." and she decides to be very sweet to him and get him to give her a cheque for a couple of pounds.

In the course of her soliloquy, Molly's thought shuttles between the images of various people, men and women, but one thing we shall mark at once, namely, that the amount of retrospective meditation that she devotes to her newly acquired lover Boylan is much inferior to the quality and quantity of the thoughts she devotes to her husband and to other people. Here is a woman who has had a brutal but more or less satisfactory physical experience a few hours ago, but her thoughts are occupied by humdrum recollecting that reverts constantly to her husband. She does not love Boylan: if she loves anyone it is Bloom.

Let us go rapidly through these close packed pages. Molly appreciates the respect Bloom has for old women and his politeness to waiters and beggars. She knows of the dirty photo of a toreador and a woman made to look like a Spanish nun which Bloom keeps in his desk; and she also suspects he has been scribbling a love letter. She meditates on his weaknesses, and she disbelieves some of the things he has told her about his day. She recalls in some detail an abortive intrigue which Bloom started with a maidservant they had: "like that slut that Mary we had in Ontario terrace padding out her false bottom to excite him bad enough to get the smell of those painted women off him once or twice I had a suspicion by getting him to come near me when I found the long hair on his coat without that one when I went into the kitchen pretending he was drinking water 1 woman is not enough for them it was all his fault of course ruining servants then proposing that she could eat at our table on Christmas if you please O no thank you not in my house. . . ." For a moment her thought switches to Boylan, when he first squeezed her hand, this mingling with fragments of song words as so often her thoughts do, but then she reverts to Bloom. Details of desirable lovemaking engage her attention and she remembers a virile-looking priest. She seems to be comparing the singular ways of Bloom, the delicate ways of a conjured-up goy (preparing the theme of Stephen), and the incense-smelling vestments of the priest—she seems to compare all this to the vulgarity of Boylan's ways: "I wonder was he satisfied with me one thing I didn't like his slapping me behind going away so familiarly in the hall though I laughed Im not a horse or an ass am I. . . ." She craves, poor girl, for delicate tenderness. The rich liquor Boylan had tasted at the Ormond bar emits its perfume on his breath and she wonders what it was: "Id like to sip those richlooking green and yellow expensive drinks those stagedoor johnnies drink with the opera hats" and the potted meat, remnants of which Bloom encountered in the bed, is accounted for now: "he had all he could do to keep himself from falling asleep after the last time we took the port and potted meat it had a fine salty taste." We learn that the thunder of the ten o'clock thunderstorm which one hears with Bloom in the hospital chapter awoke Molly after her first beauty sleep upon Boylan's departure, a Joycean synchronization. She recalls various physiological details concerning Boylan's lovemaking.

Her thoughts shift to Josephine Powell, now Mrs. Breen, whom Bloom met, as he told her, during the day. She is jealous about what she thinks was Bloom's interest in Josie—before their marriage—which she imagines could be continuing. Then she recalls Bloom as he was before their marriage and his conversation, which was on a higher cultural level than hers. And she conjures up his proposal of marriage, but her memories of Bloom at that time are all mixed up with her jealous satisfaction about Josie's unfortunate marriage and that lady's dotty husband who is as likely as not to go to bed with his muddy boots on. A murder case, a woman poisoning her husband, is also recalled, and back we go to the beginning of her romance with Bloom, and to a singer who kissed her, and to the way Bloom looked in those days, his brown hat and his gypsy-bright muffler. And then, in connection with some early lovemaking with Bloom, Gardner is mentioned for the first time, a former lover of hers, unknown to Bloom. We hear reminiscences of her marriage to Bloom, and the eight poppies he sent because she was born on 8 September 1870, and the marriage took place on 8 October 1888, when she was eighteen, a nice litter of *eights*. Again Gardner is evoked as a better lover than Bloom, and she switches to thoughts about her next date with Boylan, at four o'clock on Monday. There are allusions to things we know, such as the port and peaches Boylan sent to her, the Dedalus girls coming from school, and the one-legged sailor singing his song to whom she has thrown a penny.

She thinks of the planned concert trip, and the thought of a train trip reminds her of an amusing incident: "the time going to the Mallow Concert at Maryborough [Bloom] ordering boiling soup for the two us then the bell rang out he walks down the platform with the soup splashing about taking spoonfuls of it hadnt he the nerve and the waiter after him making a holy show of us screeching and confusion for the engine to start but he wouldnt pay till he finished it the two gentlemen in the 3rd class carriage said he was quite right so he was too hes so pigheaded sometimes when he gets a thing into his head a good job he was able to open the carriage door with his knife or theyd have taken us on to Cork I suppose that was done out of revenge on him O I love jaunting in a train or car with lovely soft cushions I wonder will he [Boylan] take a 1st class for me I might want to do it in the train by tipping the guard well. . . ." Gardner—Lieutenant Stanley Gardner—who died of enteric (intestinal) fever in South Africa some five years earlier, and their last kiss, are charmingly recalled: "he was a lovely fellow in khaki and just the right height over me Im sure he was brave too he said I was lovely the evening we kissed goodbye at the canal lock my Irish beauty he was pale with excitement about going away. . . ." We get back to Boylan and to some disgusting details of those and other ardors, and Boylan's rage "like a perfect devil for a few minutes after he came back with the stoppress tearing up the tickets and swearing blazes because he lost 20 quid he said he lost over that outsider that won and half he put on for me on account of Lenehans tip, cursing him to the lowest pits. . . ." She remembers how Lenehan "was making free with me after the Glencree dinner coming back that long joult over the featherbed mountain after the Lord Mayor looking at me with his dirty eyes," an episode that Lenehan had recounted to M'Coy with some glee. Items of lingerie are evoked and the visit of the Prince of Wales to Gibraltar where she spent her childhood and youth: "he was in Gibraltar the year I was born I bet he found lilies there too where he planted the tree he planted more than that in his time he might have planted me too if hed come a bit sooner then I wouldnt be here as I am. . . ." Money matters intrude: Bloom "ought to chuck that Freeman with the paltry few shillings he knocks out of it and go into an office or something where hed get regular pay or a bank where they could put him up on a throne to count the money all the day of course he prefers pottering about the house so you cant stir with him any side. . . ."

Physiological and anatomical details tumble along and there is even a glint of *metempsychosis*, the word Molly had asked Bloom about when he brought her her breakfast that morning and she was reading: "and that word met something with hoses in it and he came out with some jawbreakers about the incarnation he never can explain a thing simply the way a body can understand then he goes and burns the bottoms out of the pan all for his Kidney. . . ." More physiology and anatomy, and a train whistles by in the night. Back to Gibraltar and a girl friend Hester Stanhope (whose father had courted Molly a little) and then Mulvey's photo, Mulvey her first love. A novel by Wilkie Collins, *The Moonstone* (1868), and the novel *Moll Flanders* (1722) by Defoe are mentioned.

Then the things about signs, messages, and letters, and thus to Lieutenant Mulvey's love letter, which was the first she had ever received, back in Gibraltar: "I wanted to pick him up when I saw him following me along the Calle Real in the shop window then he tipped me just in passing I never thought hed write making an appointment I had it inside my petticoat bodice all day reading it up in every hole and corner while father was up at the drill instructing to find out by the handwriting or the language of stamps singing I remember shall I wear a white rose and I wanted to put on the old stupid clock to near the time he was the first man kissed me under the Moorish wall my sweetheart when a boy it never entered my head what kissing meant till he put his tongue in my mouth his mouth was sweetlike young I put my knee up to him a few times to learn the way what did I tell him I was engaged for fun to the son of a Spanish nobleman named Don Miguel de la Flora and he believed that I was to be married to him in 3 years time. . . ." Flora is rather like Bloom, whom of course she did not know yet, but "theres many a true word spoken in jest there is a flower that bloometh. . . ." There is a very detailed recollection of her first assignation with young Mulvey but she has difficulty remembering his first name, "Molly darling he called me what was his name Jack Joe Harry Mulvey was it yes I think a lieutenant. . . . " Her rambling thought associations go from him to her wearing his peaked cap for fun and then to an old bishop discoursing about the higher function of women "about girls now riding the bicycle and wearing peak caps and the new woman bloomers God send him sense and me more money I suppose theyre called after him I never thought that would be my name Bloom . . . youre looking blooming Josie used to say after I married him. . . ." And back to Gibraltar, to its peppertrees and white poplars and Mulvey and Gardner.

Another train whistles. Bloom and Boylan, Boylan and Bloom, the concert tour, are conjured up, and back to Gibraltar again. She supposes it is past four o'clock in the morning now, but it is only after two by the clock later on. The cat is mentioned and then fish—Molly likes fish. A picnic with her husband is recalled and she thinks about her daughter Milly and the two damn fine cracks across the ear she gave Milly for being insolent. She visualizes Bloom bringing Stephen Dedalus into the kitchen, and soon she realizes that her menstrual discharge has started. She gets out of the jingling bed. The repetition of the word *easy* half a dozen times refers to her being afraid the article on which she crouches will break under her—all this very unnecessary. Bloom, we discover, kneels down to it instead of sitting on it. A last "easy" and she gets back into bed. More thoughts about Bloom and then about Dignam's funeral which he had attended. This leads through Simon Dedalus and his fine voice to Stephen Dedalus, who, Bloom has told her, has seen her photo. Rudy would be eleven today. She tries to imagine Stephen, whom she saw as a little boy. She thinks of poetry—as she understands poetry—and imagines an affair with young Stephen. Boylan's vulgarity is evoked in contrast, and their recent ardors are again recalled. Her husband is lying in bed with his feet where his head should be. He likes it that way: "O move over your big carcass out of that for the love of Mike" Molly reflects. Motherless Stephen returns to her thoughts: "itd be great fun supposing he stayed with us why not theres the room upstairs empty and Millys bed in the back room he could do his writing and studies at the table in there for all the scribbling he [Bloom] does at it and if he [Stephen] wants to read in bed in the morning like me as hes [Bloom] making the breakfast for 1 he can make it for 2 Im sure Im not going to take in lodgers off the street for him if he takes a gesabo of a house like this Id love to have a long talk with an intelligent welleducated person Id have to get a nice pair of red slippers like those Turks with the fez used to sell [*Bloom's and Stephen's twin dream!*] or yellow and a nice semitransparent morning gown that I badly want. . . ."

Bloom's breakfast that she is to make for him that morning continues to fill her thoughts, with some other familiar items all mixed up—Bloom and the things he does not know, Stephen (Boylan's vulgar sexuality now dismissed), and Mulvey, and Gibraltar—in romantic Molly's last litany of affirmation before she too dozes off: "a quarter after what an unearthly hour I suppose theyre just getting up in China now combing out their pigtails for the day well soon have the nuns ringing the angelus theyve nobody coming in to spoil their sleep except an odd priest or two for his night office the alarmclock next door at cockshout clattering the brains out of itself let me see if I can doze off 1 2 3 4 5 . . . better lower this lamp and try again so as I can get up early Ill go to Lambes there beside Findlaters and get them to send us some flowers to put about the place in case he brings him home tomorrow today I mean no no Fridays an unlucky day first I want to do the place up someway the dust grows in it I think while Im asleep then we can have music and cigarettes I can accompany him first I must clean the keys of the piano with milk whatll I wear shall I wear a white rose . . . of course a nice plant for the middle of the table Id get that cheaper in wait wheres this I saw them not long ago I love flowers Id love to have the whole place swimming in roses God of heaven theres nothing like nature the wild mountains then the sea and the waves rushing then the beautiful country with fields of oats and wheat and all kinds of things and all the fine cattle going about that would do your heart good to see rivers and lakes and flowers all sorts of shapes and smells and colours springing up even out of the ditches primroses and violets nature it is as for them saying theres no God I wouldnt give a snap of my two fingers for all their learning . . . they might as well try to stop the sun from rising tomorrow the sun shines for you he [Bloom] said the day we were lying among the rhododendrons on Howth head in the grey tweed suit and his straw hat the day I got him to propose to me yes first I gave him the bit of seedcake out of my mouth and it was leapyear like now yes . . . he said I was a flower of the mountain yes so we are flowers all a womans body yes that was one true thing he said in his life and the sun shines for you today yes that was why I liked him because I saw he understood or felt what a woman is and I knew I could always get round him and I gave him all the pleasure I could leading him on till he asked me to say yes and I wouldnt answer first only looked out over the sea and the sky I was thinking of so many things he didnt know of Mulvey and Mr Stanhope and Hester and father and old captain Groves . . . and the sentry in front of the governors house with the thing round his white helmet poor devil half roasted and the Spanish girls laughing in their shawls and their tall combs . . . and the poor donkeys slipping half asleep and the vague fellows in the cloaks asleep in the shade on the steps and the big wheels of the carts of the bulls and the old castle thousands of years old yes and those handsome Moors all in white and turbans like kings asking you to sit down in their little bit of a shop and Ronda with the old windows of the posadas glancing eyes a lattice hid for her lover to kiss the iron and the wineshops half open at night and the castanets and the night we missed the boat at Algeciras the watchman going about serene with his lamp and O that awful deepdown torrent O and the sea the sea crimson sometimes like fire and the glorious sunsets and the figtrees in the Alameda gardens yes and all the queer little streets and pink and blue and yellow houses and the rosegardens and the jessamine and geraniums and cactuses and

Gibraltar as a girl where I was a Flower of the mountain yes when I put the rose in my hair like the Andalusian girls used or shall I wear a red yes and how he [Mulvey] kissed me under the Moorish wall and I thought well as well him [Bloom] as another and then I asked him with my eyes to ask again yes and then he [Bloom] asked me would I yes to say yes my mountain flower and first I put my arms around him yes and drew him down to me so he could feel my breasts all perfume yes and his heart was going like mad and yes I said yes I will Yes."

Yes: Bloom next morning will get his breakfast in bed.

The Art of Literature
and Commonsense

Now and then, in the course of events, when the flow of time turns into a muddy torrent and history floods our cellars, earnest people are apt to examine the interrelation between a writer and the national or universal community; and writers themselves begin to worry about their obligations. I am speaking of an abstract type of writer. Those whom we can imagine concretely, especially those on the elderly side, are too vain of their gifts or too reconciled with mediocrity to bother about obligations. They see very clearly, in the middle distance, what fate promises them—the marble nook or the plaster niche. But let us take a writer who does wonder and worry. Will he come out of his shell to inspect the sky? What about leadership? Will he, should he, be a good mixer?

There is a lot to be said for mingling now and then with the crowd, and he must be a pretty foolish and shortsighted author who renounces the treasures of observation, humor, and pity which may be professionally obtained through closer contact with his fellow men. Likewise it may be a good cure for certain puzzled authors, groping for what they hope are morbid themes, to charm themselves back into the sweet normality of their little hometowns or to converse in apostrophic dialect with husky men of the soil, if such exist. But taken all in all, I should still recommend, not as a writer's prison but merely as a fixed address, the much abused ivory tower, provided of course it has a telephone and an elevator just in case one might like to dash down to buy the evening paper or have a friend come up for a game of chess, the latter being somehow suggested by the form and texture of one's carved abode. It is thus a pleasant and cool place with a grand circular view and plenty of books and lots of useful gadgets. But before building oneself an ivory tower one must take the unavoidable trouble of killing quite a few elephants. The fine specimen I intend to bag for the benefit of those who might like to see how it is done happens to be a rather incredible cross between an elephant and a horse. His name is— commonsense.

In the fall of 1811 Noah Webster, working steadily through the C's, defined commonsense as "good sound ordinary sense . . . free from emotional bias or intellectual subtlety . . . horse sense." This is rather a flattering view of the creature, for the biography of commonsense makes nasty reading. Commonsense has trampled down many a gentle genius whose eyes had delighted in a too early moonbeam of some too early truth; commonsense has back-kicked dirt at the loveliest of queer paintings because a blue tree seemed madness to its well-meaning hoof; commonsense has prompted ugly but strong nations to crush their fair but frail neighbors the moment a gap in history offered a chance that it would have been ridiculous not to exploit. Commonsense is fundamentally immoral, for the natural morals of mankind are as irrational as the magic rites that they evolved since the immemorial dimness of time. Commonsense at its worst is sense made common, and so everything is comfortably cheapened by its touch. Commonsense is square whereas all the most essential visions and values of life are beautifully round, as round as the universe or the eyes of a child at its first circus show.

It is instructive to think that there is not a single person in this room, or for that matter in any room in the world, who, at some nicely chosen point in historical space-time would not be put to death there and then, here and now, by a commonsensical majority in righteous rage. The color of one's creed, neckties, eyes, thoughts, manners, speech, is sure to meet somewhere in time or space with a fatal objection from a mob that hates that particular tone. And the more brilliant, the more unusual the man, the nearer he is to the stake. *Stranger* always rhymes with *danger*. The meek prophet, the enchanter in his cave, the indignant artist, the nonconforming little schoolboy, all share in the same sacred danger. And this being so, let us bless them, let us bless the freak; for in the natural evolution of things, the ape would perhaps never have become man had not a freak appeared in the family. Anybody whose mind is proud enough not to breed true, secretly carries a bomb at the back of his brain; and so I suggest, just for the fun of the thing, taking that private bomb and carefully dropping it upon the model city of commonsense. In the brilliant light of the ensuing explosion many curious things will appear; our rarer senses will supplant for a brief spell the dominant vulgarian that squeezes

Sinbad's neck in the catch-as-catch-can match between the adopted self and the inner one. I am triumphantly mixing metaphors because that is exactly what they are intended for when they follow the course of their secret connections—which from a writer's point of view is the first positive result of the defeat of commonsense.

The second result is that the irrational belief in the goodness of man (to which those farcical and fraudulent characters called Facts are so solemnly opposed) becomes something much more than the wobbly basis of idealistic philosophies. It becomes a solid and iridescent truth. This means that goodness becomes a central and tangible part of one's world, which world at first sight seems hard to identify with the modern one of newspaper editors and other bright pessimists, who will tell you that it is, mildly speaking, illogical to applaud the supremacy of good at a time when something called the police state, or communism, is trying to turn the globe into five million square miles of terror, stupidity, and barbed wire. And they may add that it is one thing to beam at one's private universe in the snuggest nook of an unshelled and well-fed country and quite another to try and keep sane among crashing buildings in the roaring and whining night. But within the emphatically and unshakably illogical world which I am advertising as a home for the spirit, war gods are unreal not because they are conveniently remote in physical space from the reality of a reading lamp and the solidity of a fountain pen, but because I cannot imagine (and that is saying a good deal) such circumstances as might impinge upon the lovely and lovable world which quietly persists, whereas I can very well imagine that my fellow dreamers, thousands of whom roam the earth, keep to these same irrational and divine standards during the darkest and most dazzling hours of physical danger, pain, dust, death.

What exactly do these irrational standards mean? They mean the supremacy of the detail over the general, of the part that is more alive than the whole, of the little thing which a man observes and greets with a friendly nod of the spirit while the crowd around him is being driven by some common impulse to some common goal. I take my hat off to the hero who dashes into a burning house and saves his neighbor's child; but I shake his hand if he has risked squandering a precious five seconds to find and save, together with the child, its favorite toy. I remember a cartoon depicting a chimney sweep falling from the roof of a tall building and noticing on the way that a sign-board had one word spelled wrong, and wondering in his headlong flight why nobody had thought of correcting it. In a sense, we all are crashing to our death from the top story of our birth to the flat stones of the churchyard and wondering with an immortal Alice in

Wonderland at the patterns of the passing wall. This capacity to wonder at trifles—no matter the imminent peril—these asides of the spirit, these footnotes in the volume of life are the highest forms of consciousness, and it is in this childishly speculative state of mind, so different from commonsense and its logic, that we know the world to be good.

In this divinely absurd world of the mind, mathematical symbols do not thrive. Their interplay, no matter how smoothly it works, no matter how dutifully it mimics the convolutions of our dreams and the quantums of our mental associations, can never really express what is utterly foreign to their nature, considering that the main delight of the creative mind is the sway accorded to a seemingly incongruous detail over a seemingly dominant generalization. When commonsense is ejected together with its calculating machine, numbers cease to trouble the mind. Statistics pluck up their skirts and sweep out in a huff. Two and two no longer make four, because it is no longer necessary for them to make four. If they had done so in the artificial logical world which we have left, it had been merely a matter of habit: two and two used to make four in the same way as guests invited to dinner expect to make an even number. But I invite my numbers to a giddy picnic and then nobody minds whether two and two make five or five minus some quaint fraction. Man at a certain stage of his development invented arithmetic for the purely practical purpose of obtaining some kind of human order in a world which he knew to be ruled by gods whom he could not prevent from playing havoc with his sums whenever they felt so inclined. He accepted that inevitable indeterminism which they now and then introduced, called it magic, and calmly proceeded to count the skins he had bartered by chalking bars on the wall of his cave. The gods might intrude, but he at least was resolved to follow a system that he had invented for the express purpose of following it.

Then, as the thousands of centuries trickled by, and the gods retired on a more or less adequate pension, and human calculations grew more and more acrobatic, mathematics transcended their initial condition and became as it were a natural part of the world to which they had been merely applied. Instead of having numbers based on certain phenomena that they happened to fit because we ourselves happened to fit into the pattern we apprehended, the whole world gradually turned out to be based on numbers, and nobody seems to have been surprised at the queer fact of the outer network becoming an inner skeleton. Indeed, by digging a little deeper somewhere near the waistline of South America a lucky geologist may one day discover, as his spade rings against metal, the solid barrel hoop of the equator. There is a species of butterfly on the hind wing of which a large eyespot imitates a drop of liquid with such uncanny perfection that a line which crosses the wing is slightly displaced at the exact stretch where it passes through—or better say under—the spot: this part of the line seems shifted by refraction, as it would if a real globular drop had been there and we were looking through it at the pattern of the wing. In the light of the strange metamorphosis undergone by exact science from objective to subjective, what can prevent us from supposing that one day a real drop had fallen and had somehow been phylogenetically retained as a spot? But perhaps the funniest consequence of our extravagant belief in the organic being of mathematics was demonstrated some years ago when an enterprising and ingenious astronomer thought of attracting the attention of the inhabitants of Mars, if any, by having huge lines of light several miles long form some simple geometrical demonstration, the idea being that if they could perceive that we knew when our triangles behaved, and when they did not, the Martians would jump to the conclusion that it might be possible to establish contact with those oh so intelligent Tellurians.

At this point commonsense sneaks back and says in a hoarse whisper that whether I like it or not, one planet plus another does form two planets, and a hundred dollars is more than fifty. If I retort that the other planet may just as well turn out to be a double one for all we know, or that a thing called inflation has been known to make a hundred less than ten in the course of one night, commonsense will accuse me of substituting the concrete for the abstract. But this again is one of the essential phenomena in the kind of world I am inviting you to inspect.

This world I said was good—and "goodness" is something that is irrationally concrete. From the commonsensical point of view the "goodness," say, of some food is just as abstract as its "badness," both being qualities that cannot be perceived by the sane judgment as tangible and complete objects. But when we perform that necessary mental twist which is like learning to swim or to make a ball break, we realize that "goodness" is something round and creamy, and beautifully flushed, something in a clean apron with warm bare arms that have nursed and comforted us, something in a word just as real as the bread or the fruit to which the advertisement alludes; and the best advertisements are composed by sly people who know how to touch off the rockets of individual imaginations, which knowledge is the commonsense of trade using the instruments of irrational perception for its own perfectly rational ends.

Now "badness" is a stranger to our inner world; it eludes our grasp; "badness" is in fact the lack of something rather than a noxious presence;

and thus being abstract and bodiless it occupies no real space in our inner world. Criminals are usually people lacking imagination, for its development even on the poor lines of commonsense would have prevented them from doing evil by disclosing to their mental eye a woodcut depicting handcuffs; and creative imagination in its turn would have led them to seek an outlet in fiction and make the characters in their books do more thoroughly what they might themselves have bungled in real life. Lacking real imagination, they content themselves with such half-witted banalities as seeing themselves gloriously driving into Los Angeles in that swell stolen car with that swell golden girl who had helped to butcher its owner. True, this may become art when the writer's pen connects the necessary currents, but, in itself, crime is the very triumph of triteness, and the more successful it is, the more idiotic it looks. I never could admit that a writer's job was to improve the morals of his country, and point out lofty ideals from the tremendous height of a soapbox, and administer first aid by dashing off second-rate books. The writer's pulpit is dangerously close to the pulp romance, and what reviewers call a strong novel is generally a precarious heap of platitudes or a sand castle on a populated beach, and there are few things sadder than to see its muddy moat dissolve when the holiday makers are gone and the cold mousy waves are nibbling at the solitary sands.

There is, however, one improvement that quite unwittingly a real writer does bring to the world around him. Things that commonsense would dismiss as pointless trifles or grotesque exaggerations in an irrelevant direction are used by the creative mind in such a fashion as to make iniquity absurd. The turning of the villain into a buffoon is not a set purpose with your authentic writer: crime is a sorry farce no matter whether the stressing of this may help the community or not; it generally does, but that is not the author's direct purpose or duty. The twinkle in the author's eye as he notes the imbecile drooping of a murderer's underlip, or watches the stumpy forefinger of a professional tyrant exploring a profitable nostril in the solitude of his sumptuous bedroom, this twinkle is what punishes your man more surely than the pistol of a tiptoeing conspirator. And inversely, there is nothing dictators hate so much as that unassailable, eternally elusive, eternally provoking gleam. One of the main reasons why the very gallant Russian poet Gumilev was put to death by Lenin's ruffians thirty odd years ago was that during the whole ordeal, in the prosecutor's dim office, in the torture house, in the winding corridors that led to the truck, in the truck that took him to the place of execution, and at that place itself, full of the shuffling feet of the clumsy and gloomy shooting squad, the poet kept smiling.

That human life is but a first installment of the serial soul and that one's individual secret is not lost in the process of earthly dissolution, becomes something more than an optimistic conjecture, and even more than a matter of religious faith, when we remember that only commonsense rules immortality out. A creative writer, creative in the particular sense I am attempting to convey, cannot help feeling that in his rejecting the world of the matter-of-fact, in his taking sides with the irrational, the illogical, the inexplicable, and the fundamentally good, he is performing something similar in a rudimentary way to what [*two pages missing*] under the cloudy skies of gray Venus.

Commonsense will interrupt me at this point to remark that a further intensification of such fancies may lead to stark madness. But this is only true when the morbid exaggeration of such fancies is not linked up with a creative artist's cool and deliberate work. A madman is reluctant to look at himself in a mirror because the face he sees is not his own: his personality is beheaded; that of the artist is increased. Madness is but a diseased bit of commonsense, whereas genius is the greatest sanity of the spirit—and the criminologist Lombroso when attempting to find their affinities got into a bad muddle by not realizing the anatomic differences between obsession and inspiration, between a bat and a bird, a dead twig and a twiglike insect. Lunatics are lunatics just because they have thoroughly and recklessly dismembered a familiar world but have not the power—or have lost the power—to create a new one as harmonious as the old. The artist on the other hand disconnects what he chooses and while doing so he is aware that something in him is aware of the final result. When he examines his completed masterpiece he perceives that whatever unconscious cerebration had been involved in the creative plunge, this final result is the outcome of a definite plan which had been contained in the initial shock, as the future development of a live creature is said to be contained in the genes of its germ cell.

The passage from the dissociative stage to the associative one is thus marked by a kind of spiritual thrill which in English is very loosely termed *inspiration*. A passerby whistles a tune at the exact moment that you notice the reflection of a branch in a puddle which in its turn, and simultaneously, recalls a combination of damp green leaves and excited birds in some old garden, and the old friend, long dead, suddenly steps out of the past, smiling and closing his dripping umbrella. The whole thing lasts one radiant second and the motion of impressions and images is so swift that you cannot check the exact laws which attend their recognition, formation, and fusion—why this pool and not any pool, why this sound and not another—and how exactly are all those parts correlated; it is like a jigsaw puzzle that instantly comes together in your brain with the brain itself unable to observe how and why the pieces fit, and you experience a shuddering sensation of wild magic, of some inner resurrection, as if a dead man were revived by a sparkling drug which has been rapidly mixed in your presence. This feeling is at the base of what is called inspiration—a state of affairs that commonsense must condemn. For commonsense will point out that life on earth, from the barnacle to the goose, and from the humblest worm to the loveliest woman, arose from a colloidal carbonaceous slime activated by ferments while the earth was obligingly cooling down. Blood may well be the Silurian sea in our veins, and we are all ready to accept evolution at least as a modal formula. Professor Pavlov's bell-hopping mice and Dr. Griffith's rotating rats may please the practical minds, and Rhumbler's artificial amoeba can make a very cute pet. But again it is one thing to try and find the links and steps of life, and it is quite another to try and understand what life and the phenomenon of inspiration really are.

In the example I chose—tune, leaves, rain—a comparatively simple form of thrill is implied. Many people who are not necessarily writers are familiar with such experiences; others simply do not bother to note them. In my example memory played an essential though unconscious part and everything depended upon the perfect fusion of the past and the present. The inspiration of genius adds a third ingredient: it is the past and the present *and* the future (your book) that come together in a sudden flash; thus the entire circle of time is perceived, which is another way of saying that time ceases to exist. It is a combined sensation of having the whole universe entering you and of yourself wholly dissolving in the universe surrounding you. It is the prison wall of the ego suddenly crumbling away with the nonego rushing in from the outside to save the prisoner—who is already dancing in the open.

The Russian language which otherwise is comparatively poor in abstract terms, supplies definitions for two types of inspiration, *vostorg* and *vdokhnovenie*, which can be paraphrased as "rapture" and "recapture." The difference between them is mainly of a climatic kind, the first being hot and brief, the second cool and sustained. The kind alluded to up to now is the pure flame of *vostorg*, initial rapture, which has no conscious purpose in view but which is all-important in linking the breaking up of the old world with the building up of the new one. When the time is ripe and the writer settles down to the actual composing of his book, he will rely on the second serene and steady kind of inspiration, *vdokhnovenie*, the trusted mate who helps to recapture and reconstruct the world.

The force and originality involved in the primary spasm of inspiration is directly proportional to the worth of the book the author will write. At the bottom of the scale a very mild kind of thrill can be experienced by a minor writer noticing, say, the inner connection between a smoking factory chimney, a stunted lilac bush in the yard, and a pale-faced child; but the combination is so simple, the threefold symbol so obvious, the bridge between the images so well-worn by the feet of literary pilgrims and by cartloads of standard ideas, and the world deduced so very like the average one, that the work of fiction set into motion will be necessarily of modest worth. On the other hand, I would not like to suggest that the initial urge with great writing is always the product of something seen or heard or smelt or tasted or touched during a long-haired art-for-artist's aimless rambles. Although to develop in one's self the art of forming sudden harmonious patterns out of widely separate threads is never to be despised, and although, as in Marcel Proust's case, the actual idea of a novel may spring from such actual sensations as the melting of a biscuit on the tongue or the roughness of a pavement underfoot, it would be rash to conclude that the creation of all novels ought to be based on a kind of glorified physical experience. The intitial urge may disclose as many aspects as there are temperaments and talents; it may be the accumulated series of several practically unconscious shocks or it may be an inspired combination of several abstract ideas without a definite physical background. But in one way or another the process may still be reduced to the most natural form of creative thrill—a sudden live image constructed in a flash out of dissimilar units which are apprehended all at once in a stellar explosion of the mind.

When the writer settles down to his reconstructive work, creative experience tells him what to avoid at certain moments of blindness which overcome now and then even the greatest, when the warty fat goblins of convention or the slick imps called "gap-fillers" attempt to crawl up the legs of his desk. Fiery *vostorg* has accomplished his task and cool *vdokhnovenie* puts on her glasses. The pages are still blank, but there is a miraculous feeling of the words all being there, written in invisible ink and clamoring to become visible. You might if you choose develop any part of the picture, for the idea of sequence does not really exist as far as the author is concerned. Sequence arises only because words have to be written one after the other on consecutive pages, just as the reader's mind must have time to go through the book, at least the first time he reads it. Time and sequence cannot exist in the author's mind because no time element and no space element had ruled the initial vision. If the mind were constructed on optional lines and if a book could be read in the same way as a painting is taken in by the eye, that is without the bother of working from left to right and without the absurdity of beginnings and ends, this would be the ideal way of appreciating a novel, for thus the author saw it at the moment of its conception.

So now he is ready to write it. He is fully equipped. His fountain pen is comfortably full, the house is quiet, the tobacco and the matches are together, the night is young . . . and we shall leave him in this pleasurable situation and gently steal out, and close the door, and firmly push out of the house, as we go, the monster of grim commonsense that is lumbering up the steps to whine that the book is not for the general public, that the book will never never——And right then, just before it blurts out the word *s*, *e*, *double-l*, false commonsense must be shot dead.

L'Envoi

To some of you it may seem that under the present highly irritating world conditions it rather is a waste of energy to study literature, and especially to study structure and style. I suggest that to a certain type of temperament—and we all have different temperaments—the study of style may always seem a waste of energy under any circumstances. But apart from this it seems to me that in every mind, be it inclined towards the artistic or the practical, there is always a receptive cell for things that transcend the awful troubles of everyday life.

The novels we have imbibed will not teach you anything that you can apply to any obvious problems of life. They will not help in the business office or in the army camp or in the kitchen or in the nursery. In fact, the knowledge I have been trying to share with you is pure luxury. It will not help you to understand the social economy of France or the secrets of a woman's heart or of a young man's heart. But it may help you, if you have followed my instructions, to feel the pure satisfaction which an inspired and precise work of art gives; and this sense of satisfaction in its turn goes to build up a sense of more genuine mental comfort, the kind of comfort one feels when one realizes that for all its blunders and boners the inner texture of life is also a matter of inspiration and precision.

In this course I have tried to reveal the mechanism of those wonderful toys—literary masterpieces. I have tried to make of you good readers who read books not for the infantile purpose of identifying oneself with the characters, and not for the adolescent purpose of learning to live, and not for the academic purpose of indulging in generalizations. I have tried to teach you to read books for the sake of their form, their visions, their art. I have tried to teach you to feel a shiver of artistic satisfaction, to share not the emotions of the people in the book but the emotions of its author—the joys and difficulties of creation. We did not talk around books, about books; we went to the center of this or that masterpiece, to the live heart of the matter.

Now the course comes to a close. The work with this group has been a particularly pleasant association between the fountain of my voice and a garden of ears—some open, others closed, many very receptive, a few merely ornamental, but all of them human and divine. Some of you will go on reading great books, others will stop reading great books after graduation; and if a person thinks he cannot evolve the capacity of pleasure in reading the great artists, then he should not read them at all. After all, there are other thrills in other domains: the thrill of pure science is just as pleasurable as the pleasure of pure art. The main thing is to experience that tingle in any department of thought or emotion. We are liable to miss the best of life if we do not know how to tingle, if we do not learn to hoist ourselves just a little higher than we generally are in order to sample the rarest and ripest fruit of art which human thought has to offer.

Appendix

The following are sample questions from Nabokov's exams on *Bleak House* and *Madame Bovary*.

BLEAK HOUSE

1. Why did Dickens need to give Esther three suitors (Guppy, Jarndyce, and Woodcourt)?

2. If you compare Lady Dedlock and Skimpole, which of them is the author's greater success?

3. Discuss the structure and style of *Bleak House*.

4. Discuss John Jarndyce's house. (Mangles? Surprised birds?)

5. Discuss the visit to Bell Yard (Neckett's children; and Mr. Gridley).

6. Give at least four examples of the "child theme" in *Bleak House*.

7. Is the personality of Skimpole also representative of the "child theme"?

8. What kind of place was Bleak House—give at least four descriptive details.

9. Where was Bleak House situated?

10. Give at least four examples of Dickensian imagery (comparisons, vivid epithets, and the like).

11. How is the "bird theme" linked up with Krook?

12. How is the "fog theme" linked up with Krook?

13. Whose style are we reminded of when Dickens raises his voice?

14. What is the story of Esther's beauty in the course of the novel?

15. Give the structural scheme of *Bleak House* in terms of its main thematic centers and their interconnecting lines.

16. What emotions did Dickens expect the reader (minor or major, gentle or critical) to derive from *Bleak House*?

17. One aspect of Dickens' approach is individualization of characters through their manner and mannerisms of speech: select three characters in *Bleak House* and describe their idioms.

18. The social side ("upper class" versus "lower class" etc.) is the weakest one in *Bleak House*. Who was Mr. George's brother? What part did he play? Should a major reader skip those pages, even if they are weak?

19. John Jarndyce's Bleak House: list a few specific details.

20. Discuss the style of Dickens and that of Mrs. Allan Woodcourt.

21. Follow Mr. Guppy through *Bleak House*.

MADAME BOVARY

1. What was Homais' version of Emma's taking the poison—describe that event.

2. Describe briefly Flaubert's use of the counterpoint technique in the County Fair scene.

3. Analyze Flaubert's devices in the Agricultural Show chapter (grouping of characters, interplay of themes).

4. Answer the following five questions:
   i. Who wrote the *Genie du Christianisme*?
   ii. What was Leon's first view of Emma?
   iii. What was Rodolphe's first view of her?
   iv. How did Boulanger transmit his last letter to her?
   v. Who was Felicie Lempereur?

5. There are numerous thematic lines in *Madame Bovary*, such as

"Horse," "Plaster Priest," "Voice," "The Three Doctors." Describe these four themes briefly.

6. Give some details of the "counterpoint" theme in the following settings: a. The Golden Lion, b. The Agricultural Show, c. The Opera, d. The Cathedral.

7. Discuss Flaubert's use of the word "and."

8. What character in *Madame Bovary* behaves in very much the same way as a character in *Bleak House* does under somewhat similar circumstances? The thematic clue is: "devotion."

9. Is there a Dickensian atmosphere about Flaubert's description of Berthe's infancy and childhood? (Be specific.)

10. The features of Fanny Price and Esther are pleasantly blurred. Not so with Emma. Describe her eyes, hair, hands, skin.

11. a) Would you say that Emma's nature was hard and shallow?
    b) "Romantic" but not "artistic"?
    c) Would she prefer a landscape peopled with ruins and cows to one that contained no allusions to people?
    d) Did she like her mountain lakes with or without a lone skiff?

12. What had Emma read? Name at least four works and their authors.

13. All translations of *Madame Bovary* are full of blunders; you have corrected some of them. Describe Emma's eyes, hands, sunshade, hairdo, dress, shoes.

14. Follow the purblind vagabond through *Madame Bovary*.

15. What makes Homais ridiculous and repulsive?

16. Describe the structure of the Agricultural Show chapter.

17. What ideal is Emma striving for? What ideal is Homais striving for? What ideal is Leon striving for?

18. Although the construction of *Bleak House* is a great improvement on Dickens's previous work, still he had to conform to the exigencies of serialization. Flaubert ignored all matters extraneous to his art when writing *Madame Bovary*. Mention some of the structural points in *Madame Bovary*.

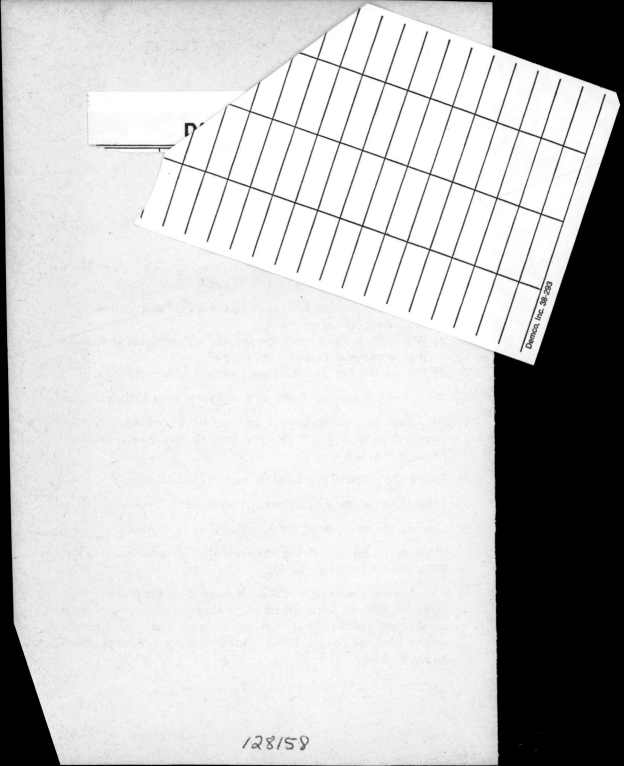